新时代英语
实用教材丛书

● 本书获福建技术师范学院2022年度职业教育教材立项资助
● 本书为国家外文局"福建省地方特色文化对外翻译标准化术语库建设项目"（18SYK09）的部分研究成果

Practical Tourism Coursebook
A Bilingual Insight

旅游实务
双语教程

韦忠生　编著

厦门大学出版社　国家一级出版社
XIAMEN UNIVERSITY PRESS　全国百佳图书出版单位

图书在版编目(CIP)数据

旅游实务双语教程 ＝ Practical Tourism
Coursebook：A Bilingual Insight / 韦忠生编著.
厦门：厦门大学出版社，2024． -- ISBN 978-7-5615
-9436-0

Ⅰ．F59

中国国家版本馆 CIP 数据核字第 2024YE5355 号

责任编辑　高奕欢　苏颖萍
责任校对　白　虹
美术编辑　张雨秋
技术编辑　许克华

出版发行　*厦门大学出版社*
社　　址　厦门市软件园二期望海路 39 号
邮政编码　361008
总　　机　0592-2181111　0592-2181406(传真)
营销中心　0592-2184458　0592-2181365
网　　址　http://www.xmupress.com
邮　　箱　xmup@xmupress.com
印　　刷　厦门市竞成印刷有限公司

开本　787 mm×1 092 mm　1/16
印张　14.75
插页　1
字数　430 千字
版次　2024 年 7 月第 1 版
印次　2024 年 7 月第 1 次印刷
定价　45.00 元

厦门大学出版社
微信二维码

厦门大学出版社
微博二维码

前言
PREFACE

　　党的二十大报告强调，"全面贯彻党的教育方针，落实立德树人根本任务，培养德智体美劳全面发展的社会主义建设者和接班人"，对"培养什么人，怎样培养人，为谁培养人"这一根本问题，提出明确要求。党的二十大报告明确提出"加强教材建设和管理"，认为"育人的根本在于立德"。教材建设工作要体现政治性、思想性，体现教育理念、教学理念的统一，其中政治性是"立德"的根本。要妥善处理思想性与科学性、理论与实际、知识和技能的广度与深度等多方面关系。本教材就是基于党的二十大报告对教材建设的要求而编写的，旨在落实立德树人的根本任务。

　　党的二十大报告强调职业教育的重要性。为了突出教材的真实性和实用性，本教材基于对旅游企业的调研和对学生学习水平和需求的分析，从实用的角度出发，整体框架以涉外旅游工作者的工作流程为主线，以工作情境中的典型工作任务为操练模块，使学生熟悉工作情境中语言交流和表达的目标，从而使学生熟练地掌握未来职业岗位需要的语言技能和职业技能。基于以上分析，本教材按旅游业务与接待流程分为 10 个单元，每个单元按主题设计 5 个学习任务，包括情景对话、角色扮演训练等模块。

　　本教材为基于工作过程的双语教程。该教材以项目为导向，以任务作为驱动因素，力图将以教师为主体的教学模式，转变为以学生为主、教师为辅的教学模式。全书分为入境旅游业务与接待、酒店业务与接待、出境旅游业务与接待三大项目，涉及相关的许多任务模拟实训，从单一的知识讲解转变为语言知识、文化知识、旅游业务知识、酒店业务知识等相互融合的工作岗位知识体系建构,将福建船政文化、建筑文化、非遗文化等内容融入其中,旨在弘扬中国特色文化,培养家国情怀。

《旅游实务双语教程》是福建技术师范学院 2022 年度职业教育教材立项项目。本书得以完成,首先要感谢福建技术师范学院教务处的经费支持。我还要对厦门大学出版社领导对本书的出版给予的鼎力支持深表谢意。感谢闽南科技学院提供了继续开展高等职业教育和教材建设的平台,践行新时代高等教育理念。感谢参考文献的所有作者,我从他们的作品中得到了许多启发和灵感。

本教材可作为旅游管理专业、旅游管理与服务教育专业、酒店管理专业、英语专业、非英语专业(公共外语英语拓展课程)的"旅游英语""旅游口译"等课程的教学用书,读者对象为研究生、本科生和高职高专学生以及其他对旅游英语感兴趣的英语学习者。

目 录
CONTENTS

项目 ❶ 入境旅游业务与接待
Project ❶ Inbound Tourism Business and Reception

第❶单元 入境旅游业务(1)
Unit ❶ Inbound Tourism Business(1)

📖 **教学目标**

⇨了解入境旅游的界定
⇨了解旅行社的分类和种类
⇨了解旅行社产品的类型
⇨掌握旅行社外联业务和客户管理
⇨掌握旅游报价分类和计算

📖 **Teaching objectives**

⇨To learn about the definition of the inbound tour
⇨To understand the classification and types of travel agencies
⇨To understand the types of travel agency products
⇨To master liaison of travel agency and customer management
⇨To master classification and calculation of tourism quotations

1.1 情景对话

A. 福州一家旅行社的李先生
B. 美国旅行社的莫里斯先生

A:早上好,我是中国环球旅行社的李先生。我可以找一下莫里斯先生吗?

B:早上好,我是莫里斯。

A:你好,莫里斯,我想和你讨论一下你的 8 天福建之行。9 月 8 日至 9 月 11 日正好是厦门的国际投资贸易洽谈会,因此酒店的房价会更高。你能重新安排行程吗?

B:我明白了。我会为我的团队重新安排行程,并传真给你新的行程。

1.1 Situational dialogue

A. Mr. Li from a travel agency in Fuzhou
B. Mr. Morris from an American travel agency

A: Good morning, this is Mr. Li from Global Travel Agency in China. May I speak to Mr. Morris, please?

B: Good morning, this is Morris speaking.

A: Hi, Morris, I would like to discuss your 8-day trip to Fujian. The time from September 8 to September 11 happens to be China International Fair for Investment and Trade in Xiamen, so the hotel room rates will be higher. Could you rearrange your itinerary?

B: I get it. I will rearrange the itinerary for my group and fax you a new itinerary.

1.2 角色扮演训练

任务 1:假设一个美国团队计划前往福建的福州、泉州、厦门和武夷山开

1.2 Role play training

Task 1: Suppose an American group plans to go to Fuzhou, Quanzhou, Xiamen and Wuyishan in Fujian for an

展 8 日全包价游,要求你设计旅游行程并报价。一些景点信息如下所示。

福州:西湖公园、三坊七巷、鼓山;泉州:清源山、开元寺;厦门:鼓浪屿、南普陀寺、湖里山炮台、厦门园林植物园;武夷山:九曲溪、天游峰、朱熹纪念馆、宋街。

任务 2:假设一个加拿大团队计划前往北京、上海、杭州、苏州、桂林和西安开展 15 日全包价游,要求你设计旅游行程并报价。一些景点信息如下所示。

北京:故宫博物院、天坛、颐和园、定陵、八达岭长城;上海:玉佛寺、豫园、外滩;杭州:西湖、六和塔、灵隐寺、飞来峰;苏州:拙政园、狮子林、寒山寺、虎丘山;桂林:漓江、象鼻山、芦笛岩、阳朔西街;西安:兵马俑博物馆、陕西历史博物馆、西安城墙、大雁塔、华清宫、半坡博物馆。

1.3 入境旅游知识聚焦

1.3.1 中国旅行社的类型

《旅行社管理暂行条例》在 1985 年 5 月 11 日由国务院颁布。这是我国旅行法制建设史上第一个行政法规。该条例将旅行社按其经营业务范围的不同,分为三类:一、二类为国际旅行社,三类为国内旅行社。[①]

2001 年国务院关于修改《旅行社管理条例》的决定,将第五条第一款修改为:"旅行社按照经营业务范围,分

8-day package tour. You are requested to design the tour itinerary and make a quotation. Information for certain scenic spots is listed as follows.

Fuzhou:West Lake Park, Three Lanes & Seven Alleys, Drum Mountain;Quanzhou: Qingyuan Mountain, Kaiyuan Temple;Xiamen: Kulangsu Island, Nanputuo Temple, Hulishan Fort, Xiamen Botanical Garden;Wuyishan:Nine-Bend Stream, Heavenly Tour Peak, Zhu Xi Memorial Hall, Street in Song Style.

Task 2: Suppose a Canadian group plans to travel to Beijing, Shanghai, Hangzhou, Suzhou, Guilin, and Xi'an for a 15-day package tour. You are requested to design the tour itinerary and provide a quotation. Information for some scenic spots is listed as follows.

Beijing:The Palace Museum, Temple of Heaven, Summer Palace, Dingling Mausoleum, Badaling Section of Great Wall; Shanghai:Jade Buddha Temple, Yu Garden, the Bund; Hangzhou:West Lake, Six Harmonies Pagoda, Lingyin Temple, Flying Peak;Suzhou: Humble Administrator's Garden, Lion Grove, Hanshan Temple, Tiger Hill;Guilin: Lijiang River, Elephant Trunk Hill, Reed Flute Cave, Yangshuo's West Street;Xi'an: Museum of Qin Terra-cotta Warriors and Horses, Shaanxi History Museum, Xi'an City Wall, Big Wild Goose Pagoda, Huaqing Palace, Banpo Museum.

1.3 Inbound tourism knowledge focus

1.3.1 Types of Chinese travel agencies

The Provisional Regulations on the Administration of Travel Agencies was promulgated by the State Council on May 11, 1985. This is the first administrative regulation in the history of legal system construction for China's tourism. The regulations divide travel agencies into three categories according to their business scope: The first and second categories are international travel agencies, and the third category is domestic travel agencies.

In 2001, the State Council revised the first paragraph of Article 5:"Travel agencies are divided into international travel agencies and domestic travel agencies according to their

---

[①] 朱晔,问建军 主编,《旅行社经营与管理业务》,西安:西安交通大学出版社,2014:7.

为国际旅行社和国内旅行社。"①国际旅行社的经营范围包括入境旅游业务、出境旅游业务和国内旅游业务，国内旅行社的经营范围仅限于国内旅游业务。

business scope." The business scope of international travel agencies includes inbound tour business, outbound tour business, and domestic tour business; the business scope of domestic travel agencies is limited to domestic tour business.

🎴 1.3.2 旅行社组织机构的种类

旅行社组织机构的种类可以分为职能性组织结构、事业部制组织结构和旅行社集团组织结构模式三种类型。②

按职能设置的部门体现了旅行社常见的组织结构，亦称为直线制组织结构，适合规模不大、业务较为简单的旅行社。旅行社的事业部制组织结构中，每一个业务部门均具有外联、计调、接待等功能，可以基于不同客源市场开展全部旅游经营业务，因此各个部门具有销售、采购和接待功能。旅行社管理层具有事业发展决策权、资金分配权和人事安排权。我国规模较大的旅行社成立了旅行社集团，如国旅集团、中旅集团、青旅集团等，每个子公司采取直线性组织结构或事业部制组织结构③。

🎴 1.3.3 中国的旅行社的职能性组织结构

中国的旅行社的职能性组织结构可以分为按照业务流程设置的旅行社组织结构、按照客源市场设置的旅行社组织结构和按照业务类别设置的旅行社组织结构。

按照业务流程设置的旅行社组织结构一般有：总经理室、副总经理室、

🎴 1.3.2 Types of travel agency organizations

The types of travel agencies organizations can be divided into three types: functional organizational structure, organizational structure based on business division, and organizational structure model based on travel agency group.

The departments established according to their functions are the reflection of common organizational structures of travel agencies, also known as linear organizations, which is suitable for travel agencies with a small scale and relatively simple business. In the organizational structure of the business division system of travel agencies, each business department has the functions of liaison, planning and dispatching, reception, etc. It can carry out all tourism business based on different source markets. Consequently, each department has the functions of sales, procurement and reception. The management of the travel agency involves the right to make decisions on business development, allocate funds and arrange personnel. Large-scale travel agencies in China have established travel agency groups, such as CITS, China Travel Service Group and China Youth Travel Service Group. Each subsidiary adopts a linear organizational structure or an organizational structure based on business division.

🎴 1.3.3 Functional organizational structure of China's travel agencies

The functional organizational structure of China's travel agencies can be divided into three types: established according to the business process, according to the source market and according to the business category.

The travel agency's organizational structure established according to the business process generally includes: office of the general manager, office of deputy general manager, liaison department, planning department, comprehensive business

---

① 国务院关于修改《旅行社管理条例》的决定，中央人民政府网站，http://www. gov. cn/gongbao/content/2002/content_61771. htm，2024/6/9.

② 叶娅丽，陈学春 主编，《旅行社经营与管理》，北京：北京理工大学出版社，2018：34-36.

③ 叶娅丽，陈学春 主编，《旅行社经营与管理》，北京：北京理工大学出版社，2018：36.

外联部、计调部、综合业务部、行政办公室、人力资源部、财务部。

外联部：有些旅行社又叫它市场部、销售部或者市场营销部。主要业务是设计和销售旅行社产品。

计调部：全称为计划调度部，主要负责接待服务的计划工作和调度工作。

综合业务部：是旅行社多功能的、带有拓展业务性质的综合部门，它同时具有某些职能部门的特征。主要承担上述三科旅游业务和票务工作。

接待部：导游就是在这个部门，由不同语种的导游人员为主体组成，主要负责具体接待计划的制定与落实，为旅游者（团）提供导游和陪同服务。

另外就是人力资源部和财务部。一般旅行社就是由上述的这些部门组成的。

按照客源市场设置的旅行社组织结构一般有：总经理室、副总经理室、行政办公室、人力资源部、财务部、东南亚部、欧洲部、美洲部。

按照业务类别设置的旅行社组织结构一般有：总经理室、副总经理室、行政办公室、人力资源部、财务部、入境部、出境部、国内部。

📖 1.3.4 旅行社的事业部制组织结构

事业部制组织结构是旅行社对具有独立的产品和市场、独立的责任和利益的部门实行分权管理的一种组织形态。有些旅行社将采购功能从各个业务部门中分离出来，单独设立一个采购部门，负责整个旅行社的对外采购任务。

旅行社的事业部制组织结构一般可以分为：总经理室、副总经理室、行

department, executive office, human resources department and financial department.

Liaison department: Some travel agencies also call it market department, sales department or marketing department. The main business is to design and sell the travel agency's products.

Planning department: The full name of the planning department is planning and dispatching department with its main duty being planning and dispatching of the reception service.

Comprehensive business department: It is a multi-functional and comprehensive department which aims to expand business of travel agencies, and it also enjoys the characteristics of some functional departments. It is mainly responsible for the tourism business, ticket-booking of the three branches mentioned above.

Reception department: Tour guides belong to this department, which is mainly composed of tour guides who speak different languages. It is mainly responsible for the formulation and implementation of specific reception plans and provides tour guide and escort service for tourists (groups).

In addition, there are human resources department and finance department. Generally, travel agencies are composed of these departments discussed above.

The organizational structure of travel agencies set up according to the source market generally includes: office of the general manager, office of deputy general manager, executive office, human resources department, financial department, Southeast Asia department, Europe department and America department.

The organizational structure of travel agencies built according to business categories generally includes: office of general manager, office of deputy general manager, executive office, human resources department, finance department, inbound tour department, outbound tour department and domestic tour department.

📖 1.3.4 Organizational structure of travel agencies based on business division

The organizational structure based on business division is an organizational form in which travel agencies implement decentralized management for the departments with independent products and markets, and independent responsibilities and interests. Some travel agencies separate the procurement function from each business department and set up a separate procurement department to be responsible for the external procurement tasks of the entire travel agency.

The organizational structure of travel agencies based on business division can generally be divided into: office of the general manager, office of deputy general manager, executive

政办公室、人力资源部、财务部、A 区部(外联部、计调部、接待部)、B 区部(外联部、计调部、接待部)、C 区部(外联部、计调部、接待部)、市场部(外联部、计调部、接待部)。

office, human resources department, financial department, the departments in area A (the liaison department, planning and dispatching department, and reception department), the departments in area B (the liaison department, planning and dispatching department, and reception department), the departments in area C (the liaison department, planning and dispatching department, and reception department), marketing department (the liaison department, planning and dispatching department, and reception department).

▦ 1.3.5 旅行社集团组织结构

我国规模较大的旅行社成立了旅行社集团,如国旅集团、中旅集团、青旅集团等,每个子公司采取直线性组织结构或事业部制组织结构。

旅行社集团组织结构一般有:总裁室、副总裁室、集团总部;子公司 1、子公司 2、子公司 3;办公室、人力资源部、财务部、入境部、出境部、国内部。

旅行社设置的主要岗位:行政管理岗位(涉及旅行社的办公室、人力资源部和财务部相关岗位)、销售岗位(同行销售岗位、服务网点的直客销售岗位)、计调岗位(组团计调、接待计调)、导游岗位(出境游领队、全程陪同导游人员、地方陪同导游人员)。

▦ 1.3.5 Organizational structure of the travel agency group

Large-scale travel agencies in China have established travel agency groups, such as CITS Group, China Travel Service Group and China Youth Travel Service Group. Each subsidiary adopts a linear organizational structure or an organizational structure based on business division.

The organizational structure of the travel agency group generally includes: office of the president, offices of vice presidents and group headquarters; subsidiary 1, subsidiary 2, subsidiary 3; executive office, human resources department, finance department, inbound tour department, outbound tour department and domestic tour department.

The main posts set up by the travel agency include administrative posts (related to the office of the travel agency, the human resources department and the finance department), sales posts (peer sales posts and direct customer sales posts at service outlets), planning and dispatching posts (group planning as well as reception planning and dispatching) and travel guide posts (outbound tour escorts, national tour guides and local tour guides).

1.4　入境旅游业务

《旅行社条例实施细则》第二条所称入境旅游业务,是指旅行社招徕、组织、接待外国旅游者来我国旅游,香港特别行政区、澳门特别行政区旅游者来内地旅游,台湾地区居民来大陆旅游,以及招徕、组织、接待在中国内地的外国人,在内地的香港特别行政区、澳门特别行政区居民和在大陆的台湾地区居民在境内旅游的业务。[①]

1.4　Inbound tourism business

The inbound tourism business mentioned in Article 2 of *The Detailed Rules for the Implementation of the Regulations on Travel Agencies* refers to the business of soliciting, organizing and receiving foreign tourists to visit China, and the tourists from the Hong Kong Special Administrative Region and Macao Special Administrative Region and the residents from the Taiwan region to visit Chinese mainland. It also involves soliciting, organizing and receiving foreigners staying in Chinese mainland, the residents of the Hong Kong Special Administrative Region, Macao Special Administrative Region and Taiwan region staying in Chinese mainland to travel within Chinese mainland.

---

① 《旅行社条例实施细则》,国家文化和旅游部网站,https://zwgk.mct.gov.cn/zfxxgkml/zcfg/bmgz/202012t20201204_905330.html,2024/6/9。

1.5 旅行社产品的类型

1.5 Types of travel agency products

从旅游经营者的角度来说,旅行社产品是指旅行社为满足旅游者旅游过程中的需要,而凭借一定的旅游景点和旅游设施向旅游者提供的各种有偿服务。这种服务具有不可感知性,也不涉及所有权的转移,但可以满足旅游者的需求。

From the perspective of tourism operators, travel agencies' products refer to various paid services provided by the travel agencies to tourists with certain tourist attractions and facilities in order to meet the needs of tourists in the process of tourism. This kind of service is imperceptible and does not involve the transfer of ownership; nevertheless, it can satisfy the needs of tourists.

1.5.1 团体包价旅游和半包价旅游

1.5.1 Group package tour and semi-package tour

团体全包价旅游产品指的是旅行社在旅游活动开始之前向参加旅游团队的旅游者收取所有旅游费用并负责安排旅游活动过程中所涵盖的所有服务的旅游产品,其服务包含:①饭店客房;②早餐、正餐和饮料;③市内游览用车与城市间的交通;④交通集散地接送服务;⑤导游服务;⑥行李服务;⑦游览点门票;⑧文娱活动入场券。① 团款一次性付清。

All-inclusive group travel products refer to the tourism products through which travel agencies charge the tourists joining the tourist group all travelling expenses and are responsible for arranging all services covered in the process of tourism activities before the start of tourism activities, including: ① hotel rooms; ② breakfast, lunch, dinner and beverage; ③ intra-city sightseeing vehicles and inter-city transportation; ④ transportation hub transfer service; ⑤ tour guide service; ⑥ luggage-transfer service; ⑦ ticket-booking; ⑧ the entrance ticket for cultural and recreational activities. The group payment shall be paid in lump sum.

团体半包价旅游产品指的是旅行社在旅游活动开始之前向参加旅游团队的旅游者收取除午、晚餐费用以外的所有旅游费用的旅游产品。

Semi-package group tourism products refer to the tourism products through which travel agencies charge the tourists joining the tourist group all travelling expenses except lunch and dinner fees before the start of tourism activities.

1.5.2 团队小包价旅游(可选择性旅游)

1.5.2 Mini-package group tour (optional tour)

团队小包价旅游产品由非选择部分和可选择部分组成,是一种选择性很强的旅游产品。非选择部分包括住房、早餐、机场(车站、码头)接送至酒店和城市间的交通费用,其费用由旅游者在旅行前预付。可选择部分包括导游服务、午晚餐、风味餐、参观游览、欣赏文艺节目等,其费用由旅游者在旅行前预付或现付。②

Mini-package group tourism products are composed of non-optional parts and optional parts, which are highly optional tourism products. The non-optional part includes the hotel, breakfast, transfer from the airport, station and dock to hotel, and inter-city transportation costs, which are prepaid by tourists before travel. The optional parts include tour guide service, lunch and dinner, special meals, sightseeing, appreciation of programs of entertainment, etc. The expenses are paid by tourists in advance or in cash before traveling.

---

① 叶娅丽,陈学春 主编,《旅行社经营与管理》,北京:北京理工大学出版社,2018:49.
② 叶娅丽,陈学春 主编,《旅行社经营与管理》,北京:北京理工大学出版社,2018:49-50.

1.5.3　团体零包价旅游(多见于发达国家)

零包价旅游是一种独特的产品形态。旅游者参加这种形式的旅游时，必须随旅游团前往和离开旅游目的地。到达目的地后，旅游者可以自由活动，不受旅游团的束缚。零包价旅游的特点是：①旅游者可以享受团体机票的优惠价格；②可由旅行社统一代办旅游签证手续。①

1.5.4　散客旅游产品

散客旅游产品是指旅游人数低于10人的旅游产品。一般散客出游前都会向旅行社咨询有关旅游行程中的食、住、行、游、购、娱方面的情况，旅行社产品种类，旅游项目价格等。旅行社则要及时开展咨询服务，向前来咨询的散客提供相关的建议、旅游方案和信息等。旅游咨询服务业务形式可分为：电话咨询、信函咨询、人员咨询、网络咨询。

▶ 1.5.4.1　散客包价旅游产品

散客包价旅游产品与团体包价旅游产品的区别在于旅游者的人数不同。散客包价旅游产品又可以分为单人包价旅游产品、2～5人全包价旅游产品和6～9人全包价旅游产品。散客包价旅游也可分为散客全包价旅游产品、散客半包价旅游产品和散客小包价旅游产品。

▶ 1.5.4.2　单项委托服务

单项委托服务是指旅行社为散客

1.5.3　Zero-fare group tour (mostly seen in developed countries)

The zero-fare tour is a unique product form. When participating in this form of tour, tourists must go to and leave the destination with the tourist group. After arriving at the destination, tourists can move freely without being bound by tourist groups. The characteristics of the zero-fare tour are：①tourists can enjoy the preferential price of group air tickets；②Travel agencies can handle tourist visa formalities on their behalf.

1.5.4　Individual tourist products

Individual tourist products refer to tourism products with less than 10 tourists. Generally, individual tourists will consult the travel agency about the food, accommodation, transportation, travel, shopping and entertainment in the tourism itinerary, the types of the travel agency's products, and the price of tourism items. Travel agencies are required to carry out consulting service in a timely manner, and provide relevant suggestions, tourism programs and information for individual tourists who come to consult. The business forms of tourism consulting service can be divided into：telephone consulting, letter consulting, face-to-face consulting, and online consulting.

▶ 1.5.4.1　Individual package tourism products

The difference between individual package tourism products and group package tourism products lies in the number of tourists. Individual package tourism products can also be divided into package tourism products for one person, package tourism products for 2-5 persons and package tourism products for 6-9 persons. Individual package tourism can also be divided into individual full package tourism products, individual semi-package tourism products and individual mini-package tourism products.

▶ 1.5.4.2　Individual entrusted service

Individual entrusted service refers to various optional

---

① 叶娅丽，陈学春 主编，《旅行社经营与管理》，北京：北京理工大学出版社，2018：50.

提供的各种按单项计价的可供选择的服务。这类服务主要有:抵离接送,行李提取、保管和托运,代订机、车票和饭店,代租汽车,代办出入境、过境临时居住和旅游签证,代向海关办理申报检验手续,代办国内旅游委托、导游服务等。单项委托服务分为受理散客来本地旅游的委托、办理散客赴外地旅游的委托和受理散客在本地的各种单项服务委托。[①]

services priced by individual items and provided by travel agencies for individual tourists. Such service mainly includes: the transfer of arrival and departure, the collection, storage and consignment of baggage, the booking of air tickets, train tickets, coach tickets, etc. and hotels, the renting of cars, the handling of the formalities to leave or enter a country, temporary residence for transit and tourist visas, the handling of customs declaration and inspection procedures, the handling of domestic tourism entrustment, tour guide service, etc. Individual entrusted service is divided into the entrustment of individual tourists to travel locally, the entrustment of individual tourists to travel to other places, and the entrustment of individual tourists to handle all kinds of local services.

1.6 旅行社外联业务

旅行社外联业务就是旅行社与旅游客户包括旅游者、旅游中间商和其他旅行社联络,通过市场分析,设计开发旅行社线路产品并直接销售的业务。[②] 旅行社外联业务是指旅行社通过各种直接或间接的手段,将开发组合的旅游产品转移到旅游者手中,也就是通过各种销售手段使旅游者来购买旅游产品。

外联部作为公司业务职能部门,是公司对外宣传的活广告,其工作人员身兼发展公司现有业务、开拓公司未来旅游市场的双重任务。外联人员就是旅行社业务销售人员,相对于计调内勤性质的工作,外联工作是外部公关销售工作。

1.6.1 旅行社外联业务的主要内容

收集信息,掌握市场动态:旅行社外联人员收集的信息,内容广泛,涉及政治、经济、文化等层面的信息,也包括产品、中间商、竞争对手方面的信息以

1.6 The task of liaison for travel agencies

The task of liaison for travel agencies is to contact tourism customers, including tourists, travel intermediaries and other travel agencies, and to design and develop the products of the travel agency through market analysis and direct sales. The task of liaison for travel agencies refers to the transfer of tourism products developed and combined by travel agencies to tourists through various direct or indirect means, that is, to make tourists purchase tourism products through various sales means.

As the company's business department, the liaison department is the company's effection advertisement for external publicity. Its staff has a dual task of developing the company's existing business and exploring the company's future tourism market. The staff of this department is the sales staff of the travel agency's business. Compared with the internal work of planning and dispatching, the task of the liaison department is the external work of sales and public relations.

1.6.1 Main tasks of travel agency's liaison

Collecting information and mastering the market dynamics: The travel agency's liaison personnel collects a wide range of information, including political, economic, cultural and other aspects of information, as well as the information about products, intermediaries, competitors and changes in

①　赵爱华 主编,《旅行社计调业务》,北京:中国旅游出版社,2021:138-139.
②　高燕 主编,《旅行社经营管理与实务》,杭州:浙江大学出版社,2014:126.

及旅游需求变化等方面的信息。只有在基于大量信息的分析与研究的基础上，才能有针对性地开展市场营销活动。

制定业务目标：旅行社外联人员针对市场信息的分析，在旅行社总体目标的指导下制定该部门的业务目标。该业务目标将成为旅行社外联人员进行市场开发、组织客源和推介产品的行动指南。

合理设计旅游产品线路：合理的旅游产品线路设计是外联销售成功的重要因素之一。旅游产品线路的内容需要体现其特色，线路编排上需要体现其合理性，具体体现在城市间和景点之间的交通路线需要考虑其经济性、便捷性和安全性，游览景点需要合理搭配，具有市场竞争力。

建立对外销售渠道：建立一个高效的旅行社招徕客源的业务网络是外联销售成功的重要一环。业务网络建成之后，外联人员需要加强对该业务网络的管理，确保销售渠道畅通无阻。

业务洽谈，推介产品：业务洽谈是外联部门与客户为实现旅游产品交易而进行的协商活动，是旅行社与客户建立业务联系的重要途径。事先了解洽谈对象和竞争对手，采取合适的谈判技巧有助于谈判的成功。

签订书面协议：外联部门与客户就共同关心的问题如旅游产品的内容、价格、付款方式和优惠条件进行协商并达成一致意见，最后签订合作意向书、合同书或委托书等书面协议，以便在此基础上开展相关业务合作。

1.6.2 外联业务洽谈工作程序

寻找客户：客户分为已有客户和潜在客户。外联部需要巩固老客户，

tourism demand. Only by relying on the research and analysis based on a large amount of information can we carry out targeted marketing activities.

Developing business objectives：On the basis of the analysis of market information, the travel agency's liaison personnel will develop the business objectives of the department under the guidance of the travel agency's overall objectives, which will become the action guide for the travel agency's liaison personnel to carry out market development, organize customer sources and promote products.

Reasonable design of tourism products：Reasonable design of tourism products is one of the important factors for the success of outbound sales. Tourist products need to reflect their characteristics, and the route arrangement needs to demonstrate its rationality as well. Specifically, the transportation routes between cities and scenic spots need to consider its economy, convenience and safety. Tourist attractions need to be reasonably matched and have market competitiveness.

Establishing external sales channels：Establishing an efficient business network for travel agencies to attract customers is an important part of the success of external sales. After the completion of the business network, liaison personnel need to strengthen the management of the business network to ensure that the sales channels are unblocked.

Business negotiation and product promotion：Business negotiation is a negotiation activity between the liaison department and customers to fulfill the transaction of tourism products. It is an important way for travel agencies to establish business relations with customers. Knowing the negotiation object and competitors in advance and adopting appropriate negotiation skills will help the success of negotiation.

Signing a written agreement：The liaison department negotiates with customers and reaches an agreement on the issues of common concern, such as the itinerary, price, terms of payment and preferential conditions of tourism products, and finally the two parties sign a written agreement such as a letter of intent, contract or letter of authorization, so as to carry out relevant business cooperation on this basis.

1.6.2 Working procedures for the business negotiation of liaison

Seeking customers：Customers are divided into existing

利用老客户以及企事业单位代表的协助上门拜访,通过各种旅游展销会和博览会、旅游协会结识同业客户和企事业客户。外联部还需要对潜在的客户进行分类,开展相应的促销活动,介绍产品。

建立客户关系涉及业务洽谈。外联业务洽谈的模式可以分为当面洽谈和通讯洽谈两种。旅行社在通讯洽谈中所采用工具主要有函件、电话、传真、新媒体(微信等),在这几种工具中传真已经成为旅行社外联业务中使用最为广泛的一种工具。

旅行社业务谈判人员在谈判开始后首先应该向对方详细介绍旅行社产品并作解答,内容涉及产品的内容、特点、销售价格、购买方式、付款条件等。在谈判中谈判人员应在事先拟定的方案基础上,吸收旅游客户提出的合理意见,适当修改相关内容,既维护旅行社的利益,也可以与对方达成协议。

签订书面协议:外联部门与旅游客户经过洽谈,就旅游产品的内容、价格、付款方式和优惠条件进行协商并达成一致意见,最后签订合作意向书、合同书或委托书等书面协议,建立业务合作关系。

customers and potential customers. The liaison department is required to consolidate old customers, make use of the assistance of old customers and the representatives of enterprises and institutions to pay door-to-door visits, and meet clients in the same industry, enterprises and institutions through various tourism fairs and expositions and tourism associations. The liaison department is also required to classify potential customers, carry out corresponding promotional activities and introduce products

Establishing customer relationship involves business negotiation. The negotiation mode of liaison can be divided into face-to-face negotiation and communication-based negotiation. The tools used by travel agencies in communication-based negotiation mainly include correspondence, telephone, fax, and new media (WeChat, etc.). Among these tools, fax has become the most widely used tool in travel agencies' business of liaison.

After the negotiation, the travel agency's business negotiators should first introduce the travel agency's products to the other party in detail and give answers, including the itinerary, characteristics, sales price, purchase method, payment terms, etc. In the negotiation, the negotiators should adopt the reasonable opinions put forward by customers and modify the relevant contents on the basis of the plan prepared in advance, so as to safeguard the interests of the travel agency and reach an agreement with the other party.

Signing a written agreement: After negotiation with customers, the liaison department will negotiate and reach an agreement on the itinerary, price, payment terms and preferential conditions of tourism products, and finally sign a written agreement such as a letter of intent, contract or letter of authorization to establish a business cooperation relationship.

1.7 旅游线路报价分类

朱晔和问建军基于报价对象、内容、线路产品的类型、报价方式以及旅游者年龄等因素详细讨论了旅游线路报价分类[①]。根据报价对象不同,他们将旅游线路报价分为:组团报价(组团社向旅游者报价)、地接报价(地接社向组团社报价)。根据内容不同,他们

1.7 Quotation classification of tourism itinerary

Zhu Ye and Wen Jianjun discussed in detail the classification of tourism itinerary quotations on the bassis of factors such as quotation objects, content, the type of the itinerary, quotation methods, and age of tourists. According to different quotation targets, they divide the tourism itinerary quotation into: the quotation offered by the tour wholesaler and the quotation offered to the tour wholesaler by the local tour operator. According to different contents, they divide the

① 朱晔,问建军 主编,《旅行社经营与管理业务》,西安:西安交通大学出版社,2014:64.

将旅游线路报价分为:总体报价和明细报价。前者只体现线路产品整体性的内容和整体性的价格;后者反映的不仅是整体性的内容和价格,还有各种细分的、具体的单项内容和价格。

根据线路产品的类型不同,他们将旅游线路报价分为:①团体旅游线路报价和散客旅游线路报价;②国内旅游线路报价、入境旅游线路报价、出境旅游线路报价;③常规旅游线路报价、专项旅游线路报价;④豪华旅游线路报价、标准等旅游线路报价、经济等旅游线路报价。

根据报价方式的不同,他们将旅游线路报价分为:邮寄报价、传真报价、媒体报价、上门报价、门市报价和展销报价六种。其中邮寄报价、传真报价、门市报价在实际运用中最为普遍。媒体报价和门市报价主要针对旅游者,而其余的报价主要针对旅游中间商或者组团旅行社。

他们还根据其他因素对旅游报价进行了分类。根据旅游者年龄不同,旅游线路报价分为:成人报价和儿童报价。根据时间上的不同,旅游线路报价可以分为:年度报价、季度报价、月度报价。根据客源地的不同,旅游线路报价可以分为:外宾报价和内宾报价。根据旅游季节的不同,旅游线路报价可以分为:淡季报价和旺季报价。

1.8 旅游线路报价的计算

朱晔和问建军详细讨论了旅游线路报价的计算方法,涉及各种费用,如综合服务费、房费、餐费、城市间交通费和专项附加费,以及其他费用①。

tourism itinerary quotation into the overall quotation and detailed quotation. The former only reflects the overall contents and overall price of the product; the latter reflects not only the overall content and price, but also various segmented and specific individual content and prices.

According to the different types of the tourism itinerary, they divide the quotation of the tourism itinerary into: ①the quotation for the group tourism itinerary and for the individual tourism itinerary; ②the quotation for the domestic tourism itinerary, for the inbound tourism itinerary and for the outbound tourism itinerary; ③the quotation for the conventional tourism itinerary and the special tourism itinerary; ④the quotation for the luxury tourism itinerary, for the standard tourism itinerary and for the economical tourism itinerary.

According to different pricing methods, they divide tourism itinerary quotations into six types: the mail quotation, fax quotation, media quotation, door-to-door quotation, market quotation and exhibition quotation. Among them, the mail quotation, fax quotation and market quotation are the most common in practice. Media quotations and market quotations are mainly targeted at tourists, while the rest are mainly aiming at travel intermediaries or tour wholesalers.

They also classified tourism quotations based on other factors. According to the age of tourists, the quotation of the tourism itinerary can be divided into the quotation for adults and quotation for children. According to the time, the quotation of the tourism itinerary can be divided into the annual quotation, quarterly quotation and monthly quotation. According to different places of the tourist origin, the quotation of the tourism itinerary can be divided into: the quotation for foreign guests and the quotation for domestic guests. According to the different tourist seasons, the quotation of the tourism itinerary can be divided into: the off-season quotation and peak season quotation.

1.8 Calculation of quotation for tourism itinerary

Zhu Ye and Wen Jianjun discussed in detail the calculation method of tourism itinerary quotations, which involves various expenses such as comprehensive service fees, room fees, meals, inter-city transportation fees, and special surcharges,

---

① 朱晔,问建军 主编,《旅行社经营与管理业务》,西安:西安交通大学出版社,2014:64-65.

以下各式子中,综合服务费、房费、餐费、城市间交通费和专项附加费的计算单位均为"元/人天"。

综合服务费总额＝实际接待人数的综合服务费

房费总额＝实际入住天数的房费

餐费总额＝实际用餐天数的餐费

城市间交通费总额＝实际乘坐交通工具客票费

专项附加费总额＝汽车超公里费＋特殊门票费

旅游线路报价的计算公式:

旅游线路报价＝综合服务费＋房费＋餐费＋城市间交通费＋专项附加费

旅行社为旅游者安排的住宿为双人标准房或三人房。有时旅游团由于人数与性别原因可能出现自然单间现象,房费差额根据协议由组团社或接待社承担。旅游团的成年旅游者人数若超过 16 人,1 人的综合服务费免收,全陪仅收取城市间交通费、房费,其余费用免收。12 岁以下儿童在不占床位和座位的情况下仅收取 30%～50% 综合服务费,12 岁以上儿童按成年人收取全额综合服务费。①

旅游线路报价一般不包括各地机场建设费、旅游意外保险费(自愿投保)、火车上用餐费用、各地特殊自费旅游项目。超公里费指的是汽车长途客运的收费,各地收费标准不一致,如上海一地是以 8 小时、80 公里为基价计算的。旅游线路报价在实施过程中若发生不可抗力因素造成实际旅费超过报价的(如行程延期),所产生的额外

as well as other expenses.

The unit of calculation is "RMB /per person and per day" for all items in the following formulas.

Total comprehensive service fee ＝ comprehensive service fee for the actual number of people received

Total room charge ＝ room charge for actual occupancy days

The total meal cost refers to the meal cost for the whole journey.

Total inter-city transportation cost ＝ actual vehicle fare

Total special surcharge ＝ extra kilometers ＋ special admission fees

Calculation formula of quotation for tourism itinerary (the calculation unit is "RMB / per person and per day"):

Quotation for tourism itinerary ＝ comprehensive service fee ＋ room fee ＋ meal fee ＋ inter-city transportation fee ＋ special surcharge

The accommodation arranged by the travel agency for tourists is a standard room for two or three people. Sometimes, due to the number of people and gender, the tour group may have a natural single room, and the difference between the room fees shall be borne by the tour agency or reception agency according to the agreement. If the number of adult tourists in the tourist group is more than 16, the comprehensive service fee for one person will be exempted, and only the inter-city transportation fee and room fee will be charged for the national guide, and the rest will be exempted. Children under 12 years old and without occupying the bed and seat will only be charged 30%-50% of the comprehensive service fee, and children over 12 years old will be charged a full comprehensive service fee as adults.

The quotation of the tourism itinerary generally does not include airport construction fees, tourism accident insurance fees (voluntary insurance), meals on the train, and special self-funded tourism projects. Extra-kilometer fees refer to the charge for long-distance passenger transport by the tourist coach. The charging standards are different in different places. For example, the standard of Shanghai is based on 8 hours and 80 kilometers. If the actual travelling expenses exceed the quoted price due to force majeure (such as travel delay) during the implementation of the quotation for the tourism itinerary, the extra expenses incurred shall be borne by the tourists themselves or shared by the travel agency and the tourists. The local tour

① 朱晔,问建军 主编,《旅行社经营与管理业务》,西安:西安交通大学出版社,2014:65.

费用由旅游者自行承担或旅行社与旅游者分担费用。地接旅行社在旅游线路报价中需要包括团队确认方式以及结算方式的具体要求。[①]

operator needs to include the specific requirements for tourist group's confirmation method and payment terms in the quotation for the tourism itinerary.

1.9　知识拓展

1.9.1　旅行社外联部客户管理

狭义的客户指的是旅行社的客源,即旅游者。广义的客户指的是与旅行社有业务来往的供应商、其他服务机构和旅游者。外联部承担对外营销的重要职能,因此基于广义客户的概念开展市场开发、产品设计、市场营销、产品创新关系旅行社经营业务的成败。旅行社外联部对客户实施科学的管理显得尤其重要。旅行社外联部客户管理包括客户的选择和建立客户档案。

1.9.1.1　客户的选择

首先,合作旅行社的实力,即人力、物力和财力是客户选择的重要依据之一。其次,资金信誉也是一个重要的因素。资金信誉指的是按时付款。作为海外旅行社,必须在旅游团抵达之前半个月内将团款汇到接团社的账户上;国内组团社应提前 10 天将团款汇到接团社的账户上。务必遵守"先付款后接团"的原则,避免延期付款。

1.9.1.2　建立客户档案

客户档案是旅行社在经营过程中与供应商、分销商、旅游者、其他相关

1.9　Knowledge expansion

1.9.1　Customer management of travel-agency's liaison department

In a narrow sense, customers refer to the source of tourists of travel agencies, namely tourists. In a broad sense, customers refer to suppliers, other service organizations and tourists who have business relations with travel agencies. The liaison department undertakes the important function of external marketing. Therefore, market development, product design, marketing and product innovation based on the concept of customers of a broad sense are related to the success or failure of the travel agency's business. It is particularly important for the travel agency's liaison department to implement scientific management on customers. The customer management of this department includes the selection of customers and the establishment of customer files.

1.9.1.1　Selection of cooperative travel agencies

The strength of cooperative travel agencies, namely human, material and financial resources, is one of the important bases for customers to choose. Secondly, financial credibility is also an important factor. Financial credibility refers to timely payment. An overseas travel agency must remit the group's expenses to the account of the local tour operator within half a month before the arrival of the tourist group; domestic tour wholesalers should remit the travelling expenses to the account of the local tour operator 10 days in advance. Always follow the principle of "payment before receiving tourist groups" to avoid delay in payment.

1.9.1.2　Establishment of customer files

Customer archives are the historical records of business cooperation between travel agencies and suppliers, distributors,

① 朱晔,问建军 主编,《旅行社经营与管理业务》,西安:西安交通大学出版社,2014:65.

部门与企业开展业务合作的历史记录。建立客户档案有助于旅行社选择合适的合作伙伴,建立独特的合作模式,也有助于旅行社及时、有效地调整经营策略,规避经营风险。

分门别类是建立客户档案的基础,可以按照供应商、分销商、传媒、旅游者来分类建立客户档案。建立重要客户档案也是重要的一环,主要涉及信誉好与规模较大的供应商、具有丰富旅游新产品推介经验的传媒、有稳定支付能力的企事业单位与个人,其档案要求尽可能详尽并及时更新。

客户关系的巩固对旅行社的可持续发展具有更重要的意义。可以采用多样化的策略,如及时回访客户、组织联谊会或答谢会(冷餐会或鸡尾酒会＋文艺节目＋参与趣味性活动＋抽奖或纪念品的形式)、设立年度奖励积分制度(在一定时间内免费享用一定数量的特色旅游产品)、对某些忠诚的重要客户给予优惠性奖励(包括累积优惠和数量优惠)、倾听客户的意见与建议、提供专门化和个性化的产品和服务、邮递印刷品推介新产品。

▶ 1.9.1.3 客户的评估

对客户的评估需要采用统一的标准,可以将评估内容以表格的形式呈现,列出评估的详细项目,使用项目计分法进行评估。对客户的评估需要基于以往的客户档案的详尽信息和数据的分析,从而保证评估的客观性。应由外联部的专业人员集体开展客户评估,从而避免由其他部门的工作人员进行操作或者个人喜好等其他因素而导致的误差。

tourists, other relevant departments and enterprises in the course of operation. The establishment of customer files helps travel agencies to select suitable partners and establish unique cooperation models, and also helps travel agencies to adjust their business strategies in a timely and effective manner to avoid business risks.

Categorization is the basis for establishing customer files, which can be classified according to suppliers, distributors, media and tourists. The establishment of important customer files is also an important part, mainly involving suppliers with a good reputation and large scale, media with rich experience in the promotion of new tourism products, and enterprises, institutions and individuals with a stable payment capacity. Their files are required to be as detailed and updated as possible.

The consolidation of customer relationship is of greater significance to the sustainable development of travel agencies. Diversified strategies can be adopted, such as timely return visits to customers, organizing reunion or thank-you parties (buffet or cocktail party ＋ programs of entertainment ＋ participatory fun activities ＋ lottery draw or souvenirs), establishing an annual bonus point system (where customers can enjoy a certain number of characteristic tourism products for free within a certain period of time), giving preferential rewards (including cumulative and quantity discounts) to some loyal and important customers, listening to customers' opinions and suggestions, providing specialized and personalized products and services, and promoting new products by mailing printing material.

▶ 1.9.1.3 Customer evaluation

The evaluation of customers needs the adoption of unified standards. The evaluation contents can be presented in the form of tables, the detailed items of the evaluation can be listed, and the project scoring method can be used for evaluation. The evaluation of customers needs to be based on the analysis of detailed information and data of previous customer files to ensure the objectivity of the evaluation. The professional staff of the liaison department will conduct the customer evaluation collectively, so as to avoid errors caused by other factors such as operation by staff from other departments or personal preferences.

❀ Exercises

Ⅰ. Fill in the blanks with proper forms of the words.

1. All-inclusive group travel products refer to the tourism products that travel agencies charge the tourists _____ (join) the tourist group all travelling expenses and are responsible for arranging all services _____ (cover) in the process of tourism activities before the start of tourism activities.

2. From the perspective of tourism operators, travel agencies' products refer to various _____ (pay) services _____ (provide) by the travel agencies to tourists with certain tourist attractions and facilities in order to meet the needs of tourists in the process of tourism.

3. Secondly, financial _____ (credible) is also an important factor. Financial credibility refers to _____ (time) _____ (pay). Always follow the principle of "payment before _____ (receive) tourist groups" _____ (avoid) delay in payment.

4. If the number of adult tourists in the tourist group is more than 16, the comprehensive service fee for one person _____ (exempt), and only the inter-city transportation fee and room fee _____ (charge) for the national guide.

Ⅱ. Translate the following Chinese sentences into English.

1. 中国的旅行社的职能性组织结构可以分为按照业务流程设置的旅行社组织结构、按照客源市场设置的旅行社组织结构和按照业务类别设置的旅行社组织结构。

2. 有些旅行社将外联部称为市场部、销售部或者市场营销部。主要业务是设计和销售旅行社产品。

3. 计调部的全称为计划调度部,主要负责接待服务的计划工作和调度工作。

4. 对客户的评估需要基于以往的客户档案的详尽信息和数据的分析,从而保证评估的客观性。

Ⅲ. Translate the following English sentences into Chinese.

1. Individual tourist products refer to tourism products with less than 10 tourists.

2. The consolidation of customer relationship is of greater significance to the sustainable development of travel agencies. Diversified strategies can be adopted.

3. Customer archives are the historical records of business cooperation between travel agencies and suppliers, distributors, tourists, other relevant departments and enterprises in the course of operation.

4. After negotiation with customers, the liaison department will negotiate and reach an agreement on the itinerary, price, payment terms and preferential conditions of tourism products, and finally the two parties sign a written agreement such as a letter of intent, contract or letter of authorization to establish a business cooperation relationship.

Ⅳ. Questions and answers.

1. How do you understand the group package tour, semi-package tour and zero-fare tour?

2. What is the difference between individual package tourism products and group package tourism products?

第❷单元　入境旅游业务(2)
Unit ❷　Inbound Tourism Business(2)

📖 **教学目标**

⇨掌握入境旅游线路报价相关内容

⇨掌握计调部职能相关内容

⇨掌握计调人员分类相关内容

⇨掌握计调部采购业务基本流程

⇨掌握旅游采购合同范本撰写方法

📖 **Teaching objectives**

⇨To master related knowledge of the quotation of inbound tour itinerary

⇨To master related knowledge of the functions of the planning and dispatching department

⇨To master related knowledge of the classification of planning and dispatching personnel

⇨To master the basic procurement process of the planning and dispatching department

⇨To master the way of writing tourism procurement contract templates

2.1　情景对话

> A. 福州一家旅行社的李先生
> B. 美国旅行社的马克

A：下午好,我是李先生。请问你是哪位?

B：下午好,我是马克。我想讨论一下8月8日至8月18日文化交流团的一些特殊要求。你能安排一场关于中国高等教育的讲座和另一场关于针灸效果的讲座吗? 此外,我的团队还想参观一家中医院。

A：好的,我会安排两次讲座和参观一家中医院。这两次讲座将由两位著名学者主讲。我将征得医院的许可,安排参观针灸治疗室,以便你们的团队更好地了解针灸是如何产生作用并对健康产生积极影响的。

B：好的,太棒了。下次再聊。

2.1　Situational dialogue

> A. Mr. Li from a travel agency in Fuzhou
> B. Mark from an American travel agency

A: Good afternoon, this is Mr. Li. May I ask who is calling, please?

B: Good afternoon, this is Mark speaking. I would like to discuss some special requirements of the cultural exchange group from August 8 to August 18. Could you arrange a lecture on Chinese higher education and another lecture on the effects of acupuncture and moxibustion? Besides, my group would like to pay a visit to a traditional Chinese medicine hospital.

A: All right, I will arrange the two lectures and the visit to a traditional Chinese medicine hospital. The two lectures will be given by two well-known scholars. I will ask for the permission of the hospital to arrange a visit to the treatment room of acupuncture and moxibustion so that your group will have a better idea of how acupuncture and moxibustion work and produce positive effects on health.

B: OK, wonderful. Talk to you next time.

2.2　角色扮演训练

假设一个美国团队计划前往福建的福州、泉州、厦门、武夷山和永定开

2.2　Role play training

Suppose an American group plans to go to Fuzhou, Quanzhou, Xiamen, Wuyishan and Yongding in Fujian for a

展15日全包价文化游,请设计旅游行程并报价。

一些文化景点与文化项目信息如下。

福州:福建省博物馆、福州文庙、林则徐纪念馆、严复故居、二梅书屋。

泉州:泉州海外交通史博物馆、洛阳桥、提线木偶戏、南安蔡氏古民居。

厦门:厦门大学人类博物馆、厦门大学古建筑群、华侨博物院、鳌园石雕、郑成功纪念馆。

武夷山:闽越王城博物馆、朱子故里五夫镇(紫阳楼、宋古街、兴贤书院等)、茶艺表演。

永定:振成楼、承启楼、福裕楼等。

15-day cultural package tour. Please design the tour itinerary and make a quotation.

Information on some cultural attractions and cultural items are as follows.

Fuzhou: Fujian Provincial Museum, Fuzhou's Confucius Temple, Lin Zexu Memorial Hall, Yan Fu's Former Residence, Ermei Study.

Quanzhou: Quanzhou Maritime Museum, Luoyang Bridge, the string-controlled puppet show and Cai's ancient residence in Nan'an.

Xiamen: Museum of Mankind in Xiamen University, the ancient architectural complex of Xiamen University, Overseas Chinese Museum, Jimei Turtle Garden stone carving, Zheng Chenggong Memorial Hall.

Wuyishan: Museum for the Capital City of Minyue Regime, Wufu Town (Zhu Xi's hometown) (Ziyang Tower, Ancient Street of the Song Dynasty, Xingxian Academy, etc.), tea art performance.

Yongding: Zhencheng Building, Chengqi Building, Fuyu Building, etc.

2.3 入境旅游线路报价

对国外组团社而言,组织入境游的旅行社只是中国国内接待社;对中国国内各地的接待社而言,国外组织旅游团的旅行社则扮演着组团社的角色。对于经营入境旅游业务的国际旅行社来说,入境旅游线路的报价涉及许多技巧和策略。①

2.3 Quotation of inbound tour itinerary

For foreign travel agencies, the travel agencies that organize inbound tours are only domestic travel agencies responsible for reception in China; for the travel agencies responsible for reception in all parts of China, the foreign travel agencies organizing tourist groups play the role of a tour wholesaler. For international travel agencies operating inbound tourism business, the quotation of the inbound tour itinerary involves many skills and strategies.

2.3.1 外国游客从本地入境时的本地游览价格

如果外国游客从本地入境,只在本地游览时,其接待价格与国内游是一致的,由住宿费、餐费、门票费、租车费、导游服务费、保险费和综合服务费构成。入境接待社接待价格＝住宿费＋餐费＋门票费＋租车费＋导游服务费＋保险费＋综合服务费。②

2.3.1 Local travelling expenses for foreign tourists when entering a locality as the first point of entry in China

If foreign tourists enter the first point of entry in China and only visit the local area, the travelling expenses are the same as those of domestic tourists, which are composed of such expenses as accommodation, meals, tickets, car rental, tour guide service, insurance and comprehensive service. In this case, the reception price charged by the travel agency responsible for reception ＝ accommodation fee＋meal fee＋ticket fee＋car rental fee＋tour guide service fee＋insurance fee＋comprehensive service fee.

---

① 张春莲,盖艳秋 主编,《旅行社计调操作实务》,北京:中国旅游出版社,2017:186.

② 张春莲,盖艳秋 主编,《旅行社计调操作实务》,北京:中国旅游出版社,2017:186.

2.3.2 外国游客从本地入境时的异地游览价格

如果外国游客从本地入境,然后前往异地游览,入境接待社就变成了国内组团社。其接待价格包括城市间交通费用、全陪服务费、办证费用、各地国内接待社报价。入境接待社接待价格＝城市间交通费用＋各地国内接待社报价＋全陪服务费＋办证费用。①

2.3.3 外国游客从本地入境时的本地和异地游览价格

如果外国游客从本地入境,其旅程包括本地游览和异地游览,入境接待社同时扮演了国内组团社和入境接待社的角色,因此其报价包括以上两种情况的报价。

入境接待社接待价格＝本地接待费＋城市间交通费用＋各地国内接待社报价＋全陪服务费＋办证费用。②

2.3.4 入境旅游接待报价方法

基于综合服务费的报价:综合服务费包含市内交通费用、导游服务费用、领队减免费用、旅行社宣传费、通讯联络费用,通常做法是将其平均计算到每位旅游者身上,按照一定的标准收取费用。早期较多使用这种计算方法,现在已经较少使用。③

2.3.2 Travelling expenses for foreign tourists' visiting other places after entering a locality as the first point of entry in China

If foreign tourists enter a locality as the first point of entry in China and then travel to other places, the travel agency responsible for the inbound tour will become a domestic tour wholesaler. The reception price includes inter-city transportation fee, national guide service fee, certificate-handling fee, and the domestic reception fee in different localities. The reception price quoted by the travel agency responsible for the inbound tour＝inter-city transportation fee＋the quotation of domestic local tour operator in variou places＋national guide service fee for the whole journey＋certificate-handling fee.

2.3.3 Travelling expenses for local tour and other places' tour when foreign tourists enter a locality as the first point of entry in China

When foreign tourists enter a locality as the first point of entry in China, their journey includes the local tour and other places' tour, and the travel agency responsible for receiving the inbound tour plays the role of both the domestic tour wholesaler and the travel agency to receive the inbound tour, so their quotation includes the above two situations.

The reception price quoted by the travel agency responsible for the inbound tour＝local reception fee＋inter-city transportation fee＋the quotation of domestic local tour operator in various places＋national guide service fee for the whole journey＋certificate-handling fee.

2.3.4 Quotation method for the reception of inbound tour

The quotation based on the comprehensive service fee: the comprehensive service fee includes the intra-city transportation fee, tour guide service fee, reduction fee for outbound tour escort service, travel agency's publicity fee, and communication fee. Generally, it is calculated on average to each tourist and charged according to a certain standard. This calculation method was widely employed in the early stage; nevertheless, currently it is rarely used.

---

① 张春莲,盖艳秋 主编,《旅行社计调操作实务》,北京:中国旅游出版社,2017:186.
② 张春莲,盖艳秋 主编,《旅行社计调操作实务》,北京:中国旅游出版社,2017:187.
③ 张春莲,盖艳秋 主编,《旅行社计调操作实务》,北京:中国旅游出版社,2017:187.

成本加利润报价法[①]:旅行团的成本包含入境接待社本地接待的住宿费、餐饮费、门票费、租车费、导游服务费等费用以及前往异地游览的城市间交通费用、异地接待社费用、全陪服务费。各旅行社的利润一般设定为15%到30%。这是目前较为常用的报价方法。

2.4 计调部的职能

计调部是旅行社的核心部门,计调部工作直接影响旅行社的正常运营。计调就是计划与调度之意,其主要任务就是旅游服务采购以及按照接待计划落实旅游团的食宿行游购娱等方面的具体事宜。计调部的职能主要在以下几个层面得以体现:选择职能、签约的职能、联络与协调职能、统计职能。[②]

选择职能:旅行社计调部通过与信誉好的旅游相关企业建立业务联系,向旅游者提供服务,如航空、酒店、餐厅、铁路、运输公司等以及各地的接待旅行社。

签约的职能:旅行社计调部需要与旅游相关企业和相关行业发生业务往来,如酒店、餐厅、各地的接待旅行社、航空、铁路、车船运输、保险等,通常采取签订合同的方式开展业务合作,以便从旅游供应商那里获得更多的优惠价格。

The quotation method based on the cost plus profit: The cost of a tourist group includes the fees for accommodation, catering, ticket, car rental, tour guide service and other fees for the local reception of the inbound tour by the travel agency, as well as the inter-city transportation fee for the visit to other places, the fee for the reception of travel agencies in other places, and national guide service fee. The profit of travel agencies is generally set at 15% to 30%. This is a commonly used quotation method at present.

2.4 Functions of the planning and dispatching department

The planning and dispatching department is the chief department of the travel agency, and its work directly affects the normal operation of the travel agency. "计调" means planning and scheduling, and its main task is to purchase tourism services and implement specific matters such as catering, accommodation, travelling, shopping, and entertainment for the tour group according to the reception plan. The functions of this department are mainly reflected in the following aspects: the function to select, the function to sign contracts, the function to communicate and coordinate and the function to collect statistics.

The function to select: This department of the travel agency provides services to tourists by establishing business contacts with creditworthy tourism-related enterprises, such as airlines, hotels, restaurants, railways, transportation companies, as well as local travel agencies to receive tourist groups.

The function to sign contracts: This department of the travel agency needs to conduct business transactions with tourism-related enterprises and related industries, such as hotels, restaurants, travel agencies in various places, airlines, railways, vehicle and ship transportation, insurance, etc. , and usually carries out business cooperation by signing contracts in order to obtain more preferential prices from tourism suppliers.

---

① 张春莲,盖艳秋 主编,《旅行社计调操作实务》,北京:中国旅游出版社,2017:187.
② 赵爱华 主编,《旅行社计调业务》,北京:中国旅游出版社,2021:2.

联络与协调职能：旅行社的组团过程乃是耗时的复杂过程，需要与旅游相关企业和相关行业保持联络、互相协调。

统计职能：计调部要对旅行社的旅游业务开展逐月、逐季逐年的定量科学分析，了解旅行社的运营情况，作为旅行社经营决策的依据，从而发现问题并设法解决。

The function to communicate and coordinate：The group-organizing process of travel agencies is a time-consuming and complex process，which involves maintaining contact and coordination with tourism-related enterprises and industries.

The function to collect statistics：The planning and dispatching department shall carry out quantitative and scientific analysis on the tourism business of the travel agency based on monthly，quarterly or yearly data，know about the operation of the travel agency，and serve as the basis for the travel agency to operate and make decision，so as to find problems and try to solve them.

2.5 计调人员的分类

按照旅游团的组成和接待过程进行划分，可以将计调分为组团型计调和接待型计调。[①]

组团型计调人员：在组团旅行社内负责组织旅游团并将其发送到异地接待旅行社的专职人员。分为国内组团型计调和出境组团型计调。

接待型计调人员：在接待旅行社中负责按照组团旅行社计划和要求安排交通工具、住宿、用餐、游览，安排导游等事宜的专职人员。分为国内接待计调和国际入境计调。

2.5 Classification of planning and dispatching personnel

According to the composition of a tourist group and the reception process，the planning and dispatching can be divided into group planning and reception planning.

Group planning and dispatching personnel of a tour wholesaler：They refer to the full-time staff of a tour wholesaler responsible for organizing tourist groups and dispatching them to be received by other travel agencies in other places. It can be divided into domestic tourist group planning and outbound tour group planning.

Reception planning and dispatching personnel：They refer to full-time personnel in the other travel agencies who are responsible for arranging transportation，accommodation，meals，tours，tour guides and other matters according to the plan and requirements of a tour wholesaler. It is divided into domestic reception planning and inbound-tour planning.

2.6 计调部采购业务基本流程

计调部采购业务指的是旅行社计调人员为组合某一旅游产品，以一定的价格向相关旅游产品供应商购买单项旅游服务产品的行为。旅行社计调凭借计调采购业务向旅游者提供各种必需的旅游服务。在旅行社产品成本中，由计调部采购的相关旅游产品成

2.6 Basic procurement process of the planning and dispatching department

The procurement business of the planning and dispatching department refers to the action of the planning and dispatching personnel of the travel agency to purchase single tourism service products from relevant tourism product suppliers at a certain price in order to combine them into a certain tourism product. The planning and dispatching staff of a travel agency provide tourists with all kinds of necessary tourism services by

---

① 赵爱华 主编，《旅行社计调业务》，北京：中国旅游出版社，2021：5.

本占了旅游团成本的较大比例。了解并掌握计调部采购业务的基本流程是旅行社计调部最重要的工作之一。

2.6.1 选择采购协作对象

组织旅行社计调人员收集同业旅行社、酒店/宾馆、交通运输企业、餐饮企业、景点、娱乐部门、购物商店、保险企业的相关资讯。实地考察基本符合旅行社要求的相关企业，初步协商合作事宜。

2.6.2 签订采购合同

与确定协作的相关企业协商并签订采购合同或合作协议书，一式两份，各持一份。已经签订的采购合同或合作协议书需要存档，并送外联部、财务部、接待部等留存备案。

2.6.3 落实采购任务

计调部制定详细的旅游团接待计划并落实各项订购任务。填写并发送各类预订单、变更单、取消单，说明旅行团的各种特殊要求。

2.6.4 采购报账结算

计调人员根据采购合同或合作协议书的相关要求，及时将费用明细账目报给财务部。财务部基于财务管理的各项规定以及合作协议书的相关要求，审核相关账目并结清费用。

virtue of planning and purchasing. In the cost of travel agency products, the cost of relevant tourism products purchased by the planning and dispatching department accounts for a large proportion of the cost of tourist groups. It is one of the most important tasks of the planning and dispatching department of travel agencies to understand and master the basic process of the procurement business of the department.

2.6.1 Select the target of procurement and collaboration

Organize the planning and dispatching personnel of the travel agency to collect the relevant information of other travel agencies, hotels, transportation enterprises, catering enterprises, scenic spots, entertainment departments, shopping stores and insurance companies. Visit relevant enterprises that basically meet the requirements of the travel agency on the spot and initially negotiate cooperation matters.

2.6.2 Sign procurement contracts

Negotiate and sign procurement contracts or cooperation agreements with the relevant enterprises that have determined to cooperate in duplicate copies, one for each. The signed procurement contract or cooperation agreement shall be filed and sent to the liaison department, finance department, reception department, etc. for keeping on file.

2.6.3 Implement procurement tasks

The planning and dispatching department works out a detailed tourist group reception plan and implements various ordering tasks. It completes and sends all kinds of advance orders, changed orders and canceled orders, and explains various special requirements of the tourist group.

2.6.4 Settle procurement reimbursement

According to the relevant requirements of the procurement contract or cooperation agreement, the planning and dispatching personnel shall timely report the detailed account of expenses to the finance department. The finance department reviews the relevant accounts and settles the expenses based on the provisions of financial management and the relevant requirements of the cooperation agreement.

2.7 知识拓展

✿ 2.7.1 旅游采购合同范本示例

旅行社与饭店合作协议①

协议编号：

甲方：_____ 饭店 　　　乙方：_____ 旅行社

一、客房套餐（每房每晚，货币单位：元）

房型	门市价	散客价	团队价	法定节假日价
普通客房				
高级客房				
豪华套房				

备注

1. 房价含中式早餐。中式早餐 ____ 元，西式早餐 ____ 元。若将中式早餐更改为西式早餐需支付差价 ____ 元。

2. 加床费用为 ____ 元。

3. 12 岁以下儿童与父母同住，不需加床者不加收费用。

4. 退房时间为 12 点之前，入住时间为 14 点以后。

5. 此价格有效期至 ____ 年 ____ 月 ____ 日止，其间价格如有变化，以双方预订确认为准。

二、订房条款

（一）团队订房（5 间成团，含 5 间）

1. 司陪房：订房 16 间可提供 1 间收费司陪房，价格为 元/间（夜晚），每团不超过 2 间。如安排团队在饭店就餐，司陪餐免费（享受旅游者预定菜式）。

2. 预订程序：乙方将订单传真给甲方市场销售部，列明旅游者名单、人数、房型、数量、抵/离店时间、联系人、联系方式等，经甲方确认之后方可生效。

3. 预订取消：乙方因故取消已确认的订单，需在 5 个工作日之前传真通知甲方，否则甲方将以以下标准收取赔偿金。

（1）提前 7 天以上（含 7 天）取消订房，不收取订房违约费用。

（2）提前 6 天取消订房，乙方需支付甲方预订客户总费用的 ____% 作为赔偿。

（3）5 个工作日内取消订房，乙方需支付甲方预订客房总费用的 ____% 作为赔偿。

（4）3 个工作日内取消订房，乙方需支付甲方总费用的 ____% 作为赔偿。

4. 预订未到：乙方需照常支付预订客房总费用的 ____%。

5. 乙方所有客房预订必须在甲方确认后两个工作日内将预订房费总额的 ____% 作为定金，汇至甲方账户，否则甲方不保留已确认的订房。

---

① 赵爱华 主编，《旅行社计调业务》，北京：中国旅游出版社，2021：47-48．个别内容有修改，英语版本为编写者所译。

（二）散客订房(5 间房以下，不含 5 间房)

1. 预订程序：乙方将订单传真给甲方市场销售部，列明旅游者名单、人数、房型、数量、抵/离店时间、联系人、联系方式等，经甲方确认之后方可生效。

2. 预订取消：乙方因故取消已确认的订单，至少需要提前 1 天传真通知甲方，得到甲方确认后方可取消预订。

三、有效期

本协议自签订之日起至 ＿＿＿ 年 ＿＿＿ 月 ＿＿＿ 日止有效。其间价格如有变动，将提前书面通知。如因一方违约或因不可抗拒的因素影响，此合约无法继续履行，则双方终止合作。本协议转让无效。

四、本协议一式两份，双方各执一份，均具同等效力。本协议解释权属甲方，未尽事宜双方协商。

单位名称：   单位名称：

销售负责人：   负责人：

联系电话：   联系电话：

传真：   传真：

盖章确认   盖章确认

日期： 年 月 日   日期： 年 月 日

2.7 Knowledge expansion

2.7.1 Tourism procurement contract (sample)

Cooperation Agreement between Travel Agency and Hotel

Agreement No.:

Party A: ＿＿＿＿＿ Hotel   Party B: ＿＿＿＿＿ Travel Agency

Ⅰ. Room package (per room and per night; currency unit: RMB)

Room type	Rack rate	Rate for individuals	Rate for tourist groups	Rate for public holiday
regular room				
superior room				
deluxe suite				

Remarks

1. The room rate includes Chinese breakfast. Chinese breakfast is ＿＿＿＿＿ RMB, while Western-style breakfast is ＿＿＿＿＿ RMB. If you would like to change Chinese breakfast into Western-style breakfast, you will need to pay a price difference.

2. The extra bed fee _____ RMB.

3. When children under the age of 12 live with their parents, there is no extra charge for them if they do not need extra beds.

4. Check-out time is before 12:00 and check-in time is after 14:00 each day.

5. The room rate is valid until the day of _____ . If there is any change in the price during the period, the reservation and confirmation of both parties shall prevail.

Ⅱ. Reservation terms

1. Room reservation for groups (the booking of 5 rooms is regarded as group booking, including 5 rooms)

(1) Room for driver and tour guide: When 16 rooms are booked for a group, one paid room for the driver and tour guide will be provided with the price of _____ RMB/per room and per night, and no more than 2 rooms for the driver and tour guide will be provided per group. If the meals of the group are arranged in the hotel, complimentary meals will be provided for the driver and tour guide (the same food as the tourist group's reservation).

(2) Reservation procedure: When Party B faxes the reservation to Party A's marketing department, listing the name list of tourists, number of people, room type, room quantity, arrival/departure time, contact person, contact information, etc. , it can take effect after Party A confirms it.

(3) Reservation cancellation: If Party B cancels the confirmed order for any reason, it shall notify Party A by fax 5 working days in advance, otherwise Party A will charge compensation according to the following standards.

a. Cancellation of reservation more than 7 days in advance (including 7 days) will not be charged for breach of contract.

b. If the reservation is canceled within 6 days, Party B shall pay Party A ____% of the total cost of the room reservation as compensation.

c. If the reservation is canceled within 5 working days, Party B shall pay Party A ____% of the total cost of the room reservation as compensation.

d. If the reservation is cancelled within 3 working days, Party B shall pay ____% of the total expenses of Party A as compensation.

(4) Reservation without check-in: Party B shall pay ____% of the total cost of the room reservation as usual.

(5) Party B must remit ____% of the total room reservation fee as a deposit to Party A's account within two working days after confirmation by Party A, otherwise Party A will not retain the confirmed room reservation.

2. Individual guest reservation (less than 5 rooms, excluding 5 rooms)

(1) Reservation procedure: Party B faxes the reservation to Party A's marketing department, listing the list of tourists, number of people, room type, room quantity, arrival/departure time, contact person, contact information, etc. , which can take effect after Party A confirms.

(2) Reservation's cancellation: If Party B cancels the confirmed reservation for any reason, it shall notify Party A by fax at least one day in advance and obtain Party A's confirmation before cancelling the reservation.

Ⅲ. Validity

This agreement starts from the date of signing and ends on _____ _____ _____ (day/month/year). If price change arises during the period, a written notice will be given in advance. If the contract cannot continue to be performed due to one party's breach of contract or the influence of force majeure, both parties shall terminate the cooperation. The transfer of this agreement is invalid.

Ⅳ. This agreement is made in duplicate, with each party holding one copy, both of which have the same effect. The right of interpretation of this agreement belongs to Party A, and matters not covered herein shall be negotiated by both parties.

Company name: Company name:
Director of sales: person in charge:
Tel: Tel:
Fax: Fax:
Seal for confirmation   Seal for confirmation
Date: (day/month/year)   Date: (day/month/year)

旅游团租车合作协议[①]

旅行社(以下简称甲方):

租赁车队(以下简称乙方):

根据《旅行社条例》《中华人民共和国道路交通安全法》的有关法律法规要求,本着平等自愿、互惠互利的原则,甲乙双方就旅游团队租车事宜达成如下协议:

一、双方合作方式

甲方根据旅游车辆需要以书面形式制定订车计划单,并附上车辆行车游览内容、租车要求(包括用车数量、时间、结算方式等)以传真方式发给乙方知悉,乙方在24小时之内以传真方式予以回复并确认。一经双方确认,任何一方不得擅自更改或取消,若有更改需经双方认可方可有效,违者将承担一切责任并赔偿损失。

---

① 吕海龙,刘雪梅 主编,《旅行社计调业务》,北京:北京理工大学出版社,2017:126-128. 内容有修改,英语版本为编写者所译。

双方在落实计划之后,任何一方必须在用车之前 3 天之内再次核对车辆租用事宜,如有更动,必须及时告知对方。至用车日若未通知对方变动情况,则按照原合同执行,具体租车价格见旅游团订车计划。

二、租车费用结算方式

每月 _____ 日凭租车单结算当月车费。

三、双方合作的责任与违约处罚

1. 甲方必须提前将租车需求以传真方式发给乙方,一经乙方确认,则表示乙方已收悉并认可,该合作有效。

2. 若团队发生退、减、增或任何变化时,甲方有责任与义务第一时间告知乙方。若由于甲方疏忽造成乙方损失,甲方负有赔偿责任。特殊情况由双方协商处理。

3. 乙方向甲方提供的车辆应经公安等部门检验年审合格并符合行业标准或合同约定标准,足额办理了乘员险、第三者责任险等保险手续费,符合交通管理部门认定的旅游目的地经营范围。

4. 乙方委派司机必须严格按照甲方拟定的团队行程执行,尊重导游的团队安排。如乙方委派司机因个人利益影响到团队的正常运行,或擅自更改行程而引发纠纷,乙方必须承担一切法律与赔偿责任。

5. 乙方若不能按照约定时间提供车辆,应提前三日书面通知甲方并支付约定车费 10% 的违约金。乙方若不能按照约定时间提供车辆,又不能及时通知甲方,应当支付 100% 的违约金。

6. 甲乙双方因不可抗力不能履行协议,不承担违约责任,然而应该提前三日通知对方并提供不能履约的充分证据;若不可抗力是在如上所述的时限之后发生的,则应当在不可抗力发生后 12 小时内通知对方并提供不能履约的充分证据。

7. 甲乙双方在执行本合同时若发生纠纷,应本着友好合作的态度协商解决。如不能协商解决,可向旅游质量监督管理所或仲裁委员会提出仲裁,也可向人民法院提出诉讼。

8. 本合同一式两份,双方各持一份,具有同等效力。甲乙双方签字盖章有效。本合同有效期从 _____ 年 _____ 月 _____ 日至 _____ 年 _____ 月 _____ 日。

四、双方合作附则

本协议未尽事宜,双方在执行中协商完善。

甲方(盖章)　　　　　　　　　　乙方(盖章)
签约代表:　　　　　　　　　　　签约代表
联系电话:　　　　　　　　　　　联系电话:
签约日期:　　　　　　　　　　　签约日期:

Cooperation Agreement on Car Rental

Travel agency (hereinafter referred to as Party A):

Car rental company (hereinafter referred to as Party B):

In accordance with the relevant laws and regulations of *The Regulations on Travel Agencies* and *Road Traffic Safety Law of the People's Republic of China*, Party A and Party B have reached the following agreement on car rental for tourist groups on the principle of equality, voluntariness, reciprocity and mutual benefit.

1. Cooperation mode of both parties

Party A shall prepare a vehicle reservation plan for the required tourist vehicles in written form, attach the itinerary and car rental requirements including the number of vehicles used, time, settlement method, etc., and send it to Party B by fax. Party B shall reply and confirm it within 24 hours by fax. Once the plan is confirmed by both parties, either party shall not change or cancel it without authorization. If a change needs to be made, it can be effective only after being approved by two parties, or the violator will bear all responsibilities and compensate for the loss.

In the process of both parties' implementing the plan, either party must re-check the vehicle rental within 3 days before using the vehicle. If there is any change, it must be informed in time. If the other party is not informed of the change on the date of using the vehicle, the original contract will still be implemented. For the specific rental price, check the tourist group's vehicle reservation plan.

2. Terms of vehicle rental fee settlement

On the day of _____ each month, the vehicle rental fee is settled on the basis of the vehicle reservation plan.

3. Responsibilities and penalties for breach of contract of both parties

(1) Party A must send a vehicle reservation plan to Party B by fax in advance. Once the plan is confirmed by Party B, it means that Party B has received and accepted it, and the cooperation is effective.

(2) Party A has the responsibility and obligation to inform Party B as soon as possible in case of any withdrawal, decrease and increase in tourist number or change of tourist groups. If Party A's negligence causes losses to Party B, Party A shall be liable for compensation. Special cases shall be handled by both parties through negotiation.

（3）The vehicles provided by Party B to Party A shall be inspected and approved by public security and other departments in annual review，and shall follow industry standards or contractual standards. They shall have fully paid insurance fees such as passenger insurance and third-party liability insurance，and shall comply with the business scope of tourist destinations recognized by the transportation regulation department.

（4）The driver/drivers appointed by Party B must strictly follow the tourist group's itinerary proposed by Party A and respect the arrangement of the tour guide. If the driver appointed by Party B affects the normal operation of the tourist group due to his/her personal interests，or changes the itinerary without authorization，Party B must bear all legal and compensation responsibilities for all arising conflicts.

（5）If Party B is unable to provide the vehicle according to the agreed time，Party B shall notify Party A in writing three days in advance and pay a penalty of 10% of the agreed fare. If Party B fails to provide the vehicle according to the agreed time and fails to notify Party A in a timely manner，Party B shall pay a penalty of 100%.

（6）If Party A and Party B are unable to perform the agreement due to force majeure，they shall not be liable for breach of contract. However，one party shall notify the other party three days in advance and provide sufficient evidence of their inability to perform；if force majeure occurs after the specified time limit mentioned above，the other party shall be notified within 12 hours of the occurrence of force majeure and sufficient evidence of inability to perform shall be provided.

（7）If any dispute arises between Party A and Party B during the execution of this contract，they shall negotiate and resolve it in a friendly and cooperative manner. If no settlement can be reached through consultation，it can be submitted to Tourism Quality Supervision and Regulation Office or Arbitration Commission for arbitration，or to the People's Court.

（8）This contract is made in duplicate，with each party holding one copy that has equal legal effect. This contract is valid from _____ （day/month/year）to _____ （day/month/year），when both parties sign and seal it.

4. Supplementary provisions for cooperation between the two parties

For the matters not covered in this contract，both parties shall negotiate and improve them in implementation.

Party A（seal）   Party B（seal）

Representative：   Representative：

Tel：   Tel：

Date：   Date：

境内旅游组团社与地接社合同①

合同编号：＿＿＿＿＿＿＿＿＿   组团社：＿＿＿＿＿＿＿＿

法定代表人（主要负责人）：＿＿＿＿＿＿＿ 职务：＿＿＿＿＿＿＿

业务经营许可证号：＿＿＿＿＿＿＿ 经营地址：＿＿＿＿＿＿＿

经办人：＿＿＿＿＿＿＿＿   职务：＿＿＿＿＿＿＿

联系电话：＿＿＿＿＿＿＿＿   传真：＿＿＿＿＿＿＿

电子邮箱：＿＿＿＿＿＿＿＿

法定代表人（主要负责人）：＿＿＿＿＿＿＿ 地接社：＿＿＿＿＿＿＿

业务经营许可证号：   职务：＿＿＿＿＿＿＿

经办人：＿＿＿＿＿＿＿＿   经营地址：＿＿＿＿＿＿＿

联系电话：＿＿＿＿＿＿＿＿   职务：＿＿＿＿＿＿＿

电子邮箱：＿＿＿＿＿＿＿＿   传真：＿＿＿＿＿＿＿

组团社将其组织的旅游者交由地接社接待，地接社按照双方确认的标准和要求，为组团社组织的旅游者提供接待服务。组团社与地接社双方经平等协商，达成如下协议：

第一条　合同构成

下列内容作为本合同的有效组成部分，与本合同具有同等法律效力：

1.《接待计划书》；

2. 双方业务往来确认；

3. 双方就未尽事宜达成的补充协议；

4. 财务确认及结算单据；

5. 其他约定：＿＿＿＿＿＿＿＿。

第二条　合同当事人

组团社和地接社是依照中华人民共和国法律、法规设立的旅行社或者分社，依法取得旅行社业务资质，且在合同有效期内双方资质有效存续。

双方均应于签订合同前向对方提供营业执照、业务经营许可证（分社备案登记证明）、旅行社责任保险单、安全管理制度、突发事件处理预案等文书复印件并加盖

---

① 境内旅游组团社与地接社合同（示范合同），中国政府网，http://www. gov. cn/govweb/foot/2014-04/17/content_2661652. htm，2022/7/5.

印章。如上述信息 _____ 发生变更，变更一方应于变更之日起 _____ 日内书面通知对方并提供更新后的材料。

第三条 《接待计划书》订立

组团社可以通过电话、传真、电子邮件等通讯方式与地接社洽谈接待相关事宜，在此过程中双方最终达成一致的事项，应形成《接待计划书》，并由双方签字盖章确认。

《接待计划书》应明确以下内容：

1. 旅游者人数及名单；

2. 接待费用，其中地接导游费用为 _____；

3. 抵离时间、航班、车次；

4. 交通、住宿、餐饮服务安排及标准；

5. 游览行程安排、游览内容及时间；

6. 自由活动次数及时间；

7. 对导游的要求；

8. 其他：_____。

第四条 《接待计划书》变更

《接待计划书》一经确认，单方不得擅自变更。

出团前如遇不可抗力或者其他原因确需变更的，经协商一致，就变更后的内容由双方签字盖章确认。紧急情况下，双方可通过电话、传真、电子邮件等通讯方式进行协商，但应在紧急情况消失之日起 _____ 日内由双方签字盖章确认。

除法律、法规规定外，出团后《接待计划书》不得变更。

第五条 接待服务要求

地接社接待服务应符合：

1.《中华人民共和国旅游法》(以下简称《旅游法》)、《旅行社条例》、《导游人员管理条例》等法律、法规；

2. 双方约定的接待服务标准；

3. 相关的国家标准和行业标准。

第六条 接待费用结算

结算方式及期限：_____。

地接社应配合组团社关于接待费用结算的要求及时填写结算单，并加盖地接社财务专用章，送达组团社财务部门。组团社应在收到地接社结算单据后 _____ 日内核对，并按约定按时足额支付接待费用。

第七条 合同义务

(一)组团社义务

1. 组团社应按约定的时限、数额支付接待费用；

2. 组团社应真实、明确说明接待要求和标准，将与旅游者达成的合同、单团《旅游行程单》的副本提供给地接社；

3. 组团社应对地接社完成接待服务予以必要协助。

(二)地接社义务

1. 地接社应严格按照双方约定安排旅游行程、旅游景点、服务项目等,不得因与组团社团款等纠纷擅自中止旅游服务;

2. 未经组团社书面同意,地接社不得以任何方式将组团社组织的旅游者与其他旅游者合并接待,或者转交任何第三方接待;

3. 地接社应选择合格且具有相应接待能力的供应商;

4. 地接社应积极配合组团社做好接待服务质量测评工作,按约定通报团队动态和反馈接待服务质量信息,服务质量测评方式及达标标准双方约定为: _____;

5. 要求导游引导旅游者健康、文明旅游,劝阻旅游者违法和违反社会公德的行为。

(三)双方共同义务

1. 双方约定的接待费用不应低于接待和服务成本;

2. 双方的约定应遵守《旅游法》《消费者权益保护法》等法律、法规,不应损害旅游者的合法权益;

3. 一方违约后,对方应采取适当措施防止损失的扩大;

4. 双方均应保守经营活动中获取的商业秘密;

5. 旅游行程中旅游者主张解除合同的,旅行社应当协助旅游者返回出发地或者旅游者指定的合理地点。

第八条　风险防范

1. 组团社和地接社均应按法律、法规规定足额投保旅行社责任保险;

2. 组团社应提示其组织的旅游者购买人身意外伤害保险;

3. 地接社为组团社组织的旅游者安排的车辆及司机必须具备合法有效资质,地接社选择的客运经营者应已购买承运人责任保险,且保险金额不低于 _____ 万元;

4. 组团社和地接社均应保证旅游者的安全,对于可能危及旅游者人身及财产安全的事项,应做出真实的说明和明确的警示,并采取必要措施防止危害发生和扩大;

5. 地接社接待过程中,旅游者受到人身、财产损害的,地接社应采取救助措施并先行垫付必要费用,及时向组团社反馈信息,收集和保存相关证据,组团社和地接社在责任划分明确后 _____ 日内根据各自承担的责任进行结算,属于第三方责任的,地接社应协助旅游者索赔。

第九条　旅游纠纷处理

1. 旅游者在地接社接待过程中提出投诉的,地接社应尽力在当地及时解决,并将处理情况书面通知组团社,未能在当地解决的,应及时书面通知组团社。地接社应积极配合组团社处理旅游者投诉、仲裁、诉讼等服务质量纠纷,及时提供所需证据材料。

2. 组团社和地接社应根据调查情况,划分各自应承担的赔偿责任,并于责任划分

明确后 _____ 日内进行结算。因组团社原因导致的行程延误、更改、取消等所造成的经济损失由组团社承担,因地接社接待服务质量问题造成的经济损失由地接社承担。

3. 因地接社接待服务质量问题而产生的经济赔偿,组团社依照或者参照如下标准做出赔偿后,地接社应在组团社提出追索请求并提供相关证明后 _____ 日内对组团社予以全额赔偿:

(1)依照组团社和旅游者约定的赔偿标准;

(2)参照国家旅游局制定的《旅行社服务质量赔偿标准》;

(3)依照法院、仲裁机构裁决所确定的数额标准。

第十条   不可抗力

1. 因不可抗力等不可归责于合同任何一方的事由致使一方不能履行合同的,应根据影响程度,部分或者全部免除责任,但迟延履行后发生不可抗力等不可归责于合同任何一方的事由的,不能免除责任。

2. 一方因不可抗力等不可归责于合同任何一方的事由不能履行合同的,应当及时通知另一方,并在合理期限内提供证明。双方应采取合理适当措施防止损失扩大,因一方未履行相关义务造成对方损失的,应承担赔偿责任。

3. 因不可抗力等不可归责于合同任何一方的事由导致行程延滞,组团社和地接社应及时与旅游者协商、调整行程,所增加的费用,同意旅游者不承担的部分由组团社和地接社协商承担。

4. 若不可抗力等不可归责于合同任何一方的事由危及旅游者人身、财产安全,组团社和地接社应采取相应的安全救助措施,所支出的费用,同意旅游者不承担的部分由组团社和地接社协商承担。

第十一条   违约责任

1. 组团社未按合同约定按时足额支付接待费用,应以未支付团款为基数,按日 _____ ％向地接社支付违约金,违约金不足以弥补实际损失的,按实际损失赔偿。

2. 组团社因如下情形造成地接社经济损失的,应按实际损失向地接社承担违约责任:

(1)接待要求、标准等信息说明不明确或者错误;

(2)未对地接社完成接待服务予以必要协助。

3. 地接社未经组团社书面同意,将组团社组织的旅游者与其他旅游者合并接待,或者转交任何第三方接待,地接社应向组团社支付当团接待费用 _____ ％的违约金,违约金不足以弥补实际损失的,按实际损失赔偿。

4. 地接社未按合同约定选择合格且具有相应接待能力的供应商,地接社应向组团社支付当团接待费用 _____ ％的违约金,违约金不足以弥补实际损失的,按实际损失赔偿。

5. 因地接社违法违规行为导致组团社受到行政处罚的,地接社应向组团社支付当团接待费用 _____ ％的违约金,违约金不足以弥补实际损失的,按实际损失赔偿。

6. 地接社未能在当地解决旅游者提出的投诉，又未及时书面通知组团社的，地接社应就造成的损失承担赔偿责任。

7. 组团社和地接社双方或者任何一方未积极采取补救措施防止损失扩大，在各自责任范围内就扩大的损失承担赔偿责任。

8. 组团社和地接社任何一方泄露在经营活动中获取的商业秘密，违约一方应向另一方支付当团接待费用 _____ ％的违约金，违约金不足以弥补实际损失的，按实际损失赔偿。

第十二条　合同解除

1. 组团社超出约定付款期限 _____ 日以上未支付接待费用的，地接社有权解除合同，并要求组团社承担相应的赔偿责任。

2. 地接社接待服务质量未达到本合同第七条第（二）款第 4 项约定的达标标准 _____ 次（含本数）以上的，组团社有权解除合同，并要求地接社承担相应的赔偿责任。

3. 因地接社原因引发旅游者有责投诉、仲裁或者民事诉讼 _____ 次（含本数）以上，组团社有权解除合同，并要求地接社承担相应的赔偿责任。

4. 因地接社违约给组团社或者旅游者造成经济损失，地接社拒不改正或者拒绝赔偿 _____ 次（含本数）以上，组团社有权解除合同，并要求地接社承担相应的赔偿责任。

5. 双方约定合同解除的其他情形：_____。

第十三条　争议解决

组团社和地接社因单团接待业务引发的争议，可协商解决，协商不成的，按下列第 _____ 种方式解决（选择一种）：

1. 提交仲裁，双方约定仲裁委员会为 _____ （标明仲裁委员会所属地区和名称）；

2. 提起民事诉讼，双方约定诉讼管辖地为 _____ （限于被告住所地、合同履行地、合同签订地、原告住所地、标的物所在地）。

第十四条　合同效力与期限

1. 本合同一式 _____ 份，双方各持 _____ 份，具有同等法律效力。

2. 本合同自双方签字盖章之日起生效，有效期为 _____ 。一方可于合同有效期届满前 _____ 日向另一方书面提出续签合同。

3. 本合同终止或者解除时，双方在合同有效期内已确认的接待计划应当继续履行。

组团社签章：_____　　　地接社签章：_____

签约时间：_____　　　　签约时间：_____

签约地点：_____　　　　签约地点：_____

Contract Between Domestic Tour Wholesaler and Local Tour Operator①

Contract No. ：＿＿＿＿＿＿＿

Domestic tour wholesaler：＿＿＿＿＿＿＿

Legal representative (person in charge)：＿＿＿＿ Title：＿＿＿＿＿＿

Business operation license No. ：＿＿＿＿＿＿

Business address：＿＿＿＿＿＿

Handled by：＿＿＿＿＿＿ Title：＿＿＿＿＿＿

Contact number：＿＿＿＿＿＿ Fax：＿＿＿＿＿＿

E-mail：＿＿＿＿＿＿

Local tour operator：＿＿＿＿＿＿

Legal representative (person in charge)：＿＿＿＿ Title：＿＿＿＿＿＿

Business operation license No. ：＿＿＿＿＿＿

Business address：＿＿＿＿＿＿

Handled by：＿＿＿＿＿＿ Title：＿＿＿＿＿＿

Contact number：＿＿＿＿＿＿ Fax：＿＿＿＿＿＿

E-mail：＿＿＿＿＿＿

The local tour operator will receive the tourists organized by domestic tour wholesaler. The local tour operator will provide reception services for the tourists organized by the tour wholesaler according to the standards and requirements confirmed by both parties. Through negotiation on an equal basis, the two parties have reached the following agreement：

Article 1 Contract composition

As an effective part of this contract，the following contents have the same legal effect as this contract：

1. "Reception Plan"；

2. Confirmation of business transactions between both parties；

3. Supplementary agreements reached by both parties on matters not covered；

4. Financial confirmation and settlement documents；

5. Other agreements：＿＿＿＿.

Article 2 Parties to the contract

The tour wholesaler and local tour operator are the travel agencies or branches established in accordance with the laws and regulations of the People's Republic of China，which have obtained travel agency business qualifications in

---

① 原合同文本为中文版，英语版本为编写者所译。

accordance with the law, and the qualifications of both parties are valid within the validity period of the contract.

Prior to contract-signing, both parties shall provide the other party with duplicate copies of business license, license for operation (certificate of branch registration), travel agency's liability insurance policy, safety regulation system, emergency response plan and other documents and affix their seals. In case of any change in the above information, the changing party shall notify the other party in writing within _____ days from the date of the change and provide updated materials.

Article 3　Conclusion of the reception plan

The tour wholesaler can negotiate with the local tour operator on reception-related matters through telephone, fax, e-mail and other means of communication. In this process, the matters finally agreed by both parties should form a reception plan, which should be signed and sealed by both parties for confirmation.

The reception plan shall specify the following contents:

1. Number and list of tourists;

2. Reception expenses: Among them, the cost of local tour guide service is _____;

3. Arrival and departure time, flight and train number;

4. Transportation, accommodation, catering service arrangements and standards;

5. Tour itinerary, items for sightseeing and time;

6. Number and time of self-arranged activities;

7. Requirements for tour guides;

8. Others: _____.

Article 4　Change of reception plan

Once the reception plan is confirmed, it cannot be changed unilaterally.

In case of force majeure or other reasons a change really needs to be made, the changed contents shall be signed and sealed by both parties for confirmation after negotiation. In the event of emergency, both parties can negotiate through telephone, fax, e-mail and other means of communication. Nevertheless, both parties shall sign and seal for confirmation within _____ days when the emergency no longer exists.

Unless stipulated by law and regulations, the reception plan shall not be changed after the tourist group starts its journey.

Article 5　Reception service requirements

The reception service of the local tour operator shall meet the following requirements:

1. *The Tourism Law of the People's Republic of China* (hereinafter referred to as *Tourism Law*), *The Regulations on Travel Agencies*, *The Regulations on Tour Guides* and other laws and regulations;

2. The reception service standards agreed by both parties;

3. Relevant national and industrial standards.

Article 6 Settlement of reception expenses

Settlement term and deadline: _____ .

The local tour operator shall settle the reception expense on the basis of the requirements of the tour wholesaler, fill in the settlement form in time, affix its special financial seal and deliver it to the financial department of the tour wholesaler. The tour wholesaler shall check the documents of settlement within _____ days upon the receipt of it from the local tour operator, and pay the reception fee in full and on the specific date as agreed.

Article 7 Contract obligations

1. Obligations of the tour wholesaler

(1) The tour wholesaler shall pay the reception fee according to the agreed time limit and amount;

(2) The tour wholesaler shall truthfully and clearly explain the reception requirements and standards, and provide the duplicate copy of the contract with tourists and the tour itinerary for a particular group for the local tour operator;

(3) The tour wholesaler shall offer necessary assistance to the local tour operator to complete the reception service.

2. Obligations of local tour operator

(1) The local tour operator shall arrange the tour itinerary, tourist attractions, service items, etc. in strict accordance with the agreement of both parties, and shall not suspend the tourism service without authorization due to the dispute with the tourist group over travelling expenses etc.;

(2) Without the written consent of the tour wholesaler, the local tour operator shall not receive the tourists organized by the tour wholesaler together with other tourists in any way, or transfer them to any third party for reception;

(3) The local tour operator shall select qualified suppliers with corresponding reception capacity;

(4) The local tour operator shall actively cooperate with the tour wholesaler in the evaluation of reception service quality, report the tourist group's situation and give feedback on reception service quality as agreed. The approach and standard for service quality evaluation are agreed by both parties as follows: _____ ;

(5) Tour guides are required to guide tourists to travel in a sensible manner, and to discourage tourists from violating laws and social ethics.

3. Joint obligations of both parties

（1）The reception expenses agreed by both parties shall not be lower than the reception and service costs;

（2）The agreement of both parties shall comply with *Tourism Law*, *The Law on the Protection of Consumer Rights and Interests* and other laws and regulations, and shall not damage the legitimate rights and interests of tourists;

（3）After one party breaches the contract, the other party shall take appropriate measures to prevent the expansion of losses;

（4）Both parties shall keep the business secrets obtained in business activities;

（5）If a tourist claims to terminate the contract when the tour itinerary is being implemented, the tour operator shall assist the tourist to return to the place of departure or the reasonable place designated by the tourist.

Article 8 Risk prevention

1. The travel agency liability insurance shall be fully insured by the tour wholesaler and local tour operator in accordance with laws and regulations;

2. The tour wholesaler shall remind the tourists it organizes to purchase personal accident insurance;

3. The vehicles and drivers arranged by the local tour operator for the tourists organized by the tour wholesaler must have legal and valid qualifications. The passenger transport operator selected by the local tour operator should have purchased carrier liability insurance, and the insurance amount should not be less than _____ RMB (the basic calculating unit is 10 000 RMB);

4. Both the tour wholesaler and the local tour operator shall ensure the safety of tourists. As regards the matters that may endanger the personal and property safety of tourists, they shall make true explanations and clear warnings, and take necessary measures to prevent the occurrence and expansion of hazards;

5. In the reception process of the local tour operator, if the tourists suffer personal and property damage, the local tour operator shall take rescue measures and advance necessary expenses, timely feed information back to the tour wholesaler, and collect and save relevant evidence. After the division of responsibilities between the tour wholesaler and the local tour operator is made clear, settlement shall be made within _____ days according to their respective responsibilities. If it is the responsibility of a third party, the local tour operator shall assist the tourists to claim compensation.

Article 9 Settlement of tourism disputes

1. If a tourist lodges a complaint in the reception process of the local tour operator, the local tour operator shall try its best to solve it in a timely manner and notify the tour wholesaler the measures it has taken in writing. If it fails to solve it locally, it shall promptly notify the tour wholesaler in writing. The local tour

operator shall actively cooperate with the tour wholesaler to deal with the service quality disputes such as tourists' complaints, arbitration and litigation, and provide necessary evidence without delay.

2. The tour wholesaler and the local tour operator shall divide their respective liability for compensation according to investigation, and after the division of liability is clear, settlement shall be made within _____ days. The tour wholesaler is liable for the economic losses caused by its delay, change and cancellation, and the local tour operator is liable for the economic losses caused by its reception service quality problems.

3. For the economic compensation caused by the reception service quality of the local tour operator, the tour wholesaler shall make compensation to tourists according to or with reference to the following standards. After the tour wholesaler makes a claim and provides relevant evidence, full compensation shall be paid to the tour wholesaler by the local tour operator within _____ days.

The standards of compensation are listed as follows:

(1) The compensation standards agreed by the tour wholesaler and tourists;

(2) "The Compensation Standards for Service Quality of Travel Agencies" formulated by the National Tourism Administration;

(3) The amount of compensation determined by the court and arbitral institution.

Article 10 Force majeure

1. If one party is unable to implement the contract due to force majeure and other causes not attributable to either party of the contract, either party shall be exempted from liability in part or in whole according to the degree of influence. Nonetheless, if force majeure and other causes not attributable to either party of the contract occur after the delay in performance, either party shall not be exempted from liability.

2. If one party is unable to implement the contract due to force majeure or other reasons not attributable to either party of the contract, one party shall notify the other party in time and provide evidence within a reasonable period. Both parties shall take reasonable and appropriate measures to prevent the expansion of losses. If one party fails to perform relevant obligations and causes losses to the other party, it shall be liable for compensation.

3. If the tour is delayed due to force majeure and other reasons not attributable to either party of the contract, the tour wholesaler and the local tour operator shall negotiate with the tourists in time and adjust the tour itinerary. The tour wholesaler and the local tour operator shall be responsible for the increased expenses (including the partial expenses not to be borne by tourists, which are agreed by two parties) through negotiation.

4. If the personal and property safety of tourists is endangered due to force majeure and other reasons not attributable to either party of the contract, the tour wholesaler and the local tour operator shall take corresponding safety rescue measures, and pay the expenses incurred (including the partial expenses not to be borne by tourists, which are agreed by two parties) through negotiation.

Article 11 Liability for breach of contract

1. If the tour wholesaler fails to pay the reception fee in full and on time as agreed in the contract, it shall take the unpaid travelling expense as the base and pay _____% default penalty to the local tour operator. If the default penalty is not enough to cover the actual losses, compensation shall be made according to the actual losses.

2. In case of economic losses to the local tour operator due to the following circumstances, the tour wholesaler shall bear the liability for breach of contract to the local tour operator according to the actual losses:

(1) The reception requirements, standards and other information were not clear or correct;

(2) The tour wholesaler did not provide necessary assistance for the local tour operator.

3. Without the written consent of the tour wholesaler, the local tour operator shall pay the tour wholesaler _____% of the current tour reception fee if it merges the tourists organized by the tour wholesaler with other tourists or transfers them to any third party for reception. If the default penalty is not enough to cover the actual loss, the local tour operator shall be liable for compensation according to the actual loss.

4. If the local tour operator fails to select qualified suppliers with corresponding reception capacity as agreed in the contract, it shall pay _____% of the group reception fee to the tour wholesaler. If the default penalty is insufficient to pay for the actual loss, compensation will be based on the actual loss.

5. If the local tour operator is subject to administrative punishment due to its illegal acts, it shall pay _____% of the group reception fee to the tour wholesaler. If the default penalty is insufficient to cover the actual loss, compensation will depend on the actual loss.

6. If the local tour operator fails to solve the tourists' complaints locally and fails to notify the tour wholesaler in writing in time, it shall be liable for the losses caused.

7. If both or either of the tour wholesaler and the local tour operator fail/fails to actively take remedial measures to prevent the expansion of losses, they/it shall be liable for compensation for the expanded losses within their/its respective scope of responsibility.

8. If either the tour wholesaler or the local tour operator reveals the business secrets obtained in the business activities，the breaching party shall pay _____ ％ of the group reception fee to the other party. If the default penalty is insufficient to cover the actual loss，compensation will rely on the actual loss.

Article 12   Termination of the contract

1. If the tour wholesaler has not paid the reception fee during the agreed payment period for more than _____ days，the local tour operator has the right to terminate the contract and request the tour wholesaler to bear the corresponding liability for compensation.

2. If the reception service quality of the local tour operator fails to meet the standard agreed in Item 4，Paragraph 2，Article 7 of this contract more than _____ times (including this time)，the tour wholesaler has the right to terminate the contract and request the local tour operator to bear the corresponding liability for compensation.

3. If the local tour operator has been responsible for complaints，arbitration or civil litigation more than _____ times (including this time)，the tour wholesaler has the right to terminate the contract and request the local tour operator to bear the corresponding liability for compensation.

4. If the local tour operator refuses to correct its acts or compensate for the economic losses caused by its breach of contract to the tour wholesaler or tourists more than _____ times (including this time)，the tour wholesaler has the right to terminate the contract and request the local tour operator to bear the corresponding liability for compensation.

5. Other circumstances for the termination of the contract agreed by both parties：_____.

Article 13   Dispute settlement

The disputes between the tour wholesaler and the local tour operator in a single-group reception can be settled through negotiation. If the negotiation fails，one of the following approaches shall apply (choose one)：

1. Submit to arbitration. Both parties agree that the arbitration commission is _____(The region and name of the arbitration commission should be indicated.)；

2. File a civil lawsuit. Both parties agree that the jurisdiction of the lawsuit is _____(The jurisdiction of the lawsuit is limited to the defendant's domicile, the place of contract implementation，the place of contract signing，the plaintiff's domicile，and the location of the subject matter.).

Article 14   Effectiveness and duration of the contract

1. This contract is made in _____ copies. Each party holds _____ copies，with the same legal effect.

2. This contract shall come into force as of the date of signature and seal of both parties, and the term of validity is _____. Either party shall submit a written request to the other party to renew the contract _____ days prior to its expiration.

3. When the contract is terminated or canceled, the reception plan confirmed by both parties within the validity period of the contract shall continue to be performed.

Signature and seal of the tour
wholesaler: _____

Signature and seal of the local tour
operator: _____

Date: _____

Date: _____

Signed at: _____

Signed at: _____

Exercises

I. Fill in the blanks with proper forms of words.

1. If foreign tourists enter a _____ (local) as the first point of _____ (enter) in China and then travel to other places, the travel agency responsible for the inbound tour will become a domestic tour _____ (wholesale).

2. "计调" means _____ (plan) and _____ (schedule), and its main task is _____ (purchase) tourism services and implement specific matters such as _____ (cater), accommodation, travelling, shopping, and entertainment for the tour group according to the reception plan.

3. According to the relevant requirements of the _____ (procure) contract or cooperation agreement, the planning and dispatching personnel shall timely report the _____ (detail) account of expenses to the finance department.

4. If Party B cancels the _____ (confirm) order for any reason, it shall notify Party A by fax 5 working days in advance, otherwise Party A will charge _____ (compensate) according to the following standards

5. This agreement is made in duplicate, with each party _____ (hold) one copy, both of which have the same effect. The right of interpretation of this agreement belongs to Party A, and matters not _____ (cover) herein shall be negotiated by both parties.

6. The tour wholesaler and local tour _____ (operate) are the travel agencies or branches _____ (establish) in accordance with the laws and regulations of the People's Republic of China, which have obtained travel agency business qualifications in accordance with the law, and the qualifications of both parties are valid within the validity period of the contract.

Ⅱ. **Translate the following Chinese sentences into English.**

1. 计调部的职能主要以下几个层面得以体现：选择职能、签约的职能、联络与协调职能、统计职能。

2. 计调部采购业务指的是旅行社计调人员为组合某一旅游产品，以一定的价格向相关旅游产品供应商购买单项旅游服务产品的行为。

3. 如因一方违约或因不可抗拒的因素影响，此合约无法继续履行，则双方终止合作。本协议转让无效。

4. 计调部制定详细的旅游团接待计划并落实各项订购任务。填写并发送各类预订单、变更单、取消单，说明旅行团的各种特殊要求。

Ⅲ. **Translate the following English sentences into Chinese.**

1. The local tour operator shall settle reception expense based on the requirements of the tour wholesaler, fill in the settlement form in time, affix its special financial seal and deliver it to the financial department of the tour wholesaler.

2. Without the written consent of the tour wholesaler, the local tour operator shall not receive the tourists organized by the tour wholesaler together with other tourists in any way, or transfer them to any third party for reception.

3. If one party is unable to implement the contract due to force majeure or other reasons not attributable to either party of the contract, one party shall notify the other party in time and provide evidence within a reasonable period. Both parties shall take reasonable and appropriate measures to prevent the expansion of losses.

4. If the tour is delayed due to force majeure and other reasons not attributable to either party of the contract, the tour wholesaler and the local tour operator shall negotiate with the tourists in time and adjust the tour itinerary. The tour wholesaler and the local tour operator shall be responsible for the increased expenses (including the partial expenses not to be borne by tourists, which are agreed by two parties) through negotiation.

Ⅳ. Questions and answers.

1. How do you understand the classification of planning and dispatching personnel?

2. What are two main quotation methods for the reception of inbound tour?

第 ❸ 单元　入境旅游接待（1）
Unit ❸　Inbound Tourism Reception（1）

📖 教学目标

⇨学会撰写一篇结构完整的欢迎辞

⇨辨别入境旅游和出境旅游

⇨掌握福建历史与文化的一些知识

⇨掌握文本中文化因素的翻译方法

⇨了解世界自然与文化遗产的选择标准

📖 Teaching objectives

⇨To learn to write a well structured welcome speech

⇨To distinguish between inbound and outbound tourism

⇨To master some facts of Fujian's history and culture

⇨To master the translation method of cultural factors in a text

⇨To understand the selection criteria for world natural and cultural heritage sites

3.1　情景对话

🎎 机场接机

> A. 中国导游
> B. 美国领队

A：晚上好，先生，您是美国来的汤姆先生吗？

B：是的。

A：很高兴见到您，汤姆先生。我是环球旅行社的导游，我叫李闽。

B：您好，我正在找导游呢！

A：随时为您效劳，先生。对了，一路上还好吗？

B：还可以。我想我们都有点累了。

A：每个人的托运行李都取到了吗？

B：让我核对一下，对了，30 件托运行李。

A：所以我们必须尽快地送你们到酒店。希望明天早上你们都精神焕发，充满活力，因为我们明天市区旅游。

B：我们一定会的。实际上，我们正盼望着游览这个城市的美丽风光。

A：请这边走，车子正在外面等候。

B：好，走吧！

3.1　Situational dialogue

🎎 Meeting guests in the airport

> A.　Chinese tour guide
> B.　tour escort from the US

A：Good evening, sir. Are you Mr. Tom from the States?

B：Ah, yes, that's right.

A：Glad to meet you, Mr. Tom. I'm the guide from Global Travel Agency. My name is Li Min.

B：Hi, I was just looking for the guide.

A：I'm always at your service, sir. By the way, did you have a pleasant journey?

B：Not bad. I think we all feel a bit tired.

A：Has everybody got checked luggage?

B：Let me check. Yes, thirty pieces of checked luggage.

A：So we must get you to the hotel as soon as possible. I hope to see you refreshed and revitalized tomorrow morning, as we are going to have a city tour.

B：I am sure we will. Actually, we are looking forward to seeing the beautiful scenery of the city.

A：Come this way, please. The coach is waiting outside.

B：Fine, let's go.

3.2 角色扮演训练

任务 1：假设你是某国际旅行社的一名英语导游，前往福州机场迎接一个美国旅游团，请准备一个欢迎辞。你代表你所在的旅行社致辞，你的欢迎辞包括对自己和对司机的介绍，还包括福州市基本概况（市树、市花、历史、地理、经济等）的介绍。

任务 2：在前往某一景点途中，导游除了要向客人介绍本地基本概况并回答客人问题，简要介绍即将参观的景点，还必须开展沿途讲解，介绍经过的景物、街道、建筑等。假如游客沿途经过福州的镇海楼、华林寺、八一七路、三坊七巷街区、乌塔等，请做一个相应的沿途讲解。

3.3 旅游文本聚焦

3.3.1 入境和出境旅游的区别是什么

简而言之，入境旅游是指外国人或非居民访问某个国家，而出境旅游指的是某个国家的居民离开本国，访问另一个国家。

从美国的角度来看，如果一个美国人访问德国，这被认为是出境旅游。然而，如果一个德国人访问美国，这被认为是入境旅游。入境和出境旅游对一个国家的金融健康有重要影响。

3.3.1.1 入境旅游的好处

当一个国家吸引大量入境旅客时，游客会在酒店、餐饮、景点、纪念品和其他设施上花钱。这创造了就业机会，并

3.2 Role play training

Task 1：Suppose you are an English tour guide from an international travel agency who is going to Fuzhou airport to meet an American tourist group. Please prepare a welcome speech. You will make the speech on behalf of your travel agency. Your welcome speech should include an introduction to yourself and the driver, as well as a basic profile of Fuzhou (city tree, city flower, history, geography, economy, etc.).

Task 2：On the way to a certain scenic spot, the tour guide must not only give the local overview to the guests and answer their questions, briefly introduce the upcoming scenic spot, but also provide introduction along the way, introducing the scenery, streets, buildings, etc. passed by. If tourists pass by Zhenhai Tower, Hualin Temple, 817 Road, Three Lanes and Seven Alleys, Black Pagoda, etc. along the way in Fuzhou, please make corresponding introductions.

3.3 Tourism text focus

3.3.1 What is the difference between inbound and outbound tourism?[1]

In the simplest terms, inbound tourism occurs when a foreigner or non-resident visits a particular country, and outbound tourism occurs when a resident of a particular country leaves it in order to visit another one.

As an example from an American perspective, if an American visits Germany, that is considered to be outbound tourism. However, if a German visits the United States, that is considered to be inbound tourism. Inbound and outbound tourism have an important impact on a country's financial health.

3.3.1.1 The benefits of inbound tourism

When a country attracts a lot of inbound tourists, the tourists spend money on hotels, dining, attractions, souvenirs and other amenities. This creates jobs, and through consumption taxes, it adds additional money to that country's

---

[1] What Is the Difference Between Inbound and Outbound Tourism? https://www. reference. com/world-view/difference-between-inbound-outbound-tourism-6760686bcb6e64b0,2020/4/1.

通过消费税为该国的国库增加了额外的资金。随着入境旅游的增加，该国的就业机会也在增加；需要新的酒店来容纳涌入的游客；新的景点涌现出来，为游客提供吸引人的内容；出租车和租用汽车的需求等也随之增加。

coffers. As the inbound tourism increases, so does the jobs in that country. New hotels are needed to accommodate the flooding tourists, new attractions spring up to offer something enticing for visitors, the need for taxis and hired cars increases and so on.

3.3.1.2 美国入境旅游

游客们涌向美国，参观大峡谷和尼亚加拉瀑布等自然奇观，以及自由女神像、白宫和拉什莫尔山等历史地标。主题公园每年吸引数百万游客，包括华特迪士尼世界和好莱坞环球影城。美国还推出著名的年度盛事，如新奥尔良的狂欢节和圣地亚哥的国际动漫展。一般来说，外国游客在美国的花费要比国内游客高得多。这种投资有助于经济繁荣。

3.3.1.2 Inbound Tourism in the United States

Tourists flock to the United States to see natural wonders, such as the Grand Canyon and Niagara Falls, and historic landmarks like the Statue of Liberty, the White House and Mount Rushmore. Theme parks attract millions of tourists each year, including Walt Disney World and Universal Studios Hollywood. There are famous annual events, such as Mardi Gras in New Orleans and Comic-Con International in San Diego. Generally speaking, foreign tourists are known to spend a considerably higher amount of money in the United States than domestic tourists. This investment helps the economy thrive.

3.3.1.3 出境旅游

即使居民要离开前往其他地方旅游，出境旅游也会在原籍国产生一些收入。出境游客从本国购买机票、旅行保险和新的旅行服装。随着旅游趋势的变化和人们寻求专业度假，如探险旅游或健康旅游，旅游公司从采购和预订定制套餐中受益。然而，最终出境旅游将金融资源从母国转移到目的国。例如，2019 年美国的旅游出口（出境旅游）高达 2 920 亿美元，而其旅游进口（入境旅游）高达 2 390 亿美元。

3.3.1.3 Outbound tourism

Outbound tourism also generates some money in the country of origin even though the residents are leaving to visit elsewhere. Outbound tourists make purchases that include plane tickets, travel insurance and new travel clothing from their home country. As travel trends change and people look for specialized vacations, such as adventure tourism or wellness tourism, tourism companies benefit from sourcing and booking customized packages. Ultimately, however, outbound tourism takes financial resources out of the home country and gives them to the destination country. As an example, travel exports (outbound tourism) for the United States in 2019 reached $292 billion, while its travel imports (inbound tourism) reached $239 billion.

3.3.1.4 旅游贸易盈余

如果一个国家的入境旅游多于出境旅游，那么它就有旅游贸易顺差。一个具有旅游贸易顺差的国家可能认为旅游业是一个非常有利可图的出口行业。对美国来说，国际旅行作为一个整

3.3.1.4 Travel trade surplus

If a country has more inbound than outbound tourism, it has a travel trade surplus. A country with a travel trade surplus can consider tourism to be a very lucrative export. For the United States, international travel as a whole continually enhances American job growth and helps balance the country's trade, being its largest service export. In 2019, US's travel

体不断促进美国就业增长，并有助于平衡该国的贸易，这是其最大的服务出口。2019 年，美国的旅行贸易顺差达到 530 亿美元。然而，受益于高水平的入境旅游并不意味着一个国家不应该鼓励出境旅游。入境和出境旅游都有无形的影响，其中包括了解周边世界和促进国家之间的积极关系。出境旅游包括商务旅行和度假，加强其他国家之间的联系，促进每个参与国的经济。

trade surplus ran into ＄53 billion dollars. Benefiting from a high level of inbound tourism doesn't mean that a country shouldn't encourage outbound tourism, however. There are intangible effects of both inbound and outbound tourism, and these include learning about the surrounding world and fostering positive relationships between countries. Outbound tourism includes business trips as well as vacations, enhancing ties between other nations and boosting the economies of each participating country.

3.4 文化文本聚焦

3.4.1 福建文化的多元性①

闽文化的主体是由多元构成的。闽文化一方面受到汉民族文化底蕴的影响，另一方面由于独特的自然地理环境、社会经济条件以及历史背景等因素，又有一些色彩鲜明的地域文化特征，呈现出多元性的特征。纵观福建文化的发展历程，闽越文化遗风、中原文化传入、宗教文化传播和海外文化影响是其形成的主要源流。

福建文化多元性的第一层面是闽越文化。福建古为闽越地，秦汉之前，闽越文化在福建占有重要地位。随着中原汉人的逐渐南迁，闽越人的主人地位慢慢被替代，但是其悠久的历史文化传统却不同程度地被保留下来。闽越人喜欢濒临江海居住，其住屋形式应为干栏式，土坯土墙住宅是中原汉人带进福建的。

福建文化多元性的第二层面是中原文化。中原文化的传入方式是以大量移民的途径为主。中原汉人曾四次大规模进入福建。第一次是西晋末年的八姓入闽，第二次是唐初陈元光开

3.4 Cultural text focus

3.4.1 Pluralism of Fujian culture

The main body of Fujian culture is composed of multiple elements. On the one hand, Fujian culture is influenced by the culture of Han nationality; on the other hand, due to the unique natural geographical environment, social and economic conditions, historical background and other factors, there are some distinctive regional cultural characteristics, showing the feature of diversity. Throughout the development of Fujian culture, the main sources of its formation are the heritage of Minyue culture, the introduction of central China's culture, the spread of religious culture and the impact of overseas culture.

The first level of cultural diversity in Fujian is Minyue culture. Fujian used to be a place ruled by Minyue tribe in ancient times; before the Qin (221—206 B.C.) and Han (206 B.C.—220 A.D.) Dynasties, Minyue culture occupied an important position in Fujian. With the gradual southward migration of the Han people in central China, the dominant position of Minyue people was gradually replaced, but their long historical and cultural traditions had been preserved to varying degrees. Minyue people preferred to live near rivers and seas, and their dwelling was a house built above the ground on a wooden (bamboo) column base, while the residential buildings with adobe and earth wall were introduced into Fujian by the Han people in central China.

The second level of cultural diversity in Fujian is central China's culture. The introduction of central China's culture was mainly undertaken by immigrants. The Han people in central China entered Fujian on four large-scale occasions. The first was the entry of eight surnames into Fujian in the late Western Jin Dynasty (265—316), the second was the development of Zhangzhou by Chen Yuanguang in the early Tang Dynasty (618—907), the third was the reign of Wang Shenzhi in the late Tang and Five Dynasties (907—960), and

① 戴志坚. 闽文化及其对福建传统民居的影响. 南方建筑,2011,(6):25. 此处标题为编者所加。

发漳州，第三次是唐末五代王审知治闽，第四次是北宋南迁。此外，从永嘉之乱前至明清，都有中原人士陆续入闽定居。这四次大移民和陆续入闽的移民，都不同程度地带来了中原的先进文化，加快了福建的开发和进步。另外还有不少闽人北上访学，也将中原文化带回闽地。如崇安人游酢、将乐人杨时受业于理学开创者程颢、程颐，留下了"程门立雪"的故事。他们返闽后大力传播理学，后被朱熹改造发扬为"闽学"。中原文化的传入是闽文化覆盖层中最厚的一层。

福建文化多元性的第三层面是宗教文化。佛教传入福建约在吴晋之际。道教传入福建也较早。五代时由于王审知父子崇尚佛道，佛道文化在福建已影响广泛。福建一些著名的佛寺、道观就是在唐及五代时期创立的。伊斯兰教在唐中叶由海路传入泉州，宋元时有数万阿拉伯人云集泉州。穆斯林后裔在泉州生息繁衍，建造了我国最早的清真寺，留下了安葬伊斯兰先贤的灵山圣墓等。基督教在明代传入闽北，并向闽东、闽南发展，基督教建的教堂、学校、医院、慈善机构几乎遍布全省各地。福建的民间宗教颇有影响，尤其是宋元前后的民间造神运动，造就了妈祖——林默、临水夫人——陈靖姑和保生大帝——吴夲等神祇，至今在福建民间仍有广泛影响。祀奉妈祖的天后宫是福建宫观建筑中数量最多的一种。

福建文化多元性的第四层面是海外文化。海外文化的影响主要来自国际贸易、外商定居闽地、闽人越洋后回归故里等方面。福建东濒海洋，深水良港星罗棋布。福州的马尾港、泉州的后渚港、漳州的月港、厦门港是四大古港。海上交通的便利，扩大了福建

the fourth was the southward migration of the Northern Song Dynasty（960—1127）. In addition, from before the Yongjia Rebellion to the Ming（1368—1644）and Qing（1644—1911）Dynasties, people from central China came to settle in Fujian one after another. The four major immigrations and successive immigrants to Fujian introduced the advanced culture of central China to varying degrees and accelerated the development and progress of Fujian. Furthermore, numerous Fujian people went to school in the north and brought the central China's culture back to Fujian. For example, when You Zuo（1053—1123）from Chong'an and Yang Shi（1053—1135）from Jiangle became the students of Cheng Hao（1032—1085）and Cheng Yi（1033—1107）, the founders of Neo-Confucianism, they left behind the story of "waiting upon Master Cheng respectfully". After returning to Fujian, they vigorously disseminated Neo-Confucianism, which was transformed and promoted by Zhu Xi as "Min Studies". The introduction of central China's culture is the dominating component of Fujian culture.

The third level of cultural diversity in Fujian is religious culture. Buddhism was introduced into Fujian around Wu Kingdom（222—280）and Jin Dynasty（265—420）. Taoism was also introduced to Fujian early. In the Five Dynasties（907—960）, because Wang Shenzhi, the ruler of Min State（909—945）, and his son advocated Buddhism and Taoism, Buddhism and Taoism culture exerted a wide influence in Fujian. Some famous Buddhist temples and Taoist monasteries in Fujian were founded in the Tang Dynasty（618—907）and Five Dynasties. Islam was introduced into Quanzhou by sea in the middle of Tang Dynasty and tens of thousands of Arabians lived in Quanzhou in the Song（960—1279）and Yuan（1271—1368）Dynasties. Muslim descendants lived and multiplied in Quanzhou, constructed the earliest mosque in China and left behind the sacred Tomb of Lingshan Mountain where Islamic sages were buried. Christianity was introduced into north Fujian in the Ming Dynasty（1368—1644）and spread to east Fujian and south Fujian. Christian churches, schools, hospitals and charity organizations were scattered almost all over the province. Fujian's folk religion enjoyed a great impact as well: especially the folk god-making movement in the Song and Yuan Dynasties created the sea goddess Mazu（the legendary name Lin Mo）, the goddess Linshui（the legendary name Chen Jinggu）and the health-preserving god Wu Tao, and so on. They still enjoy a wide influence among the public in Fujian today. The Tianhou Temple, which worships Mazu, is one of the most numerous temples in Fujian Province.

The fourth level of cultural diversity in Fujian is overseas culture. The impact of overseas culture mainly comes from international trade, the settlement of foreign businessmen in Fujian, and the return of Fujian people to their homeland from abroad. Fujian is bordered by the sea in the east and there are numerous deep-water ports. Mawei Port in Fuzhou, Houzhu Port in Quanzhou, Yuegang Port in Zhangzhou and Xiamen Port are the four major ancient ports. The convenience of maritime

沿海地区与海外商人的贸易往来，也促使闽人特别是闽南人出海谋生，向海外如日本、朝鲜、东南亚诸国发展。随着海外交通和对外文化交流的不断发展，他国的文化风俗、民情信仰便逐渐与福建文化融汇渗透在一起。在闽南，各类中西合璧的民居建筑应运而生。

transportation expanded the trade contacts between Fujian coastal areas and overseas businessmen, and encouraged Fujian people, especially those in southern Fujian, to make a living at sea and to develop in foreign countries such as Japan, Korea and countries in southeast Asia. With the continuous development of overseas transportation and cultural exchanges with foreign countries, the cultural customs and folk beliefs of other countries gradually merged into Fujian culture. In southern Fujian, various kinds of residential buildings in a combined Chinese and Western style emerged as the times required. [1]

3.4.2 宋代福建经济文化的历史地位 [2]

宋代的福建是南方有名的文化大省之一，在科举、书院、出版等各个领域，都有杰出的成就；在无形的文化产业里，宋代福建出现了许多著名的诗人、作家、历史学家、科学家，形成了一个波澜壮阔的文化浪潮。在福建历史上，这一文化浪潮是空前绝后的。

宋代福建在中国的地位很高。宋代是福建书院大发展的时期。福建虽是开发较迟的区域，但经过唐五代的发展，迄至五代时期，福建已是国内文化较发达的区域之一，后人论及五代人物，以南唐第一、闽国排名第三。

广设书院是在南宋时期，当时，二程理学传到闽中，福建士子积极研究理学的原理，这就需要聚书讲学之处。于是，建学之风在福建各地兴起，各类书院如雨后春笋般地出现。迄至南宋末年，福建已有数十所有名的书院，其数量在全国数一数二。这一优势，一直保持到元代。福建的学校与书院之多，是宋代福建文化发达的表现。

科举事业的发达，使福建有许多人进入宋代的官僚机构，从北宋到南宋，身任宰相的闽人达50位。其中章得象、曾公亮、蔡确、李纲、陈俊卿、留

3.4.2 The historical position of Fujian's economy and culture in the Song Dynasty

Fujian in the Song Dynasty (960—1279) was one of the famous cultural provinces in the south, which made outstanding achievements in imperial examinations, academies, publishing and other fields. In the intangible cultural industry, there arose many famous poets, writers, historians and scientists in Fujian in the Song Dynasty, creating a magnificent cultural wave. In Fujian history, this cultural wave is unprecedented.

Fujian enjoyed a high status in China in the Song Dynasty. The Song Dynasty witnessed a period of great development for the Fujian academy of classical learning. Fujian used to be a region with relatively slow development, but through the development of Tang Dynasty (618—907) and Five Dynasties (907—960), up to the Five Dynasties, Fujian became one of the more advanced regions in domestic culture. When later generations discussed the historical figures of the Five Dynasties, the Southern Tang Dynasty (937—975) ranked the first and the Min State (909—945) the third.

It was in the Southern Song Dynasty (1127—1279) that Neo-Confucianism represented by Cheng Hao (1032—1085) and Cheng Yi (1033—1107), two famous scholars of Neo-Confucianism, spread to central Fujian. Fujian scholars actively pursued the principles of Neo-Confucianism, which required certain particular locations for collecting books and delivering lectures. As a result, such learning atmosphere emerged all over Fujian and various academies sprang up like mushrooms. By the end of the Southern Song Dynasty, there arose dozens of famous academies in Fujian, ranking the first in the country. This advantage was maintained until the Yuan Dynasty (1271—1368). The number of schools and academies in Fujian is a manifestation of advanced Fujian culture in the Song Dynasty.

With the development of the imperial examination, numerous people in Fujian entered the bureaucracy of the Song Dynasty. From the Northern Song Dynasty (960-1127) to the Southern Song Dynasty, 50 Fujian people acted as prime ministers successively. Among them, Zhang Dexiang (978—1048), Zeng Gongliang (998—1078), Cai Que (1037—1093), Li Gang

---

① 摘自韦忠生主持的国家外文局2018年"福建省地方特色文化对外翻译标准化术语库建设项目"，译者韦忠生，内容略有修改。

② 徐晓望，论宋代福建经济文化的历史地位，东南学术，2002，(2):149.

正等人都是宋代著名的政治家,在政治上很有影响。历宋元明清四代,闽人在政治枢要中占这么重要的地位,唯有宋代。

宋代出版业中心有三个:杭州、成都、福建。研究出版史的学者公认:杭州的版本最精,福建的版本最多,成都在两个方面都位于中游。建阳书坊、麻沙逐步成为宋代出版中心之一。

在中国思想史上,使福建占有重要地位的是宋代闽学的兴起。闽学是理学的一个流派,也是理学的顶峰。宋代福建成为理学根据地。北宋时期,福建已成为儒学文化较发达的区域。

福建在唐五代是中国佛教的中心,其寺院、僧人都是全国最多的,在宋代,这一状况仍未发生变化。宋初福建僧人达 70 000 多人,约为全国的六分之一,他们出游各地寺院,因此,全国各地的许多寺庙中,都有闽僧,这一地位迄今不变。

在史学领域,宋代闽人有两部公认的史学名著,其一是郑樵的《通志》,其二是袁枢的《通鉴纪事本末》。在自然科学方面,曾公亮参与创作《武经总要》,是宋代兵器制造、兵法集成的巨著;其次,苏颂作《新仪象法要》,并制造水运仪象台,代表了中国古代天文学的成就。此外,宋慈的《洗冤录》是法医学史上的开山名著,杨士瀛在医学理论方面的探讨引人注目。蔡襄的《荔枝谱》《茶录》都是科学史上的著名的作品。在艺术方面,蔡襄是宋代书法四大家之一,蔡京与蔡卞的《宣和书谱》与《宣和画谱》,都是艺术史上的名著,而《乐书》及《律吕新书》等音乐方面著作的出现,都是闽人献给中国艺术史的名著。

(1083—1140), Chen Junqing (1113—1186) and Liu Zheng (1129—1206) were all well-known politicians of the Song Dynasty and enjoyed great political influence. During the Song, Yuan, Ming (1368—1644) and Qing (1644—1911) Dynasties, Fujian people occupied such an important position in the political center only in the Song Dynasty.

There were three publishing centers in the Song Dynasty (960—1279): Hangzhou, Chengdu and Fujian. The scholars who study the history of publishing generally acknowledge that the Hangzhou version is well known for its delicateness and the Fujian version for its great diversity while the Chengdu version reaches intermediate level in the two aspects. Jianyang's Shufang and Masha gradually became one of the publishing centers of the Song Dynasty.

In the history of Chinese thought, the rise of the school of Min studies in the Song Dynasty enabled Fujian to occupy an important position. The school of Min studies is a school of Neo-Confucianism and the peak of its development. Fujian became the base of Neo-Confucianism in the Song Dynasty. During the Northern Song Dynasty (960—1127), Fujian became a more developed area of Confucian culture.

Fujian was the center of Chinese Buddhism in the Tang Dynasty (618—907) and the Five Dynasties (907—960) with the largest number of temples and monks in the country. In the Song Dynasty, this situation remained unchanged. At the beginning of the Song Dynasty, there were more than 70 000 monks in Fujian, about one sixth of the number of monks in the whole country. They traveled to temples all over the country. As a result, there were many Fujian monks in numerous temples all over the country. This status has not changed so far.

In the field of historiography, the Fujian people in the Song Dynasty (960—1279) boasted two well-known historical masterpieces: one was Zheng Qiao's *General History of China* and the other was Yuan Shu's *Great Events in Chinese History*. In natural science, Zeng Gonglian's *Collection of the Most Important Military Techniques* was a masterpiece of weapon manufacturing and an integration of military techniques in the Song Dynasty. Also, Su Song wrote *Principles of New Astronomic Device*. His water-powered astronomical clock tower represents the achievements of ancient Chinese astronomy. Besides, Song Ci's *Cases of Redressing Injustice* is the first famous work in the history of forensic medicine, and Yang Shiying's research on medical theory attracts attention. Cai Xiang's *Introduction to Litchi Varieties* and *The Art of Tea-Drinking* are all famous works in the history of science. In terms of art, Cai Xiang is one of the four great calligraphers in the Song Dynasty. *Collection of Calligraphic Works* and *Collection of Chinese Paintings* compiled by Cai Jing and Cai Bian are both famous works in the history of art. The emergence of music books such as *The Rules of Music* and *New Introduction to Musical Rules* are all famous works dedicated by Fujian people to the history of Chinese art. ①

① 摘自韦忠生主持的国家外文局 2018 年"福建省地方特色文化对外翻译标准化术语库建设项目",译者韦忠生,内容略有修改。

3.4.3 闽王王审知的贡献①

王审知堪称五代十国时期一位明智的政治家,其当政的 30 余年里,他以史为鉴,以民为本,在经济、农业、教育、人才培养、商业和海外贸易方面做出了卓越的贡献,极大推动了福建各方面的发展,使福建成为当时全国比较稳定繁荣的地方。因此他也被后世称为"开疆闽王",深受百姓爱戴。

闽王王审知的贡献在许多方面得以体现。在其当政的 30 余年里,正值群雄纷争、武力割据的五代十国初期。而福建从未对外邦用兵,也未受外邦侵侮,境内一片升平,成为全国经济社会发展最快、变化最大、最为安宁的地区。

经济上重视和鼓励发展生产。比如,劝农兴修水利,发展农业。亲自主持兴建或扩建了一大批骨干水利工程,如福清、长乐沿海大堤,泉州六里陂、九溪十八坝,连江东湖,晋江 40 余华里灌渠,疏浚了可达 25 平方公里的福州西湖。同时围海造田,扩大耕地。在平原推广双季稻;在武夷山区开垦茶园,种植茶树,达 1 000 余处;因地制宜发展纺织、陶瓷、冶金、铸造等工业生产。

在传播中原文明上,倡导文教,兴办学堂,培养人才,教化黎民,使闽地成了才俊辈出之乡。在发展商业和海外贸易上,可谓前无古人。免除杂税,奖励通商。躬身踏察海湾,修建码头,辟建港口。疏通百余里的闽江水道,制造出可载六七百人的大船。福州、泉州由此成为我国东南沿海的重要港口,也是当时中国最大的两个港口。

3.4.3 The contribution of Wang Shenzhi, the ruler of Min State

Wang Shenzhi（862—925）was a sensible statesman in the period of Five Dynasties（907—960）and Ten States（902—979）. During his rule of more than 30 years, he took history as a lesson and put people first. He had made outstanding contributions to economy, agriculture, education, talent training, commerce and overseas trade, and had greatly promoted the development of Fujian in all aspects, so Fujian became a relatively stable and prosperous place in the country at that time. Consequently, he was also called "the ruler of the Min State, who developed Fujian" by later generations, and was deeply loved by the people.

The contribution of Wang Shenzhi, the ruler of the Min State, is demonstrated in numerous aspects. His 30 years' rule happened to be in the early Five Dynasties and Ten States, when the whole country was divided into a group of independent states and separated by force. Fujian had never dispatched troops to foreign land or been subjected to foreign aggression at that time, so it enjoyed the fastest development, the greatest changes and became the most peaceful region in the country.

He emphasized and encouraged the development of production economically. For example, he advised farmers to construct water conservancy projects and develop agriculture. He personally presided over the construction or expansion of a large number of key water conservancy projects, such as coastal embankments in Fuqing and Changle, Liulipo water conservancy project, 18 dams for 9 streams in Quanzhou, East Lake in Lianjiang, an over 20-kilometer irrigation canal in the Jin River and dredged the West Lake of Fuzhou, which totaled 25 square kilometers. Meanwhile, he asked people to reclaim land from the sea and expand cultivated land. In the plain, double-cropping rice was promoted; in Mount Wuyi, tea plantations were reclaimed in over 1 000 locations; and the industrial production of textiles, porcelain, metallurgy and foundry was developed according to local conditions.

In disseminating the civilization of central China, he advocated culture and education, established schools, trained talents and educated the people, which had made Fujian a home for talented people. Its development of commerce and foreign trade was unprecedented. Exemption of miscellaneous taxes and incentives for trade were granted. He made inspection to bays, requested people to erect wharves and build ports. He asked people to dredge more than 50 kilometers of the Min River waterway and construct a large ship capable of carrying six or seven hundred people. Fuzhou and Quanzhou became important ports along the southeast coast of China and the two largest ports in China at that time. ②

---

① 陈榕三,王审知与闽台根亲文化的研究,现代台湾研究,2009,(2):19. 内容略有修改,此处标题为编写者所加。

② 摘自韦忠生主持的国家外文局 2018 年"福建省地方特色文化对外翻译标准化术语库建设项目",译者韦忠生,内容略有修改。

3.5　知识链接

🎲 3.5.1　世界旅游组织

世界旅游组织（UNWTO）是负责促进负责任、可持续和普遍性的旅游业发展的联合国机构。

作为旅游业领域的主要国际组织，世界旅游组织将旅游业视为经济增长、包容性发展和环境可持续性发展的驱动力，促进旅游业的发展，并在宣传世界各地的知识和推动旅游政策方面为旅游业部门提供领导和支持。

▶ 3.5.1.1　优先事项

将旅游业纳入全球议程的主流：提倡旅游业具有推动社会经济增长和发展的价值，将其作为国家和国际政策的优先事项，并为旅游业的发展和繁荣创造一个公平的竞争环境。

提高旅游业竞争力：通过知识创造和交流、人力资源开发和促进政策规划、统计和市场趋势预测、可持续旅游业发展、营销和推广、产品开发、风险和危机管理等领域的完善，提高世界旅游组织成员的竞争力。

促进可持续旅游业发展：支持可持续旅游业发展的政策和做法，即充分利用环境资源，尊重所在社区的社会文化真实性并为所有人提供社会利益和经济利益。

促进旅游业对减少贫困和发展的贡献：通过将旅游业作为发展工具并促进旅游业纳入发展议程，最大限度地发挥旅游业对减少贫困和实现可持续发展目标的贡献。

促进知识、教育和能力建设：支持各国评估和满足其在教育和培训方面的需求，并为知识创造和交流提供联动系统。

3.5　Knowledge link

🎲 3.5.1　The World Tourism Organization[①]

The World Tourism Organization （UNWTO） is the United Nations agency responsible for the promotion of responsible, sustainable and universally accessible tourism.

As the leading international organization in the field of tourism, UNWTO promotes tourism as a driver of economic growth, inclusive development and environmental sustainability and offers leadership and support to the sector in advancing knowledge and tourism policies worldwide.

▶ 3.5.1.1　Priorities

Mainstreaming tourism in the global agenda：Advocating the value of tourism as a driver of socio-economic growth and development，its inclusion as a priority in national and international policies and the need to create a level playing field for the sector to develop and prosper.

Improving tourism competitiveness：Improving UNWTO Members' competitiveness through knowledge creation and exchange, human resources development and the promotion of excellence in areas such as policy planning, statistics and market trends, sustainable tourism development, marketing and promotion, product development and risk and crisis management.

Promoting sustainable tourism development：Supporting sustainable tourism policies and practices：policies which make optimal use of environmental resources, respect the socio-cultural authenticity of host communities and provide socio-economic benefits for all.

Advancing tourism's contribution to poverty reduction and development：Maximizing the contribution of tourism to poverty reduction and achieving the SDGs by making tourism work as a tool for development and promoting the inclusion of tourism in the development agenda.

Fostering knowledge, education and capacity building：Supporting countries to assess and address their needs in education and training, as well as providing networks for knowledge creation and exchange.

Building partnerships：Engaging with the private sector, regional and local tourism organizations, academia and research institutions, civil society and the UN system to build a more sustainable, responsible and competitive tourism sector.

---

① 下载自世界旅游组织官网，https：//www. unwto. org/about-us，2022/7/1。中文文本为编写者所译。

建立伙伴关系:与私营部门、区域和地方旅游组织、学术界和研究机构、民间社会和联合国系统合作,建设一个更可持续、更负责任和更有竞争力的旅游部门。

3.5.1.2 世界旅游组织的结构

成员:世界旅游组织(UNWTO)是一个政府间组织,有 160 个成员国、6 个准成员、2 个观察员和 500 多个附属成员。

机关:联合国大会是本组织的最高机关。执行理事会与秘书长协商,采取一切措施执行联合国大会的决定和建议,并向联合国大会提交报告。

秘书处:世界旅游组织总部设在西班牙马德里。秘书处由秘书长领导,分为几个部门,涉及可持续性、教育、旅游趋势和营销、可持续发展、统计和旅游卫星账户(TSA)、目的地管理、道德和风险以及危机管理等问题。技术合作和丝绸之路部在全球 100 多个国家开展发展项目,而非洲部、美洲部、亚太部、欧洲部和中东部等区域性部门则是联合国世界旅游组织与其 160 个成员国之间的联系纽带。附属会员部代表世界旅游组织 500 多个附属会员。

3.5.2 选择标准

要被列入《世界遗产名录》,遗址必须具有突出的普遍价值,并且至少符合十项评选标准中的一项。

这些标准在《世界遗产公约实施操作指南》中均有解释。除了《公约》文本,该指南是世界遗产的主要运作依据。委员会定期修订这些标准,以反映世界遗产概念本身的演变。

直到 2004 年年底,世界遗产一直是根据六项文化和四项自然标准选定。修订后的《世界遗产公约实施操作指南》的采纳,只有一套十项标准。

选择标准

(Ⅰ)代表人类创造天才的杰作;

3.5.1.2 The structure of UNWTO

Members:An intergovernmental organization, UNWTO has 160 Member States, 6 Associate Members, 2 Observers and over 500 Affiliate Members.

Organs:The General Assembly is the supreme organ of the Organization. The Executive Council takes all measures, in consultation with the Secretary-General, for the implementation of the decisions and recommendations of the General Assembly and reports to the Assembly.

Secretariat:UNWTO headquarters are based in Madrid, Spain. The Secretariat is led by the Secretary-General and organized into departments covering issues such as sustainability, education, tourism trends and marketing, sustainable development, statistics and the Tourism Satellite Account (TSA), destination management, ethics and risk and crisis management. The Technical Cooperation and Silk Road Department carries out development projects in over 100 countries worldwide, while the Regional Departments for Africa, the Americas, Asia and the Pacific, Europe and the Middle East serve as the link between UNWTO and its 160 Member States. The Affiliate Members Department represents UNWTO's 500 plus Affiliate members.

3.5.2 The criteria for selection[①]

To be included on the World Heritage List, sites must be of outstanding universal value and meet at least one out of ten selection criteria.

These criteria are explained in the Operational Guidelines for the Implementation of the World Heritage Convention which, besides the text of the Convention, is the main working tool on World Heritage. The criteria are regularly revised by the Committee to reflect the evolution of the World Heritage concept itself.

Until the end of 2004, World Heritage sites were selected on the basis of six cultural and four natural criteria. With the adoption of the revised Operational Guidelines for the Implementation of the World Heritage Convention, only one set of ten criteria exists.

Selection criteria

(Ⅰ) to represent a masterpiece of human creative genius;

---

① 下载自联合国教科文组织官网,https://whc.unesco.org/en/criteria/,2022/7/1。中文文本为编写者所译。

（Ⅱ）反映在一段时间内或在世界文化区域内,建筑或技术、纪念性艺术、城市规划或景观设计的发展所体现的人类价值观的重要交流;

（Ⅲ）为一种文化传统或一种仍然存在或已经消失的文明提供独特的或至少是特殊的证据;

（Ⅳ）是一类建筑、建筑或技术组合或景观的杰出范例,体现了人类历史上的一个或多个重要阶段;

（Ⅴ）特别是当环境在不可逆转的变化的影响下变得脆弱时,成为代表一种或多种文化或人类与环境互动的传统人类定居点、土地使用或海洋使用的杰出例子;

（Ⅵ）与具有突出普遍意义的艺术和文学作品直接或有形地联系在一起（委员会认为,这一标准最好与其他标准一起使用）;

（Ⅶ）包含最高级的自然现象或具有非凡自然美和美学重要性的区域;

（Ⅷ）是代表地球历史主要阶段的杰出范例,包括生命记录、地貌发展中重要的持续变化的地质过程或重要的地貌或地貌特征;

（Ⅸ）在陆地、淡水、沿海和海洋生态系统以及动植物群落的进化和发展过程中,成为重要的持续变化的生态和生物过程的杰出范例;

（Ⅹ）包含生物多样性原位保护最重要的自然栖息地,包括从科学或保护角度来看具有突出普遍价值的濒危物种。

财产的保护、管理、真实性和完整性也是重要的考虑因素。自1992年以来,人们与自然环境之间的重要互动被视为文化景观。

（Ⅱ）to exhibit an important interchange of human values, over a span of time or within a cultural area of the world, on developments in architecture or technology, monumental arts, town-planning or landscape design;

（Ⅲ）to bear a unique or at least exceptional testimony to a cultural tradition or to a civilization which is living or which has disappeared;

（Ⅳ）to be an outstanding example of a type of building, architectural or technological ensemble or landscape which illustrates (a) significant stage(s) in human history;

（Ⅴ）to be an outstanding example of a traditional human settlement, land-use, or sea-use which is representative of a culture (or cultures), or human interaction with the environment especially when it has become vulnerable under the impact of irreversible change;

（Ⅵ）to be directly or tangibly associated with events or living traditions, with ideas, or with beliefs, with artistic and literary works of outstanding universal significance (The Committee considers that this criterion should preferably be used in conjunction with other criteria);

（Ⅶ）to contain superlative natural phenomena or areas of exceptional natural beauty and aesthetic importance;

（Ⅷ）to be outstanding examples representing major stages of earth's history, including the record of life, significant on-going geological processes in the development of landforms, or significant geomorphic or physiographic features;

（Ⅸ）to be outstanding examples representing significant on-going ecological and biological processes in the evolution and development of terrestrial, fresh water, coastal and marine ecosystems and communities of plants and animals;

（Ⅹ）to contain the most important and significant natural habitats for in-situ conservation of biological diversity, including those containing threatened species of outstanding universal value from the point of view of science or conservation.

The protection, management, authenticity and integrity of properties are also important considerations. Since 1992, significant interactions between people and the natural environment have been recognized as cultural landscapes.

操作指南(年份)	文化标准						自然标准			
2002	（Ⅰ）	（Ⅱ）	（Ⅲ）	（Ⅳ）	（Ⅴ）	（Ⅵ）	（Ⅰ）	（Ⅱ）	（Ⅲ）	（Ⅳ）
2005	（Ⅰ）	（Ⅱ）	（Ⅲ）	（Ⅳ）	（Ⅴ）	（Ⅵ）	（Ⅷ）	（Ⅸ）	（Ⅶ）	（Ⅹ）

Operational Guidelines (year)	Cultural criteria						Natural criteria			
2002	（Ⅰ）	（Ⅱ）	（Ⅲ）	（Ⅳ）	（Ⅴ）	（Ⅵ）	（Ⅰ）	（Ⅱ）	（Ⅲ）	（Ⅳ）
2005	（Ⅰ）	（Ⅱ）	（Ⅲ）	（Ⅳ）	（Ⅴ）	（Ⅵ）	（Ⅷ）	（Ⅸ）	（Ⅶ）	（Ⅹ）

3.6 文本中文化因素的翻译

相关论文作者从不同视角探析福建省地方特色文化词语的翻译,体现了研究视角的多样性。本节内容从词条译文的统一性、译文对史实的尊重、历史朝代和历史人物的翻译、古代官职的翻译、特殊文化词语的翻译等五个层面展开讨论①。

3.6.1 译文的统一性

福建省地方特色文化对外翻译标准化术语库建设项目总词条 300 余条,每个词条的长度为 300~500 字或以上。保持词条译文的统一性,是标准化翻译的一项重要内容。标准化翻译也是旅游翻译的一项重要内容。中文文本中出现了"福建船政局"、"福州船政局"和"马尾船政局"三种不同表述,实际上均指代当时的马尾造船厂,在译文中保持了同一种译文:Fuzhou's Mawei Shipyard in Fujian,如例 1 和例 2。"三坊七巷"均保持了 Fuzhou's Three Lanes and Seven Alleys 的译文,实词首字母均为大写,作为一个专有名词而存在。

【例 1】 1866 年(清同治五年),闽浙总督左宗棠在福州马尾创办了福建船政局,轰轰烈烈地开展了建船厂、造兵舰、制飞机、办学堂、引人才、派学童出洋留学等一系列"富国强兵"活动,培养和造就了一批优秀的中国近代工业技术人才和杰出的海军将士。②

3.6 Translation of cultural factors in the text

The authors of relevant papers explore the translation of local cultural words with distinctive characteristics of Fujian Province from different perspectives, reflecting the diversity of research perspectives. This section discusses such topic from five aspects: the unity of translation of entries, respect for historical facts, translation of historical dynasties and figures, translation of ancient official positions, and translation of special cultural words.

3.6.1 Unification of translation

The Project for Terminological Database Construction of Standardized Translation of Local Characteristic Cultures in Fujian Province has a total of over 300 entries, each with a length of 300-500 words or more. Maintaining consistency in the translation of entries is an important aspect of standardized translation. Standardized translation is also an important aspect of tourism translation. There are three different expressions in the Chinese text, namely "福建船政局", "福州船政局", "马尾船政局", which actually refer to the Mawei Shipyard at that time and thus are translated as the same version: Fuzhou's Mawei Shipyard in Fujian, as is shown in Example 1 and Example 2. "三坊七巷" is translated into Fuzhou's Three Lanes and Seven Alleys as a proper noun, with the first letter of each word capitalized, except "and".

【译】 In 1866 (the fifth year of Tongzhi period in the Qing Dynasty), Zuo Zongtang (1812—1885), the governor of Fujian and Zhejiang, founded Fuzhou's Mawei Shipyard in Fujian. He vigorously carried out a series of activities in order to make China rich and its military force efficient such as building shipyards, constructing warships, manufacturing aircraft, operating schools, attracting talents and sending schoolchildren abroad for further study. He trained and cultivated numerous excellent modern Chinese industrial and technical talents as well as outstanding naval officers.

---

① 本节例 1 至例 10 及对应译文均摘选自韦忠生所主持的国家外文局 2018 年"福建省地方特色文化对外翻译标准化术语库建设项目",译者均为韦忠生。

② 下载自中国船政文化博物馆网站,http://www.czwh.org.cn/xiu-bncz-1?templateId=1&containChild=1,2022/7/1。

【例2】 马尾船政局创立后,左宗棠、沈葆桢都很重视创办传授西方长技的学校,以培养各种专业人才。1877 年、1886 年、1897 年,福州船政学堂共派出了 80 余人,赴英法留学。①

【译】 After the establishment of <u>Fuzhou's Mawei Shipyard</u> in Fujian, Zuo Zongtang(1812—1885)and Shen Baozhen(1820—1879)attached great importance to the establishment of schools to teach Western skills in order to cultivate various professionals. In 1877, 1886 and 1897, Fuzhou Ship-Building School dispatched more than 80 students to study in Britain and France.

3.6.2 译文对史实的尊重

对史实的尊重是翻译的一个重要原则。有些书刊将"洋务运动"翻译为 Westernization Movement,显然是误译。这是由于译者没有深入了解洋务运动的历史背景,因而无法实现对原文的真正理解。英语中的 westernization 似乎具有贬义的色彩,具有盲目模仿之嫌,弱化了洋务运动的积极意义。因此例 3 将"洋务运动"译为 the Self-Strengthening Movement、把"洋务派"翻译为 the advocators of the Self-Strengthening Movement 是对史实的尊重,彰显了洋务运动具有推动中国科技发展的重要意义,虽败犹荣。"中体西用"的英语译文 "making Chinese culture as a foundation and Western culture as a reference"正好体现了洋务运动的积极意义:中国文化为主,西方文化为辅。例 4 将"闽国国王"翻译为 the ruler of the Min State 也是对史实的尊重,这是由于五代十国时期,王审知并未称帝,因此译为 ruler(统治者),而不是 emperor。

3.6.2 Respect for historical facts in translation

The respect for historical facts is an important principle in translation. Some books and journals have translated "洋务运动" into Westernization Movement, which is obviously a mistranslation. This is because the translators did not have a profound understanding of the historical background of "洋务运动", so they failed to achieve a true understanding of the original text. "Westernization" in English seems to have a derogatory color, with an implication of blind imitation, weakening the positive significance of "洋务运动". Therefore, in Example 3, the translation of "洋务运动" into "the Self-Strengthening Movement" and the translation of "洋务派" into "the advocators of Self-Strengthening Movement" is a respect for historical facts, which highlights the great significance of "洋务运动" in promoting China's scientific and technological development. The translation of "中体西用" into "making Chinese culture as a foundation and Western culture as a reference" just reflects the positive significance of "洋务运动": Chinese culture is the main part, and Western culture is the auxiliary part. In Example 4, the translation of "闽国国王" as "the ruler of the Min State" is also a respect for historical facts. This is because during the Five Dynasties and Ten Kingdoms period, Wang Shenzhi did not declare himself emperor, so "国王" is translated into "ruler" rather than "emperor".

【例3】 福州船政学堂成立于 1867 年 1 月,是近代中国第一所海军制造学校,也是洋务派继设立京师同文馆等外国语学堂之后,创立最早的一所以培养航海、轮船、制造等科技人

【译】 Founded in January 1867, Fuzhou Shipbuilding School is the first naval manufacturing school in modern China. It is also the earliest new school set up by <u>the advocators of the Self-Strengthening Movement</u> after the establishment of foreign language schools such as Imperial

---

① 陈东.船政文化在近代中国文化重组中的作用.闽江学院学报,2005,(4):72-73.

才为目标的新型学堂。①

Tongwen College. The school aimed to train scientific and technological talents in navigation, shipping and manufacturing.

【例4】 福州闽王祠,是位于中国福建省福州市庆城路的一座祠堂建筑,主祀五代闽国国王王审知。

【译】 The Shrine for the ruler of the Min State (909—945) is an ancestral hall located in Qingcheng Road, Fuzhou City, Fujian Province and constructed in memory of Wang Shenzhi, the ruler of the Min State in the Five Dynasties (907—960).

【例5】 古代,中国传统文化的内容相对来说比较单一,基本上是以儒学或儒、释、道为其主要内容,洋务运动中,中国人进一步认识到还要学习西方的科学技术。在"中体西用"的旗号下,西方的自然科学技术和经济技术最先被吸收进来,成为近代文化的基本内容。②

【译】 In ancient times, the content of traditional Chinese culture was relatively monotonous, basically based on Confucianism or the combination of Confucianism, Buddhism and Taoism. In the Self-Strengthening Movement, the Chinese people further realized that they should learn Western science and technology. Under the banner of "making Chinese culture as a foundation and Western culture as a reference", the natural science, technology and economic technology of the West were first absorbed and became the basic content of modern culture.

3.6.3 历史朝代和历史人物的翻译

历史朝代和历史人物也是福建地方特色文化翻译中需要特别关注的文化信息。例6对历史年代的简单叙事显然不能满足目的语读者的叙事认知欲,需要补充具体的年代以满足其对叙事时间的求知欲望。例6涉及明代和清代,清代还涉及两个不同皇帝的统治时间。译文中,明代后添加了时间括注,翻译清顺治二年和道光间时则将具体年份作为主要信息,而将清顺治二年和道光间置于圆括号内作为补充信息,分别翻译为 In 1645 (the second year of Shunzhi period of the Qing Dynasty) 和 During 1821—1851 (Daoguang period of the Qing Dynasty)。

3.6.3 Translation of historical dynasties and historical figures

Historical dynasties and historical figures are also cultural information that needs special attention in the translation of Fujian local culture. The simple narrative of the historical age in Example 6 obviously cannot satisfy the target language readers' desire for knowledge, and it is necessary to add the specific time to satisfy their desire for knowledge of narrative time. Example 6 involves the Ming Dynasty and the Qing Dynasty, and the Qing Dynasty mentioned here also includes the ruling time of two different emperors. "The Ming Dynasty" is followed by an annotation of time, and the specific year is taken as the main information when translating the time "the 2nd year of Shunzhi period" and "Daoguang period", while the time "the 2nd year of Shunzhi period" and "Daguang period" is placed in the parenthesis as the supplementary information, so the translation is "In 1645 (the 2nd year of Shunzhi period of the Qing Dynasty)" and "During 1821—1851

---

① 王冬凌,福州船政学堂及其科学教育,大连海事大学学报(社会科学版),2004,(1):72.
② 陈东,船政文化在近代中国文化重组中的作用,闽江学院学报,2005,(4):73.

历史人物唐王朱聿键,也就是隆武政权的皇帝,成为理解的难点。如果仅仅将其翻译为 Zhu Yujian (1602—1646, the ruler of Longwu regime) 似乎还不能提供足够的历史背景了解这个历史人物,因此加了一个尾注,详细地介绍了其历史背景,从而扫清了目的语读者理解的障碍。大理寺为古代专管重大刑事案件复审复核的机关,也添加了括注予以解释性翻译。

【例6】 林聪彝故居始建于明代,清顺治二年(1645 年),唐王朱聿键①在福州即帝位时,在此设大理寺衙门。道光间,为林则徐次子林聪彝所购置。他曾职朝廷,后担任浙江省地方官员。他晚年居此,直至病终。①

注释①:崇祯帝在北京自缢后,明朝宗室在江南建立了南明政权。1644 年福王朱由崧建立了弘光政权。1645 年弘光帝被清军俘获亦死,郑芝龙、黄道周等人扶朱聿键于福州登基称帝,改元为隆武,后世称为隆武帝,也称唐王。

📖 3.6.4　古代官职的翻译

由于与现代官职迥然不同,古代官职成为福建地方特色文化翻译的难点,因此需要详细查阅,在其后添加括注或人名之后添加同位语予以解释性翻译。光禄卿为官名。南朝梁置光禄卿,北齐以后称光禄寺卿,主要掌管皇室的膳食。历代沿置,清末始废。太

(Daoguang period of the Qing Dynasty)".

The historical figure Zhu Yujian, the emperor of Longwu regime, is also a difficult point to understand. If it is only translated as "Zhu Yujian (1602—1646, the ruler of Longwu regime)", it seems that it cannot provide enough historical background to understand this historical figure; hence an endnote is added to introduce its historical background in detail, clearing the obstacles for target readers to understand. 大理寺 is an ancient organ specializing in the review of major criminal cases, and an annotation has also been added for explanatory translation.

【译】 Lin Congyi's former residence was first built in the Ming Dynasty (1368—1644). In 1645 (the second year of Shunzhi period of the Qing Dynasty) when Zhu Yujian① (1602—1646) ascended the throne in Fuzhou, Dalisi Yamen (equivalent to today's highest court, the highest appeal organ in the country) was established here. During 1821—1851 (Daoguang period of the Qing Dynasty) it was purchased by Lin Zexu's second son, Lin Congyi (1824—1878). He served in the court and later as a local official in Zhejiang Province. He lived here in his old age until his death.

Note [1]: After Emperor Chongzhen hanged himself in Beijing, the imperial family of the Ming Dynasty (1368—1644) established Nanming regime in the south of the Yangtze River. In 1644, Zhu Yousong (1607—1646), Emperor Fu, established Hongguang regime. In 1645, Emperor Hongguang was captured and killed by the Qing army. Zheng Zhilong (1604—1661), Huang Daozhou (1585—1646) and others helped Zhu Yujian to ascend the throne in Fuzhou and called him Emperor Longwu. Later generations called him Emperor Longwu, also known as Emperor Tang.

📖 3.6.4　Translation of ancient official positions

Because they are very different from modern official positions, ancient official positions have become a difficult point in the translation of Fujian local culture. Therefore, it is necessary to check in detail and add annotations or appositives following the names as interpretative translation. "光禄卿" is an official name. In the Southern Dynasties, such an official name was set up by Liang Regime and after the Northern Qi Dynasty, it was called "光禄寺卿". The official under the title

---

① 下载自三坊七巷官网,https://www.fzsfqx.com.cn/,2022/7/5。

守是秦朝至汉朝时期对郡守的尊称。明清则专称知府。提学是"提督学政"的简称。古代设有专门负责文化教育的高级地方行政官。提督为古代军队中官名,明清时多为一省之最高武官。总兵,官名。明初,镇守边区的统兵官有总兵和副总兵,无定员。知府,也称太守,是中国古代的地方职官名,州府最高行政长官。

例 7 和例 8 的光禄卿、提学、提督、总兵、知府被分别翻译为 Guangluqing（chief officer in charge of catering in the court）、an educational official responsible for the implementation of Confucianism education and its effectiveness measurement、provincial commander-in-chief、commanding officer of garrison troops、a prefecture chief。

【例 7】 北宋熙宁间(1068—1077年)光禄卿程师孟任福州太守,他扩建城池,疏通河道、湖泊,修建桥梁,救济灾民,在民间口碑非常好。程师孟在闲暇时经常游法祥寺,特别喜欢登石远望,吟诗作赋,寺僧便给该石头起名为"光禄吟台",并请程师孟题写了这四字篆书,字径有一米左右。①

【例 8】 明万历年间举人林有台,明崇祯年间提学许豸,康熙年间提督何傅,总兵何勉,嘉庆年间知府齐鲲,光绪年间著名翻译大师林纾,道光年

was mainly in charge of royal diet. It was inherited from past dynasties and abolished in the late Qing Dynasty. "太守"is the honorific title for the head of the prefecture from the Qin Dynasty to the Han Dynasty; it was called "知府" in the Ming and Qing Dynasties. "提学" is the abbreviation of "提督学政". In ancient times, there were senior local administrators specializing in cultural education. "提督" was the official name in the ancient army and was the highest military officer of a province in the Ming and Qing Dynasties. "总兵" is an official name. In the early Ming Dynasty, the commanders guarding the border area were known as generals and deputy generals, without fixed members. "知府", also known as "太守", was a local official name in ancient China and the highest executive of a prefecture center.

"光禄卿、提学、提督、总兵、知府" in Example 7 and Example 8 were translated into "Guangluqing (chief officer in charge of catering in the court), an educational official responsible for the implementation of Confucianism education and its effectiveness measurement, provincial commander-in-chief, commanding officer of garrison troops and a prefecture chief" respectively.

【译】 During 1068—1070 (Xining period of the Northern Song Dynasty), Cheng Shimeng (1015—1083) who worked as Guangluqing (chief officer in charge of catering in the court) was appointed the prefecture chief of Fuzhou. He expanded the city, dredged rivers, lakes, constructed bridges and relieved victims. He had a good reputation among the people. He often paid his visits to Faxiang Temple in his spare time and particularly liked to climb stones, look far away, chant poems and write fu (a rhymed style in ancient China between poetry and prose). Thus the monk of the temple named the stones Guanglu Yintai (the chanting platform for Guangluqing), and asked him to inscribe the four words in seal characters, which are about one meter each in diameter.

【译】 It used to be the residential house for the following celebrities: Lin Youtai, a successful candidate in the imperial examinations at the provincial level during Wanli period (1573—1620) of the Ming Dynasty; Xu Zhi, an educational official responsible for the implementation of Confucianism education and

---

① 下载自三坊七巷官网,https://www.fzsfqx.com.cn/,2022/7/5。

间著名学者郭柏苍都先后住在这里。①

its effectiveness measurement during Chongzhen period（1628—1644）of the Ming Dynasty（1368—1644）；He Fu，provincial commander-in-chief during Kangxi period（1662—1722）of the Qing Dynasty（1644—1911）；He Mian，commanding officer of garrison troops and Qi Kun，a prefecture chief during Jiaqing period（1796—1820）of the Qing Dynasty；Lin Shu，a famous translation master during Guangxu period（1875—1908）of the Qing Dynasty；and Guo Baicang，a famous scholar during Daoguang period（1821—1850）of the Qing Dynasty.

3.6.5　特殊文化词语的翻译

"文化负载词"（culturally-loaded words）蕴含丰富的文化内涵，在目的语中找不到对等的表述方式，导致文化缺省现象。目的语读者不熟悉源语文化的文化语境，从而难以建立起话语理解所必需的语义连贯。因此对于文化缺省现象，需要提供足够的文化语境，即进行归化性解释性翻译以体现文化负载词的文化含义并实现文化语义的连贯，消弭目的语言读者的理解障碍。解释性翻译无疑是文化负载词的翻译策略。

例 9 中的府、州、军为北宋和南宋时期福建省的行政编制。例 10 的"苏武牧羊"。为历史典故，出自班固《汉书·苏武传》："苏武牧羊"，西汉时期，汉武帝派大臣苏武等为使者出使西域同匈奴单于修好。由于汉朝降将鍭侯王的反叛，单于大怒，扣押了苏武等人，劝其投降。苏武宁死不屈，坚决不降，被迫沦为匈奴的奴隶在茫茫草原上放羊，19 年后才回到汉朝。其字面意义是苏武宁死不屈，情愿牧羊也不投降匈奴，其文化含义为即使在艰难的时期仍然忠于祖国。

"岳母刺字"的典故最早出自清乾

3.6.5　Translation of special cultural words

Culturally-loaded words contain rich cultural connotations and we cannot find equivalent expressions in the target language，resulting in cultural default. The target readers are not familiar with the cultural context of the original culture. Consequently it is difficult to establish the semantic coherence necessary for discourse understanding. Therefore，for the phenomenon of cultural default，it is necessary to provide sufficient cultural context，that is，to adopt domesticated interpretive translation approach to reflect cultural meaning of culturally-loaded words and realize the coherence of cultural semantics，so as to eliminate the understanding obstacles of target language readers. Explanatory translation is undoubtedly the translation strategy of cultureally loaded words.

"府、州、军" in Example 9 are the administrative establishments of Fujian Province in the Northern Song Dynasty and the Southern Song Dynasty. "苏武牧羊" in Example 10 is a Chinese historical allusion derived from Bangu's The Book of Han-Biography of Su Wu: During the Western Han Dynasty，Emperor Wu of Han sent ministers such as Su Wu as envoys to the Western Regions to reconcile with Chan Yu of the Xiongnu. Due to the rebellion of the Han Dynasty's surrendered general，Houhou Wang，Chan Yu became furious and detained Su Wu and others，urging them to surrender. Su Wu would rather die than surrender，determined not to surrender，and was forced to become slaves of the Xiongnu，herding sheep on the vast grasslands. It was only 19 years later that he returned to the Han Dynasty. Its literal meaning is that Su Wu would rather die or herd sheep than surrender to the Xiongnu，an ancient nationality in China and its cultural meaning is to remain loyal to the motherland even in difficult times.

The allusion of "Yue Fei mother's tatooed four words

---

① 下载自三坊七巷官网，https://www.fzsfqx.com.cn/，2022/7/5。

隆年间杭州钱彩评《精忠说岳》。岳飞的母亲姚太夫人,古代四大贤母之一,在国家危亡之际,励子从戎,精忠报国,被传为佳话,世尊贤母。"岳母刺字"的文化含义为时刻报效国家。从例9到例10的文化负载词均采用了括注的方式进行解释性翻译,体现了其文化含义。

'loyalty to our country' on Yue's back" originated from Qian Cai's review of Story of Yue Fei during the Qianlong period of the Qing Dynasty. Yue Fei's mother, Lady Yaotai, was one of the four great virtuous mothers in ancient times. During the crisis of the country, she encouraged her son to join the military and serve the country with great loyalty. This was passed down as a beautiful story and she was honored as a virtuous mother. The cultural meaning of the story is to serve the country at all times. The culturally-loaded words from Example 9 to Example 10 are all rendered through explanatory translation to reflect their cultural connotations.

【例9】 "八闽"之称始于宋,最具有代表性的说法是,"北宋时期,置福建路,行政区划为福、建、泉、漳、汀、南剑六州及邵武、兴化二军"。南宋孝宗时升建州为建宁府。福建路因此包括一府五州二军;府、州、军实际是同一级行政机构,共计八个,故福建号称"八闽"。①

【译】 The name of "Bamin" (literally Eight Min) began in the Song Dynasty (960—1279). The most representative saying is that "Fujian Lu"[lu, an administrative division of Fujian in the Northern Song Dynasty (960—1127)], equivalent to the province of the Ming Dynasty (1368—1644) and the Qing Dynasty (1644—1911), was established in the Northern Song Dynasty with the administrative divisions known as the six Zhou (zhou, a local administrative division in the Song Dynasty) of Fu, Jian, Quan, Zhang, Ting and the two Jun (jun, a local administrative division in the Song Dynasty) of Shaowu and Xinghua. In the Southern Song Dynasty (1127—1279), the name of Jian Zhou was changed into Jianning Fu (fu, a local administrative division in the Song Dynasty). Fujian Lu therefore included one Fu, five Zhou and two Jun. Fu, Zhou, Jun were actually the same administrative organ at the same level; the organs total eight, so Fujian is known as "Eight Min".

【例10】 闽南民居中常以广为流传的忠贞人物事迹为装饰题材。常见有苏武牧羊、岳母刺字等。②

【译】 Faithful people's deeds are widely circulated as the themes of the decorations in the folk houses of southern Fujian, such as Su Wu's sheep-herding (a symbolization of loyalty to one's native country even under harsh situations) and Yue Fei mother's tattooing on his back (a symbolization of always being ready to serve one's country), etc.

3.7 知识拓展

3.7 Knowledge expansion

3.7.1 福建土楼

福建土楼位于福建省西南部,台湾

3.7.1 Fujian tulou③

Fujian tulou is a property of 46 buildings constructed

---

① 福建省地方志编纂委员会编,《福建省志》,北京:方志出版社,2002:9.
② 蔡雄彬,从明清时期装饰艺术看当时闽南民居文化,广东园林,2012,(6):35.
③ 下载自联合国教科文组织官网,https://whc.unesco.org/en/list/1113,2022/7/5。中文文本为编写者所译。

海峡西岸的内陆地区,方圆 120 公里,由 46 栋建筑组成,建于 15 世纪至 20 世纪。分布在水稻、茶叶和烟草田之间的土楼是土屋。它们有几层楼高,沿着一个内倾的圆形或方形建造,一座土楼最多可容纳 800 人。它们是为了防御目的而建造的,围绕着一个中央开放式庭院,只有一个入口,窗户仅位于一楼上方。整个家族就居住在这些房子里,这些房子发挥了村庄的作用,被称为"家族的小王国"或"繁忙的小城市"。它们的特点是具有高大的加固泥墙,屋顶铺设着宽大的高悬的屋檐。

最精致的建筑可以追溯到 17 世纪和 18 世纪。这些建筑为各个家庭设置了垂直的空间,每个家庭在每一层拥有两到三个房间。与它们朴素的外表形成鲜明对比的是,土楼的内部非常舒适,而且往往具有精美的装饰。它们被列为建筑传统及功能的特殊范例,体现了一种特殊类型的群居生活和防御组织,就其与环境的和谐关系而言,是人类定居点的杰出范例。

▶ 3.7.1.1 突出的普遍价值

福建土楼是中国东南部山区的土楼中最具代表性和保存最好的例子。这些规模宏大、技术复杂且引人注目的防御性土楼建于 13 世纪至 20 世纪之间,周围群山绿水环抱,位于肥沃的山谷中,是群体对定居点长期以来持续存在的反应的最佳体现。土楼及相关的大量文献档案反映了七个世纪以来杰出的土楼艺术的出现、创新和发展。精心划分的内部空间,其中一些表面装饰精美,满足了群体的物质和精神需求,并以非凡的方式反映了一个复杂社会在偏远和潜在敌对环境中的发展。大型建筑与其景观的关系体现了风水原理和景观美与和谐的理念。

between the 15th and 20th centuries over 120 km in south-west of Fujian province, inland from the Taiwan Strait. Set amongst rice, tea and tobacco fields the tulou are earthen houses. Several storeys high, they are built along an inward-looking, circular or square floor plan as housing for up to 800 people each. They were built for defence purposes around a central open courtyard with only one entrance and windows to the outside only above the first floor. Housing a whole clan, the houses functioned as village units and were known as "a little kingdom for the family" or "bustling small city." They feature tall fortified mud walls capped by tiled roofs with wide over-hanging eaves.

The most elaborate structures date back to the 17th and 18th centuries. The buildings were divided vertically between families with each disposing of two or three rooms on each floor. In contrast with their plain exterior, the inside of the tulou were built for comfort and were often highly decorated. They are inscribed as exceptional examples of a building tradition and function exemplifying a particular type of communal living and defensive organization, and, in terms of their harmonious relationship with their environment, an outstanding example of human settlement.

▶ 3.7.1.1 Outstanding universal value

The Fujian tulou are the most representative and best preserved examples of the tulou of the mountainous regions of south-eastern China. The large, technically sophisticated and dramatic earthen defensive buildings, built between the 13th and 20th centuries, in their highly sensitive setting in fertile mountain valleys, are an extraordinary reflection of a communal response to settlement which has persisted over time. The tulou, and their extensive associated documentary archives, reflect the emergence, innovation, and development of an outstanding art of earthen building over seven centuries. The elaborate compartmentalised interiors, some with highly decorated surfaces, met both their communities' physical and spiritual needs and reflect in an extraordinary way the development of a sophisticated society in a remote and potentially hostile environment. The relationship of the massive buildings to their landscape embodies both Feng Shui principles and ideas of landscape beauty and harmony.

标准（Ⅲ）：土楼见证了一种悠久的文化传统，即群体居住的防御性建筑反映了复杂的建筑传统以及和谐与协作的理念，并随着时间的推移得以充分记录。

标准（Ⅳ）：土楼在规模、建筑传统和功能方面都是独一无二的，反映了社会对更大区域内经济和社会历史各个阶段的反应。

标准（Ⅴ）：土楼作为一个整体，特别是被提名的福建土楼，就其形式而言，是群体生活和防御需求的独特反映，就其与环境的和谐关系而言，是人类定居点的杰出典范。

土楼的真实性涉及维持土楼本身及其建筑传统，还涉及与土楼相关的农田景观环境和森林景观环境的结构和形成过程。土楼的完整性不仅与它们作为建筑的完整性有关，而且也与周围的农田景观和森林景观的完整性相关——根据风水原理，土楼被精心安置在其中。

对提名区域及其缓冲区的法律保护是充分的。尽管需要更好地制定尊重当地农业传统和林业传统的景观可持续性计划，然而土楼的总体管理体系是充分的，涉及政府行政机构和当地社区。

🏵 3.7.2 泉州：中国宋元的世界商贸中心

泉州的一系列遗址展示了宋元时期（公元 10—14 世纪）泉州作为一个海上商业中心的活力，以及它与中国腹地的联系。泉州在亚洲海上贸易的重要时期得以繁荣。这些遗址包括宗教建筑，如公元 11 世纪的清净寺，这是中国最早的伊斯兰建筑之一，还有

Criterion (Ⅲ): The tulou bear an exceptional testimony to a long-standing cultural tradition of defensive buildings for communal living that reflect sophisticated building traditions and ideas of harmony and collaboration, well documented over time.

Criterion (Ⅳ): The tulou are exceptional in terms of size, building traditions and function, and reflect society's response to various stages in economic and social history within the wider region.

Criterion (Ⅴ): The tulou as a whole and the nominated Fujian tulou in particular, in terms of their form are a unique reflection of communal living and defensive needs, and in terms of their harmonious relationship with their environment, an outstanding example of human settlement.

The authenticity of the tulou is related to sustaining the tulou themselves and their building traditions as well as the structures and processes associated with their farmed and forested landscape setting. The integrity of the tulou is related to their intactness as buildings but also to the intactness of the surrounding farmed and forested landscape—into which they were so carefully sited in accordance with Feng Shui principles.

The legal protection of the nominated areas and their buffer zones are adequate. The overall management system for the property is adequate, involving both government administrative bodies and local communities, although plans for the sustainability of the landscape that respect local farming and forestry traditions need to be better developed.

🏵 3.7.2 Quanzhou: Emporium of the world in Song-Yuan China[①]

The serial site of Quanzhou illustrates the city's vibrancy as a maritime emporium during the Song and Yuan periods (10th—14th centuries AD) and its interconnection with the Chinese hinterland. Quanzhou thrived during a highly significant period for maritime trade in Asia. The site encompasses religious buildings, including the 11th century AD Qingjing Mosque, one of the earliest Islamic edifices in China, Islamic tombs, and a wide range of archaeological

① 下载自联合国教科文组织官网，https://whc.unesco.org/en/list/1561，2022/7/5。中文文本为编写者所译。

伊斯兰陵墓以及大量的考古遗迹：行政建筑、对商业和防御极为重要的石砌码头、陶瓷和铁制品生产地、城市交通网络的组成部分、古代桥梁、佛塔、铭文。泉州在公元10至14世纪的阿拉伯语和西方文本中被称为刺桐。

➋ 3.7.2.1 突出的普遍价值

简要介绍

位于中国东南沿海，泉州宋元中国商贸中心所拥有的一系列遗产以一种独特的方式反映了生产、运输和营销相结合的空间结构，机构、社会和文化因素促成了泉州在公元10—14世纪作为东亚和东南亚贸易网络的海上枢纽的崛起和繁荣。宋元泉州中心以位于江海交界处的城市为中心并以其为动力，东南部的海洋将其与世界相连，西北部的山脉为其提供生产，水陆交通网络将城市、海洋、山脉连接在一起。

该遗产的组成部分和构成要素包括行政建筑和结构、宗教建筑和雕像、文化纪念场所和纪念碑、陶瓷和钢铁生产场所以及由桥梁、码头和引导旅行者的佛塔组成的交通网络。它们全面反映了宋元泉州独特的领海、社会文化和贸易结构。

标准（Ⅳ）：泉州宋元中国商贸中心通过其组成部分，突出地说明了区域一体化结构和关键的机构、交通、生产、营销和社会文化因素在公元10至14世纪亚洲海上贸易的高度繁荣时期促使泉州成为了一个全球的商贸中心和主要的商业枢纽。该遗产展示了泉州对东亚和东南亚经济和文化发展的巨大贡献。

完整性

该系列遗产包括必要的组成部分和属性，反映了泉州作为公元10至14

remains: administrative buildings, stone docks that were important for commerce and defence, sites of ceramic and iron production, elements of the city's transportation network, ancient bridges, pagodas, and inscriptions. Known as Zayton in Arabic and western texts of the 10th to 14th centuries AD.

➋ 3.7.2.1 Outstanding universal value

Brief synthesis

Located on the southeast coast of China, the serial property Quanzhou: Emporium of the World in Song-Yuan China reflects in an exceptional manner the spatial structure that combined production, transportation and marketing and the key institutional, social and cultural factors that contributed to the spectacular rise and prosperity of Quanzhou as a maritime hub of the East and South-east Asia trade network during the 10th—14th centuries AD. The Song-Yuan Quanzhou emporium system was centred and powered by the city located at the junction of river and sea, with oceans to the south-east that connected it with the world, with mountains to the far north-west that provided for production, and with a water-land transportation network that joined them all together.

The component parts and contributing elements of the property include sites of administrative buildings and structures, religious buildings and statues, cultural memorial sites and monuments, production sites of ceramics and iron, as well as a transportation network formed of bridges, docks and pagodas that guided the voyagers. They comprehensively reflect the distinguishing maritime territorial, socio-cultural and trade structures of Song-Yuan Quanzhou.

Criterion (Ⅳ): Quanzhou, Emporium of the World in Song-Yuan China outstandingly illustrates, through its component parts, the territorial integrated structure and the key institutional, transportation, production, marketing and socio-cultural factors that turned it into a global-level emporium and key commercial hub during a highly prosperous stage of Asia's maritime trade in the 10th—14th centuries AD. The property demonstrates Quanzhou's great contributions to the economic and cultural development of East and South-east Asia.

Integrity

The serial property includes the necessary components and attributes that reflect Quanzhou as a premier maritime emporium of the world of the 10th—14th centuries AD. The component parts and contributing elements maintain close functional, social, cultural and spatial links with each other, altogether illustrating the integrated territorial system and key facets and factors of Quanzhou's maritime trade system in the

世纪世界上首屈一指的海上商贸中心的地位。组成部分和重要要素之间保持着密切的功能、社会、文化和空间联系，全面阐述了宋元时期泉州海上贸易体系的整体地域体系、主要方面、重要因素。该遗产的直接背景、重要观点和其他支持区域或属性都包含在缓冲区中；对视觉冲击和背景环境敏感的区域显示出与该系列遗产的整体关联，这些区域都包含在划定的更广阔的设置区域中，并受到有效保护。通过一套保护和管理措施，城市发展压力、气候变化的影响、自然威胁和旅游业压力似乎得到了有效控制。

真实性

该系列遗产作为一个整体，由其组成部分和要素组成，真实地描述了宋元时期泉州作为全球海上商贸中心的总体布局、宋元时期的贸易体系的功能、历史和社会结构、史实。遗存的原始位置，能够清楚识别和理解的历史功能信息，在实物遗迹及其历史记录中得以反映的形式、材料、工艺、传统维护机制和技术系统的历史信息以及这些纪念碑和遗址所承载的遗存信仰和文化传统，所有这些都证明了组成部分的高度真实性和可靠性。这些物证可以在大量的历史文献以及中国和国际研究成果中得以印证。

保护和管理要求

泉州市系列遗产的所有组成部分均受到国家和省级相关法律法规（《中华人民共和国文物保护法》及其实施条例和《福建省文物保护管理条例》）的保护。它们都属于国家所有，根据有关历史文化名城、宗教事务、海洋事务和风景名胜区的法律法规，通常被授予多重保护性名称。传统的维护和

Song and Yuan periods. The immediate setting of the property, important views and other supporting areas or attributes, are all included in the buffer zone; areas sensitive to visual impacts and background environments demonstrating overall association with the serial property are all contained in demarcated wider setting areas and placed under effective protection. Urban development pressures, impacts from climate change, natural threats, and tourism pressures appear under effective control, through a set of protective and management measures.

Authenticity

The series as a whole, comprised of its component parts and contributing elements, credibly conveys the overall territorial layout, functions of the historical trade system, historical social structure, and historical chronological information of Quanzhou as a global maritime emporium in the Song and Yuan periods. Surviving original locations; information of historical functions that can be clearly recognized and understood; historical information of forms, materials, processes and traditional maintenance mechanisms and technical systems reflected in physical remains and their historical records, as well as surviving beliefs and cultural traditions that these monuments and sites carry; all testify to a high degree of authenticity and credibility of the component parts. The physical evidence can be confirmed by a wealth of historical documentation and Chinese and international research results.

Protection and management requirements

All the component parts of the serial property of Quanzhou are subject to the protection of relevant laws and regulations at the national and provincial level (*Law of the People's Republic of China on the Protection of Cultural Relics* and its *Implementation Regulations* and *The Regulations of Fujian Province on the Protection and Management of Cultural Property*). They are all owned by the state and granted with often multiple protective designations as per laws and regulations governing Famous Historical and Cultural Cities, religious affairs, marine affairs, and Scenic Areas. Traditional maintenance and conservation mechanisms also play an active role in this regard. For protection and management effectiveness, the buffer zone and the wider setting have been incorporated into the property's

保护机制也在这方面发挥积极作用。为了保护和管理的有效性，缓冲区和更广泛的设置已被纳入遗产的保护和管理系统，并纳入已制定和实施的《泉州系列遗产管理规划》和修订的《福建省"古泉州（刺桐）史迹遗址"文化遗产保护管理办法》。

该遗产管理系统是按照中国的文化遗产管理机制设计的，并纳入国家、省、市/县和遗产四级管理框架。它基于不同级别指定的责任、本地化管理和社区积极参与的原则。市一级的协调管理系统将各组成部分的管理措施和实施计划结合起来。管理工作组每季度召开一次会议，确保全面协调。管理实体提供充分的财务、人力和技术保障，并能够持续和适当地保护整个系列遗产及其各组成部分的真实性和完整性。已为该系列制定了一项长期保护和管理战略，指明了具体要求，其逐步实施对总体管理成效至关重要。

protection and management system and are covered by *The Management Plan for the Serial Property of Quanzhou*, prepared and implemented, and *The Rules of Fujian Province for the Protection and Management of Historic Monuments and Sites of Ancient Quanzhou (Zayton)*, as revised.

The property's management system is designed following China's administrative mechanism for cultural heritage and incorporated into the four-level administrative framework at national, provincial, city/county, and property levels. It is based on the principles of responsibilities designated at different levels, localized administration, and active community participation. A coordinated management system at the municipal level integrates management measures and implementation plans for each component part. A management working group meets quarterly and guarantees overall coordination. Management entities provide sufficient financial, human and technical guarantees and enable continuous and proper conservation of the authenticity and integrity of the serial property as a whole and each of its component parts. A long-term protection and management strategy, indicating specific requirements, has been prepared for the series and its progressive implementation is crucial for the overall management effectiveness.

❋ Exercises

Ⅰ. Fill in the blanks with proper forms of words.

1. In the history of Chinese thought, the rise of Min Studies _____ (represent) by Zhu Xi in the Song Dynasty enabled Fujian _____ (occupy) an important position.

2. In _____ (disseminate) the civilization of central China, Wang Shenzhi advocated culture and education, established schools, trained talents and educated the people, which had made Fujian a home for _____ (talent) people.

3. The World Tourism Organization (UNWTO) is the United Nations agency responsible for the promotion of responsible, sustainable and universally _____ (access) tourism. As the leading international organization in the field of tourism, UNWTO promotes tourism as a _____ (drive) of economic growth, inclusive development and environmental _____ (sustainable) and offers leadership and support to the sector in advancing knowledge and tourism policies worldwide.

4. The Fujian Tulou are the most _____ (represent) and best _____ (preserve) examples of the tulou of the _____ (mountain) regions of south-eastern China. The large, _____ (technical) sophisticated and dramatic earthen _____ (defend)

buildings, built between the 13th and 20th centuries, in their highly sensitive setting in fertile mountain valleys, are an extraordinary _____ (reflect) of a communal response to settlement which has persisted over time.

Ⅱ. Translate the following Chinese sentences into English.

1. 纵观福建文化的发展历程,闽越文化遗风、中原文化传入、宗教文化传播和海外文化影响是其形成的主要源流。

2. 宋代的福建是南方有名的文化大省之一,在科举、书院、出版等各个领域,都有杰出的成就;在无形的文化产业里,宋代福建出现了许多著名的诗人、作家、历史学家、科学家,形成了一个波澜壮阔的文化浪潮。

3. 王审知堪称五代十国时期一位明智的政治家,在其当政的30余年里,他以史为鉴,以民为本,在经济、农业、教育、人才培养、商业和海外贸易方面做出了卓越的贡献,极大推动了福建各方面的发展,使福建成为当时全国比较稳定繁荣的地方。因此他也被后世称为"开疆闽王",深受百姓爱戴。

4. "文化负载词"蕴含丰富的文化内涵,在目的语中找不到对等的表述方式,导致文化缺省现象。解释性翻译无疑是文化负载词的翻译策略。

Ⅲ. Translate the following English sentences into Chinese.

1. In the simplest terms, inbound tourism occurs when a foreigner or non-resident visits a particular country, and outbound tourism occurs when a resident of a particular country leaves it in order to visit another one.

2. When a country attracts a lot of inbound tourists, the tourists spend money on hotels, dining, attractions, souvenirs and other amenities. This creates jobs, and through consumption taxes, it adds additional money to that country's coffers.

3. If a country has more inbound than outbound tourism, it has a travel trade surplus. A country with a travel trade surplus can consider tourism to be a very lucrative export. For the United States, international travel as a whole continually enhances American job growth and helps balance the country's trade, being its largest service export.

4. The series as a whole, comprised of its component parts and contributing elements, credibly conveys the overall territorial layout, functions of the historical trade system, historical social structure, and historical chronological information of Quanzhou as a global maritime emporium in the Song and Yuan periods.

Ⅳ. **Questions and answers.**

1. How is pluralism of Fujian culture reflected?

2. Why is the historical position of Fujian's economy and culture in the Song Dynasty important?

3. How much do you know about the contribution of Wang Shenzhi，the ruler of the Min State?

4. What are the criteria for the selection of world cultural and natural heritage?

第❹单元　入境旅游接待(2)
Unit ❹　Inbound Tourism Reception(2)

📖 **教学目标**
⇨ 掌握景点介绍的要点
⇨ 辨别非物质文化遗产的概念
⇨ 了解福建非物质文化遗产项目
⇨ 了解福建地方特色文化的内涵
⇨ 掌握文本中文化意象的翻译策略
⇨ 掌握非物质文化遗产文本的文化因素翻译方法

📖 **Teaching objectives**
⇨ To master key points of introducing scenic spots
⇨ To distinguish the concept of intangible cultural heritage
⇨ To know about intangible cultural heritage projects in Fujian
⇨ To understand connotations of local characteristic culture in Fujian
⇨ To master translation methods strategies of cultural images in a text
⇨ To master translation methods of cultural factors in intangible cultural heritage texts

4.1 情景对话

▦▦ **旅游行程核对**

> A. 陈先生,福州一家旅行社的全陪
> B. 斯蒂芬,美国一家旅行团的领队

A:你好,斯蒂芬,你能抽出点时间检查并讨论一下我们的旅游行程安排吗?

B:好的,稍等一下。我要拿一份福建文化之旅的 15 天旅游行程。

A:我们比较一下我们的旅游行程,查看一下是否有任何出入,好吗?

B:好的,在我们开始旅行之前最好先检查一下。

A:我同意。如果我们以后发现我们的行程不一致,我们可能会遇到麻烦。

B:我认为我们在福州第二天的行程安排太满了。我们能稍微调整一下吗? 这样我们的团队就有时间在三坊七巷自由漫步,看看周围的情况。我们在

4.1 Situational dialogue

▦▦ **Verification of tour itinerary**

> A. Mr. Chen, a national guide from a travel agency in Fuzhou
> B. Stephen, a foreign tour escort from a travel agency in the US

A: Hi, Stephen, could you spare some time to check and discuss the arrangement of our tour itinerary?

B: OK, just a second. Let me get a tour itinerary for our 15-day cultural tour in Fujian.

A: Shall we compare our tour itinerary to find out whether there is any discrepancy?

B: Fine, it had better be checked now before we start our trip.

A: I agree. If we found out some discrepancy between our itineraries later, we might get into trouble.

B: I think our schedule for the second-day tour in Fuzhou is too full. Could we adjust it a little bit so that our group may have some time to have a free walk in Three Lanes and Seven Alleys and look around themselves? Similar problems seem to exist in the arrangement of our tour itinerary in other places. We need save some time for the members of the tourist group

其他地方的旅游行程安排似乎也存在类似的问题。我们需要节省一些时间，让旅游团的成员在每个城市走动一下。

A：好的。我会在三坊七巷安排一个半小时的自由漫步。我还将努力为他们节省 1～2 个小时，让他们有点时间在每个城市自由漫步，这样他们就有机会与当地人交流，更好地了解每个地方。可以吗？

B：太好了。谢谢你这么做。

A：不客气。无论何时团队有任何特殊要求，请告诉我。

to walk around in each city.

A: All right. I will arrange one and half hours' free walk there. I will also try to save 1—2 hours for them to have a free walk in each city so that they can have a chance to communicate with the local people and have a better idea of each place. Is it okay?

B: Cool. Thank you for doing that.

A: It is my pleasure. Whenever there is any special requirement for the group, just let me know.

4.2　角色扮演训练

景点介绍的要点

如果是自然景观，介绍内容的重点需要聚焦于景点地理位置、景点基本信息、景点特点、景点价值以及面临的问题等内容。如果是人文景观需要聚焦于景点基本信息、历史价值、奇特之处、有趣的故事以及面临的问题等。在景点讲解中，导游需要根据游客的文化层次等不同，因人而异地选择好讲解内容。对于文化层次较高的游客，导游人员需要深入讲解；对于文化层次较低的游客，导游人员需要采用更为通俗的语言，不必开展深入的介绍。在运用导游技巧上也是如此。比如对一般的游客，导游可多运用虚实结合法、问答法、借用故事法、拟人比喻法以及活用数字法等等。而对文化层次较高的游客可运用画龙点睛法、制造悬念法、设置疑问法、故事穿插法以及含蓄幽默法等等。请任意选择一处自然景观或人文景观予以介绍。

4.2　Role playing training

Key points of introduction of a scenic spot

If it is a natural landscape, the introduction should focus on the geographical location of the scenic spot, its basic information, its characteristics, its value and the problems it faces. If it is a place of cultural interest, the introduction needs to focus on the basic information, historical value, uniqueness, interesting stories, and problems it faces. In the explanation of scenic spots, tour guides need to choose the content of the introduction according to tourists' differences like the varying cultural levels of the tourists, and according to different places. For tourists with higher cultural levels, tour guides need to make in-depth introduction, while for tourists with lower cultural levels, tour guides need to use more colloquial language and do not need to make in-depth introductions. The same applies to the use of tour guide skills. For example, for ordinary tourists, tour guides can use methods such as the combination of the folklore and basic information of a scenic spot, question and answer, story borrowing, the application of personification, and flexible use of numbers. For tourists with higher cultural levels, they can use finishing touches, creating suspense, setting questions, mixture of storytelling and scenic spot introduction, and implicit humor, among others. Please choose any natural landscape or place of cultural interest in your introduction.

4.3   文本聚焦：非物质文化遗产

4.3.1   什么是非物质文化遗产？

近几十年来，"文化遗产"一词的内容发生了很大变化，部分原因是教科文组织制定了一些文书。文化遗产不仅包括历史遗迹和收藏品，还包括从我们的祖先那里继承下来并传承给我们后代的传统或生活方式的表达，如口头传统、表演艺术、社会实践、仪式、节日活动、关于自然和宇宙的知识和实践，或传统手工艺的知识和技能。

面对日益发展的全球化，非物质文化遗产虽然脆弱，但却是保持文化多样性的重要因素。了解不同社区的非物质文化遗产有助于跨文化对话，并鼓励相互尊重生活方式。

非物质文化遗产的重要性不在于其文化表现形式本身，而在于其代代相传的知识财富和技能财富。这种知识传播的社会价值和经济价值与少数群体和国家内的主流社会群体有关，对发展中国家和发达国家同样重要。

4.3.1.1   非物质文化遗产是：

传统、当代实践和生活方式。非物质文化遗产不仅代表继承过去的传统，也代表不同文化群体参与的当代农村和城市的实践。

4.3.1.2   包容性

我们可以分享类似于其他人实践的非物质文化遗产的表现形式。无论它们是来自邻近的村庄，还是来自世界另一端的城市，或是被移民和定居在不同地区的人们所适应，它们都是非物质文化遗产：它们是一代又一代人传承下

4.3   Text focus：Intangible cultural heritage

4.3.1   What is intangible cultural heritage? ①

The term "cultural heritage" has changed content considerably in recent decades, partially owing to the instruments developed by UNESCO. Cultural heritage does not end at monuments and collections of objects. It also includes traditions or living expressions inherited from our ancestors and passed on to our descendants, such as oral traditions, performing arts, social practices, rituals, festive events, knowledge and practices concerning nature and the universe or the knowledge and skills to produce traditional crafts.

While fragile, intangible cultural heritage is an important factor in maintaining cultural diversity in the face of growing globalization. An understanding of the intangible cultural heritage of different communities helps with intercultural dialogue, and encourages mutual respect for other ways of life.

The importance of intangible cultural heritage is not the cultural manifestation itself but rather the wealth of knowledge and skills that is transmitted through it from one generation to the next. The social and economic value of this transmission of knowledge is relevant for minority groups and for mainstream social groups within a State, and is as important for developing States as for developed ones.

4.3.1.1   Intangible cultural heritage is：

Traditional, contemporary and living at the same time：intangible cultural heritage does not only represent inherited traditions from the past but also contemporary rural and urban practices in which diverse cultural groups take part；

4.3.1.2   Inclusive

We may share expressions of intangible cultural heritage that are similar to those practised by others. Whether they are from the neighbouring village, from a city on the opposite side of the world, or have been adapted by peoples who have migrated and settled in a different region, they all are intangible cultural heritage：they have been passed from one generation to another, have evolved in response to their

---

① 下载自联合国教科文组织官网，https：//ich. unesco. org/en/what-is-intangible-heritage-00003，2022/7/5。中译文由编写者翻译。

来的,随着环境的变化而演变,它们有助于赋予我们一种认同感和延续感,将我们的过去、现在和未来连接起来。非物质文化遗产不会产生这样的问题:某些实践是否为某一文化所特有。它有助于形成社会凝聚力,鼓励认同感和责任感,促使个人感受到自己是一个或不同社区的一部分,并感受到自己是整个社会的一部分。

▶ 4.3.1.3 代表性

在比较的基础上,非物质文化遗产不仅仅因为其独特性或特殊价值而被视为一种重要的文化产品。它在社区中蓬勃发展,并依靠那些将自己所拥有的传统、技能和习俗等知识代代相传给社区的其他人或其他社区的人们。

▶ 4.3.1.4 以社区为基础

非物质文化遗产只有在得到创造、维护和传播它的社区、团体或个人承认时才能成为遗产——如果没有他们的承认,任何其他人都不能为他们决定某一特定表达或实践是他们的遗产。

▦ 4.3.2 非物质文化文本聚焦
▶ 4.3.2.1 乌龙茶制作技艺(铁观音制作技艺)

福建安溪产茶历史悠久,始于唐末,兴于明清,盛于当代。安溪茶农吸取红茶全发酵和绿茶不发酵的原理,发明了半发酵的制茶工艺。安溪铁观音是我国六大茶类之一乌龙茶。安溪铁观音传统制作技艺都是手工操作,在我国制茶界中独树一帜,从而形成了铁观音茶文化。①

为何产于安溪的茶叶具有奇特的

environments and they contribute to giving us a sense of identity and continuity, providing a link from our past, through the present, and into our future. Intangible cultural heritage does not give rise to questions of whether or not certain practices are specific to a culture. It contributes to social cohesion, encouraging a sense of identity and responsibility which helps individuals to feel part of one or different communities and to feel part of society at large;

▶ 4.3.1.3 Representative

Intangible cultural heritage is not merely valued as a cultural good, on a comparative basis, for its exclusivity or its exceptional value. It thrives on its basis in communities and depends on those whose knowledge of traditions, skills and customs are passed on to the rest of the community, from generation to generation, or to other communities;

▶ 4.3.1.4 Community-based

Intangible cultural heritage can only be heritage when it is recognized as such by the communities, groups or individuals that create, maintain and transmit it—without their recognition, nobody else can decide for them that a given expression or practice is their heritage.

▦ 4.3.2 Focus on intangible cultural text
▶ 4.3.2.1 Oolong tea production techniques (Tieguanyin production techniques)

Anxi tea production in Fujian enjoys a long history, which began in the late Tang Dynasty (618—907), developed in the Ming (1368—1644) and Qing (1644—1911) Dynasties and flourished in the contemporary era. The tea growers in Anxi absorbed the principle of the full fermentation of black tea and the non-fermentation of green tea, and invented a semi-fermented tea-making process. Anxi Tieguanyin is one of the six major types of tea in China. The traditional production techniques of Anxi Tieguanyin tea are all based on manual operation unique to China's tea industry, thus forming Tieguanyin tea culture.

---

① 下载自福建省非物质文化遗产保护中心,http://www.fjfyw.net/daibiaozuo/2015-01-16/1270.html,2022/7/5。

名称"铁观音"？清代雍正、乾隆年间，因安溪所产茶品质特异，乌润结实，沉重似铁，香韵形美，犹如观音，故此得名"铁观音"。

安溪铁观音传统制作技艺由采摘、初制、精制三个部分组成。采摘前先要确定采摘期，制定采摘标准，然后再熟练运用技术进行采摘。制茶时，要根据季节、气候和叶的鲜嫩程度等各种情况灵活处理。制作安溪铁观音，先要以晒青、凉青、摇青等方法控制和调节茶青，使之发生一系列物理、生物变化，形成"绿叶红镶边"和独特的色、香、味；再以高温杀青，制止酶的活性；最后进行揉捻和反复多次的包揉、烘焙，形成带有天然兰花香和特殊韵味的高雅茶品。安溪铁观音传统制作技艺是安溪茶农长期生产经验和劳动智慧的结晶，具有较高的科学价值。①

💠 4.3.2.2　武夷岩茶(大红袍)制作技艺③

武夷岩茶的制作可追溯到汉代，经历代的发展沿革，到清代初年出现了岩茶制作的完善技艺，首开乌龙茶制作的先河。武夷岩茶(大红袍)独有的"岩骨花香"是由武夷山独特的生态环境、气候条件和精湛的传统制作技艺造就的。其传统制作流程共有10道工序，环环相扣，不可或缺，其中对茶质起关键作用的是"双炒双揉"、"低温久烘"等环节。

武夷山为红茶、乌龙茶的发源地，

Why does the tea produced in Anxi have a unique name "Tieguanyin"? In Yongzheng period (1723—1735) and Qianlong period (1736—1795) of the Qing Dynasty (1644—1911), because the tea produced in Anxi was special in its quality, dark in appearance and firm in its texture, heavy and iron-like in its weight, fragrant in its taste and beautiful in its shape, and alike the image of Guanyin (a Bodhisattva), hence the name of the tea.

The traditional production technique of Tieguanyin in Anxi consists of picking, preliminary production and refinement. Before picking, we should first determine the picking time, establish the picking standard, and then skillfully use the technique to pick. Tea-making should be handled flexibly according to season, climate, and the fresh and tender degree of leaves. In order to produce Tieguanyin in Anxi, a series of physical and biological changes should be made to control and regulate the tea's green color by means of sun-drying, cooling and shaking so as to form the unique color of "a green leaf with a red edge", fragrance and taste. Then, the enzyme activity should be restrained by killing the green color at a high temperature. Finally, the high-quality tea with a natural orchid fragrance and special flavor can be produced by rolling, repeated rubbing and drying over a fire. Anxi Tieguanyin traditional production technique is the crystallization of Anxi tea farmers' long-term production experience and labor wisdom, so it enjoys a high scientific value. ②

💠 4.3.2.2　Production techniques of Wuyi rock tea

The production of Wuyi rock tea can be traced back to the Han Dynasty (206 B. C. —220 A. D. Through the development in different dynasty, in the early Qing Dynasty (1644—1911) there appeared the perfect technique of producing rock tea, which marked the beginning of oolong tea production. Its special taste is created by the unique ecological environment and climate conditions of Mount Wuyi and exquisite traditional production techniques. Its traditional production process follows 10 interlocking and indispensable processes, of which the key for the quality of tea is to "double-frying and double-rubbing" and "long drying under a low temperature" and other processes.

Mount Wuyi is the birthplace of black tea and oolong tea. The tea custom accompanied by Wuyi rock tea production

---

① 下载自中国非物质文化遗产网，http://www. ihchina. cn/project_details/14620/，2022/7/5。
② 摘自韦忠生主持的国家外文局 2018 年"福建省地方特色文化对外翻译标准化术语库建设项目"，译者韦忠生。
③ 下载自中国非物质文化遗产网，http://www. ihchina. cn/project_details/14373/，2022/7/5。

与武夷岩茶制作技艺相伴而生的茶俗有浓郁的地方特色,喊山、斗茶赛、茶艺等风俗,拥有广泛的群众基础。

国家技术监督部门已经批准武夷岩茶为原产地保护产品,国家商标总局(2018年更名为国家知识产权局商标局)也批准其使用"武夷山大红袍"商标。但由于茶商受到市场经济利益的驱使,机械生产工艺带来了冲击,加上老艺人疏于传技,传统岩茶制作工艺出现濒危迹象,急需加以保护。①

🔊4.3.2.3　福建客家擂茶制作工艺

福建将乐、宁化等地的客家人制作擂茶的习俗相传已久。如今这一传统习俗已渗透客家人日常生活的方方面面,造屋乔迁、婚姻喜事、生日寿诞、开业庆典、欢庆佳节等等,都要宴请擂茶,以款待佳宾。由于擂茶中有青草药、芝麻、炒米、炒豆等多种佐料,故擂茶具有清香、爽口、独特的口感,不仅能解渴、充饥,还能清凉降火、消痰化气、健脾养胃,深受客家人的亲睐。②

擂茶是客家人为了求生存、避免南方瘴病侵袭而产生的一种驱瘟疫防病毒的特殊饮茶文化。1996年初客家擂茶窑址在福建将乐县被发现,以实物证明了客家擂茶文化在将乐有着较浓厚的积淀。同时,也为研究擂茶的历史提供了丰富的材料。

擂茶是我国茶叶最早的制作方法之一,同时,"食擂茶"又是我国最早的饮茶方式之一,是中国饮食文化尤其是茶文化的一个重要组成部分。尽管

technique enjoys strong local characteristics. The customs of shouting to mountain to bless a bumper harvest of tea production, the tea contest and tea ceremony, etc. are popular among the public in this area.

Relevant national technical supervision department has approved Wuyi rock tea as a product of origin protection and National Trademark Administration (renamed Trademark Office of China National Intellectual Property Administration in 2018) has also approved the application of "Wuyi Dahongpao" (Big Red Robe) trademark. However, because tea merchants are driven by market economic interests, challenges are brought about by mechanical production technique and the transmission of skills are neglected by old artisans, the traditional rock tea production techniques show signs of endangerment, and urgently need to be protected. ①

🔊4.3.2.3　Production techniques of Hakka pestled tea in Fujian Province

The Hakka people in Jiangle, Ninghua and other places in Fujian Province have been producing pestled tea for a long time. Nowadays, this traditional custom has permeated every aspect of Hakkas' daily life, such as house-building and relocation, marriage and the wedding, birthday, opening ceremony, celebration of festivals and so on. On such occasions pestled tea is offered to entertain guests. As there are many kinds of ingredients in pestled tea, such as herbal medicine, sesame, fried rice, fried beans and so on, the tea enjoys a fragrant, refreshing and unique taste. It not only quenches thirst and allays hunger, but also cools down the body, eliminates phlegm, invigorates the spleen and stomach, so it is deeply loved by Hakka people.

Pestled tea represents a special tea culture produced by Hakkas in order to survive and avoid the attack of southern plague. At the beginning of 1996, the old production site for Hakkas' pestled tea was unearthed in Jiangle County, Fujian Province, which proves that the culture of pestled tea enjoys a long history in Jiangle. Meanwhile, it also provides abundant materials for the study of the history of pestled tea.

Pestling tea is one of the earliest methods of tea production in China. Meanwhile, "eating pestled tea" is one of the earliest tea drinking methods in China, and is an important part of Chinese

---

① 摘自韦忠生主持的国家外文局2018年"福建省地方特色文化对外翻译标准化术语库建设项目",译者韦忠生。
② 福建省非物质文化遗产保护中心,http://www.fjfyw.net/daibiaozuo/2015-01-16/1381.html,2022/7/5。

随着科技的进步、社会的发展,茶叶的制作方法和饮茶方式有所改善,但我们从来无法否认或低估擂茶。自古人们已习惯于通过茶联络感情、招待客人、祭祀神祖、洽谈生意等等,此种文化背景使擂茶能在客家人中代代传承。①

food culture, especially tea culture. With the progress of science and technology as well as the development of society, the methods of making and drinking tea have been improved, but pestled tea can never be denied or underestimated. Since ancient times, people have been accustomed to making friendly contacts through drinking tea on such occasions as entertaining guests, offering sacrifices to gods and ancestors, negotiating business, and so on. This cultural background enables the pestled tea to be passed down from generation to generation among the Hakka people. ②

4.4　文化文本聚焦

🔖 福建土楼的文化内涵③

隐藏在崇山峻岭里的福建土楼坚固封闭,高大对称,除了客观上具有自卫御敌、适宜居住和光宗兴业等实际功能外,还蕴含着丰富的人文信息,具有深厚的文化内涵。福建土楼丰富的文化内涵体现了儒家文化、道家哲学观、生态美学思想、风俗文化和民俗艺术的精髓。

福建土楼的文化内涵在多个层面得以体现。第一,土楼建筑的向心性、对称性以及族人按血缘性聚居等特征,正是儒家文化和宗族精神的一个缩影。一座土楼就是一个家族的凝聚中心,这种强调同宗血缘凝聚力的集体聚居的特殊性,反映了中国传统文化中强大的家族伦理制度。几世同堂的大家族制度在古代中国是自上而下、随处可见的习俗制度,但像土楼那样,至今保持了富于共同协作的家族观念的大家族制度,确属罕见。方楼圆寨均在中轴线,中心置建一高大厅堂,作全楼的中枢和向心点,楼内每环每层每间房朝向中枢,体现了家族向心力和统一性。

4.4　Cultural text focus

🔖 Cultural connotations of Fujian tulou

Fujian tulou hidden among high mountains are solid, closed, tall and symmetrical. They not only objectively enjoy the practical functions of self-defense, protection against enemies, suitability for living, glorifying ancestors and revitalizing old business, but also contain abundant humanistic information and profound cultural connotations. The rich cultural connotation of Fujian tulou embodies the essence of Confucian culture, Taoist philosophy, ecological aesthetics, custom and culture, and folk art.

The cultural connotation of Fujian tulou is revealed in numerous aspects. Firstly, the centripetal as well as symmetrical nature of tulou, and the characteristics of people's living together according to blood relationship symbolize Confucianism and the clan spirit. A tulou represents the cohesion of a family. The particularity of the collective settlement, which emphasizes the cohesion of consanguinity, reflects the strong family ethics system in traditional Chinese culture. In ancient China, a large family system of several generations was a top-down and ubiquitous custom. However, it is rare to see a large family system that has so far maintained such a strong collaborative family concept like the tulou. Both square tulou and round tulou are located on the central axis. A high hall is constructed in the center to serve as the pivot and centripetal point of the whole building. Every room on every floor in every ring in the building faces the center, which reflects the centripetal force and unity of the family.

---

① 林更生,客家擂茶探源,茶叶科学技术,2009,(1):51-52.
② 摘自韦忠生所主持的国家外文局2018年"福建省地方特色文化对外翻译标准化术语库建设项目",译者韦忠生。
③ 邓文金,马照海,福建土楼文化三论,闽台文化研究,2009,(1):59.题目为编写者所加。

第二，八卦原则运用于土楼建造中，体现了深刻的道家哲学观。八卦是中国古代最具特色，也是最神圣的文化符号，对古代社会的政治、经济、军事、哲学、医学、文学、宗教、建筑、养生等方面都产生了极大影响。在土楼建造中，八卦的运用可谓精妙绝伦，不仅八卦土楼完全以八卦精髓为建楼指南，而且其他类型的土楼建造亦多用八卦择地定位，镇宅辟邪，出煞保安。现存有名的八卦楼有在田楼、振成楼、八卦堡等。

第三，土楼内设学堂、题对联诗文，具有浓厚的人文气息。秉承中原汉民族尊师重教的传统，许多土楼内专设学堂或以祠堂祖堂兼作学堂，供本楼及邻近子弟学习文化。在土楼成群的永定，兴学之风极盛，以至一座土楼涌现出几个至几十个成功成名的人才。楼内随处可见的对联无时不在激励后辈学子求上进。这些自勉或勉励后人的知书识礼成大事的家训，是土楼文化传承儒家文化的典型代表。

第四，福建土楼依山傍水而建，充分利用自然地貌又与自然融合无间，体现了天人合一的生态美学思想。大大小小的土楼循着起伏的山势错落有致，仿佛慈母背上的婴孩、怀中的爱子，而且有水为乐有林为朋，仿佛造化使然，奇异幽美秀丽。华安二宜楼正大厅的两副对联形象地描述了圆楼与周围环境的和谐之美。

第五，土楼文化是一部内容非常丰富的风俗文化书。各朝各代的中原汉民族不断涌入福建，他们举家南迁，建造土楼，共同生活，繁衍后代，同祀一列祖宗，从而使黄河或长江风俗文化一代又一代地保留下来。有学者指出"福建是中国风俗文化的荟萃地。

Secondly, the Eight Diagrams Principle is applied to the construction of tulou, which embodies the profound Taoist philosophy. The eight diagrams are the most distinctive and sacred cultural symbols in ancient China, which have exerted great influence on the politics, economy, military, philosophy, medicine, literature, religion, architecture and health preservation of ancient society. In the construction of tulou, the application of the Eight Diagrams Principle is exquisite. Not only is the essence of the eight diagrams the guide for building octagonal tulou, but also the guide for selecting a site, driving out evil spirits and ensuring safety in constructing other types of tulou. Existing well-known octagonal tulou include Zaitian Building, Zhencheng Building, the Octagonal Fortress and so on.

Thirdly, schools are attached to tulou in which you can see the decorations such as couplets of poems with a strong humanistic flavor. Adhering to the tradition of respecting teachers and emphasizing education of the Han nationality in central China, the owners of numerous tulou have established special schools in tulou or converted one function of ancestral halls into that of the schools for their own buildings and their neighboring children to learn culture. In Yongding, where tulou are clustered, learning atmosphere is so strong that several to dozens of successful talents emerge in a single tulou. The couplets that can be seen everywhere in the buildings are always encouraging the younger students to strive for progress. These family precepts, which encourage people themselves or future generations to be a well-educated model of propriety and make great achievement in future, are the typical representative of tulou culture to inherit Confucianism.

Fourthly, Fujian tulou are constructed along mountains and rivers, making full use of natural landforms and blending with nature, which embodies the ecological aesthetic thought of harmony between man and nature. The tulou, large and small, are scattered among undulating mountains, like a baby on the back of a loving mother and a beloved child in her arms. Additionally, they offer you the pleasure of having water and forest as friends, as if those fantastic and beautiful views are created by nature. Two pairs of couplets in the main hall of Hua'an's Eryi Building vividly depict the beauty of harmony between the round tulou and its surroundings.

Fifthly, tulou culture is a book on rich customs culture. The Han nationality in central China had been migrating to Fujian constantly in all dynasties. Their families moved south, constructed tulou, lived together, reproduced and worshiped the same series of ancestors, thus preserving the customs and cultures of the Yellow River or the Yangtze River from generation to generation. Some

别地有的风俗这里有,别地没有的风俗这里也有,别地古代盛行而现在消失或已经演变而面目全非的风俗现象在这里仍旧保留着它的古朴风貌"。

第六,土楼丰富的文化内涵还体现在建筑装饰的精巧华丽、具有独特性的民俗艺术上。土楼的内部融汇了雕梁、壁画、彩绘、书法多种艺术。壁画彩绘保护专家对二宜楼的壁画彩绘进行了详细普查,结果计有壁画 593 平方米、226 幅,彩绘 99 平方米、214 幅。

scholars argued that "Fujian is a gathering place of Chinese customs and culture, where you can experience all kinds of old customs. Some of the customs are already extinct in other places or have evolved to enjoy completely different features here and some still retain the simple and unsophisticated style".

Sixthly, the rich cultural connotations of tulou are also reflected in the exquisite and gorgeous architectural decoration and unique folk art. The interior of tulou combines a variety of art forms such as carved beams, murals, colored paintings and calligraphy works. An expert in the protection of murals and colored paintings conducted a detailed survey of the murals and colored paintings in Eryi Building. The results showed that there were 226 murals covering 593 square meters and 214 colored paintings covering 99 square meters respectively. [1]

4.5　文本中文化意象的翻译

文化意象的两个构成要素是物象(physical image)和寓意(connotation)。物象是信息的载体,体现了人们对某一物体的感知;寓意则是物象在特定文化语境中的引申意义或文化含义,是文化意象的映现。文化意象是与特定文化语境紧密关联的文化符号,具有独特的文化内涵。由于中英两种语言文化背景各不相同,各自的文化意象所传递的文化内涵也迥然不同,文化意象也因此成为翻译中的难点之一。

4.5　Translation of cultural images in texts

The two constituent elements of cultural image are physical images and connotation. The physical image is a carrier of information, reflecting people's perception of a certain object; the connotation refers to the extended meaning or cultural meaning of objects in a specific cultural context, which is the reflection of cultural image. Cultural image is a cultural symbol closely related to a specific cultural context, with unique cultural connotations. Due to the different cultural backgrounds between Chinese and English languages, the cultural connotations conveyed by their cultural images are also vastly different, making cultural images one of the difficulties in translation.

4.5.1　保留物象与文化意象阐释

文化意象的对等移植就是保留源语中的物象与文化意象阐释,这是由于源语已经提供了文化意象阐释,其文化语境显而易见,体现了语用意义,即文化含义,因此目的语读者不必进行语境推测,从而减少了目的语读者所付出的阅读努力,也没有必要进行语境重构。

4.5.1　Preserving physical images and cultural image interpretation

The equivalent transplantation of cultural images is to preserve the physical image and cultural image interpretation in the source language. This is because the source language has already provided cultural image interpretation, and its cultural context is obvious, reflecting the pragmatic meaning, i. e. cultural meaning. Therefore, target language readers do not need to engage in contextual speculation, which reduces the reading effort put in by target language readers, and there is

---

① 摘自韦忠生主持的国家外文局 2018 年"福建省地方特色文化对外翻译标准化术语库建设项目",译者韦忠生,内容略有不同。

例1的源语文本已经解释了喜鹊与梅花、白鹭与莲花搭配的文化意象，因此译文只要将其完整地翻译出来即可。译文仅对汉语同音词添加了个别内容。英汉语中动物词语文化意象的错位现象可以分为两类：其一，有些动物词语在两种文化中具有迥然不同的文化意象；其二，某些动物词语在一种文化语境具有文化意象，而在另一种文化中全然不存在任何文化意象。喜鹊在中国文化中是"喜庆"的象征。"喜鹊踏梅"是传统的吉祥画。然而喜鹊在英语文化中是不吉利的征兆。凤、鹤、鹿、白鹭等均为中国文化特有的文化意象，在英语文化中不具有任何文化意象，原文指出它们都具有吉祥的寓意，因此在译文中既保留其物象，也保留了源语对其文化意象的阐释，为目的语读者提供了足够的文化语境，实现了文化意象的传递。

【例1】 闽南民居中动物的吉祥寓意也随处可见。在闽南传统民宅中，以凤、鹤、鹿、喜鹊等出现频率最高，龙、麒麟则因规制等原因使用较少。神灵瑞兽常与植物组合出现，如喜鹊与梅花搭配，取其"喜"之谐音，寓意"喜上眉梢"。白鹭常与莲花搭配，取其"路"之谐音，寓意"一路连科"。①

4.5.2 舍弃物象、保留文化意象

物象一般来说较好理解，然而由于在不同文化体系里语言的文化背景存在巨大差异，文化意象的转换成为

no need for contextual reconstruction.

The source language text of Example 1 has already explained the cultural image of the combination of "the magpie and plum blossom" and "the egret and lotus", so we only need to fully translate it. Only some contents are added to explain the Chinese homophones. The misplacement of cultural images of animal words in English and Chinese can be divided into two categories: first, some animal words have very different cultural images in the two cultures; secondly, certain animal words have cultural images in one cultural context, while in another there is no cultural image at all. The magpie is a symbol of "festivity" in Chinese culture. "Magpie stepping on plum blossoms" is a traditional painting with auspicious meaning. However, the magpie is an unlucky sign in English culture. The phoenix, crane, deer, egret, etc. are all unique cultural images of Chinese culture, and do not have any cultural images in English culture. The source language points out that they all have auspicious meanings. Therefore, in the translation, both their physical images and the interpretation of their cultural images in the source language are preserved, providing sufficient cultural context for target language readers and achieving the transmission of cultural images.

【译】 The auspicious implication of animals in the local-style dwelling houses of southern Fujian can also be seen everywhere. Among the traditional local-style dwelling houses in southern Fujian, the phoenix, crane, deer and magpie, etc. enjoy the highest frequency of occurrence in house decoration while the dragon and Chinese unicorn are less frequently utilized because of relevant rules. Deities and auspicious beasts usuallly appear in the combination with plants, such as the matching of magpies and plum blossoms, where "xi"(happy) in "xique"(magpie) is used, implying "looking very happy". Egrets are often paired with lotus flowers, using the homonyms of "lu" in "bailu"(egret) and "lu"(road), which symbolizes "a great success in the imperial examination". ②

4.5.2 Abandoning physical images and preserving cultural images

The physical image is generally easy to understand. However, due to the significant differences in the cultural

---

① 蔡雄彬，从明清时期装饰艺术看当时闽南民居文化，广东园林，2012，(6)：34-35.
② 摘自韦忠生主持的国家外文局2018年"福建省地方特色文化对外翻译标准化术语库建设项目"，译者韦忠生.

翻译的难点之一,因而翻译过程中出现文化意象的缺失和错位现象,因此需要建构关联的语境。例 2 中源语的"海滨邹鲁"和"衣锦还乡"中的"邹鲁"和"衣锦"均为中国文化中特有的物象,具有含义丰富的文化意象。邹鲁为古代邹国、鲁国的并称,因孟子生于邹国,孔子生于鲁国,故以"邹鲁"指文化昌盛之地、礼义之邦,体现了其文化意象。在"衣锦还乡"中,"衣锦"为物象,具有两层意义:其字面意义是穿着华丽的衣服回到故乡,其文化意象是荣归故里。这两个物象在目的语中均未保留,仅将其文化意象移植到目的语中,分别将其翻译为"glorious homecoming after having won high honors and social recognition"和"a coastal city where its culture flourishes"。

backgrounds of languages between different cultural systems, the transformation of cultural images has become one of the difficulties in translation. As a result, there are phenomena of missing and misplaced cultural images in the translation process, and therefore, it is necessary to construct relevant contexts. In Example 2, "邹鲁" and "衣锦" in the source language "海滨邹鲁" and "衣锦还乡" are both unique physical images in Chinese culture, with rich cultural connotations. Zoulu("邹鲁") is a combination of Zou State and Lu State in ancient time. Because Mencius was born in Zou State and Confucius was born in Lu State, later, the term "Zoulu" was used to refer to the land of cultural prosperity and the state of etiquette and righteousness, reflecting its cultural image. In "衣锦还乡", "衣锦" is a physical image with two meanings: its literal meaning is to return to one's hometown wearing gorgeous clothes; its cultural image is returning to one's hometown with honor. These two physical images are not retained in the target language and only the cultural images are transplanted into the target language. They are translated as "a coastal city where its culture flourishes" and "glorious homecoming after having won high honors and social recognition", respectively.

【例 2】 唐末五代宋初,北方汉人入迁莆仙地区进入高峰期,莆仙平原的开发逐渐从莆田中部向沿海及山区推进。经济发展带动文化教育兴盛,莆仙地区人才辈出,素称"海滨邹鲁"、"文献名邦"。科举文化在莆仙之发达世所罕见,历代世家名宦辈出,人才济济、衣锦还乡、光宗耀祖是他们的追求。体现在传统民居中,受中原京城居住文化影响至深。①

【译】　At the end of the Tang Dynasty (618—907) and the beginning of the Song Dynasty (960—1279), the migration of northern Han people to Puxian (Putian and Xianyou) area reached its peak. The development of Puxian Plain was gradually promoted from central Putian to coastal and mountainous areas. Economic development resulted in the prosperity of culture and education. Men of talent came out in succession, so it is known as "a coastal city where its culture flourishes" and "a region with a long history, a well-developed culture and a large number of talented people". Imperial examination culture was unique in Puxian, famous clans emerged in all dynasties and a galaxy of talents appeared. Glorious homecoming after having won high honors and social recognition as well as making one's ancestors illustrious were their pursuit. It is embodied in the traditional local-style dwelling houses, which are deeply influenced by the residential culture of the capital city of central China. ②

4.5.3　保留物象并阐释文化意象

源语文本和目的语文本之间的关系是一种原始文本和生成文本之间的

4.5.3　Preserving physical images and interpreting cultural images

The relationship between the source language text and the

---

① 戴志坚.闽文化及其对福建传统民居的影响,南方建筑,2011,(6):26-28.
② 摘自韦忠生主持的国家外文局 2018 年"福建省地方特色文化对外翻译标准化术语库建设项目",译者韦忠生.

关系。在文化意象缺失的情况下,纯粹的文化移植难以让目的语读者理解译文的含义。由于文化缺省是一种具有鲜明文化特性的交际现象,不具有源语文化语境知识的目的语读者面对这样的文化缺省时经常无法理解其文化含义。为了既保留源语文化信息,同时有助于目的语读者理解源语文化意象,保留物象并加注释的翻译手法无疑为一种移植源语文化意象的翻译策略。

例3中的"石敢当"是流行于闽南地区的一种辟邪的建筑装饰,具有独特的文化意象。译例中的"石敢当",除了保留其源语中的物象,还进行了语境重构,增加了阐释性的内容,即明示了其文化寓意,将其翻译为"'Shigandang',small stone steles placed outside houses or in streets and lanes against evil spirits"。

target language text is a relationship between the original text and the generated text. In the absence of the cultural image, pure cultural transplantation makes it difficult for target readers to understand the meaning of the translation. Since cultural default is a communicative phenomenon with distinct cultural characteristics, target language readers without knowledge of the cultural context of the source language cannot understand its cultural connotation when faced with such cultural default. In order to preserve the cultural information of the source language and help the target readers understand the cultural images of the source language, the translation technique of retaining the physical image and adding annotations is undoubtedly a translation strategy of transplanting the cultural images of the source language.

"石敢当" in Example 3 is an architectural decoration popular in the southern Fujian region to ward off evil spirits, with its unique cultural image. In the translation example, "Shigandang" not only retains the physical image in its source language, but also undergoes contextual reconstruction, adding explanatory content, which clearly indicates its cultural connotation. In the example, the phrase "石敢当" is translated as "'Shigandang', small stone steles placed outside houses or in streets and lanes against evil spirits".

【例3】 闽南民居中的第二类镇宅厌胜物是制冲性厌胜物。房屋或者是聚落面对路口、桥头、港口等交通要道,民间认为通衢要道人车往来频繁,影响聚落和民宅的安宁,破坏了人与自然和谐,此现象谓之"犯冲",需要设法破解。常见做法就是安置"石敢当"或竖立"石雕符号",金门地区也设置风狮爷于路口或者是在面对要道的墙壁设置镶壁风狮爷。①

【译】 The second type of talismans to guard the local-style dwelling houses of southern Fujian are the talismans against disturbance of peace. For houses or settlements facing major traffic routes such as intersections, bridges and ports, people think that the frequent flow of pedestrians and vehicles in thoroughfares affects the peace, hence destroying the harmony between human beings and nature. This phenomenon is known as "disturbance of peace" and needs to be solved. The common practice is to install "Shigandang", small stone steles placed outside houses or in streets and lanes against evil spirits or erect "symbols of stone carving". In Jinmen area, stone lions are also placed at the intersection or mounted on the wall facing the main road. ②

4.5.4 重构文化意象

创造性翻译主要体现在,当源语

4.5.4 Reconstructing cultural images

The technique of creative translation is mainly employed

---

① 蔡雄彬.从明清时期装饰艺术看当时闽南民居文化.广东园林,2012,(6):34-35.
② 摘自韦忠生主持的国家外文局2018年"福建省地方特色文化对外翻译标准化术语库建设项目",译者韦忠生。

中的词语或表达方式的概念意义无法在目的语中找到对等的词语或表达方式时,译者必须根据自己所处的文化语境在目的语中创造与源语语境中概念对等的新词语或新的表达方式。例4源语中的"颠沛流离"为汉语成语,其喻义为生活艰难,四处流浪。可以翻译为"vagrant life, wander from place to place, be a vagabond"等。例4将"颠沛流离"翻译为 exodus 可以更好地体现其文化寓意,移植其文化意象,这是由于该词涉及圣经文化,而圣经文化乃是西方文化的重要来源之一。《出埃及记》(*The Book of Exodus*)中描述了以色列人大规模离开埃及的过程,历经千辛万苦。客家人五次大迁徙,饱经各种艰辛与磨难,与犹太人出走埃及有许多相似之处。

【例4】 在饱尝颠沛流离的痛苦之后,客家人更加巩固和加强了宗族、家族观念,聚族而居、敬祖睦宗显得十分突出。①

on occasions when the conceptual meaning of words or expressions in the source language is not equivalent to that in the target language. The translator must create new words or expressions in the target language that are equivalent to the concepts in the source language context on the basis of his/her own cultural context. The phrase "颠沛流离" in Example 4 is a Chinese idiom, which means living in hardship and wandering around. It can be translated as "vagrant life, wander from place to place, be a vagabond", etc. In Example 4 "颠沛流离" is translated into "exodus", which can better reflect its cultural connotations and transplant its cultural image. This is because the term involves biblical culture, which is one of the important sources of Western culture. *The Book of Exodus* describes the process of the Israelites leaving Egypt on a large scale, going through countless hardships. The Hakka people underwent five major migrations, enduring various hardships, which had many similarities with the Israelites exodus from Egypt.

【译】 Hakka people have consolidated and strengthened their clan and family concepts after experiencing the misery of exodus, so it is prominent that they live together and respect their ancestors. ②

4.6 非物质文化文本中文化因素的翻译

2021年"延平郡王信俗"被列为第5批国家级非物质文化遗产代表性项目。郑成功信俗是闽南文化的重要组成部分,也是联系两岸民众的文化纽带。因此,厦门的延平郡王信俗具有重要的意义。以下文本中的"南明"和"思明州"是非物质文化文本中的文化因素。如果直译而不加以解释将给读者造成理解上的困难,因此添加注解无疑是翻译此类文化因素的途径。

4.6 Translation of cultural factors in intangible cultural texts

In 2021, "Folk Belief to Worship Zheng Chenggong" was listed as a representative project of the fifth batch of national intangible cultural heritage. The folk belief is an important component of culture in southern Fujian and a cultural link that connects people on both sides of the Taiwan Strait. Therefore, the folk belief in Xiamen is of great significance. The terms "Nanming" and "Siming Prefecture" in the following text refer to cultural factors in texts of intangible culture. If translated directly without explanation, it will cause difficulties for readers to understand, so adding annotations is undoubtedly a good way to translate such cultural factors.

---

① 戴志坚,闽文化及其对福建传统民居的影响,南方建筑,2011,(6):26-28.
② 摘自韦忠生主持的国家外文局2018年"福建省地方特色文化对外翻译标准化术语库建设项目",译者韦忠生。

延平郡王信俗①

郑成功率军驱逐了荷兰殖民者，组织大批汉族军民开拓台湾，是海峡两岸民众共同景仰的民族英雄。因为南明[1]永历帝封他为延平郡王，故又称郑延平。延平郡王信俗可上溯至清朝光绪元年（1875），其间台湾地区官方建立延平郡王祠堂祀奉郑成功；随后厦门也建立延平王祠堂。郑成功在海峡两岸享有极高的威望，台湾有 58 座延平郡王祠。

在今思明区内，有郑成功操练水师、誓师东征的水操台，有练兵的演武场、演武池，有屯兵的嘉兴寨，有太平岩郑成功读书处，有先锋营、洪本部、国姓井、延平公园、延平郡王祠等遗迹。特别是位于鸿山公园半山腰"嘉兴古寨"景点内的"荥阳通祠"（郑氏祠堂），是与台南"延平郡王祠"同时期设立的"郡王祠"旧址。

每年春秋二季，或逢郑成功生辰、逝世纪念日，或郑成功建立思明州[2]的时间，官方或民间都会组织相关的纪念活动。

注释：

[1] 南明（1644 年—1683 年）是明朝京师顺天府失陷后，由明朝宗室在南方建立的若干政权。

[2] 明末清初（1650 年），民族英雄郑成功为了抗清复明，驻军厦门时，把厦门改为思明州（蕴含"思念大明"之意）。

Folk belief to worship Zheng Chenggong

Zheng Chenggong (1624—1662) led the army to expel the Dutch colonists and organized a large number of Han people to open up Taiwan. He is a national hero admired by the people on both sides of the Taiwan Strait. Because Emperor Yongli (1623—1662) of Nanming Regime[1] (1644—1683) made him the ruler of Yanping Prefecture, he is also known as Zheng Yanping. The belief of Yanping Prefecture's ruler can be traced back to 1875 (the first year of Guangxu period in the Qing Dynasty), in which the official Temple of Yanping Prefecture's Ruler was established in Taiwan to worship Zheng Chenggong, and then a similar temple was set up in Xiamen as well. Zheng enjoys great prestige on both sides of the Taiwan Strait. There are 58 such temples in Taiwan.

In today's Siming District, Xiamen, there are historical remains such as water platform for Zheng's training of sailors and swearing their oaths before the eastern expedition, martial arts field and martial arts pool for military training, Jiaxing Village for stationing troops, the reading place located on Taiping Rock, Xianfeng Camp, Hongbenbu Alley, Guoxing Well, Yanping Park and Temple of Yanping Prefecture's Ruler. In particular, "Xingyang Tong Ci" (Zheng's Ancestral Hall), located in the scenic spot of "Jiaxing Ancient Village" on the hillside of Hongshan Park, is the old site of "Temple of Yanping Prefecture's Ruler" which was erected at the same time as the similar temple in Tainan.

Every spring and autumn, or on the anniversary of Zheng's birth and death, or at the time when he established Siming Prefecture[2], official or civil organizations will organize relevant commemorative activities.

Note:

[1] Nanming Regime (1644—1683) refers to a number of regimes established by the imperial clan of the Ming Dynasty (1368—1644) in the south after the collapse of Shuntianfu (the supreme local administration of the capital city) in Beijing in the Ming Dynasty.

[2] In 1650 (the end of the Ming Dynasty and the beginning of the Qing Dynasty), Zheng Chenggong, a national hero, changed the name of Xiamen into Siming Prefecture when he stationed his troop in Xiamen in order to fight against the the Qing Dynasty (1644—1911) and restore the Ming Dynasty (1368—1644). The name Siming Prefecture implies the meaning of "missing the Ming Dynasty". ②

4.7　知识链接

🔲 三坊七巷民居建筑的装饰题材分类①

　　三坊七巷民居建筑内部以木结构为主,各种形式的精湛木雕艺术成为民居最重要的建筑装饰特色之一,其融合了明清时期南方建筑的艺术精华,透露出当地特有的审美气息和细腻的工艺技术,体现出建筑的美感和性格。三坊七巷民居建筑的装饰题材主要可分为植物类、动物类、人文类和器物类。

　　三坊七巷民居建筑的装饰题材分类显而易见,植物和花卉图案便是例证。三坊七巷古民居中还有很多地方运用了梅、兰、桂等花卉图案。兰花清雅芳香,花质素洁,喻君子高洁之品质;桂有及第折桂之意,喻子孙科举及第,仕途昌达。桂花与兰花组成"兰桂齐芳"的纹样,寓意子孙仕途昌达、尊荣显贵。

　　动物灵兽是装饰中常用的图案题材,如象征吉祥灵瑞的龙、凤、麒麟、蝙蝠,威猛镇邪的狮、虎、象、豹,以及其他众多的飞禽、走兽、虫鱼等题材。在三坊七巷古民居建筑中除了能经常看见采用鹿、蝙蝠、鹤等图案的雕刻外,还不时有其他意外的发现。位于宫巷11号的北洋海军总长刘冠雄宅厅两侧的门扇上各有4块装饰木雕,其中一侧为虾、鱼、蟹、蚝四种海里动物,另一侧则为蜻蜓、知了、甲虫、金蝉四种昆虫,形态逼真,工艺精湛,把这些自然界里的小生物刻画得栩栩如生、呼之欲出。

4.7　Knowledge link

🔲 Classification of decoration subject of local-style dwelling houses in Three Lanes and Seven Alleys

The interior of local-style dwelling houses in Three Lanes and Seven Alleys is dominated by wood structure. The exquisite wood carving art of various forms has become one of the most important architectural decorative features of the houses. It integrates the artistic essence of southern architecture in the Ming (1368—1644) and Qing (1644—1911) Dynasties, reveals the unique local aesthetic flavor and exquisite craftsmanship, and reflects the beauty and character of the buildings. The decoration themes for local-style dwelling houses in Three Lanes and Seven Alleys can be divided into plants, animals, culture and utensils.

The classification of decoration subject of local-style dwelling houses in Three Lanes and Seven Alleys is only too evident: plant and flower patterns are examples. There are many places in the ancient dwellings of Three Lanes and Seven Alleys which apply flower patterns as their decoration such as plum, orchids and osmanthus. The orchid is elegant and fragrant, and it is well known for its snow-white flower, which symbolizes the noble quality of a gentleman; the orchid carries the implication of passing an imperial examination, and is applied as a metaphor to wish descendants success in the imperial examination and a prosperous official career. Osmanthus and orchids form the pattern of "the fragrance of osmanthus and orchids", which implies that the future generations will have a successful official career and honorable life.

Animals and mythological animals are commonly utilized in decorative patterns, such as dragons, phoenixes, Chinese unicorns and bats, which symbolize auspiciousness, as well as fierce and evil-dispelling lions, tigers, elephants and leopards. Likewise, many other birds, animals, insects and fish are also employed as subject matters in decorative patterns. In the ancient local-style dwelling houses of Three Lanes and Seven Alleys, besides the carvings of deer, bats and cranes, there are other unexpected discoveries from time to time. There are four decorative wood carvings on the doors along both sides of the hall of the former residence of Liu Guanxiong, the navy commander of Beiyang Government (1912－1928), located at No. 11 Gong Lane. One side is decorated with shrimp, fish, crab and oysters, and the other side is decorated with dragonflys, cicadas, beetles and golden cicadas. They are vivid in shape and exquisite in craftsmanship. These small creatures

---

① 卓娜.福建民居三坊七巷的装饰木雕艺术.南京工程学院学报(社会科学版),2010,(3):33-34. 此处标题为编写者所加。

在三坊七巷民居建筑木雕中，人文类装饰图案题材主要包括文学典故、戏曲故事、民间传说、日常生活、民俗风情等。如福禄寿三星、三国演义、闹元宵、看花灯、招亲祝寿，以及表现日常生活的孩童嬉戏、渔樵耕读等图景画意。这类雕饰题材与人们的生活情感十分贴近，表达了人们对美好生活的向往之情。同时，一些雕饰还宣传忠义孝悌，褒扬报效国家，具有一定社会伦理色彩，达到道德教化的目的。

in nature are vividly portrayed. [1]

In the woodcarving works of local-style dwelling houses in Three Lanes and Seven Alleys, the cultural themes of the decorative patterns mainly include literary allusions, dramatic stories, folklore, daily life and folk customs, etc., such as the three gods of fortune, prosperity and longevity, *Romance of the Three Kingdoms*, the celebration of the lantern festival, the watching of the lantern show, the wedding ceremony and birthday congratulations, as well as the pictures associated with children's fun in daily life, and life after retirement in ancient time (literally fishing, woodcutting, farming and studying). This kind of theme in carving is very close to people's life and emotion, expressing people's yearning for a better life. Meanwhile, some carving works also emphasize loyalty, filial piety and praise one's service to his/her country, so they are endowed with a certain social ethical color to achieve the purpose of moral education.

4.8 知识拓展

🔲 4.8.1 鼓浪屿

鼓浪屿是一个小岛，位于九龙江口，与厦门市相望。随着 1843 年厦门商埠的开放，以及 1903 年该岛作为公共租界的建立，这个位于中国南部海岸的岛屿突然成为中外交流的重要窗口。鼓浪屿是这些交流中产生的文化融合的一个特例，这些交流在其城市结构中仍然清晰可见。这里混合了不同的建筑风格，包括传统闽南风格、西方古典复兴风格和殖民地外廊式风格。各种风格影响得以融合的最好的证明是一场新的建筑运动，即厦门装饰艺术风格的崛起，它是 20 世纪早期现代主义风格和装饰艺术的融合。

▶ 突出的普遍价值

简要介绍

鼓浪屿的遗产反映了一个现代定居点的复合性质。该定居点由 931 座

4.8 Knowledge expansion

🔲 4.8.1 Kulangsu [2]

Kulangsu is a tiny island located on the estuary of the Chiu-lung River, facing the city of Xiamen. With the opening of a commercial port at Xiamen in 1843, and the establishment of the island as an international settlement in 1903, this island off the southern coast of the Chinese empire suddenly became an important window for Sino-foreign exchanges. Kulangsu is an exceptional example of the cultural fusion that emerged from these exchanges, which remain legible in its urban fabric. There is a mixture of different architectural styles including Traditional Southern Fujian Style, Western Classical Revival Style and Veranda Colonial Style. The most exceptional testimony of the fusion of various stylistic influences is a new architectural movement, the Amoy Deco Style, which is a synthesis of the Modernist style of the early 20th century and Art Deco.

▶ Outstanding Universal Value

Brief synthesis

The heritage of Kulangsu Island reflects the composite nature of a modern settlement composed of 931 historical

---

① 摘自韦忠生主持的国家外文局 2018 年"福建省地方特色文化对外翻译标准化术语库建设项目"，译者韦忠生。

② 下载自联合国教科文组织网站，https://whc.unesco.org/en/list/1541/，2022/7/5。中文文本为编写者所译。

具有各种当地和国际建筑风格的历史建筑、自然景观、具有历史意义的街道网络和花园组成。

经过当地中国人、归国华侨和来自多个国家的外国居民的共同创造，鼓浪屿发展成为一个具有卓越文化多样性和现代生活品质的国际性定居点。它也成为活跃在东亚和东南亚的华侨和精英的理想居住地，也是 19 世纪中期至 20 世纪中期现代人居理念的体现。

鼓浪屿是这些交流产生的文化融合的一个特殊例子，在几十年来形成的有机城市结构中，文化融合始终清晰可见。各种风格影响得以融合的最好证明是一场真正的新建筑运动——从岛上兴起的厦门装饰风格。

标准（Ⅱ）：鼓浪屿在其建筑特征和风格中展示了中国、东南亚和欧洲建筑和文化价值观与传统的交流，这些价值观和传统是由定居在该岛的外国居民或归国华侨所创造的。创建的定居点不仅反映了定居者从他们的原籍地或故居带来的各种影响，还合成了一种新的混合风格——所谓的厦门装饰风格，这种风格在鼓浪屿发展，并对东南亚沿海地区乃至更远的地区产生了影响。在这方面，该定居点说明了在亚洲全球化早期阶段，不同价值观的碰撞、互动和融合。

标准（Ⅳ）：鼓浪屿是厦门装饰风格的起源和最佳代表。厦门装饰风格（Amoy Deco Style）以厦门当地的方言"Amoy"命名，指的是一种建筑风格和类型，最早出现在鼓浪屿，体现了来自当地建筑传统、早期西方尤其是现代主义的影响以及闽南移民文化的灵感的融合。基于这些，厦门装饰风格展示了传统建筑类型向新形式的转变，后来在整个东南亚被作为参照物，并在更广泛的地区流行。

buildings of a variety of local and international architectural styles, natural sceneries, a historic network of roads and historic gardens.

Through the co-creation of local Chinese, returned overseas Chinese, and foreign residents from many countries, Kulangsu developed into an international settlement with outstanding cultural diversity and modern living quality. It also became an ideal dwelling place for the overseas Chinese and elites who were active in East Asia and Southeast Asia as well as an embodiment of modern habitat concepts of the period between mid-19th and mid-20th century.

Kulangsu is an exceptional example of the cultural fusion, which emerged from these exchanges, which remain legible in an organic urban fabric formed over decades constantly integrating more diverse cultural references. Most exceptional testimony of the fusion of various stylistic influences is a genuinely new architectural movement the Amoy Deco Style, which emerged from the island.

Criterion （Ⅱ）: Kulangsu Island exhibits in its architectural features and styles the interchange of Chinese, Southeast Asian and European architectural and cultural values and traditions produced in this variety by foreign residents or returned overseas Chinese who settled on the island. The settlement created did not only mirror the various influences settlers brought with them from their places of origin or previous residence but it synthesized a new hybrid style—the so-called Amoy Deco Style, which developed in Kulangsu and exerted influences over a far wider region in Southeast Asian coastal areas and beyond. In this, the settlement illustrates the encounters, interactions and fusion of diverse values during an early Asian globalization stage.

Criterion （Ⅳ）: Kulangsu is the origin and best representation of the Amoy Deco Style. Named after Xiamen's local Hokkien dialect name Amoy, Amoy Deco Style refers to an architectural style and typology, which first occurred in Kulangsu and illustrates the fusion of inspirations drawn from local building traditions, early western and in particular modernist influences as well as the southern Fujian Migrant culture. Based on these the Amoy Deco Style shows a transformation of traditional building typology towards new forms, which were later referenced throughout Southeast Asia and became popular in the wider region.

完整性

具有历史意义的景观的完整性得以保持，主要是由于对具有历史意义的建筑结构的持续保护和对新建筑的高度、体积和形式的有效开发控制。建筑和绿地之间的由来已久的关系也有助于整体景观的完整性，包括保存完好的悬崖和岩石的自然景观、历史性花园及其附属庭院、独立的私人花园。

该遗产的完整性体现在整个岛屿的划界上，包括其周围的沿海水域，延伸到珊瑚礁边缘，这促使岛屿的建筑结构和自然环境形成了一个和谐的整体。早期对这种和谐的认识阻止了该岛周围水域的大量开发，而在其他岛屿或附近大陆可以看到这种大量的开发。对这座岛屿的价值至关重要的是，它从未通过交通基础设施与厦门相连，只能通过渡轮抵达。如今，这一限制构成了游客管理流程的重要组成部分，确保了该岛的持续完整。

旅游压力是一个可能影响岛屿完整性的问题，因此需要严格控制。每天最多允许 35 000 名游客进入鼓浪屿。这一数字需要予以密切监测，以确保足以防止大量游客产生的负面影响。

真实性

鼓浪屿在形式和设计、位置和环境、岛屿材料和物质的许多元素以及在较低程度上的使用和功能方面都保持了其真实性。无论是城市居住模式还是建筑结构，都保留了其独特的布局和风格特征。后者仍然是岛上各种建筑风格以及它所创造的厦门装饰风格的可信的代表。

鼓浪屿保留了它独特的位置和自然景观，并保护了理想居住区的环境

Integrity

The integrity of the historic landscape has been maintained, primarily as a result of consistent conservation of historic architectural structures and effective development controls regarding height, volume and form of new buildings. The historic relationship of built-up and green spaces also contributes to the overall landscape integrity which includes the preserved natural sceneries of cliffs and rocks and the historic gardens, both affiliated courtyard and independent private gardens.

The completeness of the property is demonstrated in the delimitation of the entire island including its surrounding coastal water until the edge of the reef, which underpins that the built structures and the natural setting of the island form one harmonious whole. The early recognition of the harmony has prevented extensive development in the waters surrounding the island, which can be witnesses on other islands or the nearby mainland. Essential for the recognition of the value of the island is that it was never connected to Xiamen via traffic infrastructure and remains solely accessible by ferry. Today, this restriction constitutes an essential element of visitor management processes ensuring the continued intactness of the island.

Tourism pressures are a concern that could affect the integrity of the island and hence require strict controls. A maximum number of 35 000 visitors per day will be allowed to access Kulangsu, a number that will require close monitoring to ensure it suffices to prevent negative impacts of large visitor flows.

Authenticity

Kulangsu Island has retained its authenticity in form and design, location and setting and in many elements of the island material and substance as well as—to a lower extent—use and function. Both the urban settlement patterns as well as the architectural structures have retained their characteristic layout and stylistic features. The latter remain credible representations of the various architectural styles the island unites as well as the Amoy Deco Style it created.

Kulangsu retains its original location and natural landscape setting and has preserved the atmospheric qualities of an ideal residential settlement with a wide range of public services, which continue to serve their original function. The urban structures retain protected by the original legal context, which was created for the establishment of the international settlement in 1903 and remains valid until present. The various spatial contexts of the island, both natural and built-up retain

质量,提供了广泛的公共服务,这些服务将继续发挥原来的功能。城市结构仍然受到原来的法律保护。该法律是1903年为建立租借地而创立的,直到现在仍然有效。该岛的各种空间环境,无论是自然的还是人工的,都保留了其原有的连接和关系,包括道路连接和景观之间的关系。

保护和管理要求

1988年,鼓浪屿被国务院认定为国家风景名胜区。51处具有代表性的历史性建筑、花园、建筑物和文化遗址被列入遗产名录:19处为国家级遗产,8处为省级遗产,24处为区级遗产。此外,所有省级和区级保护遗址将被列入第八批国家遗产名录①。

《鼓浪屿文化遗产地保护管理规划》于2011年正式通过,政府自2014年开始实施。该规划基于对该遗产地的状况和威胁的广泛分析,制定了管理战略和行动计划。这些战略性文件还将所有其他计划和保护条例的规定纳入一个综合管理系统,使所有相关管理利益相关者之间的合作制度化。2014年通过的《鼓浪屿商业业态控制导则》遵循了该保护和管理计划,这是必要的。这些文件为岛上商业服务的规模和质量保证措施发挥了引导作用,尤其是旅游业服务的规模和质量保证措施。

根据《鼓浪屿风景区2017年容量计算报告》,岛上的最佳人数被设定为25 000人,而绝对最大人数被设定为每天50 000人。由于这一数字包括了岛上的居民和通勤者,包括高峰日在内,岛上的有效最大游客人数目前被控制在35 000人。

their original links and relations including road connections and sight relations.

Protection and management requirements

Kulangsu was recognized by the State Council as a National Scenic Area in 1988 under the National Scenic Area framework. Fifty-one representative historic buildings, gardens, structures and cultural sites are included in Heritage lists: nineteen as National Heritage Sites, eight as Provincial Heritage Sites, and twenty-four as County Heritage Sites. Moreover, all the provincial and county protected sites will be added to the 8th Tranche of the National Heritage List.

The Conservation and Management Plan for Kulangsu Cultural Heritage was officially adopted 2011 and is being implemented by the Government since 2014. The plan establishes management strategies and actions based on an extensive analysis of the property's conditions and threats. The strategic documents also integrate the provisions of all other plans and protective regulations into a comprehensive management system institutionalizing the cooperation between all concerned management stakeholders. Indicated as a necessity, the Conservation and Management Plan is supported by Guidelines on Control of Commercial Activities on Kulangsu, which have been adopted in 2014. These guide scale and quality assurance measures for commercial services on the island, in particular those in the tourism sector.

Following the 2017 Capacity Calculation Report of Kulangsu Scenic Zone, the optimum number of people on the island is set at 25 000 while the absolute maximum lies at 50 000 people per day. Since this number includes the residents and commuters to the island, the effective maximum number of visitors is now controlled at 35 000 visitors, including on peak days.

---

① 厦门市下属的行政区划是区级,该段落的两个county均译为"区",英语中的district似乎更为确切。

4.8.2 武夷山

武夷山是中国东南部生物多样性保护最为突出的地区,也是大量古代残存的物种的避难所,其中许多是中国特有物种。九曲溪令人印象深刻的峡谷的宁静之美,以及众多的寺庙和道观(尽管许多现在已成为废墟),为理学思想的发展和传播提供了环境。自11世纪以来,理学思想一直在东亚文化中具有影响力。公元前1世纪,汉朝统治者在城村附近修建了一座大型行政首府。它巨大的城墙环绕着一个具有重要意义的考古遗址。

◆ 突出的普遍价值

简要介绍

武夷山位于中国东南部的福建省,是中国亚热带森林和华南雨林多样性的最大、最具代表性的保护得最好的森林。对于生物多样性保护来说,这片土地具有极其重要的意义,它是许多古老的、残存的植物物种的避难所,其中许多是中国特有的,并拥有极为丰富的动植物群,包括大量的爬行动物、两栖动物和昆虫。

九曲溪拥有令人印象深刻的峡谷的宁静之美,光滑的悬崖与清澈的深不可测的水面交相辉映,其美景名闻遐迩。沿着这条河流,有许多寺庙和道观,其中许多现在已成为废墟,这为理学的发展和传播提供了环境。理学是一种自11世纪以来在东亚文化中非常具有影响力的政治哲学。值得一提的是,从北宋到清朝(公元10至19世纪),兴办了多达35所的古代儒家书院。此外,该地区还拥有可以追溯到商朝(公元前2世纪)的墓葬、铭文、放置木船棺的岩石掩体以及60多座道观和寺院的遗迹。

4.8.2 Mount Wuyi[①]

Mount Wuyi is the most outstanding area for biodiversity conservation in south-east China and a refuge for a large number of ancient, relict species, many of them endemic to China. The serene beauty of the dramatic gorges of the Nine Bend River, with its numerous temples and monasteries, many now in ruins, provided the setting for the development and spread of Neo-Confucianism, which has been influential in the cultures of East Asia since the 11th century. In the 1st century B. C. , a large administrative capital was built at nearby Chengcun by the Han dynasty rulers. Its massive walls enclose an archaeological site of great significance.

◆ Outstanding universal value

Brief synthesis

Mount Wuyi, located in China's south-east province of Fujian, contains the largest, most representative example of a largely intact forest encompassing the diversity of the Chinese Subtropical Forest and the South Chinese Rainforest. Of enormous importance for biodiversity conservation, the property acts as a refuge for an important number of ancient, relict plant species, many of them endemic to China, and contains an extremely rich flora and fauna, including significant numbers of reptile, amphibian and insect species.

The serene beauty of the dramatic gorges of the Nine-Bend River is of exceptional scenic quality in its juxtaposition of smooth rock cliffs with clear, deep water. Situated along this river are numerous temples and monasteries, many now in ruins, which provided the setting for the development and spread of Neo-Confucianism, a political philosophy which has been very influential in the cultures of East Asia since the 11th century. In particular there are no fewer than 35 ancient Confucian academies dating from the Northern Song to Qing Dynasties (10th to 19th centuries CE). In addition the area contains tombs, inscriptions and rock shelters with wooden boat coffins dating back to the Shang Dynasty (2nd century BCE), and the remains of more than 60 Taoist temples and monasteries.

In the 1st century BCE a large administrative capital was built at nearby Chengcun by the Han Dynasty rulers. Its massive walls enclose an archaeological site of great significance.

---

① 下载自联合国教科文组织网站,https://whc.unesco.org/en/list/911/,2022/7/5。中文文本为编写者所译。

公元前 1 世纪,汉朝统治者在城村附近修建了一座大型行政首府。它巨大的城墙环绕着一个具有重要意义的考古遗址。

该遗产由四个保护区组成:西部是武夷山国家级自然保护区,中部是九曲溪生态保护区,东部的武夷山风景名胜区是毗邻的,而汉代古城遗址保护区是一个单独的区域,距离东南约 15 公里。总面积 107 044 公顷,周围是 40 170 公顷的缓冲区。该遗产由于其文化价值、绚丽的风景和生物多样性价值而被列入世界文化和自然遗产名录。

标准(Ⅲ):武夷山是一个被保护了十多个世纪的美丽景观。它拥有一系列特殊的考古遗址,包括公元前 1 世纪建立的汉城,以及与公元 11 世纪理学诞生相关的一些寺庙和研究中心。

标准(Ⅵ):武夷山是理学的摇篮,理学在东亚和东南亚国家占据主导地位长达几个世纪,并影响了世界大部分地区的哲学和政府。

标准(Ⅶ):九曲溪(下游的峡谷)周围东部风景区的壮观地貌具有非凡的景观质量,以孤立的、单面的本地红色砂砾岩巨石群而著称。它们沿着河流 10 公里曲折河段向前绵延,位于河床上方 200~400 米处,终止于清澈的深水中。古老的悬崖痕迹是该遗址的一个重要侧面,让游客可以"鸟瞰"河流。

标准(Ⅹ):武夷山是世界上最杰出的亚热带森林之一。这是国内规模最大、最具代表性、保护得最好的森林,其中国亚热带森林和华南雨林的多样性,植物多样性高。它是许多古老的、残存的植物物种的避难所,其中许多是中国特有的,在中国其他地方也很罕见。它还具有杰出的动物多样性,尤其是爬行动物、两栖动物和昆虫。

The property consists of four protected areas: Mount Wuyi National Nature Reserve in the west, Nine-Bend Stream Ecological Protection Area in the centre and Mount Wuyi National Scenic Area in the east are contiguous, and the Protection Area for the Remains of Ancient Han Dynasty is a separate area, about 15 km to the south-east. Totalling 107 044 ha, the property is surrounded by a buffer zone of 40 170 ha and has been inscribed for cultural as well as scenic and biodiversity values.

Criterion (Ⅲ): Mount Wuyi is a landscape of great beauty that has been protected for more than twelve centuries. It contains a series of exceptional archaeological sites, including the Han City established in the 1st century BCE and a number of temples and study centres associated with the birth of Neo-Confucianism in the 11th century CE.

Criterion (Ⅵ): Mount Wuyi was the cradle of Neo-Confucianism, a doctrine that played a dominant role in the countries of Eastern and South-eastern Asia for many centuries and influenced philosophy and government over much of the world.

Criterion (Ⅶ): The spectacular landforms in the eastern scenic area around Nine-Bend Stream (lower gorge) are of exceptional scenic quality, with isolated, sheer-sided monoliths of the local red sandstone. They dominate the skyline for a tortuous 10 km section of the river, standing 200—400 m above the riverbed, and terminate in clear, deep water. The ancient cliff tracks are an important dimension of the site, allowing the visitor to get a 'bird's-eye-view' of the river.

Criterion (Ⅹ): Mount Wuyi is one of the most outstanding subtropical forests in the world. It is the largest, most representative example of a largely intact forest nationwide, encompassing the diversity of the Chinese Subtropical Forest and the South Chinese Rainforest, with high plant diversity. It acts as a refuge for a large number of ancient, relict plant species, many of them endemic to China and rare elsewhere in the country. It also has an outstanding faunal diversity, especially with respect to its reptile, amphibian and insect species.

完整性

武夷山具有高度的生态和景观完整性，以及保护区管理的悠久历史。自 1979 年以来，该地区一直处于严格的保护状态，在此之前，省级和中央政府对该地区发布了许多保护法令，可以追溯至 1 000 多年以前。它是一个拥有广阔范围的遗产，所有描述其价值的必要元素都包含在列入世界文化和自然遗产的区域的边界之内，并具有有效的缓冲区。该遗产位于福建省省级行政区内。1999 年该遗产被列入世界文化和自然遗产名录时，武夷山国家级自然保护区内几乎没有居民居住；武夷山的 22 700 名居民（2012年为 24 500 人）分散在主要位于九曲溪生态保护区和武夷山国家风景区的14 个村庄。居民茶叶生产活动增加导致的水土流失具有一定的影响，是管理的挑战。

真实性

九曲溪河沿岸东部地区的文化景观保存了相当程度的真实性，这在很大程度上是由于 8 世纪以来一千多年的捕鱼和林业作业禁令的严格执行。然而，由于使用和重建的大量变化，该地区完整的文化遗产在很大程度上失去了其设计、材料和功能的真实性。相比之下，考古遗址——城村古镇遗址、船棺以及被拆毁或倒塌的寺庙、书院和道观的遗迹——具有完全的真实性。

保护和管理要求

武夷山世界文化和自然遗产地完全由中华人民共和国政府拥有。根据《森林法》（1998 年）、《文物保护法》（2002 年）、《野生动物保护法》（2004年）和《风景名胜区条例》（2006 年），它被列为国家级自然保护区、国家级风景名胜区、森林公园和国家级文物

Integrity

Mount Wuyi has a high level of ecological and landscape integrity, as well as a long history of management as a protected area. It has had strict protective status since 1979, prior to which provincial and central governments had issued protective edicts over the area for more than 1 000 years. It is a large property with all elements necessary to express its values included within the boundaries of the inscribed area, and has an effective buffer zone. The property lies within one provincial administration of Fujian, and in 1999 when the property was inscribed, few inhabitants lived within the Mount Wuyi National Nature Reserve; the 22 700 inhabitants (24 500 in 2012) in Mount Wuyi being scattered through 14 villages primarily in Nine-Bend Stream Ecological Protection Area and Mount Wuyi National Scenic Area. The water and soil loss caused by the increased tea production activities of inhabitants has certain impact and is a challenge for management.

Authenticity

The cultural landscape in the eastern zone, along the Nine-Bend River, has conserved a remarkable degree of authenticity, largely owing to the strict application over more than a millennium of the 8th century ban on fishing and forestry operations. However, the intact cultural properties in this region have to a considerable extent lost their authenticity in design, materials, and function as a result of numerous changes of use and reconstructions. By contrast, the archaeological sites—the Chengcun ancient town site, the boat coffins, and the remains of demolished or collapsed temples, academies, and monasteries—possess full authenticity.

Protection and management requirements

The Mount Wuyi World Heritage property is wholly owned by the government of the People's Republic of China. It is listed as a state-level nature reserve, a state-level scenic area, a forest park and a state-level cultural relics protection unit, thus assuring the safeguarding of both the cultural and natural values of the property, under a number of national laws including: *the Forestry Law* (1998), *the Environmental Protection Law* (2002), *Regulations on Nature Reserves* (2002), *Cultural Relics Protection Law* (2002), *the Law on the Protection of Wildlife* (2004), and *Scenic Areas Ordinance* (2006). Regulations relating specifically to Mount Wuyi were promulgated by the National Government in 1982, 1988, 1990, 1995, and 1996. The property was designated as a

保护单位,从而确保了遗产的文化价值和自然价值的保护。1982 年、1988 年、1990 年、1995 年和 1996 年,国家政府颁布了专门针对武夷山的法规。该遗产地于 1987 年被指定为联合国教科文组织人与生物圈计划(MAB)的生物圈保护区,使其获得了附加的国际和国家保护地位。

在省级层面,福建省发布了《福建省武夷山世界文化和自然遗产保护条例》和其他有关保护武夷山世界遗产的特别地方法规。已为该遗产的四个保护区编制了总体规划或保护计划,并为该遗产设立了包括现场监测中心在内的特别行政组织。监测中心定期监测遗产的文化和自然资源状况、遗产的整体生态环境以及旅游压力对其造成的潜在损害。该中心还负责对亚热带森林生态系统、生物多样性保护和附近社区的可持续发展进行研究。这一持续监测和研究计划为政策审查提供了信息,以加强对遗产完整性和真实性的保护。

未来的管理优先事项包括:减少生活污水和固体废物对九曲溪水质的影响;利用地理信息系统(GIS)技术改进森林火灾管理,改进消防设施并培训专业人员;减少岩石铭文的风化;以及采取措施实现茶产业可持续发展。

UNESCO (MAB) Biosphere Reserve in 1987, giving it additional international and national protection status.

At the provincial level, Fujian Province has issued the Regulations of Fujian Province on the Protection of Mount Wuyi World Cultural and Natural Heritage and other special local regulations relating to the protection of Mount Wuyi as a World Heritage property. A master plan or a protection plan has been compiled for each of the four protected areas of the property. Special administrative organizations, including an on-site Monitoring Center, have been set up for the property. The Monitoring Center conducts periodic monitoring on the condition of the property's cultural and natural resources, the overall ecological environment of the property, and the potential damage to the property resulting from the pressures of tourism. The Center is also responsible for conducting research on the subtropical forest ecosystem, biodiversity protection, and sustainable development of the nearby community. This ongoing monitoring and research programme informs policy review to enhance the safeguarding of the property's integrity and authenticity.

Future management priorities include: reduction of the impacts from domestic sewage and solid waste on the water quality of the Nine-Bend River; improved forest fire management taking advantage of GIS technology, improving fire control facilities and training professional staff; reduction of the weathering of rock inscriptions; and measures to achieve sustainable development of the tea industry.

Exercises

Ⅰ. Fill in the blanks with proper forms of words.

1. The tea growers in Anxi absorbed the principle of the full _____ (ferment) of black tea and the _____ (non-ferment) of green tea, and invented a _____ (semi-ferment) tea-making process.

2. Because tea merchants are driven by market economic interests, challenges are brought about by mechanical production technique and the transmission of skills are neglected by old artisans, the traditional rock tea production techniques show signs of

_____ (endanger), and urgently need to be protected.

3. _____ (Pestle) tea represents a special tea culture _____ (produce) by Hakkas in order to survive and avoid the attack of southern plague.

4. Fujian tulou _____ (hide) among high mountains are solid, closed, tall and _____ (symmetry). They not only _____ (objective) enjoy the practical functions of self-defense, protection against enemies, suitability for living, _____ (glorify) ancestors and revitalizing old business, but also contain abundant _____ (human) information and profound cultural connotations.

Ⅱ. Translate the following Chinese sentences into English.

1. 武夷山为红茶、乌龙茶的发源地,与武夷岩茶制作技艺相伴而生的茶俗有浓郁的地方特色,喊山、斗茶赛、茶艺等风俗,拥有广泛的群众基础。

2. 安溪茶农吸取红茶全发酵和绿茶不发酵的原理,发明了半发酵的制茶工艺。安溪铁观音是我国六大茶类之一乌龙茶。

3. 擂茶是客家人为了求生存、避免南方瘴病侵袭而产生的一种驱瘟疫防病毒的特殊饮茶文化。

4. 文化意象的两个构成要素是物象和寓意。物象是信息的载体,体现了人们对某一物体的感知;寓意则是物象在特定文化语境中的引申意义或文化含义,是文化意象的映现。

Ⅲ. Translate the following English sentences into Chinese.

1. Mount Wuyi is one of the most outstanding subtropical forests in the world. It is the largest, most representative example of a largely intact forest encompassing the diversity of the Chinese Subtropical Forest and the South Chinese Rainforest, with high plant diversity.

2. Mount Wuyi was the cradle of Neo-Confucianism, a doctrine that played a dominant role in the countries of Eastern and South-eastern Asia for many centuries and influenced philosophy and government over much of the world.

3. Kulangsu Island exhibits in its architectural features and styles the interchange of Chinese, Southeast Asian and European architectural and cultural values and traditions produced in this variety by foreign residents or returned overseas Chinese who settled on the island. The settlement created did not only mirror the various influences settlers brought with them from their places of origin or previous residence but it synthesized a new hybrid style—the so-called Amoy Deco Style, which developed in Kulangsu and exerted influences over a far wider region in Southeast Asian coastal areas and beyond.

4. The integrity of the historic landscape has been maintained, primarily as a result of consistent conservation of historic architectural structures and effective development controls regarding height, volume and form of new buildings.

Ⅳ. **Questions and answers.**

1. What is intangible cultural heritage?

2. What is the cultural connotation of Fujian tulou?

项目❷　酒店业务与接待
Project ❷　Hotel Business and Reception

第❺单元　酒店业务（1）
Unit ❺　Hotel Business (1)

📖 **教学目标**

⇨掌握旅游团办理入住手续的基本程序
⇨掌握酒店类型分类相关知识
⇨掌握酒店等级分类相关知识
⇨掌握酒店客房类型相关知识
⇨了解酒店管理模式
⇨了解 2022 年世界酒店排名

📖 **Teaching objective**

⇨To master the basic procedures for check-in of a tourist group
⇨To master related knowledge of the classification of hotel types
⇨To master related knowledge of the level classification of hotels
⇨To master related knowledge of the types of hotel rooms
⇨To know about hotel management models
⇨To know about 2022 world hotel rankings

5.1　情景对话

🈂 **在前台办理团体登记**

A. 当地导游
B. 前台接待员

B：晚上好，欢迎光临我们的酒店。今天我能为你做些什么？

A：我是福州环球旅行社的王先生。我们的旅行社为 0807 英国学术交流团预订了今明两天的 13 间双人间和 2 间大床房。

B：请稍等。我查一下登记表。谢谢你的等待。你的团队预订了 13 间双人间和 2 间大床房，共住两晚。你能给我你们的团体名单和团体签证吗？

A：给你。我想确保所有的房间都是无烟房，因为我们团队没有人吸烟。

B：让我查一下。是的，都是无烟

5.1　Situational dialogue

🈂 **Group check-in at front desk**

A. local tour guide
B. receptionist at front desk

B：Good evening, welcome to our hotel. How can I help you today?

A：I am Mr. Wang from Global Travel Agency in Fuzhou. Our travel agency has reserved 13 double rooms and 2 king-sized rooms for British Academic Exchange Group 0807 for today and tomorrow.

B：Just a second, please. I will check the registration list. Thank you for your waiting. Your group has a reservation of 13 double rooms and 2 king-sized rooms for two nights. Could I have the name list of your group and group visa?

A：Here you are. I would like to make sure all the rooms are non-smoking rooms since nobody in my group smokes.

B：Let me check. Yes, they are all non-smoking rooms.

房。你能为旅游团填写一下登记表吗？

　　A：好的，你能把所有的登记表都给我吗？以便我可以将表格分发给旅游团成员填写。

　　B：当然。团队明天上午何时预订叫醒时间？

　　A：6：30。我们团队的行李什么时候可以送到我们的房间？

　　B：它将在大约30分钟后送到你们的房间。这是你们的钥匙卡和团队早餐券。

　　A：西餐厅在哪里？

　　B：在第二层，7点开门。如果有任何问题或要求，请告诉我。

　　A：谢谢。

　　B：不客气。

5.2　角色扮演训练

　　请根据相应任务创造对话。

　　任务 1：假如你是一家酒店的前台服务人员，有一个澳大利亚旅游团的客人由于房间朝向不好，想调整到一个朝向更好、可以看到部分市容市貌的房间，你需要如何处理？

　　任务 2：如果你是酒店的前台工作人员，有外国散客前往办理住宿事宜，你需要注意那些事项？

　　以下是一些可供使用的句子，必要时需要做些调整。

　　1.晚上好，前台。今天我能为你做些什么？

　　2.请稍等。让我检查一下是否有这样的房间。

　　3.有一个朝南的房间，阳光充足，可以看到城市的部分景色。你可以看到一个美丽的公园，有一个湖和大面积的绿树。但房间在另一层，10楼。你想换个房间吗？

　　4.我明白了。可以告诉我你的名字和房间号码吗？

Could you fill in the registration form for the group?

　　A：OK，could you give me all those registration forms to me so that I can distribute them among the group members and get them finished？

　　B：Sure．Here you are．What time would you like to make for morning call tomorrow？

　　A：6：30，please．When will the luggage for our group be delivered to our room？

　　B：It will be delivered to your room in about 30 minutes．Here are the card keys and breakfast coupons for your group．

　　A：Where is the Western-style restaurant located？

　　B：It is located on the second floor and it opens at 7：00．If you have got any problems or requests，please let me know．

　　A：Thank you．

　　B：You are welcome．

5.2　Role play training

　　Please create dialogues based on the corresponding tasks.

　　Task 1：If you are a front desk staff member of a hotel and a guest of an Australian tour group wants to change to a room with a better orientation and a partial view of the city due to the poor orientation of his/her room．What do you need to do？

　　Task 2：If you are a a front desk staff member of a hotel and there are foreign individual travellers who are going to check in，what matters should you pay attention to？

　　【译】

　　The following are some useful sentences that need to be adjusted if necessary.

　　1. Good evening，front desk．How can I help you today？

　　2. Just a second，please．Let me check whether there is availability of such kind of room．

　　3. A room facing south enjoys more sunlight and a partial view of the city．You can see a beautiful park with a lake and large area of green trees．However，the room is on another floor，the 10th floor．Would you like to change your room？

　　4. I see．May I have your name and room number，please？

5. 大约20分钟后,我会派一名行李员送上新房间的钥匙卡。请您到前台填写一张换房表好吗?

6. 十一层有空房间。你需要什么样的房间?

7. 可以提供双人房,但无法提供大床房。可以吗?

8. 你想怎么付款?信用卡和旅行支票都可以。

9. 请把您的信用卡让我授权一下,可以吗?

10. 这是你的钥匙卡和早餐券。行李员会带你去你的房间。

5.3 酒店业务知识聚焦

5.3.1 酒店类型分类

酒店根据规模、位置、目标市场、服务水平、提供的设施、房间数量、所有权和隶属关系等进行分类。

5.3.1.1 规模或房间数量

- 低于200间客房—非常小
- 最多200间客房—小
- 200至399间客房—中等
- 400至700间客房—大型
- 700多间客房—超大

5.3.1.2 目标市场

酒店的目标市场很多,酒店可以根据目标市场进行分类。常见的市场类型包括商务、机场、套房、住宅、度假村、分时度假、赌场、会议酒店。

商务酒店:这些酒店是最大的酒店类型,主要面向商务旅客,通常位于市中心或商业区。虽然商务酒店主要为商务旅客服务,但许多旅行团、个人游客和小型会议团都认为这些酒店很有吸引力。商务酒店可能提供免费报纸、免费咖啡、免费本地电话、免费早餐等。

5. After about 20 minutes, I will send a bellboy with the key card of the new room. Would you please come to the front desk for filling out a Room Changing Form?

6. There are rooms available on the 11th floor. What kind of room do you need?

7. Double rooms are available, but not king-sized rooms. Is it OK for you?

8. How would you like to pay? Both credit cards and traveller's check are acceptable.

9. May I take an imprint of your credit card, please?

10. This is your key card and breakfast coupon. The bellboy will show you to your room.

5.3 Focus on hotel business knowledge

5.3.1 Classification of hotels by their type

Hotels are classified according to the hotel size, location, target markets, levels of service, facilities provided, number of rooms, ownership and affiliation, etc.

5.3.1.1 Size or number of rooms

- Below 200 rooms—Very Small
- Up to 200 rooms—Small
- 200 to 399 rooms—Medium
- 400 to 700 rooms—Large
- More than 700 rooms—Mega

5.3.1.2 Target markets

The hotel targets many markets and hotel can be classified according to target market. The common type of markets includes business, airport, suites, residential, resort, timeshare, casino and convention hotels.

Business hotels: The most hotels belong to this type. They primarily cater to business travelers and are usually located in downtown or business districts. Although business hotels primarily serve business travelers, many tour groups, individual tourists and small conference groups find these hotels attractive. Business hotels may provide complimentary newspapers, coffee, local telephone calls and breakfast, etc.

套房酒店:这类酒店是酒店业的最新趋势和增长最快的细分市场。这类酒店房型为一间客厅和一间独立的卧室。会计师、律师、商人和高管等专业人士认为套房酒店特别有吸引力,这是由于他们可以在卧室旁边的区域工作和娱乐。

长住酒店:长住酒店与套房酒店有些相似,但通常在房间内提供厨房设施。这类酒店是为那些想住一周以上,又不想在酒店设施上花钱的长期入住者而设的。

精品酒店:精品酒店(boutique hotel)一词是在开发商伊恩·施拉德(Ian Schrager)和他的合作伙伴史蒂夫·鲁贝尔(Steve Rubell)将一个小楼摩根斯(Morgans)改建成一个高档酒店时得来的。[①] 精品酒店仅指那种具有一个鲜明的与众不同的文化理念的酒店。精品酒店出现于 80 年代初期,以它那包含崭新概念的设计和独特的氛围而变得炙手可热。绝大多数精品酒店都集中在美国和欧洲等发达国家和地区。

住宅式酒店:住宅式酒店为客人提供长期或永久住宿。通常,客人与酒店签订租约,租期为一个月至一年。住宅式酒店房间通常包括客厅、卧室、厨房、私人阳台、洗衣机、厨房用具等。与普通酒店不同,住宅式酒店只提供每周一次的家政服务。

度假酒店:度假酒店通常位于山区、岛屿上或远离城市的一些其他具有异国情调的地方。这些酒店有风景,娱乐设施,供住宅进行高尔夫、网球、帆船、滑雪和游泳等运动的场所。度假村酒店提供令人愉快和难忘的客人体验,鼓励客人再次前往。

Suite hotels: This kind of hotel is the latest trend and the fastest-growing segment of the hotel industry. Such hotels provide a living room and a separate bedroom for the hotel guest. Professionals such as accountants, lawyers, businessmen and executives find suite hotels particularly attractive as they can work and also entertain in an area beside the bedroom.

Extended stay hotels: Extended stay hotels are somewhat similar to suite hotels, but usually offer kitchen amenities in the room. This kind of hotel is for long-stayers who want to stay more than a week and do not want to spend much on hotel facilities.

Boutique hotels: The name "boutique hotel" was derived from developer Ian Schrager and his partner Steve Rubell when they transformed a small building, Morgans, into a high-end hotel. Boutique hotels only refer to the ones with a distinctive cultural concept. The boutique hotel emerged in the early 1980s. With its new-concept design and unique atmosphere, it has become hot. The vast majority of boutique hotels are concentrated in developed countries and regions such as the United States and Europe.

Residential hotels: Residential hotels provide long-term or permanent accommodation for guests. Usually the guest makes a lease with the hotel for a minimum of one month up to a year. The room of residential hotels generally includes a living room, bedroom, kitchen, private balcony, washing machines, kitchen utensils, etc. Unlike normal hotels, residential hotels only provide weekly housekeeping service.

Resort hotels: Resort hotels are usually located in the mountains, on an island, or in some other exotic locations away from cities. These hotels provide scenery, recreational facilities, and sports facilities where guests can play golf, tennis, sailing, skiing and swimming. Resort hotels provide enjoyable and memorable guest experiences that encourage guests to return to the resort.

---

① Jordan Hollander, What Is a Boutique Hotel? A Clear Definition with Examples, https://hoteltechreport. com/news/boutique-hotel, 2022/7/5.

民宿:这些房子的房间被改造成住宿设施,可容纳1至14间客房,一些国家是不超过5间。民宿的老板通常留在酒店内,负责为客人提供早餐。

分时度假酒店:酒店业的另一个新类型或细分领域是分时度假酒店。分时度假酒店是指客人在特定时期内购买住宿权。业主可能租用管理公司的酒店物业。

会议酒店:这类酒店专注于与会者的住宿。它们还提供视频会议设施、视听设备、商务服务、灵活的座位安排、挂图等。这些酒店大多位于大都市区之外,拥有高尔夫球场、游泳池、网球场、健身中心、水疗中心等设施。

汽车旅馆:近年来,随着私家车车主的增加,汽车旅馆的生意也有所增长。汽车旅馆是主要供驾车者入住的酒店,位于主要高速公路附近,交通便利。

5.3.2 酒店的等级

酒店等级是指一家酒店的豪华程度、设施设备水平、服务范围、服务质量等方面所反映出的级别与水准。不少国家和地区,通常根据酒店的位置、环境、设施、服务等情况,按照一定的标准和要求对酒店进行分级,并用某种标志表示出来,在酒店显著的地方公之于众。

中国、日本、希腊、印度、埃及、土耳其、阿联酋、意大利、罗马尼亚、加拿大等是由政府主管饭店业的职能部门,如国家旅游主管部门来进行饭店等级评定的国家。瑞士、奥地利、荷兰、比利时、卢森堡等是由饭店协会或旅游业协会来进行饭店等级评定的国家。在欧洲酒店业协会(HOTREC)的支持下,奥地利、捷克、德国、匈牙利、荷兰、瑞典和瑞士的饭店协会创建了"饭店星级联盟"。2009年9月14

Homestays: These are houses with rooms converted into overnight facilities, which can accommodate 1 to 14 guest rooms (no more than 5 guest rooms in some countries). The owners of the homestays usually stay on the premises and are responsible for serving breakfast to the guest.

Timeshare hotels: Another new type or segment of the hospitality industry is the timeshare hotel. Timeshare hotels are where the guests purchase accommodations for a specific period. These owners may also have the unit rented out by the management company that operates the hotel.

Convention hotels: The type of hotel focuses on overnight accommodation for meeting attendees. They also provide a video conferencing facility, audiovisual equipment, business services, flexible seating arrangements, flipcharts, etc. These hotels are mostly located outside the metropolitan areas and have facilities like golf courts, swimming pools, tennis courts, fitness centers, spas, etc.

Motels: Motels have enjoyed an increase in their business in recent years as the increase in private car owners has materialised. A motel is a hotel mainly for motorists and located near a major motorway with convenient transportation.

5.3.2 Hotel grade

The hotel grade refers to the level and standard reflected by a hotel's luxury level, facilities and equipment level, service scope, service quality, etc. In many countries and regions, hotels are usually classified according to certain standards and requirements according to the location, environment, facilities, services, etc. of the hotel, and are marked with certain signs, which are made public in prominent places of the hotel.

China, Japan, Greece, India, Egypt, Türkiye, the United Arab Emirates, Italy, Romania, Canada, etc. are the countries where the government departments in charge of the hotel industry, such as the national tourism department, perform hotel rating. Switzerland, Austria, the Netherlands, Belgium, Luxembourg and other countries are rated by hotel associations or tourism associations. With the support of HOTREC, hotel associations in Austria, the Czech Republic, Germany, Hungary, the Netherlands, Sweden and Switzerland established the "Hotel Star Alliance". On September 14, 2009, the alliance released the hotel classification standards

日,该联盟发布了以德国标准为蓝本的饭店分级标准,自 2010 年 1 月开始在大部分欧洲国家实施①。另一种评估模式是由第三方组织负责评估。第三方组织广义上是指除去政府、饭店行业协会之外的各种组织,包括旅行批发商、旅行杂志、旅行网站、学术机构等。目前各国和地区采用的等级制度各不相同,用以表示级别的标志与名称也不一致。目前世界上有 80 多种酒店等级制,归纳起来大致有以下几种。②

(1)星级表示法。即依据一定的标准评定酒店的等级,然后用星表示出来。星越多等级越高。星级表示法在世界上被普遍采用,如中国和法国酒店分为 1~5 星级。

(2)钻石数量表达法。美国没有专门的酒店评级机构,评极标准由不同的社会组织颁布,其中有影响的主要有美国汽车协会颁布的"钻石评级体系"和福布斯旅游指南(Forbes Travel Guide)体系颁布的"星级标准"。"钻石评级体系"由一颗钻石到五颗钻石构成,代表不同的等级。

(3)字母表示法。有些国家和地区将酒店的等级用字母 A、B、C、D、E 来表示,A 为最高级,E 为最低级,如希腊、奥地利等国。

(4)数字表示法。有些国家和地区将酒店的等级用数字 1、2、3、4、5 来表示,1 为最高级,5 为最低级,如意大利、阿尔及利亚等国。

此外还有其他的一些等级分类方法。例如,瑞士的酒店以价格分为 1~6 级。日本酒店等级分类至今未采用世界通行的星级制,只分为高级酒店或一般酒店。

based on German standards, and the standards of the alliance have been implemented in most European countries since January 2010. Another evaluation mode is that the third-party organization is responsible for the evaluation. In a broad sense, third-party organizations refer to various organizations except the government and hotel industry associations, including travel wholesalers, travel magazines, travel websites, academic institutions, etc. At present, different countries and regions adopt different hierarchies, and the signs and names used to indicate the levels are also different. There are currently over 80 hotel rating systems in the world, which can be summarized as follows.

(1) Star rating system. That is to say, the hotel is rated according to certain standards, and then indicated by the star. The more stars, the higher the level. The star rating system is widely used in the world. For example, Chinese and French hotels are classified into 1—5 stars.

(2)Diamond rating system. There is no specialized hotel rating agency in the United States. The standards are issued by different social organizations. The influential ones are mainly the "diamond rating system" issued by the American Automobile Association and the "star standard" issued by the Forbes Travel Guide system. The "diamond rating system" consists of the ratings of one diamond to five diamonds, representing different grades.

(3) Alphabetic rating system. Some countries and regions use the letters A, B, C, D, E to indicate the hotel grade, such as Greece, Austria and other countries. A is the highest level and E is the lowest level.

(4) Numeric rating system. Some countries and regions use the numbers 1, 2, 3, 4 and 5 to indicate the hotel level, such as Italy, Algeria and other countries. 1 is the highest level and 5 is the lowest level.

In addition, there are some other hierarchical classification methods. For example, hotels in Switzerland are categorized into 1-6 levels by price. Up to now, Japanese hotels have not adopted the world's popular star rating system, but are only classified into high-end hotels or general hotels.

①　What Do Hotel Stars Mean in Europe? https://www.hotrec.eu/industry-projects/hotel-stars/,2022/7/5.

②　李伟清 主编,《酒店经营管理实务》,北京:中国旅游出版社,2021:12-13.

5.3.3 酒店管理模式

酒店行业发展至今，无论是本土酒店集团还是进入国内的国外酒店集团，其经营模式主要有这几种：

5.3.3.1 自主管理模式

这种模式是国内外酒店集团常用的管理模式，成立酒店管理公司，拥有自己的酒店品牌，由自己的酒管公司负责全权运营管理。大部分房地产企业下的酒店集团通常也会考虑以自主管理的方式管理自有品牌，比如万达、世茂。

酒店集团投资或收购一家全资酒店，然后自主经营，这也是早期酒店集团扩张的主要模式。美国贝斯特维斯特国际集团（Best Western International）就是这种模式的典型代表。

自主管理的优势在于酒管公司拥有酒店管理运营的决策权，与其他投资方的合作相对稳定，比较容易达成初期的运营目标；但劣势在于自主管理需要雄厚的资金支持，对于国际酒店集团来说，其发展会受到一定的制约。因此，国际酒店集团中选择自主管理模式的较少，国内房地产企业因为自身拥有大量的资金，多数会选择自主管理模式。

5.3.3.2 委托管理模式

这种模式是国内外酒店集团主流管理模式，通过酒店投资人与管理集团签署管理合同来约定双方的权利、义务和责任，以确保管理集团能以自己的管理风格、服务规范、质量标准和运营方式来向被管理的酒店输出专业技术、管理人才和管理模式，并向被管理酒店收取一定比例的品牌管理费、会员订单费等。酒店管理集团在提供

5.3.3 Hotel management mode

Since the development of the hotel industry, whether local hotel groups or foreign hotel groups entering China, their business models mainly include the following:

5.3.3.1 Independent management mode

This mode is commonly used by hotel groups at home and abroad. A hotel management company is established to manage the group's own hotel brand, and it is responsible for full operation and management. Hotel groups under most real estate enterprises usually choose to manage their own brands in an autonomous way such as Wanda and Shimao.

The hotel group invests or acquires a wholly-owned hotel and then operates independently. This is also the main expansion mode of hotel groups in the early period. Best Western International is a typical representative of this model.

The advantage of independent management is that the hotel management company has the decision-making power of hotel management and operation. The cooperation with other investors is relatively stable, and it is easier to achieve the initial operation goals. However, the disadvantage is that independent management needs strong financial support. For international hotel groups, their development is subject to certain constraints. Therefore, few international hotel groups choose the independent management mode. Most domestic real estate enterprises will choose the mode because of their large amounts of funds.

5.3.3.2 Entrusted management mode

This mode is the mainstream management mode of domestic and foreign hotel groups. The rights, obligations and responsibilities of both parties are agreed through the management contract signed by the hotel investor and the management group to ensure that the management group can introduce professional technology, management talents and the management mode to the managed hotels with its own management style, service specifications, quality standards and operation mode, and charge the managed hotels a certain proportion of brand management fee, member's reservation

委托经营服务时,既可以提供一揽子服务,也可以提供单项服务。

委托管理的优势在于管理团队拥有较丰富和较强的酒店管理经验和能力,能对下属酒店进行紧密的控制与管理,同时减少投资风险,利润较高。劣势在于业主方所需承担的人力成本较高。近年来,国内的酒店业主已经逐渐意识到了国际酒店管理品牌的高成本和外派人员与本土员工在文化等方面的差异,而业主方与酒店管理公司发生纠纷事件也层出不穷。所以,不少业主方采取短期委托管理模式以确保酒店走上经营轨道,例如锦江、华住。

▶ 5.3.3.3　特许经营模式

酒店特许经营主要有三种模式:纯粹的特许经营模式、与第三方管理公司合作的特许经营模式、中国市场特有的特许经营模式。中国市场特有的特许经营模式通过委派酒店集团管理公司培育出来的酒店总经理加入酒店业主团队协助管理。这一模式有助于酒店品牌保持原有的品质,也避免了特许经营模式在中国水土不服的问题。[①]

这种模式在国外比较流行。其是以特许经营权的转让为核心的一种经营方式,管理集团自己的专有技术、品牌与酒店业主的资本相结合来扩张经营规模。这种模式中,管理集团通过受许酒店认购特许经营权的方式将自己所拥有的具有知识产权性质的品牌名称、注册商标、经营方式、操作程序、预订系统及采购网络等无形资产的使用权转让给受许酒店,并一次性收取特许经营权转让费或初始费,以及每月根据

fee, etc. The hotel management group can provide both package services and single services when offerting entrusted operation services.

The advantage of entrusted management is that the management team has extensive experience and strong ability in hotel management, and can closely control and manage subordinate hotels, reduce investment risks and has higher profits. The disadvantage lies in the high labor cost that the owner has to bear. In recent years, domestic hotel owners have gradually realized the high cost of international hotel management brands and the cultural differences between expatriates and local employees, and disputes between the owner and hotel management companies have also emerged endlessly. Therefore, many owners adopt a short-term entrusted management mode to ensure that the hotel is on the business track, for example, Jinjiang, Huazhu.

▶ 5.3.3.3　Franchising mode

There are mainly three modes of hotel franchising: the pure franchising mode, franchising mode in cooperation with a third-party management company, and franchising mode unique to the Chinese market. The franchising mode unique to the Chinese market is to appoint the general manager of the hotel cultivated by the hotel group management company to join the hotel owner team to assist in management. This model helps to maintain the original quality of the hotel brand and also avoids the problem that the franchising model is not suitable in China.

This model is relatively popular abroad. It is a business development model that focuses on the transfer of the franchise and combines the management group's own proprietary technology as well as brand and the hotel owner's capital to expand the business scale. The mode is operated on the basis of the application right transfer of intangible assets such as brand names, registered trademarks, business methods, operating procedures, reservation systems and procurement networks owned by the management group with intellectual property rights to the licensed hotels by means of subscription for franchise rights and the collection of one-time franchise transfer fees or initial fees, as well as the management of

---

① 刘伟,《酒店管理》,北京:中国人民大学出版社,2022:17.

营业收入而浮动的特许经营服务费(包括公关广告费、员工培训费、顾问咨询费等)。

特许经营的优势在于可以有效降低扩张成本,减少直接投入和资金风险。加盟酒店有助于提高品牌影响力与市场占有率,通过特许经营权的转让,集团能够获得长期的经济收益,提高经济收入。缺点在于对成员酒店缺乏直接经营管理权,服务质量可能失去控制,引起顾客的不满,同时存在一定的潜在投资与负债风险。温德姆就是一个例子。

▶ 5.3.3.4 租赁经营

租赁经营是指酒店集团向酒店所有者租赁酒店,对酒店进行管理。长期租赁在国际酒店业中往往被视为全资拥有形式的变体。跨国酒店公司通常运用这种方式在东道国的最佳地点选择酒店,例如万豪和希尔顿的一些酒店就是以长期租赁方式进行运营的。[①] 这类租赁在大多数情况下要求做出长期的财务承诺。因此只有在仔细考虑选址、市场的长期盈利能力以及东道国保持稳定的能力的基础上才能做出选择。

租赁经营可以分为固定租赁经营模式和变动租赁经营模式。固定租赁经营模式是多数精品单体酒店或部分连锁品牌旗下直营项目常用的模式,是指租赁方与业主签订的租赁合同。优势与劣势与自营管理类似。变动租赁经营模式国外比较流行,指租赁方与业主签订根据各种情况确定租赁费变动范围的合同,租赁后管理。好处是公平且可以应对各种变化,解决当前经常出现的业主与管理公司的矛盾。国内常

franchise service fees (including public relations advertising fees, online booking fees, employee training fees, consulting fees, etc.) that fluctuate according to the operating income every month.

Operating under franchise enjoys the advantage of effectively lowering expansion cost, reducing direct investment and capital risk. Franchised hotels help to improve brand influence and market share. Through the transfer of franchise rights, the group can obtain long-term economic benefits and improve economic income. The disadvantage lies in the lack of direct operation and management right for member hotels, which may lead to the loss of control over service quality, customer dissatisfaction, and certain potential investment and liability risks. Wyndham is an example.

▶ 5.3.3.4 Lease management

Lease management refers to the hotel group's leasing hotels from hotel owners to manage hotels. Long-term leasing in the international hotel industry is often seen as a variation of the form of wholly-owned ownership. Multinational hotel companies usually employ this method to select best-located hotels in the host country. For example, some hotels of Marriott and Hilton are operated by long-term lease. In most cases, such leases require long-term financial commitment. Therefore, the choice can only be made on the basis of careful consideration of the location, long-term profitability of the market and the ability of the host country to maintain stability.

Lease operation can be divided into the fixed lease operation mode and variable lease operation mode. The fixed lease operation mode is used in most single boutique hotels or directly-operated projects under some chain brands, which refers to the the lease contract signed between the leaser and the owner. Advantages and disadvantages are similar to those of independent management. The operating mode of the variable lease is popular abroad, which means that the leaser signs a contract with the owner to determine the range of the lease fee according to various circumstances, and manages after the lease. The advantage is that it is fair and can deal with various changes, and solve the current frequent conflicts between the owner and the management company. Common

---

① 刘伟,《酒店管理》,北京:中国人民大学出版社,2022:19.

见的酒店集团中，通常会采取混合 2～3 种经营模式的管理方式，如自主管理＋委托管理；国际酒店集团中，一般会选择自主管理＋特许经营的模式进行扩张。

domestic hotel groups usually adopt a mixed management mode of 2—3 business models，like the mode of independent management ＋ entrusted management. International hotel groups generally choose the mode of independent management ＋franchise for expansion.

5.3.4　酒店客房类型

单人间：是放置一张单人床的客房，一般数量较少、面积较小。

双人间：双人间又称标准间，在房内放两张单人床，可住两位宾客，也可供一人居住。这类客房在酒店占绝大多数。单人床的常用尺寸为 2 000 mm× 1 200 mm。

大床房：是指在房内配备一张双人床的房间，适合夫妻旅游居住，也适合单身宾客居住，新婚夫妇使用时称之为"蜜月客房"。双人床的尺寸通常为 1 800 mm× 2 000 mm 或 2 000 mm×2 000 mm。

标准套间：又称普通套间，一般为连通的两个房间。一间为起居室，即会客室，起居室也可设盥洗室，可不设浴缸，一般供拜访的宾客使用；另一间为卧室，卧室中放一张大床或两张单人床，配有卫生间。

商务套房：又叫商务标准间，内部设施非常齐全，高级酒店才提供商务套房。除了卧室、卫生间，还包括客厅。部分酒店商务套房等同于行政套房。即有独立的咖啡厅、快速办理登记的前台，部分房间有传真机。

行政套房：一般指行政楼层的套房。个别酒店设置有行政楼层，专为商务客人设置，并配有专用的商务中心、咖啡厅。有独立的前台，即可快速办理入住和退房的地方。

总统套房：接待外国元首或者高级商务代表之类贵宾的客房。总统套

5.3.4　Hotel room types

Single room：A guest room with a single bed and usually in a small quantity and area.

Twin room：A twin room, also known as a standard room, has two single beds in the room, which can accommodate two guests or one person. This type of room accounts for the vast majority in hotels. The common size of a single bed is 2 000 mm×1 200 mm.

Double room：It refers to a room equipped with a double bed, suitable for couples to live in, as well as single guests. When used by newlyweds, it is called a "honeymoon room". The size of a double bed is usually 1 800 mm×2 000 mm or 2 000 mm×2 000 mm.

Standard suite：It is also known as a regular suite, usually consisting of two connected rooms. One is the living room, also known as the reception room. The living room can also have a bathroom without a bathtub, and is generally used by visiting guests; the other room is a bedroom, with one double bed or two single beds and a bathroom.

Business suite：It is also known as a business standard room, with very complete internal facilities and only high-end hotels offer business suites. In addition to the bedroom and bathroom，it also includes the living room. Some hotel's business suites are equivalent to executive suites. There is an independent coffee shop, a front desk for quick registration, and some rooms have fax machines.

Executive suite：It generally refers to the suite on the administrative floor. Some hotels have executive floors specifically designed for business guests and are equipped with dedicated business centers and coffee shops. There is an independent front desk for quick check-in and check-out.

Presidential suite：It is a guest room for guests such as foreign heads of state or senior business representatives.

房并非五星级酒店所专有,有的不大的豪华酒店,尤其是近些年发展起来的精品酒店,根据自身需要也可以设置总统套房。

Presidential suites are not exclusive to five-star hotels, and even some small luxury hotels, especially boutique hotels that have developed in recent years, can also set up presidential suites according to their own needs.

5.4　知识拓展

"品牌金融"[①]评选出"2022 年 50 强酒店"

希尔顿酒店的品牌价值大幅提升,名列前茅,而大多数酒店品牌仍低于疫情前的价值。

- 希尔顿品牌价值增长 58%,达到 120 亿美元
- 排名前 50 的酒店品牌中约有三分之二仍低于疫情前的价值
- 泰姬酒店是世界上最强大的 AAA 级酒店品牌
- 丽思卡尔顿酒店是全球增长最快的酒店品牌,今年的价值翻了一番多

➡ 希尔顿酒店品牌价值增长 58%,达到 120 亿美元

根据主要品牌评估咨询公司"品牌金融"的一份新报告,希尔顿(品牌价值增长 58%,达到 120 亿美元)已成为世界上最有价值的酒店品牌,其品牌价值现已超过第二和第三的总和:凯悦酒店(品牌价值增长 26%,达到 59 亿美元)和假日酒店(品牌价值增长 10%,达到 42 亿美元)。

每年"品牌金融"对 5 000 个最大的品牌进行评估,并发布大约 100 份报告,对所有行业和国家的品牌进行排名。该公司评选出的"2022 年 50 强酒店"排行榜中包括了全球价值最高、实力最强的 50 大酒店品牌。

当我们展望后疫情的世界时,可发现希尔顿酒店的品牌价值增长是由预测收入的增长和预期盈利的提高所驱动的。与此同时,该公司的研究发现,顾客对希尔顿的认知有所提高,大品牌在安全问题上的可靠性和可信度是一个关键因素。这促使其品牌实力指数从 80.8 上升至 88.0,提高了 7.2 个百分点,其品牌评级从 AAA-提升至 AAA。

"品牌金融"财务技术总监 Alex Haigh 表示,新冠肺炎疫情导致全球旅行中断,对品牌价值造成了重大破坏,然而客户认识到酒店也饱受新冠肺炎疫情的冲击。因此,我们看到成功的品牌能够迅速反弹,并在后疫情的世界中重新赢得客户的信任。

➡ 排名前 50 的酒店品牌中约有三分之二仍低于疫情前的价值

过去两年,为了应对新冠肺炎疫情的蔓延,全球出台了旅行限制措施,这给酒店品牌增加了巨大而明显的成本,许多品牌尚未恢复元气:在 2022 年酒店排名中的 50 个品牌中,约三分之二(即 34 个品牌)的品牌仍低于 2020 年疫情之前的估值,仅三分之一(即 16 个品牌)比大流行前估值高。

诺翰酒店的品牌价值大幅提升(品牌价值增长 47%,达到 10 亿美元)。该品牌总体上遭到了新冠肺炎疫情的严重破坏,更具体地说,是奥密克戎变异毒株。该酒店在 2021 上半年的入住率介于 20%至 30%之间,10 月份增长至 62%,而奥密克戎变异毒株是 2022 年 1 月该酒

---

① "品牌金融"是全球领先的独立品牌商业估值和战略咨询公司,在 20 多个国家开展业务。

店入住率跌至 26% 的重要原因。然而,随着该酒店的所有物业重新开业,入住率最近又恢复了 60% 以上。这些数据有助于该酒店的品牌价值在收入预测增加的情况下比疫情前的估值高出 33%。

在其他地方,洲际豪华酒店的品牌价值(品牌价值下降 1%,跌至 15 亿美元)略有下降,人们对洲际酒店的主要中国市场重新开放服务的可能延误感到忧心忡忡。尽管经历了酒店业有史以来最艰难的时期,洲际酒店仍然致力于实现其品牌承诺,即"使宾客宾至如归"。这一品牌承诺致力于使客户和员工受益,并为当地社区带来积极的影响。他们的战略包括更加专注于品牌,并为未来品牌价值提供显著增长的潜力。

雅高集团,包括品牌宜必思(品牌价值增长 24%,增加至 4.63 亿美元)和铂尔曼(品牌价值增加 20%,增加至 3.49 亿美元),今年表现强劲,品牌价值大幅增长。这两个品牌的平均房价恢复到新冠肺炎疫情之前的水平,一些酒店甚至超过了新冠肺炎疫情前的房价。虽然新冠肺炎疫情限制措施仍有一些挥之不去的后果,然而他们的酒店品牌在疫情期间保持了显著的品牌价值和品牌实力。消费者认为新冠肺炎疫情冲击了这两个品牌的业务。

➲ 泰姬酒店跃升为世界上最强大的 AAA 级酒店品牌

除品牌价值外,"品牌金融"还通过衡量营销投资、利益相关者权益和业务绩效的指标平衡计分卡来确定品牌的相对实力。根据 ISO 20671,该公司对利益相关者权益的评估纳入了来自 35 多个国家和近 30 个行业的 100 000 多名受访者的原始市场研究数据。泰姬酒店(品牌价值上升 6%,达到 3.14 亿美元)是排名中最强的品牌,品牌强度指数(BSI)得分为 88.9(满分 100),获得相应的 AAA 品牌评级。

与世界各地的其他酒店一样,新冠肺炎疫情和随后的全国封锁冲击了泰姬酒店的业绩。泰姬酒店成功地调整了策略,以便满足游客的相关需求。泰姬酒店凭借其灵活性和战略举措(如向医疗保健部门提供支持)走在了这一领域的前列。

➲ 丽思卡尔顿酒店是全球增长最快的酒店品牌,今年的价值翻了一番多

丽思卡尔顿酒店(品牌价值增长 112%,增加至 11 亿美元)是今年全球增长最快的酒店品牌,其品牌价值比疫情前的 6.32 亿美元高出 74%。这一品牌价值的增长是基于其每间可用客房的可观收入以及数量庞大的客房。作为万豪集团的一部分,丽思卡尔顿酒店已经建立了一个非常强大的品牌,其品牌实力指数从 79.6 上升到 83.2,其品牌评级现已稳居 AAA 级。

其他快速增长的品牌包括贝蒙特酒店(Baymont,品牌价值增长 97%,达到 3.82 亿美元)。该品牌因从新冠肺炎疫情中迅速恢复而重新进入这些排名。品牌价值的反弹与对其主要市场的强劲交易条件预测以及客户认知的改善有关。同样,旅居酒店(Residence Inn,品牌价值增长 92%,达到 7.6 亿美元)是增长第三快的酒店品牌。该品牌在客户认知方面取得了显著改善。与其他品牌相比,该品牌的客房数量和每间客房的收入都很可观。

表 5-1　2022 年 50 强酒店榜单

2022 年排名	2022 年品牌价值/年度价值变化	国家
1.希尔顿酒店	120.4 亿美元/+58.2%	美国
2.凯悦酒店	59.05 亿美元/+25.8%	美国

2022 年排名	2022 年品牌价值/年度价值变化	国家
3.假日酒店	41.55 亿美元/+10%	美国
4.欢朋酒店	39.28 亿美元/+37.2%	美国
5.万豪酒店	23.13 亿美元/-3.9%	美国
6.逸林酒店	21.11 亿美元/+61.9%	美国
7.香格里拉酒店	19.11 亿美元/-3.8%	中国
8.洲际酒店	14.5 亿美元/-0.8%	英国
9.尊盛酒店	14.37 亿美元/+64.4%	美国
10.皇冠假日酒店	12.71 亿美元/+4.6%	英国
11.凯富酒店		美国
12.普瑞米尔酒店		英国
13.丽思卡尔顿酒店		美国
14.温德姆酒店		美国
15.诺翰酒店		西班牙
16.万怡酒店		美国
17.美居酒店		法国
18.喜来登酒店		美国
19.皇冠酒店		澳大利亚
20.欣庭酒店		美国
21.威斯汀酒店		美国
22.斯堪的克酒店		瑞典
23.旅居酒店		美国
24.品质酒店		美国
25.华美达酒店		美国
26.拉昆塔酒店		美国
27.长住酒店		美国
28.锦江酒店		中国
29.惠庭酒店		美国
30.豪华精选酒店		美国
31.戴斯酒店		美国
32.宜必思酒店		法国
33.汉庭酒店		中国
34.斯泰布里奇套房酒店		英国
35.诺富特酒店		法国
36.JW 万豪酒店		美国
37.速 8 酒店		美国
38.万丽酒店		美国

2022 年排名	2022 年品牌价值/年度价值变化	国家
39. 万枫酒店		美国
40. 全季酒店		中国
41. 贝蒙特酒店		美国
42. 千禧酒店		新加坡
43. 铂尔曼酒店		法国
44. 巴塞罗集团		西班牙
45. 福朋酒店		美国
46. W 酒店		美国
47. 康莱德酒店		美国
48. 泰姬酒店		印度
49. 华尔道夫酒店		美国
50. 肯特伍德酒店		英国

（来源：https：//brandirectory. com/rankings/hotels/table)

5. 4　Knowledge expansion

BRAND FINANCE：HOTELS 50 2022

HILTON BRAND VALUE LEAPS AHEAD TO RETAIN TOP POSITION，WHILE MOST HOTEL BRANDS REMAIN BELOW PRE-PANDEMIC VALUES[①]

• Hilton brand value is up 58％ to US＄12. 0 billion

• Two-thirds of top 50 hotel brands remain below pre-pandemic values

• Taj Hotels is world's strongest hotels brand with AAA rating

• The Ritz-Carlton is world's fastest growing hotel brand，more than doubling in value this year

▶ Hilton brand value is up 58％ to US＄12. 0 billion

Hilton (brand value up 58％ to US＄12. 0 billion) has extended its reign as the world's most valuable hotels brand，according to a new report from the leading brand valuation consultancy，Brand Finance. Hilton has grown its lead as the most valuable hotels brand in the world，with a brand value which is now greater than 2nd and 3rd combined：Hyatt (brand value up 26％ to US＄5. 9 billion) and Holiday Inn (brand value up 10％ to US＄4. 2 billion).

Every year，Brand Finance puts 5 000 of the biggest brands to the test，and publishes around 100 reports，ranking brands across all sectors and countries. The world's top 50 most valuable and strongest hotel brands are included in the annual Brand Finance Hotels 50 2022 ranking.

As we look to a post-pandemic world，Hilton's brand value increase is driven by both an increase in forecast revenue and increased profitability expectations. At the same time，Brand

---

① 　下载自"品牌金融"网站，https：//brandirectory. com/rankings/hotels/，2023/5/14。中文版本为编写者所译。

Finance research discovered that customers improved their perception of Hilton, with the large brand's perceived reliability and credibility on safety issues being a key factor. This contributed to a 7.2 point increase on its Brand Strength Index from 80.8 to 88.0, improving its Brand Rating from AAA— to AAA.

According to Alex Haigh, Brand Finance Technical Director, the global disruption to travel due to the COVID-19 pandemic caused significant disruption to brand values—but customers recognise that hotels are not to blame for the disruption. As a result, we see that successful brands have been able to bounce back quickly and re-earn customer trust in the post-pandemic world.

▶️ Two-thirds of top 50 hotel brands remain below pre-pandemic values

Global travel restrictions over the last two years introduced in response to the spread of COVID-19 imposed significant and obvious costs on hotel brands, with many yet to recover: Of the 50 brands included in the Hotels 50 2022 ranking, two-thirds of the brands (34) remain below their pre-pandemic valuation of 2020, with just one-third (16) above their pre-pandemic valuation.

One brand to increase brand value sharply was NH Hotels (brand value up 47% to US$1.0 billion) which endured significant disruption from COVID-19 generally, and the Omicron variant more specifically. NH Hotels endured an occupancy rate of between 20% and 30% throughout the first half of 2021, growing throughout the year to 62% in October—before the Omicron variant played a key role in the occupancy rate falling back down to 26% in January 2022. However, with all NH Hotels properties now re-opened, occupancy rates have returned back over 60% more recently. These data are contributing to the NH Hotels brand value achieving a rate 33% higher than their pre-pandemic valuation on the back of increased revenue forecasts.

Elsewhere, the brand value of luxury hotel Intercontinental (brand value down 1% to US$1.5 billion) fell marginally, with significant concerns about potential delays to the reopening of services in Intercontinental's key Chinese market. Despite enduring some of the toughest periods ever endured by the hospitality industry, Intercontinental remains focused on delivering its brand promise of delivering "True Hospitality for Good". This brand promise seeks to benefit customers and staff, and to also bring positive difference to their local communities. Their strategy includes placing a sharper focus on their brand, and offers the potential of significant future brand value growth.

The Accor group, including brands Ibis (brand value up 24% to US$463 million) and Pullman (brand value up 20% to US$349 million) is having a strong year, with their brand values growing significantly this year. Average room rates across the Pullman and Ibis brands returned to their pre-COVID-19 levels, and some properties even exceeded pre-COVID-19 rates. While there are some lingering consequences of COVID-19 restrictions, their hotel brands maintained significant brand value and brand strength through the pandemic, a recognition that consumers did not blame hotels for the virus.

▶️ Taj Hotels is world's strongest hotels brand with AAA rating

In addition to brand value, Brand Finance determines the relative strength of brands through a balanced scorecard of metrics evaluating marketing investment, stakeholder equity, and business performance. Compliant with ISO 20671, Brand Finance's assessment of stakeholder equity incorporates original market research data from over 100 000 respondents in more than 35 countries and across nearly 30 sectors. Taj Hotels (brand value up 6% to US $ 314 million) is the strongest brand in the ranking with a Brand Strength Index (BSI) score of 88. 9 out of 100 and a corresponding AAA brand rating.

The pandemic and subsequent national lockdowns hit Taj like other hotels across the world, and Taj was able to successfully adjust strategies to remain relevant to the need of tourists. Taj was at the forefront of this with agility and strategic initiatives such as offering support to the healthcare sector.

▶ The Ritz-Carlton is world's fastest growing hotel brand, more than doubling in value this year

The Ritz-Carlton (brand value up 112% to US $ 1. 1 billion) is the world's fastest growing hotel brand this year, with its brand value now 74% above its pre-pandemic value of US $ 632 million. This brand value has increased based on its impressively high revenue per available room and large number of rooms. Part of the Marriott Group, the Ritz-Carlton has built an extremely strong brand, with its Brand Strength Index increasing from 79. 6 to 83. 2, with its brand rating now firmly in the AAA— band.

Other quickly growing brands include Baymont (brand value up 97% to US $ 382 million) which has re-entered these rankings as it bounces back quickly from COVID. This bounce back in brand value is associated with strong trading conditions forecast for its key markets, and improved customer perception. Similarly, Residence Inn (brand value up 92% to US $ 760 million) is the third fastest growing hotel brand, which has achieved a significant improvement in customer perception, which is leveraging a very large number of rooms and revenue per room relative to other brands.

Table 5-1　HOTELS 50 2022

2022 Rank	**2022 Brand Value/Annual Value Change**	**Country**
1. Hilton	US $ 12. 04 billion/+58. 2%	USA
2. Hyatt	US $ 5. 905 billion/+25. 8%	USA
3. Holiday Inn	US $ 4. 155 billion/+10%	USA
4. Hampton Inn	US $ 3. 928 billion/+37. 2%	USA
5. Marriott	US $ 2. 313 billion/−3. 9%	USA
6. Double Tree	US $ 2. 111 billion/+61. 9%	USA
7. Shangri-La	US $ 1. 911 billion/−3. 8%	China
8. Intercontinental	US $ 1. 45 billion/−0. 8%	UK
9. Embassy Suites	US $ 1. 437 billion/+64. 4%	USA
10. Crowne Plaza	UK $ 1. 271 billion/+4. 6%	UK
11. Comfort		USA
12. Premier Inn		USA
13. The Ritz-Carlton		USA
14. Wyndham		USA
15. NH Hotels		Spain

续表

2022 Rank	2022 Brand Value/Annual Value Change	Country
16. Courtyard		USA
17. Mercure		France
18. Sheraton		USA
19. Crown		Australia
20. Homewood Suites		USA
21. Westin		USA
22. Scandic Hotels		Sweden
23. Residence Inn		USA
24. Quality		USA
25. Ramada		USA
26. La Quinta		USA
27. Extended Stay		USA
28. Jinjiang		China
29. Home2 Suites		USA
30. Luxury Collection		USA
31. Days Inn		USA
32. Ibis		France
33. Hanting Hotel		China
34. Staybridge Suites		UK
35. Novotel		France
36. JW Marriott		USA
37. Super 8		USA
38. Renaissance Hotels		USA
39. Fairfield Inn		USA
40. JI Hotel		China
41. Baymont		USA
42. Millennium Hotels		Singapore
43. Pullman		France
44. Grupo Barcelo		Spain
45. Four Points		USA
46. W		USA
47. Conrad		USA
48. Taj		India
49. Waldorf Astoria		USA
50. Candlewood Suites		UK

(source：https://brandirectory.com/rankings/hotels/table)①

---

① 由于属于非付费用户，排名 11 以后的酒店无法显示"2022 年品牌价值/年度价值变化"（2022 Brand Value/Annual Value Change）的具体数值。

❄ Exercises

Ⅰ. Fill in the blanks with proper forms of words.

1. Although business hotels _____ (primary) serve business travelers, many tour groups, individual tourists and small conference groups find these hotels _____ (attract). Business hotels may provide _____ (compliment) newspapers, coffee, local telephone calls and breakfast, etc.

2. Convention hotels focus on overnight accommodation for meeting _____ (attend). They also provide a video _____ (conference) facility, audiovisual equipment, business services, flexible seating arrangements, flipcharts, etc. These hotels are mostly _____ (locate) outside the metropolitan areas and have facilities like golf courts, swimming pools, tennis courts, fitness centers, spas, etc.

3. The independent management mode is _____ (common) used by hotel groups at home and abroad. A hotel management company _____ (establish) to manage the group's own hotel brand, and is responsible for full operation and management. The hotel group invests or acquires a _____ (wholly-own) hotel and then operates _____ (independent). Hotel groups under most real estate enterprises usually choose _____ (manage) their own brands in an autonomous way such as Wanda and Shimao.

4. The entrusted management mode is the mainstream management mode of domestic and foreign hotel groups. The rights, obligations and responsibilities of both parties _____ (agree) through the management contract _____ (sign) by the hotel investor and the management group _____ (ensure) that the management group can introduce professional technology, management talents and the management mode to the _____ (manage) hotels with its own management style, service specifications, quality standards and operation mode, and charge the managed hotels a certain proportion of brand management fee, member's reservation fee, etc.

5. A twin room, also _____ (know) as a standard room, has two single beds in the room, which can accommodate two guests or one person. A double room refers to a room _____ (equip) with a double bed, suitable for couples _____ (live) in, as well as single guests. When _____ (use) by newlyweds, it is called a "honeymoon room".

Ⅱ. Translate the following Chinese sentences into English.

1. 套房酒店是酒店业的最新趋势和增长最快的细分市场。这类酒店房型为一间客厅和一间独立的卧室。

2. 住宅式酒店为客人提供长期或永久住宿。通常,客人与酒店签订租约,租期至少为一个月至一年。住宅式酒店房间通常包括客厅、卧室、厨房、私人阳台、洗衣机、厨房用具等。与普通酒店不同,住宅式酒店只提供每周一次的家政服务。

3. 酒店业的另一个新类型或细分领域是分时度假酒店。分时度假酒店是指客人在特定时期内购买住宿权。业主可能租用管理公司的酒店物业。

4. 行政套房一般指行政楼层的套房。个别酒店设置有行政楼层,专为商务客人设置,并配有专用的商务中心、咖啡厅。有独立的前台,即可快速办理入住和退房的地方。

Ⅲ. Translate the following English sentences into Chinese.

1. Every year, Brand Finance puts 5 000 of the biggest brands to the test, and publishes around 100 reports, ranking brands across all sectors and countries. The world's top 50 most valuable and strongest hotel brands are included in the annual Brand Finance Hotels 50 2022 ranking.

2. The name "Shangri-La" evokes the image of a remote and beautiful landscape where harmony with nature approaches perfection. We aspire to live up to this name by designing environmental sustainability into our new development projects and asset enhancement initiatives. We also strive to promote environmental stewardship in the daily operations of our hotels.

3. HUALUXE Hotels and Resorts is a hotel brand of InterContinental Hotels Group. HUALUXE Hotels and Resorts is an international premium hotel brand created with the customs of Chinese consumers in mind. At HUALUXE，we provide guests with an immersive Chinese culture experience and bring Chinese aesthetic and cultural heritage into daily life. HUALUXE exhibits the art of Chinese hospitality that revolves around "eat" and "meet".

4. It's nowadays widely known and accepted that the next step of hospitality leans towards personalization. To achieve，whatsoever，a high level of personalized services，constant yet premium communication with the guests must be preserved. Thankfully，technology has made it easier for hoteliers to communicate with their guests，as there are nowadays numerous ways to directly contact them，from social media to location-based notifications.

Ⅳ. **Questions and answers.**

1. What is the franchising mode of hotel management?

2. How much do you know about the lease management mode of hotel management besides other hotel management modes?

3. What is the difference between the double room and twin room?

第❻单元　酒店业务(2)
Unit ❻　Hotel Business(2)

📖 **教学目标**
⇨掌握会议预订的基本程序
⇨掌握客房服务和餐饮服务的表述
⇨掌握酒店各部门的划分方式
⇨了解世界主要酒店集团与品牌
⇨了解2021年世界酒店排名

📖 **Teaching objectives**
⇨To master the basic procedures for conference reservation
⇨To master expressions of room service and catering service
⇨To master the division method of hotel departments
⇨To know about major hotel groups and brands in the world
⇨To know about 2022 World Hotel Rankings

6.1　情景对话

🔠 会议预订

> A. 海上丝绸之路(福州)国际旅游节外国参与者
> B. 酒店销售代表

　　A：早上好，我们一行15人将参加海上丝绸之路(福州)国际旅游节。你们酒店可以提供什么样的房间和会议设备？

　　B：早上好，福州环球酒店销售部。我们的酒店是五星级酒店，拥有400多间客房，配有内部宽带网络，可提供标准客房、商务客房、中西风格的豪华套房、复式套房、总统套房。此外，有9间多功能宴会会议厅，提供多样的场地布置。完善的会议宴会设施，配备现代化的视听设备，无论是商务会议、高端会谈，还是中西式宴会、时尚婚礼或酒会派对、家庭聚会等，均可满足全系列服务要求。您需要什么样的房间和会议设备？

　　A：我想预订11月23日至28日14间商务客房和1间中式豪华套房，预订11月25日1间会议厅和宴会厅。会议厅提供什么样的设施？

6.1　Situational dialogue

🔠 Reservation for a conference

> A. foreign participant of Maritime Silk Road (Fuzhou) International Tourism Festival
> B. sales representative of hotel

　　A：Good morning, our group of 15 persons is going to participate in Maritime Silk Road (Fuzhou) International Tourism Festival. What kind of rooms and conference services are available in your hotel?

　　B：Good morning, sales department of Global Hotel. Our hotel is a five-star hotel of over 400 guest rooms with the internal broadband network, ranging from standard rooms and business rooms to luxury suites of Chinese and Western styles, duplex suites, presidential suites. In addition, there are 9 multi-functional banquet and conference halls, providing a variety of venue arrangements. Perfect conference and banquet facilities, equipped with modern audio-visual equipment, can meet the full range of service requirements, whether it is business meetings, high-end meetings, Chinese and Western style banquets, fashionable weddings or cocktail parties, family gatherings, etc. What kind of rooms and conference services do you need?

　　A：I would like to reserve 14 business rooms and 1 luxury suite of Chinese style from November 23 to 28, one conference room and banquet room on November 25. What kind of facilities are provided in the conference room?

B：我们在会议厅提供讲台、高射投影仪、幻灯机和无线麦克风。我会把我们的实际报价传真给你，需要您发传真确认。

　　A：谢谢。

　　B：不客气。

6.2　角色扮演训练

任务 1：假如你在客房服务中心实训，客人要求提供酒店用品、洗衣服务、修理服务等，需要熟悉相关表述。

一些可供参考的句子和表述如下。

1. 如果你忘了带房卡，你可以出示身份证，楼层服务员会开门。

2. 这是你要的《中国日报》。我能为你做点别的吗？

3. 我会立即派人去收取你洗的衣服。

4. 请把脏衣服放置在洗衣袋里。

5. 在收取洗衣单时，要注意房间号、客人的姓名以及客人的特殊要求。

6. 收取衣服时，请客人在洗衣单上注明衣服是需要熨烫、洗涤还是干洗，以及他/她想什么时候取回。

7. 洗衣店不对留在口袋里的东西负责。

8. 通常洗衣服需要两天左右。但我们提供当天可以取回衣服的快速服务。

9. 对于当天的服务，我们在上午 11 点之前收取衣服，并在当天晚上 9 点之前将其送到客人的房间；或者在下午 3 点前收取衣服，第二天中午前送到客人房间。

10. 对于快速洗衣服务，我们在下午 2 点前收取衣服，并在 4 小时内送达，额外收取 50% 的费用。

11. 如需快速洗衣服务，请勾选

6.2　Role playing training

Task 1：If you are being trained at the room service center and the guest requests hotel supplies，laundry services，repair services，etc.，you need to be familiar with the relevant expressions.

Some sentences and expressions can serve as your reference.

1. If you forget your room card with you，you can show your ID card and the floor attendant will unlock the door.

2. This is *China Daily* you asked for. Can I do anything else for you?

3. I'll send someone to collect your laundry immediately.

4. Please put your dirty clothes in your laundry bag.

5. When collecting the laundry list，pay attention to the room nunber，the name of the guest，and the special demands of the guest as well.

6. When collecting the laundry，ask the guest to make a note in the laundry whether the clothes need ironing，washing or dry-cleaning and what time he/she wants to get them back.

7. The laundry is not responsible for the things left in pocket.

8. Usually it takes about two days to have laundry done. But we also have express service for the same day.

9. For the same day service，we collect the clothes by 11：00 am and deliver them to the guests' room by 9：00 pm on the same day；or we collect the clothes before 3：00 pm and deliver them to the guests' room by noon the next day.

10. For express service，we collect the clothes by 2：00 pm and deliver them within four hours at a 50% extra charge.

11. For express service，please check off "Same Day Service".

"当日服务"。

12. 我们对快速洗衣服务加收 50％的费用。只需要 4 个小时。

13. 我现在就派人去修理。请问您的姓名和房间号是?

14. 很抱歉。我们现在派人来修,还是你想换房间?

15. 我会立即通知维修部门。他们会派人来检查的。请等几分钟。

16. 服务员在门口。任何问题请随时问她。谢谢你的来电,祝你今天愉快。

任务 2:假如你在餐饮部实训,如何接受客人点菜和处理付款等相关事宜? 一些可供参考的句子和表述如下。

1. 我们现在没有可容纳 15 人的桌子,但大约 15 分钟后就会有一张。你介意在休息室里等着喝一杯或是看报纸吗? 桌子准备好了,我会通知你的。

2. 如果您愿意等待,我们非常欢迎。

3. 很抱歉让你久等了。桌子现在准备好了。请这边走。

4. 我可以给你看一下午餐菜单吗? 请慢慢阅读。

5. 现在可以点菜了吗?

6. 你的开胃菜/主菜/甜点想要什么?

7. 你的牛排要多熟? 三成熟、五成熟,还是八成熟?

8. 这是菜单。我们既有自助餐,也有点菜。你更喜欢哪一个?

9. 我建议你尝尝洋葱牛排。这是我们餐厅的特色菜。我们有意大利酱、法国酱和千岛酱。

10. 我想向你推荐鸡汤汆海蚌,福州菜的代表菜之一。

11. 收银员会马上帮您准备好账单。您想怎么付款?

12. 您可以把它记在酒店账单上。请在账单上签上您的名字和房间号好吗? 您能出示一下您的房间钥匙吗?

12. We charge 50% more for express service. It only takes 4 hours.

13. The housemaid is at the door. Please feel free to ask her anything. Thank you for calling and have a nice day.

14. I will send someone to repair it now. Your name and room number, please?

15. Sorry for that. We'll send someone to fix it now or you want to change your room?

16. I will inform the maintenance department immediately. They'll send someone up to check it. Please wait a few minutes.

Task 2: If you are being trained in the catering department, how to take customer orders and deal with payment and other related matters? Some sentences and expressions can serve as your reference.

1. We don't have a table for 15 persons now, but one will be available after about 15 minutes. Do you mind waiting in the lounge and have a drink there or read newspapers? I will let you know when the table is ready.

2. If you would like to wait, we are more than welcome to do so.

3. Sorry to have kept you waiting. The table is ready now. This way, please.

4. May I show you lunch menu? Please take your time.

5. May I take your order now? / Are you ready to take your orders now?

6. What would you like to have for your appetizer / main dish / dessert?

7. How would you like your steak done, rare, medium or well-done?

8. Here is the menu. We have both buffet-style and a la carte dishes. Which would you prefer?

9. I recommend you to try Beef Steak with Onion. It is the specialty of our restaurant. We have Italian, French and Thousand Island dressing to go with it.

10. I would like to recommend to you Instant-boiled Sea Clam in Chicken Broth, one of the representative dishes of Fuzhou cuisine.

11. The cashier will have your bill ready in a second. How would you like to pay for it?

12. You can put it on your hotel bill. Would you sign your name and room number on your bill, please? And could you please show your room key?

6.3 酒店知识聚焦

6.3.1 酒店各部分的划分

酒店各部分的划分是根据酒店的组织原则和酒店的业务特点进行切块和分层。

6.3.1.1 酒店的上级机构

所谓的上级机构是指酒店的投资者，它对产权有最终决策权，并以所有者的身份监督并约束经营者的经营管理行为。上级机构在一些酒店可能不存在，如独资自行管理的酒店，但酒店有上级机构的体制在我国是大量存在的。

6.3.1.2 酒店内部各部门的划分

酒店有多种业务内容，根据业务内容的不同把酒店业务分成几个部。一般酒店的部门有前台部门和后台部门。前台部门是指处于一线为宾客提供面对面服务的部门，主要有销售部、公关部、前厅部、客房部、餐饮部、娱乐部、康乐部、商品部等。后台部门是指处于二线不直接和宾客接触，间接向宾客提供服务的部门，主要有人事部、财务部、工程部、保安部、采供部、办公室等。部门的划分也不是绝对的，它是根据组织原则，综合各种因素而确定的。

6.3.2 世界主要酒店集团

如果按酒店数量计算，世界上最大的连锁酒店最初都是些简陋的小酒店，他们有着远大的愿景，希望在酒店业中有所作为。通过持续以永恒的经典和现代元素为基础，他们将自己的遗产传承到现在。他们不断发展，关

6.3 Hotel knowledge focus

6.3.1 Division of various parts of the hotel

The division of each part of the hotel is based on the organizational principles of the hotel and the business characteristics of the hotel.

6.3.1.1 The superior organization of the hotel

The so-called superior organization refers to the investor of the hotel, which has the final decision-making power over the property rights, and supervises and restricts the operation and management behavior of the operator as the owner. The superior organization may not exist in some hotels, such as the hotels managed by the sole proprietorship, but the system with the superior organization exists in a large number of hotels in China.

6.3.1.2 Division of departments within the hotel

The hotel has a lot of business, and the hotel business is divided into several departments according to the different business scopes. General hotel departments include the front office department and back office department. The front office department refers to the department that provides face-to-face service for guests at the front line, mainly including the sales department, public relations department, front office department, guest room department, catering department, entertainment department, recreation department, commodity department, etc. The back office department refers to the department at the second line that does not directly contact the guests, but provides services to the guests indirectly, mainly including the human resource department, the finance department, the engineering department, the security department, the procurement and supply department, and the office. The division of departments is not absolute either. It is determined according to organizational principles and various factors.

6.3.2 Main hotel groups in the world

If calculated by the number of hotels, the largest chain hotels in the world were initially simple small hotels. They had a great vision and hoped to make a difference in the hotel industry. By continuing to base themselves on timeless classical and modern elements, they have inherited their heritage to the present. They continue to develop, care about the social problems around them, and proudly fulfill their commitment to provide

心周围的社会问题,自豪地兑现了在全球提供优质住宿的承诺。

6.3.2.1 万豪国际集团

万豪国际创建于 1927 年。万豪国际集团拥有 31 个著名酒店品牌,在全球 138 个国家经营的酒店超过 8 500 家。万豪(Marriott)酒店于 1957 年在美国华盛顿市开业,在公司的核心经营思想指导下,加之以早期成功经营的经验为基础,万豪酒店迅速成长,并取得了长足的发展。

20 世纪 80 年代,万豪根据市场的发展和特定需求,精心设计并创立了万怡(Courtyard)酒店。1983 年,第一家万怡酒店在美国正式开业。由于是广泛听取商务客人的意见,经过精心设计而推出的中等价位客房并保持高水准服务的酒店,万怡酒店一问世,即获成功。很快,它便成为其他同业中的佼佼者。

1984 年,以公司创办者的名字命名的 J. W. 万豪(J. W. Marriott)酒店在美国华盛顿市开业。J. W. 万豪酒店品牌是在万豪酒店标准的基础上升级的超豪华酒店品牌,向客人提供更为华贵舒适的设施和极有特色的高水准的服务。

此后,在 1987 年万豪公司收购了"旅居"连锁酒店(Residence Inn),其特点是:酒店房间全部为套房设施,主要为长住客人提供方便实用的套房及相应服务。同年,万豪又推出了经济型的万枫酒店(Fairfield Inn)和万豪套房酒店(Marriott Suites)两个新品牌酒店。

万豪国际集团在持续快速发展中,又于 1995 年收购了全球首屈一指的顶级豪华连锁酒店公司——丽思卡尔顿酒店(Ritz-Carlton)。这一举措使万豪成为首家拥有各类不同档次优质品牌的酒店集团。

high-quality accommodation around the world.

6.3.2.1 Marriott International Group

Founded in 1927, Marriott International Group has 31 famous hotel brands and operates over 8500 hotels in 138 countries worldwide. The first Marriott Hotel was opened in Washington, D. C. in 1957. Under the guidance of the company's core business philosophy and based on its early successful business experience, Marriott Hotel quickly grew and made considerable progress.

In the 1980s, Marriott meticulously designed and founded Courtyard Hotel according to market development and specific needs. In 1983, the first Courtyard Hotel officially opened in the United States. As Courtyard Hotel is a hotel that has listened to the opinions of business guests extensively, and has carefully designed and launched medium-priced rooms and maintained high standards of service, it was a success as soon as it was launched. Soon, it became a leader in hotel industry.

In 1984, the J. W. Marriott Hotel named after its founder opened in Washington, D. C. , USA. J. W. Marriott Hotel is a super luxury hotel brand upgraded on the basis of Marriott Hotel standards, providing guests with more luxurious and comfortable facilities and highly distinctive and high-quality services.

Since then, Marriott acquired the "Residence Inn" chain hotel in 1987, which is characterized by all suite facilities and mainly provided convenient and practical suites and corresponding services for long-term guests. In the same year, Marriott launched two new brand hotels, the economic Fairfield Inn and Marriott Suites.

In the process of continuous and rapid development, Marriott International Group acquired Ritz-Carlton, the world's leading luxury hotel chain, in 1995. This move makes Marriott the first hotel group to have various high-quality brands of different grades.

此后又在 1997 年，相继完成了对万丽连锁酒店公司(Renaissance)及其下属的新世界连锁酒店（New World），以及华美达国际连锁酒店（Ramada International)的收购。此举使万豪国际集团在全球的酒店数量实现了大幅增长，特别在亚太地区，一跃成为规模领先的酒店集团。2016 年，万豪国际收购喜达屋酒店及度假村集团（Starwood Hotels & Resorts Worldwide），开创了世界上最大的酒店集团。①

万豪国际旗下各品牌分类如下。

奢华：丽思卡尔顿（Ritz-Carlton）、豪华精选（The Luxury Collection）、瑞吉（St. Regis）、W 酒店、JW 万豪（JW Marriott）等，高级：万豪（Marriott）、喜来登（Sheraton）、威斯汀（Westin）、艾美（Le Méridien）、万丽（Renaissance）等，精选：万怡（Courtyard）、福朋喜来登（Four Points by Sheraton）、万枫（Fairfield）等，长住酒店：旅居酒店（Residence Inn）、万豪行政公寓（Marriott Executive Apartments）等。②

万豪国际集团于 1997 年进入中国酒店业市场，并于此后快速发展。万豪国际集团旗下的丽思卡尔顿酒店、JW 万豪酒店、万豪酒店、万丽酒店、万怡酒店、万豪行政公寓共 6 个酒店品牌均进入中国市场运营。

◐ 6.3.2.2　洲际酒店集团

洲际酒店集团是一个知名的全球化的酒店集团，在全球 100 多个国家和地区经营和特许经营超过 6 000 家酒店、18 个品牌，拥有超过 60 年国际酒店管理经验。③

1777 年，英国巴斯（Bass）集团成立，成为英国第一家独立注册商标的

Since 1997, it has successfully completed the acquisition of Renaissance and its subordinate New World Hotels, as well as Ramada International. This has enabled Marriott International Group to achieve a substantial increase in the number of hotels worldwide, especially in the Asia Pacific region, and become a leading hotel group. Heralding in a new era in 2016, Marriott International acquires Starwood Hotels & Resorts Worldwide, creating the world's largest hotel group.

The brands under Marriott International are categorized below.

Luxury: Ritz-Carlton, The Luxury Collection, St. Regis, W Hotel, JW Marriott, etc.; high-end: Marriott, Sheraton, Westin, Le Méridien, Renaissance, etc.; boutique: Courtyard, Four Points by Sheraton, Fairfield, etc.; extended stay: Residence Inn, Marriott Executive Apartments, etc.

Marriott International Group entered the Chinese hotel market in 1997 and has developed rapidly since then. A total of 6 hotel brands under Marriott International Group, including Ritz-Carlton, JW Marriott, Marriott, Renaissance, Marriott and Marriott Executive Apartments, have entered the Chinese market.

◐ 6.3.2.2　InterContinental Hotels Group

InterContinental Hotels Group is a famous global hotel group. It operates and franchises more than 6 000 hotels in more than 100 countries and regions around the world with 18 brands. It has more than 60 years of international hotel management experience.

In 1777, the British Bass Group was established, becoming the first independent trademark group in Britain. At

---

① Our Story of Innovation，https://www. marriott. com/about/culture-and-values/history. mi，2023/5/13.

② Explore Our Brands，https://www. marriott. com/marriott-brands. mi，2023/5/13.

③ IHG Hotel Development，https://development. ihg. com/about-us，2023/5/13.

集团。成立之初,巴斯集团主要以饮料和啤酒的生产和销售为主。至20世纪80年代末,转入酒店行业。

1988年购入国际假日酒店(Holiday Inn International),开始涉足酒店业。1990年巴斯收购了假日酒店业务在北美的剩余部分,并完全拥有这个世界著名的品牌,开始了扩张。同一年智选假日酒店(Holiday Inn Express)被并购。

1994年推出皇冠假日酒店与度假村(Crowne Plaza Hotels & Resorts),迎合高层次消费者。1997年推出斯泰布里奇套房酒店(Staybridge Suites),迎合高消费长住市场,发展迅速。1998年购入洲际酒店和度假村(InterContinental Hotels & Resorts),增加了另一个高端品牌。2000年巴斯收购澳大利亚南太平洋酒店集团(Southern Pacific Hotels Corporation)和美国酒店管理公司布里斯托尔酒店与度假村股份有限公司(Bristol Hotels & Resorts Inc.)。2001年买入欧洲波斯特豪斯连锁酒店(European Posthouse chain of hotels),在将其大部分酒店转换为假日酒店(Holiday Inn)后,巩固了假日酒店在英国和欧洲大陆的地位。

2003年,洲际酒店集团(IHG)成立,同一年增加了一个中级长住酒店品牌肯德伍德酒店(Candlewood)。2004年推出英迪格酒店(Indigo),提供实惠精品屋住宿。2007年推出假日酒店度假村(Holiday Inn Resort),作为家庭娱乐和度假的首选,并宣布斥资10亿美元更新假日酒店品牌家族,这是酒店业有史以来最大的投资。继斯泰布里奇套房酒店(Staybridge Suites)在北美取得成功后,2008年洲际酒店集团在英国利物浦和埃及开罗开设了创新性的酒店。假日酒店和智选假日酒店(Holiday Inn Express)是2012年伦敦奥运会和残奥会的官方酒店服务提供商。2018年,洲际酒店

the beginning of its establishment, Bass Group mainly focused on the production and sales of beverages and beer. By the end of 1980s, it had turned into the hotel industry.

In 1988, it bought Holiday Inn International and began to set foot in the hotel industry. In 1990, Bass bought the remaining North American part of the Holiday Inn business, so it owned the world-famous brand entirely and set its sights on expansion. Holiday Inn Express was acquired at the same year.

In 1994, Crowne Plaza Hotels & Resorts were launched to cater to high-level consumers. In 1997, it launched the Staybridge Suites, catering to the extended stay market based on high consumption, and developed rapidly. In 1998, it purchased InterContinental Hotels & Resorts, adding another high-end brand. In 2000, Bass acquired Southern Pacific Hotels Corporation in Australia and US-based hotel management company, Bristol Hotels & Resorts Inc. In 2001, it purchased European Posthouse chain of hotels. After most of the posthouse chain of hotels were converted into Holiday Inn, it consolidated the position of Holiday Inn in Britain and the European continent.

In 2003, InterContinental Hotels Group (IHG) was established and at the same year Candlewood, an intermediate extended stay hotel brand, was added. In 2004, Indigo Hotel was launched to provide affordable boutique housing. In 2007 Holiday Inn Resort was launched as a first choice for family fun and relaxation, and IHG announced a $1 billion refresh of the Holiday Inn brand family, the industry's biggest ever investment. Following the success of Staybridge Suites in North America, IHG opened ground-breaking properties in Liverpool, UK and Cairo, Egypt in 2008. Holiday Inn and Holiday Inn Express are the official hotel service providers for 2012 London Olympics and Paralympics. In 2018, IHG bought a 51% stake in the Regent Hotels & Resorts brand, securing a strong presence at the top end of the luxury segment.

集团收购了丽晶酒店与度假村(Regent Hotels & Resorts)品牌51%的股份,确保了其在高端市场的强大地位。①

洲际旗下的酒店品牌有洲际酒店及度假村(InterContinental Hotels & Resorts)、假日酒店(Holiday Inn)、皇冠假日酒店和度假村(Crowne Plaza Hotels & Resorts)、智选假日酒店(Holiday Inn Express)、斯泰布里奇套房酒店(Staybridge Suites)、英迪格酒店(Indigo)等。②

自1984年第一家假日酒店在北京开业以来,洲际酒店集团已扎根中国市场39年。作为最早进入中国的国际酒店集团之一,伴随着中国旅游业及酒店业的不断发展,洲际酒店集团始终坚守"在中国、为中国"的本土发展战略,不断加大在华投入,取得了瞩目成绩。至2023年3月31日洲际酒店集团大中华区迎来641家开业酒店里程碑,分布在北京、香港、澳门、上海、重庆、成都、南京、杭州、福州、青岛、无锡、大连等地。③

▶💿 6.3.2.3　希尔顿酒店

希尔顿是世界上最大、发展最快的酒店公司之一,拥有19个品牌,在122个国家和地区全球拥有7215处酒店。④ 希尔顿集团原来分为希尔顿国际酒店集团(HI)和希尔顿酒店管理公司(HHC)。希尔顿国际酒店集团为总部设于英国的希尔顿集团公司旗下分支,拥有除美国外全球范围内"希尔顿"商标的使用权。美国境内的希尔

The hotel brands under InterContinental Hotels Group include InterContinental Hotels & Resorts, Holiday Inn, Crowne Plaza Hotels & Resorts, Holiday Inn Express, Staybridge Suites, Indigo, etc.

Since the first Holiday Inn opened in Beijing in 1984, InterContinental Hotels Group has been rooted in the Chinese market for 39 years. As one of the first international hotel groups to enter China, with the continuous development of China's tourism and hotel industry, InterContinental Hotels Group has always adhered to the local development strategy of "in China, for China", constantly increased investment in China, and made remarkable achievements. By March 31, 2023, InterContinental Hotels Group ushered in the milestone of 600 hotels in Greater China, distributed in Beijing, Hong Kong, Macao, Shanghai, Chongqing, Chengdu, Nanjing, Hangzhou, Fuzhou, Qingdao, Wuxi, Dalian and other places.

▶💿 6.3.2.3　Hilton Hotel

Hilton is one of the largest and fastest growing hotel companies in the world, with 19 brands and 7215 hotels in 122 countries and regions. Hilton Group is originally divided into Hilton International Hotel Group and Hilton Hotel Management Company (HHC). Hilton International Hotel Group (HI), a branch of Hilton Group, headquartered in the United Kingdom, has the right to use the "Hilton" trademark worldwide except in the United States. Hilton hotels in the United States are owned and managed by Hilton Hotel Management Company.

---

① https://www.ihgplc.com/en/about-us/our-history,2023/5/13.

② https://www.ihgplc.com/en/our-brands,2023/5/13.

③ https://development.ihg.com/regions/greater-china,2023/5/13.

④ https://www.hilton.com/en/corporate/,2023/5/13.

顿酒店则由希尔顿酒店管理公司拥有并管理。①

主要品牌：希尔顿酒店（Hilton Hotels）、康莱德酒店和度假村（Conrad Hotels & Resorts）、华尔道夫酒店（Waldorf Astoria Hotels）、希尔顿逸林酒店（Double Tree Hotels）、尊盛套房酒店（Embassy Suites）、欣庭套房酒店（Homewood Suites）、花园酒店（Garden Inn）、惠庭酒店（Home2 Suites）、欢朋酒店（Hampton Hotels）、希尔顿度假俱乐部（Hilton Grand Vacations Club）等。②

1988 年希尔顿饭店在上海开业，它标志着希尔顿集团开始进入中国市场。20 世纪 90 年代由于集团发展战略主要在北美和欧洲市场，因此希尔顿在中国市场扩张步伐明显落后于其他国际饭店集团。进入新世纪，随着中国饭店市场日渐庞大，同时美国的希尔顿饭店公司收购了英国的希尔顿国际，希尔顿品牌成为统一实体后，集团发展战略重点开始转向亚洲市场，尤其是中国市场，希尔顿加速了其在中国市场的扩张步伐。目前希尔顿酒店集团在香港、北京、上海、天津、重庆、武汉、广州、西安、合肥、厦门、青岛、无锡等地拥有酒店。

Major brands: Hilton Hotels, Conrad Hotels & Resorts, Waldorf Astoria Hotels, Double Tree Hotels, Embassy Suites, Homewood Suites, Garden Inn, Home2 Suites, Hampton Hotels, Hilton Grand Vacations Club, etc.

In 1988, Hilton Hotel opened in Shanghai, which marked Hilton Group's entry into the Chinese market. In the 1990s, as the Group's development strategy was mainly based in the North American and European markets, Hilton lagged behind other international hotel groups in its expansion in the Chinese market. In the new century, with the growing Chinese hotel market and the acquisition of Hilton International from the United Kingdom by the American Hilton Hotel Company, the Hilton brand has become a unified entity. The focus of the Group's development strategy has shifted to the Asian market, especially the Chinese market, and Hilton has accelerated its expansion in the Chinese market. Currently, Hilton Hotel Group owns hotels in Hong Kong, Beijing, Shanghai, Tianjin, Chongqing, Wuhan, Guangzhou, Xi'an, Hefei, Xiamen, Qingdao, Wuxi and other places.

▶ 6.3.2.4　香格里拉酒店

香格里拉亚洲有限公司是香格里拉酒店的投资控股公司，主要业务是酒店物业、办公/零售等投资物业以及待售住宅、开发、运营和管理。1971 年第一家香格里拉酒店在新加坡开业。自那以后，它已经发展成为一个多元化的业务组合，涵盖 100 多家酒店和度假村，包括零售和商业房地产

▶ 6.3.2.4　Shangri-La Hotel

Shangri-La Asia Limited is an investment holding company of Shangri-La Hotels and its principal businesses include the development, operations and management of hotel properties, investment properties such as office / retail spaces, as well as residential developments for sale. In 1971, the first Shangri-La Hotel opened in Singapore. Since then, it has developed into a diversified business portfolio covering over 100 hotels and resorts, as well as multiple mixed-use

---

① 刘伟，《酒店管理》，北京：中国人民大学出版社，2022：53.
② https://www.hilton.com/en/corporate/，2023/5/13.

在内的多个混合用途开发项目。该公司成立于百慕大群岛,为有限责任公司,股票主要在香港联合交易所有限公司(股票代码00069)上市,并在新加坡证券交易所有限公司(证券代码S07)二次上市。①

创办人郭鹤年是马来西亚声名显赫的华人企业家,祖籍福建省福州市,有亚洲糖王之称。郭氏集团控制着超过100家公司,业务渗透到新加坡、泰国、中国、印尼、斐济和澳大利亚等地,主要经营范围从制糖、面粉、饲料、油脂、矿山,一直到金融、酒店、种植业、商贸和船运等等。1971年,他与新加坡经济发展局合资建成了新加坡第一家豪华大酒店——香格里拉大酒店,并开始在亚太地区扩张,打造香格里拉酒店品牌。他定义了亚洲的热情好客,并为奢侈品和东道主的意义设定了新的标准。

香格里拉旗下拥有4个不同品牌,分布于22个国家及地区,拥有100多家酒店与度假酒店。香格里拉酒店与度假酒店,分布在亚太、中东、北美和欧洲各大城市的黄金地段。秉承着融入社区的理念,2011年,香格里拉集团旗下首批嘉里酒店于上海及北京开业。盛贸饭店选址于亚洲和中东的主要商业中心,实为商务休闲旅客的务实与明智之选。今旅酒店(Hotel JEN)坐落于亚洲重要门户城市的优质地段,以设计和生活方式为中心,提供先进科技、灵活空间,以及24小时服务,让住客保持节奏,丰富住宿体验。②

目前香格里拉酒店集团在北京、香港、杭州、深圳、武汉、西安、成都、福州、广州、哈尔滨、沈阳、青岛、苏州等地拥有酒店。

development projects including retail and commercial real estates. The company was established in Bermuda as a limited liability company. Its shares are mainly listed on the Stock Exchange of Hong Kong Limited (stock code 00069) with a secondary listing on the Singapore Exchange Securities Trading Limited (stock code S07).

The founder Robert Kuok, a prominent Chinese entrepreneur in Malaysia, was born in Fuzhou, Fujian Province. He is known as the King of Sugar in Asia. Guok's Group controls more than 100 companies. Its business has covered Singapore, Thailand, China, Indonesia, Fiji, Australia and other places. Its main business scope includes sugar making, flour, feed, oil, mining, finance, hotels, planting, commerce and shipping, etc. In 1971, he and Singapore Economic Development Board jointly built the first luxury hotel in Singapore—Shangri-La Hotel, and began to build the hotel brand in the Asia Pacific region. He defined Asian hospitality and set new standards for luxury and what it means to be a host.

Shangri-La boasts 4 different brands, distributed in 22 countries and regions, and possesses more than 100 hotels and resort hotels. Shangri-La Hotels and Resorts are located in the prime locations of major cities in Asia Pacific, the Middle East, North America and Europe. Adhering to the concept of community integration, the first batch of Kerry Hotel under Shangri-La Group was opened in Shanghai and Beijing in 2011. Located in the main business center of Asia and the Middle East, Traders Hotel is a practical and wise choice for business and leisure travelers. Hotel JEN is located in the high-quality area of the important gateway city in Asia. Centered on design and lifestyle, Hotel JEN provides advanced technology, flexible space, and 24-hour services to keep the guests' pace and enrich the guests' accommodation experience.

At present, Shangri-La Hotel Group owns hotels in Beijing, Hong Kong, Hangzhou, Shenzhen, Wuhan, Xi'an, Chengdu, Fuzhou, Guangzhou, Harbin, Shenyang, Qingdao, Suzhou and other places.

---

① https://www.shangri-la.com/group/investors/corporate-profile, 2023/5/13.
② https://www.shangri-la.com/group/our-businesses/hotels-and-resorts, 2023/5/13.

6.3.2.5 凯悦酒店集团

1957 年企业家杰伊·普里茨克买下了洛杉矶国际机场附近的凯悦汽车旅馆。1967 年，第一家凯悦酒店在亚特兰大开业，其开创性的设计和标志性的中庭使得凯悦酒店成为酒店业的创新者。1969 年香港凯悦酒店（Hyatt Regency Hong Kong）开业，这是美国以外的第一家凯悦酒店。凯悦酒店迅速与国际旅行者建立了牢固的联系，搭建了通往亚洲的桥梁，并为数十年来在世界各地的品牌知名度奠定了基础。2009 年，凯悦的股票开始在纽约证券交易所公开交易，股票代码为 H。在其 66 年的发展过程中，许多品牌加入其中：凯悦酒店，1967；安达仕（Andaz），2007；凯悦臻选（The Unbound Collection by Hyatt），2016；汤普森酒店（Thompson Hotels）、凯悦尚选（JdV by Hyatt）、凯悦悠选（Destination by Hyatt）、阿丽拉（Alila），2018；凯悦嘉荟（Caption by Hyatt），2019。①

凯悦酒店集团旗下酒店品牌包括：柏悦（Park Hyatt）、安达仕（Andaz）、君悦（Grand Hyatt）、凯悦（Hyatt Regency）、凯悦嘉轩（Hyatt Place）以及凯悦嘉寓（Hyatt House）。柏悦酒店是专为追求私密性、个性化及高质量服务的旅行者设计的世界级豪华精品酒店品牌。君悦酒店是专为商务和休闲旅行者以及大规模会议活动服务的豪华酒店品牌，以其规模宏大、设施先进而著称。凯悦酒店是凯悦酒店集团的高档旗舰品牌，数量最多，是公司较小型的豪华饭店。②

6.3.2.5 Hyatt Hotels Group

Entrepreneur Jay Pritzker purchased the Hyatt Motel near Los Angeles International Airport in 1957. The first Hyatt Regency hotel debuted in Atlanta, its groundbreaking design and signature atrium defining Hyatt as a hospitality innovator in 1967. Hyatt Regency Hong Kong, the first Hyatt hotel outside of the United States, opened its doors in 1969. Hyatt quickly established a strong bond with international travelers, built a bridge to Asia and set the foundation for decades of brand recognition around the world. In 2009 Hyatt stock began trading publicly on the New York Stock Exchange under the ticker symbol H. During its 66-year development process, many brands have been added to its portfolio: Hyatt Regency, 1967; Andaz, 2007; The Unbound Collection by Hyatt, 2016; Thompson Hotels, JdV by Hyatt, Destination by Hyatt and Alila, 2018; Caption by Hyatt, 2019.

Hyatt Hotels Group's hotel brands include Park Hyatt, Andaz, Grand Hyatt, Hyatt Regency, Hyatt Place and Hyatt House. Park Hyatt is a world-class luxury boutique hotel brand designed for travelers who pursue privacy, personalization and high-quality service. Grand Hyatt is a luxury hotel brand dedicated to business and leisure travelers and large-scale conference activities. It is famous for its grand scale and advanced facilities. Hyatt Regency is the high-end flagship brand of Hyatt Hotels Group, with the largest number. It is a smaller luxury hotel of the company.

① https://about.hyatt.com/en/hyatthistory.html，2023/5/13.
② https://about.hyatt.com/en/hyatthistory.html，2023/5/13.

截至 2021 年 12 月,凯悦在大中华区开业酒店 109 家;旗下 19 个品牌中的 11 个已进入大中华区。在其布局的核心城市中,深耕多年的上海为凯悦发力中国市场打下良好基础。目前上海陆家嘴的三座地标中,凯悦酒店集团已进驻其中的两座——上海金茂君悦大酒店进驻上海金茂大厦,上海柏悦酒店则进驻环球金融中心。这两家标志性酒店在刷新上海酒店新高度的同时,奠定了凯悦酒店集团的行业标杆地位。

截至 2021 年底,凯悦已在上海开业 17 家旗下品牌酒店,过去两年 13 家新酒店准备落地上海,其中包括安达仕(Andaz)、凯悦尚萃(Hyatt Centric)、凯悦嘉荟(Caption by Hyatt)、凯悦臻选(The Unbound Collection by Hyatt)、阿丽拉(Alila)等品牌酒店的签约,意味着未来将有更多独具特色的品牌在此落地,与上海的多元文化碰撞出更耀眼的火花。

其中,凯悦臻选、凯悦尚选(JdV by Hyatt)和凯悦悠选(Destination by Hyatt)三个"软品牌",通过为独立品牌酒店注入凯悦集团的强大系统而显著提升竞争力,致力于为有酒店情怀和品牌梦想的业主打造独具特色的产品和实现文化传承。而即将引入的新品牌如凯悦嘉荟和汤普森酒店(Thompson Hotels)将为业主、投资者带来更多差异化、个性化的品牌选择。[①]

▶ 6.3.2.6 温德姆酒店集团

温德姆酒店及度假村是世界上最大的酒店特许经营公司,总部设于美

By December 2021, Hyatt had opened 109 hotels in Greater China; eleven of its 19 brands had entered Greater China. Among the core cities in its layout, Shanghai, which has been cultivated for many years, has laid a good foundation for Hyatt's efforts in the Chinese market. Currently, among the three landmarks in Lujiazui, Shanghai, Hyatt Hotels Group has settled in two of them; Grand Hyatt Shanghai has settled in Shanghai Jinmao Tower; Shanghai Park Hyatt Hotel is based in the World Financial Center. These two iconic hotels have established the benchmark position of Hyatt Hotels Group in the industry while refreshing the new height of hotels in Shanghai.

By the end of 2021, Hyatt had opened 17 brand hotels in Shanghai. In the past two years, 13 new hotels have been ready to be settled in Shanghai, including Andaz, Hyatt Centric, Caption by Hyatt, The Unbound Collection by Hyatt, Alila and other brand hotels, which means that more unique brands will be established here in the future. The exchanges with Shanghai's multi-culture will emit more dazzling sparks.

Among them, the Unbound Collection by Hyatt, JdV by Hyatt and Destination by Hyatt are three "soft brands" that significantly enhance their competitiveness by injecting a strong system of Hyatt Group into independent brand hotels, and are committed to creating unique products and realizing cultural inheritance for owners with hotel feelings and brand dreams. The new brands to be introduced, such as Caption by Hyatt and Thompson Hotels, will bring more differentiated and personalized brand choices to owners and investors.

▶ 6.3.2.6 Wyndham Hotel Group

Wyndham Hotels & Resorts are the largest hotel franchising company in the world. Headquartered in Parsippany, New

---

[①] 深耕中国市场,凯悦酒店集团大中华区开业 109 家酒店,网易,https://www. 163. com/dy/article/H13FAL6E05389YET. html,2022/2/26。

国新泽西州帕西帕尼,在六大洲95个国家经营22个品牌,9 000多家酒店。① 温德姆酒店集团经营模式分自主管理和特许经营两种,其中特许经营模式在温德姆酒店集团全球扩张路上发挥着巨大作用。

其旗下经营品牌从享誉全球的高档酒店品牌温德姆酒店及度假酒店(Wyndham Hotels and Resorts),到家喻户晓的舒适酒店品牌——华美达酒店(Ramada)、戴斯酒店(Days Inn)、速8酒店(Super 8)以及豪生酒店(Howard Johnson)等,一贯为不同消费群体提供多样化的酒店选择和物超所值的优质服务。②

苏州温德姆花园酒店(Wyndham Garden Suzhou)2016年隆重开业,标志着温德姆花园酒店和度假村(Wyndham Garden Hotels and Resorts)品牌首度进驻中国。在2019年末,中国首家麦客达温德姆酒店(Microtel Inn & Suites by Wyndham)正式面世。随后,麦客达温德姆酒店在杭州、合肥、贵阳、昆明、丽江和天津等不同城市相继开业。到2022年底,温德姆酒店集团在中国各大城市和新兴目的地开设20家麦客达温德姆酒店,如黄山、三亚、长沙、青岛、福州等地。华美达酒店品牌继续呈现出强劲的增长势头。温德姆酒店集团计划在中国广受欢迎的旅游胜地新开10家华美达酒店。这包括2022年开业的桂林阳朔华美达度假酒店(Ramada by Wyndham Guilin Yangshuo Resort)。③

Jersey, the United States, Wyndham Hotel Group operates 22 brands and more than 9 000 hotels in 95 countries on six continents. The business model of Wyndham Hotel Group can be divided into independent management and franchising. The franchising model plays a huge role in the global expansion of Wyndham Hotel Group.

Its operating brands range from the world-renowned high-end hotel brand Wyndham Hotels and Resorts to well-known comfortable hotel brands, such as Ramada, Days Inn, Super 8 Hotels and Howard Johnson Hotels, which have always provided diversified hotel choices and quality services for different consumer groups.

The grand opening of Wyndham Garden Suzhou in 2016 marks the first time Wyndham Garden Hotels and Resorts entered China. At the end of 2019, Microtel Inn & Suites by Wyndham, the first such hotel in China, was officially launched. Subsequently, such hotels opened in Hangzhou, Hefei, Guiyang, Kunming, Lijiang and Tianjin. By the end of 2022, Wyndham Hotel Group had opened 20 Microtel Inn & Suites by Wyndham in major cities and emerging destinations in China, such as Huangshan, Sanya, Changsha, Qingdao, Fuzhou, etc. Ramada hotel brand continues to show a strong growth momentum. Wyndham Hotel Group plans to open 10 new Ramada hotels in China's popular tourist resorts. This includes Ramada by Wyndham Guilin Yangshuo Resort, which opened in 2022.

---

① https://www.wyndhamhotels.com/,2023/5/13.
② https://www.wyndhamhotels.com/wyndham-rewards/our-brands,2023/5/13.
③ 温德姆酒店集团亚太区以强劲势头开启2022年,搜狐网,http://news.sohu.com/a/536750092_393368,2022/4/10.

6.3.2.7 雅高酒店集团

雅高酒店集团在全世界 110 个国家拥有 40 个酒店品牌、5 400 家酒店，可满足不同顾客的需要。① 集团成立于 1967 年，总部设在巴黎。雅高集团拥有酒店行业最大的品牌组合，包括国际知名的豪华和高级品牌，以及受欢迎的中端和经济型品牌。② 2016 年 7 月，雅高酒店集团收购了标志性品牌费尔蒙、莱佛士和瑞士酒店，使集团确立了全球奢华酒店市场领导者的地位。事实上，集团目前已经是全球第二大的奢华酒店运营商。雅高酒店集团的战略愿景是成为全球首屈一指的酒店经营者。费尔蒙、莱佛士和瑞士酒店品牌加入后，集团已成为一个更强大、更多元化的机构。

雅高拥有 40 个品牌。奢华品牌包括莱佛士（Raffles）、费尔蒙（Fairmont）、索菲特传奇（Sofitel Legend）、索菲特（Sofitel）等，高端品牌包括美憬阁（MGallery）、铂尔曼（Pullman）、美爵（Grand Mercure）以及瑞士酒店（Swissotel）等，中端酒店包括诺富特（Novotel）、美居（Mercure）等，经济型酒店品牌有宜必思（Ibis）、宜必思尚品（Ibis Styles）、宜必思快捷（Ibis Budget）。③

雅高集团于 1985 年进入中国，是最早进入该市场的国际酒店管理集团之一。1990 年，第一家诺富特酒店在广州开业，1993 年第一家索菲特酒店在上海开业，2004 年 4 月中国第一家宜必思酒店在天津开业。1999 年 9 月，集团与北京首旅集团签署合作协

6.3.2.7 Accor Hotels Group

Accor Hotel Group enjoys 40 hotel brands and 5 400 hotels in 110 countries worldwide，which can meet the needs of different customers. It was founded in 1967，with its headquarters in Paris. Accor offers the largest brand portfolio in the hotel industry comprised of internationally acclaimed luxury and premium brands as well as popular midscale and economy brands. In July 2016，Accor Hotels Group acquired the iconic brands Fairmont，Raffles and Swissotel，which established the group as the global leader in the luxury hotel market. In fact，it is now the second largest luxury hotel operator in the world. Accor Hotel Group's strategic vision is to become the world's leading hotel operator. With the acquisition of Fairmont，Raffles and Swissotel brands，the group has now become a more powerful and diversified organization.

Accor boasts 40 brands. Its luxury brands include Raffles，Fairmont，Sofitel Legend，Sofitel，etc；its high-end brands include MGallery，Pullman，Grand Mercure and Swissotel；its middlescale hotels include Novotel，Mercure，etc；its economy hotel brands include Ibis，Ibis Styles，Ibis Budget.

Accor Group entered China in 1985 and is one of the first international hotel management groups to enter the market. In 1990，the first Novotel Hotel opened in Guangzhou；In 1993，the first Sofitel Hotel was launched in Shanghai；In April 2004，the first Ibis Hotel in China opened in Tianjin. In September 1999，it signed a cooperation agreement with Beijing Tourism Group；In 2002，it formed a partnership with Jinjiang Group；At the beginning of 2015，Accor Hotel Group

---

① https://group. accor. com/en/group/who-we-are/about-us，2023/5/13.

② https://group. accor. com/en/hotel-development/compare-our-brands，2023/5/13.

③ https://group. accor. com/en/hotel-development/compare-our-brands，2023/5/13.

议；2002 年，与锦江集团结成合作伙伴；2015 年初，与华住酒店集团签订经济型和中端品牌的加盟商联盟协议。继成都棕榈泉费尔蒙酒店（Fairmont Chengdu）于 2017 年 1 月揭幕，成为雅高酒店集团在大中华区的第 200 家酒店，武汉泛海费尔蒙酒店（Fairmont Wuhan）2018 年开业，深圳鹏瑞莱佛士酒店（Raffles Shenzhen）2019 年开业，济南瑞士酒店（Swissotel Jinan）2020 年开业。同时，在杭州、郑州、成都、南京、长沙、西安及三亚等城市，都有这些品牌的项目计划。

▶◉ 6.3.2.8　贝斯特韦斯特国际酒店集团

贝斯特韦斯特国际酒店集团成立于 1946 年，在全球 100 多个国家和地区拥有 4 200 多家酒店，旗下 18 个集团品牌从三星到五星满足不同的客源市场。积分永不过期的酒店常旅客计划吸收了超过 3 500 万会员。在北美，超过 60% 的集团酒店被"猫途鹰"（Tripadvisor）授予"优越"评级。①

贝斯特韦斯特国际酒店集团拥有 18 个独特的酒店品牌，包括贝斯特韦斯特酒店（Best Western）、贝斯特韦斯特优质酒店（Best Western Plus）、贝斯特韦斯特精品酒店（Best Western Premier）、唯博酒店（Vīb）、格洛酒店（Glō）、贝斯特韦斯特行政酒店（Executive Residency by Best Western）、萨蒂酒店（Sadie）、艾登酒店（Aiden）、贝斯特韦斯特至尊精选酒店（BW Premier Collection）和贝斯特韦斯特品质精选酒店（BW Signature Collection）。

and Huazhu Hotel Group signed an alliance agreement for franchise of economy and midscale brands. Following its unveiling in January 2017, Fairmont Chengdu became the 200th hotel of Accor Hotel Group in Greater China. Fairmont Wuhan opened in 2018, Raffles Shenzhen opened in 2019, and Swissotel Jinan opened in 2020. At the same time, there are project plans for these brands in Hangzhou, Zhengzhou, Chengdu, Nanjing, Changsha, Xi'an and Sanya.

▶◉ 6.3.2.8　Best Western International Hotel Group

Founded in 1946, Best Western International Hotel Group has more than 4 200 hotels in more than 100 countries and regions around the world, and its 18 group brands meet different customer source markets from three-star to five-star ratings. The hotel's frequent quest program, where the guest's points never expire, has attracted more than 35 million members. In North America, more than 60% of the group's hotels are rated "superior" by "Tripadvisor".

Best Western International Hotel Group enjoys 18 unique hotel brands, including Best Western, Best Western Plus, Best Western Premier, Vib, Glō, Executive Residency by Best Western, Sadie, Aiden, BW Premier Collection and BW Signature Collection.

---

① https://www.bestwestern.com/en_US/about/press-media/best-western-timeline-and-story.html，2023/5/13.

通过收购,贝斯特韦斯特国际酒店集团现在还提供奢华系列酒店(WorldHotels Luxury)、豪华系列酒店(WorldHotels Elite)、世尊系列酒店(WorldHotels Distinctive)和匠旅系列酒店(WorldHotels Crafted)。作为其产品组合的一部分,它还提供舒尔斯泰酒店(SureStay)、舒尔斯泰优质酒店(SureStay Plus)、舒尔斯泰精选酒店(SureStay Collection)和舒尔斯泰单间公寓酒店(SureStay Studio)。每个品牌都有自己的个性和风格,但都致力于提供卓越的客户服务、卓越的价值和现代设施。①

Through acquisition, it now also provides WorldHotels Luxury, WorldHotels Elite, WorldHotels Distinctive and WorldHotels Crafted. As part of its product portfolio, it also offers SureStay, SureStay Plus, SuryStay Collection and SureStay Studio. Each brand has its own personality and style, but is committed to providing excellent customer service, exceptional value and modern facilities.

▶💿 6.3.2.9　精选国际酒店集团

精选国际酒店集团是一家世界著名的国际酒店品牌管理机构,成立于1939 年,总部位于美国马里兰州银泉。精选国际也是世界领先的酒店特许经营公司。目前在 40 多个国家和地区特许经营 7 000 多家酒店,拥有近 57 万间客房。② 精选酒店最早起源于信誉良好的品质酒店(Quality Inn)。

1981 年,随着凯富酒店(Comfort Inn)的开设和发展,精选酒店开始快速扩张。在相继收购了凯瑞酒店(Clarion)、罗德维酒店(Rodeway Inn)和依可洛奇酒店(EconoLodge)之后,精选酒店又对舒眠酒店(Sleep Inn)、门斯特套房酒店(MainStay Suites)进行了革命性的改造,使自身的业务范围全面拓展,从经济型消费到高消费,从基本服务到高档次的娱乐享受,各种服务无所不包。精选旗下拥有 11 个

▶💿 6.3.2.9　Choice Hotels International Group

Choice Hotels International Group is a world-famous brand management organization of international hotels. Founded in 1939, it is headquartered in Silver Spring, Maryland, USA. It is also a leading hotel franchise company in the world. Currently, it franchises over 7 000 hotels in over 40 countries and regions, with nearly 570 000 rooms. Choice Hotels originated from the reputable Quality Inn.

In 1981, with the opening and development of Comfort Inn, it began to rapidly expand. After successively acquiring Clarion, Rodeway Inn, and EconoLodge hotels, it has undertaken revolutionary renovations for Sleep Inn and MainStay Suites, expanding its business scope from affordable to high consumption, from basic services to high-end entertainment, and offering a wide range of services. It has 11 independent brands under its control: Comfort Inn, Comfort

---

① https://www.bestwestern.com/en_US/hotels/discover-best-western/brands.html,2023/5/13.
② https://www.choicehotels.com/about,2023/5/13.

独立的品牌[①]:凯富酒店(Comfort Inn)、凯富套房酒店(Comfort Suites)、品质酒店(Quality Inn)、凯瑞(Clarion Hotel)、舒眠酒店(Sleep Inn)、依可洛奇酒店(EconoLodge)、罗德维酒店(Rodeway Inn)、门斯特套房酒店(MainStay Suites)、郊外长住连锁酒店(Suburban Extended Stay Hotel)、坎布里亚套房酒店(Cambria Suites)和亚森精品酒店(Ascend Collection)。

21 世纪,精选国际酒店集团将旗下著名国际酒店品牌凯瑞酒店(Clarion Hotel)推进大中华区域市场,促进了中西方酒店品牌文化之间的融合与发展。2002 年初,北京第一家四星级的凯富酒店开业,开业以来取得良好的效益。目前,除北京市开业凯富酒店、亚运村的凯富套房酒店外,天津、沈阳、西安等中国重点城市均有发展。

Suites, Quality Inn, Clarion, Sleep Inn, EconoLodge, Rodeway Inn, MainStay Suites, Suburban Extended Stay Hotel, Cambria Suites and Ascend Collection.

In the 21st century, Choice Hotels International Group has promoted its renowned international hotel brand, Clarion Hotel, to the Greater China regional market, promoting the integration and development of hotel brand cultures between China and the West. In early 2002, the first four-star Comfort Hotel opened in Beijing, which has achieved good results since its opening. At present, except for Comfort Hotel opened in Beijing and Comfort Suites in the Asian Games Village, its hotels also open in Chinese key cities such as Tianjin, Shenyang, and Xi'an.

6.4 知识拓展

表 6-1　2021 年世界 100 强酒店榜单(1～40 名)

2021 年酒店集团排名	总部所在地	房间数/酒店数
1.万豪国际	美国	1 446 600/7 795
2.锦江国际集团	中国	1 239 274/11 959
3.希尔顿	美国	1 065 413/6 777
4.洲际酒店集团	英国	885 706/6 032
5.温德姆酒店集团	美国	810 051/8 950
6.雅高酒店集团	法国	777 714/5 298
7.华住酒店集团	中国	753 216/7 830
8.精选国际酒店集团	美国	575 735/7 139
9.首旅如家酒店集团	中国	475 124/5 916
10.贝斯特韦斯特国际酒店集团	美国	34 807/3 963
11.格林酒店集团	中国	337 153/4 659
12.尚美生活集团	中国	288 293/5 804

---

① https://www.choicehotels.com/about,2023/5/13.

续表

2021 年酒店集团排名	总部所在地	房间数/酒店数
13.凯悦酒店集团	美国	284 944/1 162
14.东呈国际集团	中国	254 774/3 025
15.爱姆布瑞吉	美国	226 797/1 517
16.德胧集团	中国	144 468/863
17.G6 酒店集团	美国	116 669/1 409
18.韦斯特蒙特酒店集团	美国	88 363/795
19.美利亚酒店集团	西班牙	83 772/316
20.惠特贝瑞	英国	80 000/820
21.雅诗阁	新加坡	78 000/750
22.美诺集团	泰国	75 621/527
23.东横酒店	日本	72 559/331
24.美国长住酒店	美国	71 500/650
25.海格特酒店	美国	70 002/409
26.巴塞罗酒店集团	西班牙	62 000/271
27.红屋顶汽车旅馆	美国	60 211/652
28.住友酒店集团	中国	60 000/1 000
29.凤悦酒店及度假村	中国	55 932/206
30.斯堪的克酒店	瑞典	54 265/268
31.B&B 酒店	法国	50 000/654
32.金陵连锁酒店	中国	50 000/217
33.丽屋酒店及度假村	西班牙	49 832/100
34.凯撒娱乐	美国	47 200/51
35.华特迪士尼	美国	45 940/37
36.美高梅国际酒店集团	美国	45 162/21
37.旅客之家酒店有限公司	英国	44 984/592
38.法塔尔国际酒店及度假村	以色列	44 000/229
39.基准金字塔酒店	美国	43 054/219
40.索纳斯特酒店集团	美国	42 680/1 143

表 6-2 2021 年世界 100 强酒店榜单(41～80 名)

2021 年酒店集团排名	总部所在地	房间数/酒店数
41.香格里拉酒店集团	中国	42 640/104
42.北欧之选酒店	挪威	40 250/222

2021 年酒店集团排名	总部所在地	房间数/酒店数
43. 千禧国际酒店集团	新加坡	39 924/139
44. 丽呈酒店	中国	37 107/273
45. 加维奥塔旅游集团	古巴	35 497/105
46. 君廷酒店及度假村集团	中国	35 462/167
47. 潘多克斯	瑞典	35 372/157
48. 明宇商旅	中国	35 095/181
49. 恭胜酒店集团	中国	33 777/747
50. 新月酒店和度假村	美国	31 490/118
51. 绿地酒店旅游集团	中国	29 513/116
52. HHM 酒店	美国	29 300/185
53. 波萨达斯集团	墨西哥	28 888/186
54. 中旅酒店	中国	28 158/118
55. 雷迪森酒店集团	中国	28 070/169
56. HEI 酒店及度假村	美国	26 400/95
57. DH 酒店集团	德国	25 073/124
58. 瑞雅国际	中国	25 000/125
59. 奇利特酒店集团	土耳其	25 000/19
60. 茵汤套房酒店	美国	24 895/196
61. 君澜酒店集团	中国	24 635/103
62. 万达酒店及度假村	中国	24 403/94
63. 伊波罗之星	西班牙	24 351/67
64. 大仓日航酒店管理公司	日本	24 213/78
65. 四季酒店集团	加拿大	24 200/122
66. 王子大饭店和度假村	日本	23 938/83
67. 汽车旅馆一号	德国	23 933/83
68. L＋R 酒店	英格兰	23 300/108
69. 德鲁里酒店集团	美国	22 786/135
70. 欧洲之星	西班牙	22 526/227
71. 雷明顿酒店	美国	22 437/111
72. 安徽古井酒店发展股份有限公司	中国	22 320/280
73. 协和酒店	美国	22 273/146
74. 大西洋酒店	巴西	22 000/135
75. 群岛酒店集团	印度尼西亚	21 783/153
76. 中庭酒店	美国	21 773/83

续表

2021 年酒店集团排名	总部所在地	房间数/酒店数
77. MCR 酒店	美国	21 614/142
78. GF 酒店和度假村	美国	21 392/139
79. 戴维森酒店集团	美国	21 267/78
80. 蓝钻酒店和度假村	美国	21 245/54

表 6-3　2021 年世界 100 强酒店榜单（81～100 名）

2021 年酒店集团排名	总部所在地	房间数/酒店数
81. 辉盛国际	新加坡	21 000/120
82. 酒店管理公司	美国	20 810/172
83. 瑟利纳酒店	英国	20 751/95
84. 云顶集团	马来西亚	20 585/33
85. 印度酒店有限公司	印度	19 936/170
86. 地中海俱乐部	法国	19 736/64
87. 凯宾斯基酒店	瑞士	19 500/79
88. 拉斯维加斯金沙集团	美国	19 116/8
89. TPG 度假酒店与码头投资公司	美国	18 996/131
90. 硬石国际	美国	18 660/37
91. 科勒斯莱酒店和度假村	美国	18 597/128
92. 罗塔那酒店管理公司	阿联酋	18 371/69
93. 远东酒店集团	新加坡	18 000/97
94. GCH 酒店集团	德国	17 500/120
95. 珀林酒店集团	中国	16 817/202
96. 南方太阳酒店集团	南非	16 766/105
97. 洛伊斯酒店和度假村	美国	16 445/26
98. 浮木酒店管理	美国	16 046/88
99. 怀特酒店	美国	15 736/63
100. 杰斯酒店集团	埃及	15 428/59

表 6-4　进入全球酒店 200 强之内的其他中国酒店

2021 年酒店集团排名	总部所在地	房间数/酒店数
105. 萨维尔酒店集团	中国	14 771/72
108. 世纪金源集团	中国	14 000/20
114. 香宿酒店集团	中国	12 369/236
117. 朗廷酒店集团	中国	12 255/32
139. 深圳格兰云天酒店管理有限公司	中国	10 419/43

2021 年酒店集团排名	总部所在地	房间数/酒店数
151. 瑰丽酒店集团	中国	9 361/42
154. 帝盛酒店集团	中国	9 064/32
160. 蝶来酒店集团	中国	8 873/53
166. 海逸酒店管理有限公司	中国	8 500/11
167. 文华东方酒店集团	中国	8 500/36
170. 富豪国际酒店集团	中国	8 200/16

Table 6-1　2021 World Top 100 Hotels List（1—40）

Ranking and name of hotels	Headquarters	Number of rooms/Number of hotels
1. Marriott International	USA	1 446 600/7 795
2. Jinjiang International Holdings Co., Ltd.	China	1 239 274/11 959
3. Hilton	USA	1 065 413/6 777
4. IHG Hotels & Resorts	USA	885 706/6 032
5. Wyndham Hotels & Resorts	USA	810 051/8 950
6. Accor	France	777 714/5 298
7. Huazhu Group Ltd.	China	753 216/7 830
8. Choice Hotels International	USA	575 735/7 139
9. BTG Hotels (Group) Co., Ltd.	China	475 124/5 916
10. Best Western Hotel Group	USA	34 807/3 963
11. GreenTree Hospitality Group	China	337 153/4 659
12. Qingdao Sunmei Group Co.	China	288 293/5 804
13. Hyatt Hotels Corp.	USA	284 944/1 162
14. Dossen International Group	China	254 774/3 025
15. Aimbridge Hospitality	USA	226 797/1 517
16. Delonix Group	China	144 468/863
17. G6 Hospitality LLC	USA	116 669/1 409
18. Westmont Hospitality Group	USA	88 363/795
19. Melia Hotels International	Spain	83 772/316
20. Whitbread	UK	80 000/820
21. The Ascott Ltd.	Singapore	78 000/750
22. Minor Hotel Group	Thailand	75 621/527
23. Toyoko Inn Co.	Japan	72 559/331
24. Extended Stay	USA	71 500/650
25. Highgate	USA	70 002/409
26. Barcelo Hotel Group	Spain	62 000/271
27. Red Roof Motel	USA	60 211/652

Ranking and name of hotels	Headquarters	Number of rooms/Number of hotels
28. Zhuyou Hotel Group	China	60 000/1000
29. Funyard Hotels & Resorts	China	55 932/206
30. Scandic Hotels	Sweden	54 265/268
31. B & B Hotels	France	50 000/654
32. Jinling Hotels & Resorts Corp.	China	50 000/217
33. Riu Hotels & Resorts	Spain	49 832/100
34. Caesars Entertainment	USA	47 200/51
35. Walt Disney Co.	USA	45 940/37
36. MGM Resorts	USA	45 162/21
37. Travelodge Hotels	UK	44 984/592
38. Fattal International Hotels & Resorts	Israel	44 000/229
39. Benchmark Pyramid	USA	43 054/219
40. Sonesta International Hotels Corp.	USA	42 680/1 143

Table 6-2　2021 World Top 100 Hotels List（41—80）

Ranking and name of hotels	Headquarters	Number of rooms/Number of hotels
41. Shangri-La	China	42 640/104
42. Nordic Choice Hotels	Norway	40 250/222
43. Millennium Hotels and Resorts	Singapore	39 924/139
44. Rezen Hotels	China	37 107/273
45. Grupo de Turismo Gaviota	Cuba	35 497/105
46. Barony Hotels & Resorts Worldwide	China	35 462/167
47. Pandox	Sweden	35 372/157
48. Minyoun Hospitality Corp. Ltd.	China	35 095/181
49. Gongsheng Hotel Group	China	33 777/747
50. Crescent Hotels & Resorts	USA	31 490/118
51. Greenland Hotel and Tourism Group	China	29 513/116
52. HHM	USA	29 300/185
53. Grupo Posadas	Mexico	28 888/186
54. CTG Hotel Holdings Corp. Ltd.	China	28 158/118
55. Landison Hotels & Resorts Co.	China	28 070/169
56. HEI Hotels & Resorts	USA	26 400/95
57. DH Hotel Group	Germany	25 073/124
58. Swiss Belhotel International	China	25 000/125
59. Kilit Hospitality Group	Turkey	25 000/19

续表

Ranking and name of hotels	Headquarters	Number of rooms/Number of hotels
60. InTown Suites	USA	24 895/196
61. Narada Hotel Group	China	24 635/103
62. Wanda Hotels & Resorts	China	24 403/94
63. Iberostar Hotels & Resorts	Spain	24 351/67
64. Okura Nikko Hotel Management	Japan	24 213/78
65. Four Seasons Hotels and Resorts	Canada	24 200/122
66. Prince Hotels and Resorts	Japan	23 938/83
67. Motel One	Germany	23 933/83
68. L+R Hotels	England	23 300/108
69. Drury Hotel Group	USA	22 786/135
70. Eurostars Hotel Co.	Spain	22 526/227
71. Remington Hotels	USA	22 437/111
72. Anhui Gujing Hotels Development Co., Ltd.	China	22 320/280
73. Concord Hospitality Enterprises	USA	22 273/146
74. Atlantic Hotels	Brazil	22 000/135
75. Archipelago International	Indonesia	21 783/153
76. Atrium Hospitality	USA	21 773/83
77. MCR Hotels	USA	21 614/142
78. GF Hotels & Resorts	USA	21 392/139
79. Davidson Hospitality Group	USA	21 267/78
80. Blue Diamond Hotels & Resorts	USA	21 245/54

Table 6-3   2021 World Top 100 Hotels List (81—100)

Ranking and name of hotels	Headquarters	Number of rooms/Number of hotels
81. Frasers Hospitality	Singapore	21 000/120
82. Hotel Equities	USA	20 810/172
83. Selina Hospitality	UK	20 751/95
84. Genting Group	Malaysia	20 585/33
85. The Indian Hotels Co., Ltd.	India	19 936/170
86. Club Med	France	19 736/64
87. Kempinski Hotels	Switzerland	19 500/79
88. Las Vegas Sands Corp.	USA	19 116/8
89. TPG Hotels Resorts & Marinas	USA	18 996/131
90. Hard Rock International	USA	18 660/37
91. Crestline Hotels & Resorts	USA	18 597/128

续表

Ranking and name of hotels	Headquarters	Number of rooms/Number of hotels
92. Rotana Hotel Management Corp.	UAE	18 371/69
93. Far East Hospitality	Singapore	18 000/97
94. GCH Hotel Group	Germany	17 500/120
95. Bolin Hotel Group	China	16 817/202
96. Southern Sun	South Africa	16 766/105
97. Loews Hotels & Resorts	USA	16 445/26
98. Driftwood Hospitality Management	USA	16 046/88
99. White Lodging	USA	15 736/63
100. Jaz Hotel Group	Egypt	15 428/59

Table 6-4　Other Chinese Hotels Entering the Global Top 200 Hotels List[①]

Ranking and name of hotels	Headquarters	Number of rooms/Number of hotels
105. Savile Hotel Group Co., Ltd.	China	14 771/72
108. Century Golden Resources Group	China	14 000/20
114. Xiangsu Hotel Group	China	12 369/236
117. Langham Hospitality Group	China	12 255/32
139. Shenzhen Grand Skylight Hotels Management Co., Ltd.	China	10 419/43
151. Rose Hotel Group	China	9 361/42
154. Dorsett Hospitality International	China	9 064/32
160. Deefly Hotels & Resort Group	China	8 873/53
166. Harbour Plaza Hotel Management Ltd.	China	8 500/11
167. Mandarin Oriental Hotel Group	China	8 500/36
170. Regal Hotels International	China	8 200/16

❀ Exercises

Ⅰ. Fill in the blanks with proper forms of words.

1. If _____ (calculate) by the number of hotels, the largest chain hotels in the world were _____ (initial) simple small hotels. They had a great vision and _____

[①] 表 6-1～表 6-4 的数据摘自酒店行业美国权威杂志《酒店》(HOTELS)公布的 2021 年"全球酒店 225"排行榜。《酒店》主要是对酒店管理公司进行排名,而不是酒店投资公司,那些只拥有酒店物业而不经营酒店的不动产投资公司和信托基金被排除在排名之外。

(hope) make a difference in the hotel industry. By continuing to base themselves on timeless classical and modern elements, they _____ (inherit) their heritage to the present. They continue to develop, care about the social problems around them, and proudly fulfill their _____ (commit) to provide high-quality _____ (accommodate) around the world.

2. Marriott International Group is a world-famous hotel management company and an enterprise _____ (list) in the Fortune Global 500. Marriott International Group, _____ (found) in 1927, is _____ (headquarter) in Washington, USA. It _____ (select) as the most outstanding company in the hotel industry by world-famous business magazines and media for many times.

3. J. W. Marriott Hotel is a super luxury hotel brand _____ (upgrade) on the basis of Marriott Hotel standards, _____ (provide) guests with more luxurious and comfortable facilities and _____ (high) distinctive and high-quality services.

4. In 1994, Crowne Plaza Hotels & Resorts _____ (launch) to cater to high-level consumers. In 1997, it launched the Staybridge Suites, catering to the _____ (extend) stay market based on high consumption, and developed rapidly, and its total number amounted to more than 50 hotels in the United States.

5. Since the first Holiday Inn opened in Beijing in 1984, InterContinental Hotels Group _____ (root) in the Chinese market for 39 years. As one of the first international hotel groups _____ (enter) China, with the continuous development of China's tourism and hotel industry, InterContinental Hotel Group _____ always _____ (adhere) to the local development strategy of "in China, for China", constantly increased investment in China, and made remarkable achievements.

6. By December 2021, Hyatt _____ (open) 109 hotels in Greater China; eleven of its 19 brands _____ (enter) Greater China. Among the core cities in its layout, Shanghai, which _____ (cultivate) for many years, _____ (lay) a good foundation for Hyatt's efforts in the Chinese market.

II. Translate the following Chinese sentences into English.

1. 万豪国际集团旗下的丽思卡尔顿酒店、JW 万豪酒店、万豪酒店、万丽酒店、万怡酒店、万豪行政公寓共 6 个酒店品牌均进入中国市场运营。万豪国际集团还有望在 2023 年初迎来中国第 500 家酒店开业,进一步彰显万豪国际持续深耕中国市场的承诺。

2. 洲际酒店集团是一个知名的全球化的酒店集团,在全球 100 多个国家和地区经营和特许经营超过 6 000 家酒店、18 个品牌,拥有超过 60 年国际酒店管理经验。

3. 希尔顿是世界上最大、发展最快的酒店公司之一,拥有 19 个品牌,在 122 个国家和地区全球拥有 7 215 处酒店。希尔顿国际酒店集团(HI)为总部设于英国的希尔顿集团公司旗下分支,拥有除美国外全球范围内"希尔顿"商标的使用权。

4. 雅高酒店集团在全世界 110 个国家拥有 40 个酒店品牌、5 400 家酒店,可满足不同顾客的需要。集团拥有酒店行业最大的品牌组合,包括国际知名的豪华和高级品牌,以及受欢迎的中端和经济型品牌。

Ⅲ. Translate the following English sentences into Chinese.

1. Guests are still customers even after they leave a property. That means hoteliers shouldn't cease all communication. Follow-up communication helps to build brand trust and loyalty.

2. Send a thank-you email after departure. It's critical to follow up with guests directly after they leave a property. Give them a way to send direct feedback. If the experience was poor, this gives the opportunity to save the hotel from a negative online review and hoteliers can begin service recovery (which builds loyalty). If guests have feedback for the hotel, it's equally important to act on that feedback. When guests know hoteliers are listening and adapting to their needs, they will build loyalty with the brand.

3. Hyatt's culture is built upon the practice of empathy, grounded in listening and fueled by care. We strive to create a sense of belonging and community: We value relationships with each other, with our guests, and with our community and we live our values of Respect, Integrity, Creativity, Humility, Empathy, and Fun every day.

4. ETOA is the trade association for tour operators and suppliers in European destinations, from global brands to local independent businesses. The membership includes tour and online operators, intermediaries and wholesalers, European tourist boards, hotels, attractions, technology companies and other tourism and business service providers.

Ⅳ. Questions and answers.

1. Do hotels always have their superior organization?

2. What do the front office department and back office department refer to?

3. What are the main hotel management groups in the world and the chief brands they represent?

第❼单元　酒店接待
Unit ❼　Hotel Reception

📖 **教学目标**

⇨掌握特殊要求客房预订的基本程序

⇨掌握市场营销部代表的工作职责

⇨掌握市场营销部旅游团队接待程序

⇨掌握预订的种类与管理相关知识

⇨掌握订房纠纷的控制方法

⇨掌握客房价格体系与平均房价计算相关知识

⇨掌握总台接待与销售管理相关知识

📖 **Teaching objectives**

⇨To master the basic procedures for booking rooms with special requirements

⇨To master the job responsibilities of representatives in the marketing department

⇨ To master the marketing department's reception procedures for the tourist group

⇨To master related knowledge of the types and management of reservations

⇨To master the controlling methods of booking disputes

⇨To master related knowledge of the room price system and average room rate calculation

⇨To master related knowledge of front desk reception and sales management

7.1　情景对话

🔲 **办理有特殊要求的入住手续**

> A. 布朗，一家德国公司的商业代表
> B. 酒店前台接待员

B：早上好，先生。今天我能为你做什么？

A：我是布朗。前几天我与你们酒店的销售部预订了两间商务套房。

B：请稍等。我需要查一下预订表。（检查后一会）是的，您预订了一年的住宿，从 2023 年 3 月 5 日到 2024 年 3 月 5 日。我们酒店的销售部确认了这一点。它们是两间毗邻的商务套房，面向公园，景色优美。你喜欢较高楼层的房间还是较低楼层的房间？

A：我更喜欢较高楼层的房间，但不要太高。8 楼到 10 楼的房间是一个更好的选择。

B：让我查一下。10 楼的两间相

7.1　Situational dialogue

🔲 **Handling check-in with special requirements**

> A.　Brown, a business representative of a German company
> B.　receptionalist at front desk of a hotel

B：Good morning, sir. How can I help you today?

A：I am Brown. I had a reservation of two business suites with the sales department of your hotel the other day.

B：Just a second, please. I need to check the registration list. (a little while after the check) Yes, you had a reservation for a one-year stay starting from March 5, 2023 until March 5, 2024. It was confirmed by the sales department of our hotel. They are two adjoining business suites facing the park with a beautiful view. Do you like the rooms on a higher floor or lower floor?

A：I prefer the rooms on a higher floor, but not too high. The rooms on the 8th floor to 10th floor are a better choice.

B：Let me check. Are the two adjoining business suites on the 10th floor, Room 1008 and Room 1009, OK for you? They

邻的商务套房,1008 室和 1009 室,可以吗? 它们面对的是西湖公园,步行即可到达。

A:太好了,可以。一间用作工作室套房,另一个用作家庭套房。从酒店到公园有多远?

B:步行大约 10 分钟。另一个优点是公园没有门票。一大早,成群的人在那里晨练。

A:太棒了! 也许我以后有机会加入他们。

B:这是你的房卡,电梯在那里。我会让行李员把你的行李送到你的房间。

A:谢谢。

B:不客气。

7.2 角色扮演训练

任务 1: 如果你正在一家酒店的销售部门实习,一个由 34 人组成的英国旅行团有 13 对夫妻要求你预订大床房和双床房,你将如何处理预订? 在英国大床房(a double room)配有一张可睡一或两个人的大床,双床房(twin room)是指有两张单人床的房间。在欧洲,一些双人间配有特大号床,被称为特大号床房。

任务 2: 如果你正在酒店商务中心实习,你将如何应对各种情况? 一些有用的句子可以应用于相关的情况。

1. 当然可以。你想把它传真到哪里?

2. 请你写下国家代码、区号和传真号码好吗?

3. 线路占线。请稍等。

4. 我刚把你的文件打好。打印前请下来校对一下。

5. 这是你的原稿和打印稿。请检查一下。

6. 既然如此,我现在就帮你打印

are facing West Lake Park, which is within walking distance.

A: Great, I will take them. One will be used as studio suite and the other as family suite. How far is it from the hotel to the park?

B: Just about 10 minutes' walk. The other advantage is that the admission is free. Early in the morning, crowds of people do morning exercise there.

A: Awesome! Maybe I will have a chance to join them later.

B: Here are your room cards and the elevators are over there. I will ask the bellboy to deliver your luggage to your room.

A: Thanks.

B: It is my pleasure.

7.2 Role play training

Task 1: If you are having an internship in the sales department of a hotel and 13 couple in a British tour group of 34 persons request you to book the double room or twin room fo them, how will you handle the booking? In UK double rooms come with one big bed that sleeps one or two and the twin room refers to a room with two single beds. In Europe, some double rooms are equipped with a king-size bed and they are known as king-size rooms.

Task 2: If you are having an internship in the business center of a hotel, how will you deal with all kinds of situations? Some useful sentences can be applied in relevant situations.

1. Sure. Where do you want to fax it to?

2. Would you please write down the country code, the area code and fax numbers?

3. The line is busy. Just a second, please.

4. I have just finished typing your documents. Please come down to proof read it before printing.

5. Here is your original script and the typed one. Please check it.

6. In this case, let me print it for you now. Could you please wait for a few seconds?

出来。你能稍候片刻吗？

7.扫描件已发送到您的电子邮件中，您现在可以查看了。

8.我们刚刚收到一份给你的传真，我们的工作人员会马上把它送到你的房间。

9.这是你的传真记录。请在这里签名。

10.您可以用现金支付，也可以由我们计入您的房间账单。

11.你能出示一下你的房间卡或房间钥匙吗？

7.3　酒店销售部代表的工作职责

1.了解并掌握酒店的经营政策、价格体系、对外销售制度，贯彻执行部门经理安排的对外销售工作，积极开展酒店的宣传、推广工作。

2.协助开展酒店会议、团队业务的洽谈及接待，对外促销酒店客房、餐饮以及其他各项服务，参与酒店各类大型活动的宣传与促销。

3.密切联系国内外客户，了解市场供求情况、客户意向和需求，积极参加国内外的旅游宣传、促销活动。与各地区客户建立长期稳定的良好合作关系，不断开拓新市场、新客源。

4.经常走访客户，征求客户意见。分析销售动态，根据市场变化提出改进方案，把握酒店的营销政策，提高酒店平均房价和市场占有率。

5.协调各部门之间的关系，加强横向沟通，配合做好接待、销售工作。负责客户档案资料的管理工作。

6.协助处理酒店的公共关系事务，与新闻媒体、关系单位、业务部门建立并保持良好的公共关系。

7.完成部门经理交办的其他工作任务。

7. The scanned copy has been sent to your email and you can check it now.

8. We just received one fax for you and our staff will send it to your room in a moment.

9. Here is your fax record. Please sign here.

10. You can pay in cash or we can put it on your room bill.

11. Can you show me your room card or room key?

7.3　Job responsibilities of representatives from hotel's sales department

1. Understand and master the hotel's operating policies, pricing system, and external sales system, implement the external sales work arranged by the department manager, and actively carry out the hotel's publicity and promotion work.

2. Assist in the negotiation and reception of hotel meetings and group business, promote hotel rooms, catering, and other services externally, and participate in the publicity and promotion of various large-scale events of the hotel.

3. Strengthen contact with domestic and foreign customers, learn about market supply and demand, customer intentions and needs, actively participate in tourism publicity and promotional activities at home and abroad. Establish long-term and stable good cooperative relationships with customers in various regions, and continuously explore new markets and customer sources.

4. Regularly visit customers, solicit their opinions. Analyze sales trends, propose improvement plans based on market changes, grasp the hotel's marketing policies, and increase the average room price and market share of the hotel.

5. Coordinate the relationships between various departments, strengthen horizontal communication, and cooperate in reception and sales work. Be responsible for managing customer files and materials.

6. Assist in handling hotel public relations affairs, and establish and maintain good public relations with news media, related organizations and business departments.

7. Complete other tasks assigned by the department manager.

7.4 酒店销售部旅游团队接待程序

草拟合同前,先要了解该年度淡旺季的团体房价、司陪房价、散客房价。合同拟好后,先呈相关领导审阅,批复后送商务中心打印。合同取回后,要认真审核,确信准确无误后,盖上本部印章,呈相关领导签署。签后,复印一份存档,把签好的合同寄发相关方(或让对方到店签署)。收到签复合同后,在登记册上分类登记,复印一式三份,一份交前厅部,两份交财务部。

接到国内外旅行社传真,先与前厅部联系,了解要求的订房日期是否能安排,回复传真,确认订房。将传真置于该旅行社的档案中,注意其订房的时间变更及人数增减,及时与前厅部联系,通知变更情况。回复传真时,要注意检查电文,特别是报价传真,一定要审核价格是否准确,以防止出现漏洞。回复传真后,需要复印一份交前厅部订房,然后存档。

按照对方订房单(机票、车票、接送服务等)要求,与各部门联系落实。变更时一定要通知有关部门。团队抵达前(尤其是一些重要团队及一些代理人)要检查房间是否按要求安排好;落实订餐,记录该团队进餐的地点;检查机票、车票及提出的要求是否落实。来往文件、书信、传真、计划要按日期次序存档。凡各人处理完的文件,一定要签署,以便查核。参加洽谈后,要及时编写备忘录。

7.4 Tourist group's reception procedure for hotel's sales department

Before drafting a contract, it is necessary to learn about room rates for groups, tour guides and drivers and individual tourists for that year in the peak season and off-season. After the contract is drafted, it is first submitted to relevant leaders for review and approval, and then it is sent to the business center for printing. After the contract is taken back, it should be carefully reviewed and confirmed to be accurate. After that, it should be stamped with the seal of the department and submitted to relevant leaders for signature. After signing, make a copy for archiving and send the signed contract to relevant parties (or have the other party sign it in the hotel). After receiving the signed contract, classify and register it in the registering book, and make three copies, one for the front office department and two for the finance department.

Upon receiving a fax from domestic and foreign travel agencies, contact the front office department first to inquire if the required booking date can be arranged. Reply to the fax and confirm the booking. Place the fax in the file of the travel agency, pay attention to the changes in the booking time and the increase or decrease in the number of people, and promptly contact the front office to notify the changes. When replying to a fax, it is important to check the message, especially the quotation fax, and ensure that the price is reviewed for accuracy to prevent loopholes. After replying to the fax, you need to make a copy and submit it to the front office for booking, and then keep it on file.

According to the requirements of the other party's booking form (such as the air ticket, train ticket, shuttle service, etc.), you should contact various departments and implement them. Be sure to notify relevant departments when changes occur. Before the group arrives (especially some important groups and agents), it is necessary to check whether the reservations for rooms, meals, air tickets and train tickets are arranged as required and whether proposed requirements are implemented. Documents, letters, faxes, and plans should be archived in a chronological order. All documents processed by everyone must be signed for verification. After participating in the negotiation, it is necessary to write a memorandum in a timely manner.

7.5 酒店预订的种类

刘伟将酒店预订的种类分为非保证类客房预订和保证类预订并开展了详细的讨论。①

7.5.1 非保证类客房预订

7.5.1.1 临时性（口头）预订

它指的是客人在抵达酒店之前的短时间内或者抵达的当天所提出的预订。在这种情况下的预订通常没有酒店的确认函,客人也未付订金,只能予以口头承诺。通常酒店会将客房保留到 18:00,若到时客人未到,该预订将被取消。

7.5.1.2 确认性预订

确认性预订通常是指以书面形式确认,然而尚未支付预付款或者订金的预订。对于已作确认性预订的前来登记住宿的客人,向他们收取欠款的风险比较小。

对于确认类预订,酒店可以事先声明为客人保留客房至某一具体时间。过了规定时间,客人如未前来住宿,也未与酒店联系,则酒店有权将客房出租给其他客人。

7.5.2 保证类客房预订

为了避免客人预订后临时取消订房,造成客房不能出租而引起损失,饭店会要求客人预付定金或以其他方式来保证其订房要求,这就是保证类预订。

保证类预订有三种形式:预付款担保、信用卡担保、合同担保。②

7.5 Types of hotel reservations

Liu Wei divides hotel reservation into non-guaranteed room reservation and guaranteed reservation and provides detailed explanations.

7.5.1 Non-guaranteed room reservations

7.5.1.1 Temporary（verbal）reservation

It refers to the reservation made by the guest shortly before or on the day of arrival at the hotel. In this case, reservations usually do not have a confirmation letter from the hotel, and the guest has not paid the deposit and can only make verbal promises. Usually, hotels reserve rooms until 18:00. If the guest does not arrive by then, the reservation will be canceled.

7.5.1.2 Confirmed reservation

The confirmed reservation usually refers to the reservation that is confirmed in writing, but the guest has not yet made the advance payment or paid deposit. For guests who have made confirmed reservations and come to register for accommodation, the risk of collecting debt from them is relatively low.

For the confirmed reservation, the hotel can declare in advance that the room will be reserved until a specific time. If a guest does not come to stay or contact the hotel after the specified time, the hotel has the right to rent the room to other guests.

7.5.2 Guaranteed room reservations

In order to prevent guests from temporarily canceling their reservations and causing losses due to the failure to rent out their rooms, hotels may require guests to prepay a deposit or use other means to ensure their booking requirements. That is called guaranteed reservations.

There are three forms of guaranteed reservations: the advance payment guarantee, credit card guarantee and contract guarantee.

① 刘伟,《酒店管理》,北京:中国人民大学出版社,2022:293.
② 刘伟,《酒店管理》,北京:中国人民大学出版社,2022:293.

预付款担保：预付款担保指的是客人凭借支付预付款而获得酒店的订房保证。

信用卡担保：如果酒店没有足够的时间向客人收取预付款，可以要求客人在预订酒店客房时使用信用卡作为担保。

合同担保：合同担保不如预付款担保和信用卡担保常用，然而也是一种有效的担保方式。酒店与经常预订该酒店的商业公司签订合同。

7.6 预订业务管理

具有一定规模的酒店中，酒店的销售部负责客房的预订。同时，总台也接受客房的预订。前厅预订是一项非常重要的工作。

1.接受预订。首先要查阅记录簿或电脑，如有空房，则立即填写预订单。注明客人姓名、抵离店日期及时间、房间类型、价格、结算方式以及餐食标准、种类等内容。

2.确认预订。在接到客人的预订要求后，要立即查询是否可以提供住房，决定是否能够接受客人的预订。如果可以接受，就要对客人的预订加以确认。

3.拒绝预订。如果酒店无法接受客人的预订，就应对预订加以婉拒，并主动提出一系列可供客人选择的建议。

4.核对预订。为了提高预订的准确性和酒店的开房率，在客人到店前，要提前与客人进行多次核对，问清客人是否能够如期抵店、住宿人数、时间和要求等是否有变化。核对工作通常要进行三次。

5.预订的取消。由于各种缘故，

Advance payment guarantee：It refers to the guarantee where a guest obtains a hotel reservation by making the advance payment.

Credit card guarantee：If the hotel does not have enough time to collect advance payment from guests, they can be required to use their credit card as a guarantee when booking hotel rooms.

Contract guarantee：The contract guarantee is not as commonly used as the advance payment guarantee and credit card guarantee, but it is also an effective guarantee method. The hotel signs contracts with commercial companies that frequently book the hotel.

7.6 Reservation management

For hotels with a certain scale, the sales department of the hotel is responsible for booking rooms. At the same time, the front desk also accepts room reservations. The reservation is a very important task of the front desk.

1. Accept the reservation. Firstly, check the record book or computer, and if there are available rooms, immediately fill out the advance order. Indicate the guest's name, arrival and departure dates and time, room type, price, settlement method as well as food standards and types.

2. Confirm the reservation. After receiving a reservation request from a guest, it is necessary to immediately check if the room is available and decide whether the guest's reservation can be accepted. If it is acceptable, the guest's reservation must be confirmed.

3. Refuse the reservation. If the hotel is unable to accept a guest's reservation, the staff should politely decline the reservation and proactively provide a series of suggestions for the guest to choose from.

4. Check the reservation. In order to improve the accuracy of reservations and the occupancy rate of the hotel, it is necessary to conduct multiple checks with the guests before they arrive at the hotel. The staff should ask if the guest can arrive on schedule, whether there are any changes in the number of people staying, time and requirements, etc. The check is usually conducted three times.

5. Cancel the reservation. Due to various reasons, guests may cancel their reservation before arriving at the hotel. When

客人可能在抵店之前取消订房。接受订房的取消时,不能在电话里表露出不愉快,而应使客人明白,他今后随时都可光临酒店,并受到欢迎。正确处理取消订房,对于酒店巩固自己的客源市场具有重要意义。

6.预订的变更。预订的变更是客人在抵达之前临时改变预计的日期、人数、要求、期限、姓名和交通工具等。预订变更后,要及时调整。

7.7　订房纠纷的产生及控制方法

7.7.1　订房纠纷的原因

1.宾客订房时未说明通讯地址或联系方法,酒店无法告知当时客满的情况。

2.宾客抵店时间已超过规定的留房时间,事先又未通知酒店,导致抵店后酒店无法提供客房。

3.宾客打电话到酒店订房,预订员接受预订后未给予书面确认,宾客抵店后无房间提供。

4.宾客声称自己办理了订房手续,但酒店没有订房记录。

5.宾客不理解酒店住房方面的政策及有关规定,或在价格上发生争执,从而对酒店不满。

7.7.2　减少预订纠纷的方法

1.加强对预订员及其他有关人员的培训教育,提高其工作责任心和业务素质。

2.酒店应该应用订房单记录宾客的订房要求。如是电话或当面预订,应复述宾客的预订内容,解释酒店专用术语的确切含义及有关规定,避免

accepting a cancellation of a reservation, the staff should not express displeasure over the phone, but rather make the guest understand that they can visit the hotel at any time in the future and be welcomed. The correct handling of canceling reservations is of great significance for hotels to consolidate their customer market.

6. Change the reservation. The change of the reservation refers to a temporary change in the expected date, number of people, requirements, deadline, name, and transportation of the guest before arrival. After the reservation is changed, it should be adjusted in a timely manner.

7.7　Generation and controlling methods of room reservation disputes

7.7.1　Reasons for reservation disputes

1. Guests did not specify their mailing address or contact information when booking, and the hotel was unable to inform them of the full occupancy at that time.

2. The guest's arrival time has exceeded the specified room retention time, and the guest did not notice the hotel in advance, resulting in the hotel's failure to provide rooms upon the guest's arrival.

3. The guest called the hotel to reserve a room, but the reservation staff did not provide written confirmation after accepting the reservation. No room is available upon the guest's arrival.

4. The guest claimed to have made a reservation, but the hotel did not have a booking record.

5. Guests did not understand the hotel's housing policies and regulations, or had disputes over prices, resulting in dissatisfaction with the hotel.

7.7.2　Approaches to reducing reservation disputes

1. Enhance the training of booking staff and other relevant personnel to improve their sense of responsibility and professional quality.

2. The booking staff should use a room reservation form to record the guest's booking requirements. If it is a phone call or face-to-face booking, the guest's booking information should be repeated, and the exact meaning and relevant regulations of

出现误解、错误或遗漏。

3. 建立健全与前台接待组等部门保持有效沟通的制度,接待组应正确统计可售房的数量,及时掌握预订未到、提前抵店、延期离店、未经预订直接抵店、临时取消及住店宾客换房等用房变化情况,每天应按时将上述统计数字通知预订处。

4. 平时加强预订工作的检查,避免错误地存放预订资料。

5. 对订房的变更及取消预订的受理工作应予重视。

6. 加强与酒店销售部、订房代理处的沟通。

7. 结合本酒店实际及行业惯例,完善预订政策、预订工作程序及有关报表及规定。

7.8 客房价格体系

为了确保酒店的收益,酒店会规范定价程序,制定客房等酒店产品的定价体系,并控制好其收入。酒店定价系统取决于酒店的价格定位,价格定位涉及诸多因素:酒店的位置、成本、供求关系、竞争对手的价格、季节性、定价目标等。[①]

1. 门市价就是标准价,又被称为散客价,一般不含餐、服务费等,只含客房价格。

2. 协议价是指公司与酒店签协议时,商定该机构或公司的客人或员工入住该酒店时,所享受的一个优惠价。

3. 团队价是酒店针对旅行社所组织的团队的优惠价格,旨在与旅行社建立良好关系、保证酒店具有稳定的

the hotel's specific terms should be explained to avoid misunder standing, errors, or omissions.

3. Establish and improve the system for maintaining effective communication with the front desk reception team and other departments. The reception team should accurately count the number of available rooms, timely grasp the changes in room usage such as missed bookings, early arrivals, delayed departures, direct arrivals without reservations, temporary cancellations, and guest room changes. The booking office should be notified of the above statistics on a daily basis.

4. Strengthen the inspection of booking work in normal time to avoid storing booking materials incorrectly.

5. Attention should be paid to the acceptance of changes and cancellations of reservations.

6. Reinforce communication with the sales department of the hotel and booking agencies.

7. On the basis of the actual situation of this hotel, and the customary rule of the hotel industry, improve booking policies, booking procedures, and relevant reports and regulations.

7.8 Room pricing system

In order to ensure the hotel's revenue, the hotel will standardize pricing procedures, establish a pricing system for hotel products such as guest rooms, and control its revenue. The hotel pricing system depends on the hotel's price positioning, which involves many factors: the hotel location, cost, supply and demand relationship, competitor prices, seasonality, pricing goals, etc.

1. Rack rate is the standard price, also known as the price for FIT (fully individual tourist), which generally does not include meals, service fees, etc. and only includes the room price.

2. Contracted rate refers to a discounted price enjoyed by guests or employees of an organization or a company, which signs an agreement with the hotel.

3. Group rate is a discounted price offered by hotels for tourist groups organized by travel agencies, aiming at establishing good relationships with travel agencies and ensuring a stable customer basis for the hotel. The

① 刘伟,《酒店管理》,北京:中国人民大学出版社,2022:287.

客源。其价格的确定主要取决于相关旅行社的团队数量以及酒店淡旺季的客房利用率。

4.饭店提供的小包价通常包括房租费及餐费、交通费、旅游门票费。小包价旅游又称可选择性旅游,它由非选择部分和可选择部分构成。非选择部分包括接送、住房和早餐,旅游费用由旅游者在旅游前预付;可选择部分包括导游、风味餐、节目欣赏和参观游览等,旅游者可根据时间、兴趣和经济情况自由选择,费用既可预付,也可现付。

5.折扣价是酒店向常客、长住客或其他身份特殊的客人提供的优惠房价。

6.旺季价是指在旅游旺季,在标准房价的基础上将房价上浮一定的百分比,旨在获得最大的经济效益。

7.淡季价是指在旅游淡季,在标准房价的基础上将房价下调一定的百分比,旨在提高客房利用率。

8.白天租用价。酒店收取白天租用价的情况如下:钟点房。大部分酒店收取半天房费,也有些以小时计价。白天入住酒店的客人(会议类客户、误机客等)所订的房间。此类房最长时限为 6 小时,可以使酒店客房在一天内出租两次,因此在旺季出租率超出100%;夜晚 10:00 以后要求入住的客人也可享受这种优惠。这类房价通常比标准房价低30%左右,服务对象为未预订而需要等待空房的客人。

9.免费住宿:鉴于各种原因,酒店有时提供免费住宿,通常只有总经理才有权批准。

7.9 平均房价计算

RevPAR(revenue per available room)和 ADR(average daily rate)是

两个常用的指标,用于衡量酒店的收益情况。RevPAR 是指每间可用房间的平均收益,计算公式为:客房总收入÷可用客房总数。RevPAR 常常被用来衡量酒店的客房利用率,以及酒店的盈利能力。ADR 是指已租房间的平均房价,计算公式为:客房总收入÷出租的客房数。ADR 常常被用来衡量酒店的定价策略,以及酒店在相同市场条件下的竞争力。在收益管理中,这两个指标都很重要。RevPAR 可以帮助酒店管理人员了解酒店的客房利用率和盈利情况,而 ADR 则可以帮助酒店管理人员了解酒店的定价策略和竞争力。因此,在收益管理中,酒店管理人员应该同时关注这两个指标,并结合实际情况制定相应的策略来提升收益。

revenue. RevPAR is the average revenue per available room, and its calculation formula is: total room revenue ÷ total number of available rooms. RevPAR is often used to measure the utilization and profitability of the hotel. ADR is the average room rate per rented room, and its calculation formula is total room revenue ÷ number of rented rooms. ADR is often used to measure hotel pricing strategies and hotel competitiveness under the same market conditions. In revenue management, both indicators are important. RevPAR can help hotel managers learn about the utilization of hotel rooms and profitability, while ADR can help hotel managers learn about pricing strategies and competitiveness of the hotel. Therefore, in revenue management, hotel managers should pay attention to these two indicators at the same time, and formulate corresponding strategies to improve revenue on the basis of the actual situation.

7.10 前台旅游团队接待程序

7.10.1 准备工作

1. 提前 1~2 天就做好准备工作,确保团队用房。

2. 两个以上旅游团队同时抵店时应先预排级别高的重点旅游团队,再排用房数多的旅游团队。

3. 若有可能,同一旅游团队的客人所用客房尽量安排同一楼层。

4. 一时无房间预排时,可暂时等候,但最迟应在客人抵达前(一小时)排出房间。

5. 前台当班人员应清楚每个旅游团队的特殊事项并做好与销售部和客房部的沟通。

7.10 Reception procedure of front desk for tour group

7.10.1 Preparation work

1. Make preparation 1-2 days in advance to ensure the tour group's room availability.

2. When there are two or more tour groups arriving at the hotel at the same time, priority should be given to key tour groups with higher levels, followed by the tour groups with more room demand.

3. Rooms for the guests from the same tour group should be arranged on the same floor if possible.

4. When there is no room to be scheduled for a while, the staff can wait temporarily, but it should be prepared at the latest (one hour) before the guest arrives.

5. Front desk personnel on duty should be clear about special matters of every tour group and communicate well with the sales department and housekeeping department of the hotel.

🔡 7.10.2　迎候客人

1. 当团队抵达时，根据客人信息查找该团预订单。

2. 根据预订单信息与客人核对人数、房间数、是否订餐等。内容无误后，请其全陪签单。特殊情况需要增减房间时，礼貌征询全陪，并请其签字，然后通知客房部和收银处做好相应变更。

🔡 7.10.3　填单、验证、分房

请客人填写住房登记单。统一清点房卡数，由全陪分发给队员。入住资料输入电脑，并通知房务中心及总机。通知客房部全陪的姓名及房号。将团队预订单交收银留存，特别是注明结帐方式的单子。

7.11　总台销售的一般工作要求与销售技巧

🔡 7.11.1　销售准备

1. 仪表仪态要端庄，要表现高雅的风度和姿态。

2. 总台工作环境要有条理，服务台区域干净整齐，不零乱。

3. 熟悉酒店各种类型的客房及其服务质量，以便向潜在宾客介绍。

4. 了解酒店所有餐厅、酒吧、娱乐项目的特色以及各营业场所、公共区域的营业时间与分布。

🔡 7.10.2　Welcoming guests

1. When the tour group arrives, search for the group's preorder on the basis of customer information.

2. Check the number of people, number of rooms, and whether to book meals with customers on the basis of the pre-order information. After the information is confirmed correct, ask the national tour guide to sign the form. When special circumstances require room additions or reductions, politely consult with the national tour guide and ask for his/her signature, and then notify the housekeeping center and cashier to make corresponding changes.

🔡 7.10.3　Form filling, verification, and room allocation

Ask the guest to fill out the registration form. Count the number of room cards, and ask the national tour guide to distribute it to the group members. Enter the check-in information into the computer and notify the housekeeping center and the switchboard operator. Notify the housekeeping department of the name and room number of the group's national tour guide. Submit the group reservation form to the cashier for retention, especially documents indicating terms of payment.

7.11　General job requirements and sales skills for front desk

🔡 7.11.1　Sales preparation

1. The appearance and demeanor should be dignified, displaying elegant air and posture.

2. The working environment at the front desk should be organized. The service desk area should be clean and tidy.

3. Be familiar with various types of hotel rooms and their service quality so as to introduce them to potential guests.

4. Learn about the characteristics of all restaurants, bars, and entertainment programs in the hotel, as well as the operating hours and distribution of various business venues and public areas.

7.11.2 服务态度

一个礼貌、训练有素的前厅部员工是酒店经营管理中宝贵的财富,他使宾客形成的对酒店的第一印象将决定宾客的满意度和忠诚度,满意的宾客不仅会再次光顾酒店,还会为酒店宣传,扩大酒店的影响。

1.要善于用眼神和宾客交流,要表现出热情和真挚。

2.要面部常带微笑,对宾客表示欢迎。

3.要使用礼貌用语问候每位宾客。

4.举止行为要恰当、自然、诚恳。

5.回答问题要简单、明了、恰当,不要夸大住宿条件。

6.不要贬低提出异议的宾客,要耐心向宾客解释问题。

7.11.3 销售过程

1.要善于用描述性语言向宾客介绍几种客房的特点,说明能给宾客带来的好处以供宾客选择,但不要对几种客房作令人不快的比较。

2.不要直接询问宾客要求哪种价格的房间,应在描述客房情况的过程中,试探宾客要哪种。

3.要善于观察和尽力弄清宾客的要求和愿望,有目的地销售适合宾客需要的客房。

4.不要放弃对潜在宾客推销客房。必要时可派人陪同他们参观几间不同类型的客房,增进与宾客之间的了解,这将有助于对犹豫不决的宾客促成销售。

7.11.4 宾客销售技巧

1.了解宾客购买动机,灵活销售酒店产品。

7.11.2 Service attitude

A polite and well-trained front office employee is a valuable asset in hotel management. The first impression of the hotel he gives to the quest will determine the guest's satisfaction and loyalty. Satisfied guests will not only stay in the hotel again, but also promote the hotel and expand its influence.

1. Be good at communicating with guests through eye contact and demonstrate enthusiasm and sincerity.

2. Always smile and welcome guests.

3. Greet each guest with polite language.

4. Show appropriate, natural, and sincere behavior

5. Provide simple, clear, and appropriate answers, and do not exaggerate accommodation conditions.

6. Do not belittle guests who raise objections, and be patient in explaining the issue to the guests.

7.11.3 Sales process

1. Be good at using descriptive language to introduce the characteristics of several kinds of guest rooms to guests, explaining the benefits they can bring for them so that the guests can choose; however, do not make unpleasant comparisons between several guest rooms.

2. Do not directly inquire about the room rate requested by the guest. Instead, try to explore which price range the guest prefers while describing the room.

3. Be adept at observing and trying your best to understand guests' requirements and wishes, and try to sell rooms that are suitable for their needs.

4. Don't give up promoting rooms to potential guests. If necessary, send someone to accompany them to visit several different types of guest rooms to enhance mutual understanding with guests, which will help promote sales for hesitant guests.

7.11.4 Sales techniques

1. Learn about guests' purchasing motivations and flexibly sell hotel products.

2.要在销售酒店产品的同时介绍酒店周围的环境,体现附加价值,增加饭店的吸引力。

3.熟悉酒店的各项服务内容,因为附加的小利益往往起到较好的促销作用。

4.需要多一些耐心和多一番努力。

7.12   客房的重要地位

1.客房部是酒店向客人提供住宿服务的部门,也是酒店的重要营业部门。

2.客房是供客人住宿、休息、会客和洽谈业务的场所,是饭店最基本的设施,是饭店经营最主要、最基本的商品。

3.客房收入是饭店经济收入的主要来源,客房是带动酒店一切经济活动的枢纽(其营业收入占饭店营业收入的比例高、创利率高)。

4.客房服务质量与管理水平是饭店的重要标志。

5.客房部的管理直接影响饭店的运行和管理。公共区域的清洁和保养、全体员工制服的洗涤和保管、各类棉织品的提供由客房部负责,客房部员工占饭店员工总数的比例大。

7.13   知识链接

❧ 客房状态

1.住客房(Occupied,简写 OCC),即客人正在住用的房间。

2.走客房(check out,简写 C/O),表示客人已结账并已离开的客房。

3.续住房(Stay,简写 S),表示客人延长了住宿。

4.未清扫房(Vacant Dirty,简写 VD),表示该客房为没有经过打扫的空房。

7.12   The importance of guest rooms

1. The housekeeping department is the department that provides accommodation services to guests and is also an important business department of the hotel.

2. A guest room is a place for guests to stay, rest, meet visitors and negotiate business. It is the most basic facility of a hotel and the most important and basic commodity for hotel operation.

3. Room revenue is the main source of the hotel income, and rooms are the hub that drives all economic activities of the hotel (their revenue accounts for a high proportion of the hotel's revenue and creates a high profit).

4. The quality of room service and management level are important symbols of a hotel.

5. The management of the housekeeping department directly affects the operation and management of a hotel. The housekeeping department is responsible for cleaning and maintenance of public areas, washing and storage of all staff uniforms, provision of various cotton goods, and the housekeeping staff accounts for a large proportion of all the hotel employees.

7.13   Knowledge link

❧ Room status

1. Occupied, abbreviated as OCC, refers to the room in which the guest is currently staying.

2. Check out, abbreviated as C/O, refers to the room where the guest has checked out and left.

3. Stay, abbreviated as S, shows that the guest extends his or her accommodation time.

4. Vacant Dirty, abbreviated as VD, indicates that the room is an empty room that has not been cleaned.

2. When selling hotel products, it is also necessary to introduce the surrounding environment of the hotel, which reflects added value, and increases the attractiveness of the hotel.

3. Be familiar with the various services of the hotel, as additional small benefits often have a good promotional effect.

4. Sales work need more patience and effort.

5. 住客外宿房（Sleep Out，简写 S/O），表示该客房已被租用，但住客昨夜未归。为了防止逃账等意外情况，客房部应将此种客房状况通知总台。

6. 维修房或待修房（Out of Order，简写 OOO），表示该客房因设施设备发生故障，暂不能出租。

7. 已清扫房（Vacant Clean，简写 VC），又称 OK 房，表示该客房已清扫完毕，可以重新出租。

8. "请勿打扰房"（Do Not Disturb，简写 DND），表示该客房的客人因睡眠或其他原因而不愿被服务人员打扰。

9. 贵宾房（Very Important Person，简写 VIP），表示该客房住客是酒店的重要客人。

10. 长住房（Long Stay，简写 LS），即长期由客人包租的房间。

11. 请即打扫房（Make Up Room，简写 MUR），表示该客房住客因会客或其他原因需要服务员立即打扫。

12. 少量行李房（Light Baggage，简写 L/B），表示住客行李很少的房间。为了防止逃账，客房部应及时通知总台。

13. 无行李房（No Baggage，简写 N/B），表示该房间的住客无行李。这种情况应及时通知总台。

14. 准备退房（Expected Departure，简写 ED），表示该客房住客应当在当天中午 12 点以前退房，但现在还未退房。

15. 加床（Extra-bed，简写 E），表示该客房有加床。

7.14 知识拓展

▨▨ 2023 年预测一览

酒店业将继续在复苏方面取得重大进展。根据牛津经济研究院对美国

5. Sleep out (S/O) means that the room has been rented but the guest did not return the previous night. In order to prevent unexpected situations such as bill evasion, the housekeeping department should notify the front desk of such room conditions.

6. A maintenance room, also known as an Out of Order (OOO), indicates that the room cannot be rented temporarily due to a malfunction in its facilities and equipment.

7. Vacant Clean （VC）, also known as OK room, indicates that the room has been cleaned and can be re-rented.

8. Do Not Disturb (DND) means that guests in the room are unwilling to be disturbed by service personnel due to sleep or other reasons.

9. Very Important Person (VIP) means that the guests in this room are important guests of the hotel.

10. Long Stay (abbreviated as LS) refers to a room that is rented by guests for a long time.

11. Make Up Room (MUR) means that the guest in the room needs the waiter to clean it immediately due to reception or other reasons.

12. Light Baggage (abbreviated as L/B) refers to a room where guests have very little luggage. In order to prevent bill evasion, the housekeeping department should promptly notify the front desk.

13. No Baggage (N/B) means that the guests in the room have no luggage, and the front desk should be promptly notified of this situation.

14. Expected Departure, abbreviated as ED, indicates that guests in the room are expected to check out before 12:00 at noon on the same day, but have not yet checked out.

15. Extra-bed (abbreviated as E) indicates that the guest room has an additional bed.

7.14 Knowledge expansion

▨▨ 2023 Projections at a glance[1]

Hotels will continue to make significant strides toward recovery. According to an analysis for AHLA by Oxford Economics, 2023 U. S. hotel demand is projected to surpass

---

① The American Hotel & Lodging Association，A New Era for U. S. Hotels—2023 State of the Hotel Industry Report，2023：3.

酒店行业协会（AHLA）的分析，2023年美国酒店需求预计将超过 2019 年的水平，而名义收入预计将达到新的高度。

酒店经营者可能会看到价格持续上涨和供应链中断。美国酒店行业协会白金合作伙伴伊万达公司（Avendra）报告称，市场力量将继续影响酒店运营所依赖产品的定价和可用性。虽然以消费者价格指数（CPI）衡量的广义通胀率已从夏季高点回落，然而未来几个季度，酒店相关产品的通胀率将继续保持在 5% 至 10% 以上，高达历史平均水平的两倍多。

客人认为清洁、价格、灵活性和可持续性至关重要，疫情时代的预防措施不再那么重要。美国酒店行业协会白金合作伙伴艺康集团（Ecolab）的一项调查揭示了消费者在预订酒店时的偏好和关键决策因素。调查结果强调，清洁的环境、忠诚度计划和预订灵活性将使酒店更好地吸引和迎合客人。

会议和活动将强势回归。美国酒店行业协会白金合作伙伴安可公司（Encore）报告称，团体会议和活动的未来是光明的：该公司《2022 年秋季策划人意向报告》调查的 70% 的策划人要么预订了新活动。要么积极寻找新活动，61% 的策划人预计 2023 年会有更大的预算。

技术进步将推动该行业向前发展。美国酒店行业协会的技术部门——下一代酒店技术协会（HTNG）的执行领导小组表示，2023 年可能是人工智能大规模采用的转折点。此外，酒店经营者可能会越来越多地将机器人技术视为解决持续的人员短缺问题的方法，他们将密切关注与可持续性、网络安全和隐私相关的问题。

辅助服务模式将得以强势发展。根据美国酒店行业协会白金合作伙伴甲骨文酒店服务公司（Oracle Hospitality）

2019 levels while revenue is expected to reach new heights on a nominal basis.

Hoteliers can expect to see continued price increases and supply chain disruptions. AHLA Platinum Partner Avendra reports that market forces will continue to impact the pricing and availability of the products that hotels rely on to operate. While broad inflation as measured by the consumer price index (CPI) has come off its highs of the summer, inflation for hospitality-related products will continue to run 5% to upwards of 10% for the next few quarters, which is more than double the historical average.

Guests rank cleanliness, price, flexibility, and sustainability as critical; pandemic-era precautions less so. A survey from AHLA Platinum Partner Ecolab reveals consumer preferences and key decision-making factors when booking a hotel. The findings highlight that getting cleaning practices, loyalty programs, and reservation flexibility right will allow hotels to better attract and cater to guests.

Meetings and events will come back strong. AHLA Platinum Partner Encore reports that the future is bright for group meetings and events: 70% of planners surveyed for the company's Fall 2022 Planner Pulse Report were either booking or actively sourcing new events, and 61% expected to have larger budgets in 2023.

Technological advancements will propel the industry forward. The Executive Leadership Group of HTNG, AHLA's technology arm, suggests that 2023 could be a turning point for the wide-scale adoption of artificial intelligence. In addition, hoteliers may increasingly consider robotics as a solution to ongoing staffing shortages and they will be paying close attention to issues related to sustainability, cybersecurity, and privacy.

The ancillary service model will gain momentum. According to an analysis by AHLA Platinum Partner Oracle Hospitality, special amenities and upselling are increasingly critical to a hotelier's revenue strategy. Operators are adopting

的分析,特殊设施和追加销售对酒店经营者的收入战略越来越重要。运营商正在采用技术提供个性化优惠,并满足客人的独特需求。

technology to personalize offers and cater to the unique desires of their guests.

❋ Exercises

Ⅰ. Fill in the blanks with proper forms of words.

1. Before _____ (draft) a contract, it is necessary to learn about room rates for groups, tour guides and drivers and free individual tourists for that year in the peak season and off-season. After the contract _____ (draft), it _____ first _____ (submit) to relevant leaders for review and _____ (approve), and then it is sent to the business center for printing. After the contract is _____ (take) back, it should be carefully reviewed and confirmed to be accurate. After that, it should be stamped with the seal of the department and submitted to relevant leaders for signature.

2. Before the group arrives (especially some important groups and agents), it is necessary to check whether the reservations for rooms, meals, air tickets and train tickets are arranged as _____ (require) and whether proposed requirements _____ (implement). All documents _____ (process) by everyone must be signed for _____ (verify).

3. When _____ (accept) a cancellation of a reservation, the staff should not express displeasure over the phone, but rather make the guest _____ (understand) that they can visit the hotel at any time in the future and be welcomed. The correct handling of _____ (cancel) reservations is of great significance for hotels _____ (consolidate) their customer market.

4. Group rate is a discounted price _____ (offer) by hotels for tourist groups _____ (organize) by travel agencies, _____ (aim) at establishing good relationships with travel agencies and _____ (ensure) a stable customer basis for the hotel. The _____ (determine) of the price mainly depends on the number of the tourist group from relevant travel agencies and the hotel's room _____ (utilize) during peak and low seasons.

5. RevPAR can help hotel managers learn about the utilization of hotel rooms and profitability, while ADR can help hotel managers learn about _____ (price) strategies and _____ (competitive) of the hotel. Therefore, in revenue management, hotel managers should pay attention to these two _____ (indicate) at the same time, and formulate _____ (correspond) strategies to improve revenue on the _____ (base) of the actual situation.

Ⅱ. Translate the following Chinese sentences into English.

1. 确认性预订通常是指以书面形式确认，然而尚未支付预付款或者订金的预订。对于已作确认性预订的前来登记住宿的客人，向他们收取欠款的风险比较小。

2. 为了避免客人预订后临时取消订房，造成客房不能出租而引起损失，饭店会要求客人预付定金或以其他方式来保证其订房要求，这就是保证类预订。

3. 为了提高预订的准确性和酒店的开房率，在客人到店前，要提前与客人进行多次核对，问清客人是否能够如期抵店、住宿人数、时间和要求等是否有变化。核对工作通常要进行三次。

4. 具有一定规模的酒店中，酒店的销售部负责客房的预订。同时，总台也接受客房的预订。前厅预订是一项非常重要的工作。

Ⅲ. Translate the following English sentences into Chinese.

1. AHLA (American Hotel & Lodging Association) is the singular voice representing every segment of the hotel industry including major chains, independent hotels, management companies, REITs (real estate investment trusts), bed and breakfasts, industry partners, and more. AHLA strives to be an indispensable resource serving,

supporting and advocating on behalf of the American hospitality industry in order to build a vibrant and united hospitality industry that powers America's economy.

2. American hotels support 8.3 million American jobs, which is equivalent to nearly one in 25 U. S. jobs, according to an economic analysis released on June 4, 2023 by the American Hotel & Lodging Association and Oxford Economics. The study, which includes a breakdown of the hotel industry's economic impact in every state and congressional district, provides a comprehensive look at how hotels are contributing to communities across the nation.

3. The components of direct hotel industry impacts are:

Hotel operations: representing the revenue of hotels (e. g., rooms, food and beverage, and others) plus certain taxes (taxes on lodging and other sales taxes); ancillary hotel guest spending: representing spending by hotel guests at other businesses in the destination; capital investment: representing the construction of new hotels, renovations, and ongoing capital spending on the upkeep of existing hotels.

IV. Questions and answers.

1. RevPAR (revenue per available room) and ADR (average daily rate) are two commonly used indicators to measure hotel revenue. How do you calculate them?

2. How do you understand the importance of guest rooms?

3. If you are working at the front desk，how will you employ the sales techniques?

项目❸ 出境旅游业务与接待
Project ❸ Outbound Tour Business and Reception

第❽单元 出境旅游业务（1）
Unit ❽ Outbound Tour Business（1）

📖 **教学目标**

⇨掌握出境旅游业务的界定
⇨了解经营出境旅游的旅行社资质要求
⇨了解出境旅游的构成部分
⇨掌握出境旅游需要的证件的相关知识
⇨掌握签证的申请程序
⇨掌握旅游保险的申请的相关知识

📖 **Teaching objectives**

⇨To master the definition of the outbound tour business
⇨ To learn about qualification requirements for travel agencies operating the outbound tour
⇨To understand the components of the outbound tour
⇨To master related knowledge of the necessary documents for the outbound tour
⇨To master the procedure for visa application
⇨ To master related knowledge of the application for tourism insurance

8.1 情景对话

多次入境签证的申请

> A. 范女士，中国出境游领队
> B. 曼谷机场的签证办理工作人员

A：早上好，先生，我是中国出境游领队，我泰国的签证即将到期。由于时间限制，我回中国后没有时间申请新签证。我的旅行社要求我在曼谷机场申请多次入境签证。申请贵国新签证是在这里吗？需要什么材料？

B：是的，是在这里办理。为了发展泰国旅游业，积极应对东盟一体化进程，泰国向外国游客发放了多次入境旅游签证。手续费为 5 000 泰铢。

8.1 Situational dialogue

Application for multi-entry visa

> A. Mrs. Fan, a Chinese outbound tour escort
> B. visa processing staff at Bankgok airport

A: Good morning, sir. I am a Chinese outbound tour escort. My visa to Thailand is going to expire soon. Due to the time limit, there is no time for me to apply for a new visa when I return to China. My travel agency asked me to apply for a multi-entry visa at the Bangkok airport. Is it the right place I make an application for a new visa to your country? What is needed for the application?

B: Yes, this is the right place. In order to develop Thailand's tourism industry and actively respond to the ASEAN integration process, Thailand has issued the multiple entry tourism visa（METV）to foreign tourists. You are

该签证允许游客在 6 个月内多次进出泰国，每次停留时间不超过 60 天。需要提供有效的护照，填写申请表并提交两张照片。

A：谢谢。（在填写完申请表后一点时间）这是我的护照、申请表、照片和费用。我要等多久？

B：大约 30 分钟。

A：谢谢。

B：（30 分钟后）办好了。

A：多谢。

B：不客气。

8.2　角色扮演训练

回应客人出境游问询

任务 1：假如一家位于某一城市或某一县城的旅行社不具备出境旅游经营资格，客人可以前往报名参加出境游吗？

提示：客人可以前往不具备出境旅游经营资格的旅行社报名，然而由于该旅行社不具备出境旅游经营资格，所以只能接受客人的报名、收取旅游费用并将客人转给具备出境旅游经营资格的旅行社。该旅行社可以收取一定的手续费。

任务 2：假如持中国公民有效护照经香港前往其他国家或地区的过境旅客参加 15 天的新马泰港游，进入香港除了出示护照还需要其他材料吗？

提示：在这种情况下，客人在进入香港时，除了护照，还需要出示前往他国的签证和国际机票。

8.3　出境旅游管理文本聚焦

8.3.1　出境旅游业务的界定

按照《旅行社条例实施细则》[①]，出

required to pay a processing fee of 5 000 baht. This visa allows tourists to enter and exit Thailand multiple times within six months, with each stay not exceeding 60 days. You need to provide your valid passport, fill in the application form and submit two photos.

A：Thank you. (a little while after finishing the filling of the application form) This is my passport, application form, photos and processing fee. How long shall I have to wait?

B：About 30 minutes.

A：Thank you.

B：(after 30 minutes) Your new visa is ready.

A：I appreciate it.

B：You are welcome.

8.2　Role play training

Responding to customers' inquiries about outboud tour

Task 1：If a travel agency located in a certain city or county does not have the qualification to operate the outbound tour, can customers register for the outbound tour there?

Hint：Guests can register with travel agencies that do not have the qualification to operate the outbound tour. However, as the travel agency does not have the qualification to operate the outbound tour, the travel agency can only accept customer's registration and collect traveling expenses and transfer them to travel agencies that have the qualification to operate the outbound tour. The travel agency can charge a certain handling fee.

Task 2：If the transit passengers who pass through Hong Kong with valid passports of Chinese citizens to other countries or regions join a 15-day tour to Singapore, Malaysia, Thailand and Hong Kong, do they need to show other materials besides the passport?

Hint：In this case, guests need to present not only their passport, but also their visa and international flight ticket to other countries when entering Hong Kong.

8.3　Focus on outbound tour management text

8.3.1　Definition of outbound tour

According to *The Detailed Rules for the Implementation*

---

① 《旅行社条例实施细则》，国家文化和旅游部网站，https://zwgk.mct.gov.cn/zfxxgkml/202012/t20201204_905330.html，2023/2/9。

境旅游业务，是指旅行社招徕、组织、接待中国内地居民出国旅游，赴香港特别行政区、澳门特别行政区和台湾地区旅游，以及招徕、组织、接待在中国内地的外国人、在内地的香港特别行政区、澳门特别行政区居民和在大陆的台湾区居民出境旅游的业务。

8.3.2 经营出境旅游的旅行社资质要求

《旅行社条例》①对经营出境旅游的旅行社资质提出了相应的要求。

第八条 旅行社取得经营许可满两年，且未因侵害旅游者合法权益受到行政机关罚款以上处罚的，可以申请经营出境旅游业务。

第九条 申请经营出境旅游业务的，应当向国务院旅游行政主管部门或者其委托的省、自治区、直辖市旅游行政管理部门提出申请，受理申请的旅游行政管理部门应当自受理申请之日起20个工作日内作出许可或者不予许可的决定。予以许可的，向申请人换发旅行社业务经营许可证；不予许可的，书面通知申请人并说明理由。

第十三条 旅行社应当自取得旅行社业务经营许可证之日起3个工作日内，在国务院旅游行政主管部门指定的银行开设专门的质量保证金账户，存入质量保证金，或者向作出许可的旅游行政管理部门提交依法取得的担保额度不低于相应质量保证金数额的银行担保。

经营国内旅游业务和入境旅游业务的旅行社，应当存入质量保证金20万元；经营出境旅游业务的旅行社，应当增存质量保证金120万元。质量保

of the *Regulations on Travel Agencies*, the outbound tour refers to the tour in which travel agencies solicit, organize and receive the residents of Chinese mainland to travel abroad and to travel to Hong Kong Special Administrative Region, Macao Special Administrative Region and Taiwan. It also refers to the tour in which travel agencies solicit, organize and receive the foreigners staying in Chinese mainland and the residents of Hong Kong Special Administrative Region, Macao Special Administrative Region as well as Taiwan staying in Chinese mainland to travel outbound.

8.3.2 Qualification requirements for travel agencies operating the outbound tour

The *Regulations on Travel Agencies* set corresponding requirements for the qualifications of travel agencies operating the outbound tour.

Article 8 If a travel agency has obtained a business license for more than two years and has not been fined or punished by the administrative organ for infringing upon the legitimate rights and interests of tourists, it may apply for operation of the outbound tour.

Article 9 An application for the operation of the outbound tour shall be submitted to the tourism administrative department of the State Council or the entrusted tourism administrative department of the province, autonomous region or municipality directly under the Central Government. The tourism administrative department that accepts the application shall make a decision on whether to approve it or not within 20 working days from the date of accepting the application. If the approval is granted, the travel agency's business operation permit shall be renewed to the applicant; if the permit is not granted, the applicant shall be notified in writing and the reasons shall be explained.

Article 13 A travel agency shall, within 3 working days from the date of obtaining the travel agency's business operation license, open a special quality deposit account at the bank designated by the tourism administration department under the State Council, deposit the quality deposit, or submit a bank guarantee with a legally obtained amount of guarantee no less than the corresponding amount of quality deposit to the tourism administration department that issues the license. Travel agencies operating domestic and inbound tourism businesses shall deposit a quality guarantee deposit of 200 thousand RMB; The travel agencies operating the outbound

---

① 《旅行社条例》，国家文化和旅游部网站，https://zwgk.mct.gov.cn/zfxxgkml/zcfg/xzfg/202012/t2020120，2023/2/9。

证金的利息属于旅行社所有。

第十五条 有下列情形之一的,旅游行政管理部门可以使用旅行社的质量保证金:

(一)旅行社违反旅游合同约定,侵害旅游者合法权益,经旅游行政管理部门查证属实的;

(二)旅行社因解散、破产或者其他原因造成旅游者预交旅游费用损失的。

第十七条 旅行社自交纳或者补足质量保证金之日起三年内未因侵害旅游者合法权益受到行政机关罚款以上处罚的,旅游行政管理部门应当将旅行社质量保证金的交存数额降低50%,并向社会公告。旅行社可凭省、自治区、直辖市旅游行政管理部门出具的凭证减少其质量保证金。

第十八条 旅行社在旅游行政管理部门使用质量保证金赔偿旅游者的损失,或者依法减少质量保证金后,因侵害旅游者合法权益受到行政机关罚款以上处罚的,应当在收到旅游行政管理部门补交质量保证金的通知之日起5个工作日内补足质量保证金。

第二十五条 经营出境旅游业务的旅行社不得组织旅游者到国务院旅游行政主管部门公布的中国公民出境旅游目的地之外的国家和地区旅游。

8.4 出境旅游的构成部分

出境旅游是中国入境旅游业务、国内旅游业务、出境旅游业务三种旅游业务中出现最晚的一种旅游业务。中国公民出境旅游由港澳台游、出国游、边境游三大部分组成。

tour shall deposit an additional 1. 2 million RMB as the quality deposit. The interest of the quality deposit belongs to the travel agency.

Article 15 Under any of the following circumstances, the tourism administrative department may use the quality deposit of the travel agencies:

(1) The travel agency violates the travel contract and infringes upon the legitimate rights and interests of tourists, which is verified by the tourism administrative department;

(2) The loss of tourists' prepaid traveling expenses has been caused by the dissolution, bankruptcy or other reasons of the travel agency.

Article 17 If a travel agency has not been fined or punished by the administrative organ for violating the legitimate rights and interests of tourists within three years from the date of paying or making up the quality deposit, the tourism administrative department shall reduce the amount of the quality deposit of the travel agency by 50% and deliver a public announcement. The travel agency may reduce its quality deposit by the certificate issued by the tourism administrative department of the province, autonomous region or municipality directly under the Central Government.

Article 18 After the tourism administrative department employs the quality deposit to compensate for the loss of tourists, or reduces the quality deposit according to law, if the travel agency is fined or punished by the administrative organ for infringing on the legitimate rights and interests of tourists, it shall make up the quality deposit within 5 working days from the date of receiving the notice from the tourism administrative department to make up the quality deposit.

Article 25 The travel agencies operating the outbound tour shall not organize tourists to travel to countries and regions other than the outbound tour destinations of Chinese citizens announced by the tourism administration department of the State Council.

8.4 Components of outbound tour

The outbound tour is the latest mode of tour among China's inbound tour, domestic tour and outbound tour. Chinese citizens' outbound tour consists of the Hong Kong, Macao and Taiwan tour, overseas tour and border tour.

The Hong Kong and Macao tour is the first kind of outbound tour launched by Chinese mainland. In November 1983, Guangdong Province was the first to allow its residents

港澳游是中国内地率先开办的出境旅游业务。1983 年 11 月,广东省最先开放该省居民赴香港探亲旅游。1984 年,国务院批准开放内地居民赴港澳地区的探亲旅游。

1987 年 11 月,国家旅游局和对外经济贸易部批准了辽宁省丹东市对朝鲜新义州市的"一日游",开始了中国边境旅游的发展。其后,国家相继批准了在黑龙江、内蒙古、辽宁、吉林、新疆、云南、广西等省、自治区与俄罗斯、蒙古、朝鲜、哈萨克斯坦、吉尔吉斯斯坦、缅甸、老挝、越南等国家开展边境旅游。为统一规范对边境旅游的管理,1996 年 3 月 8 日,国务院批复了《边境旅游暂行管理办法》,1997 年 10 月 15 日由国家旅游局、外交部、公安部、海关总署联合发布施行。该办法中规定,我国公民均可参加边境旅游,这标志着中国边境旅游发展开始进入成熟期。

1988 年,为了满足归侨、侨眷及相关人员的探亲需要,经国务院批准,规定由海外亲友付费、担保,允许公民赴泰国探亲旅游。这是我国出国旅游的起点。其后,在 1992 年 10 月,增加新加坡、马来西亚;1992 年 7 月,增加菲律宾为探亲旅游目的地。

1997 年 7 月 1 日,经国务院批准,由国家旅游局和公安部联合发布的《中国公民自费出国旅游管理暂行办法》正式实施。它标志着出国旅游开始走向成熟发展的阶段,中国出境旅游业务全面展开。更重要的是,它标志着中国旅游业初步形成了入境旅游、国内旅游、出境旅游三足鼎立的市场格局。该办法确定了国家关于出国旅游的发展原则:有组织、有计划、有控制。有组织是指中国公民自费出国须以团队形式进行,不办理散客出国旅游业务,要求整团出入国境;有计划是指国家根据入境

to visit relatives in Hong Kong. In 1984, the State Council approved family visits of Chinese mainland residents in Hong Kong and Macau regions.

In November 1987, National Tourism Administration and Ministry of Foreign Economic Relations and Trade approved the "one-day tour" from Dandong City, Liaoning Province, to Sinuiju City, DPRK, and began the development of China's border tour. Since then, China has successively approved the development of the border tour in Heilongjiang, Inner Mongolia, Liaoning, Jilin, Xinjiang, Yunnan, Guangxi and other provinces and autonomous regions with Russia, Mongolia, DPRK, Kazakhstan, Kyrgyzstan, Myanmar, Laos, Vietnam and other countries. In order to standardize the management of the border tour, the State Council approved *The Interim Measures for the Administration of Border Tour* on March 8, 1996, which was jointly issued and implemented by the National Tourism Administration, the Ministry of Foreign Affairs, the Ministry of Public Security and the General Administration of Customs on October 15, 1997. The measures stipulate that all Chinese citizens can participate in the border tour, which marks the beginning of the mature period of China's border tour development.

In 1988, in order to satisfy the needs of returned overseas Chinese, the family members of overseas Chinese and relevant persons to visit their relatives, the State Council stipulated that Chinese citizens were allowed to visit relatives and travel in Thailand with payment and guarantee made from overseas relatives and friends. This is the starting point of China's outbound tour. Subsequently, in October 1992, Singapore and Malaysia were added; in July 1992, the Philippines was increased as a tour destination of the same kind.

On July 1, 1997, *The Interim Measures for the Administration of Chinese Citizens Traveling Abroad at Their Own Expenses*, jointly issued by the National Tourism Administration and the Ministry of Public Security, was officially implemented with the approval of the State Council. It marks the beginning of the mature development of the outbound tour, and China's outbound tour was in full swing. More importantly, it marks a tripartite market pattern of the inbound tour, domestic tour and outbound tour that China's tourism industry has initially formed. The measures define the national development principles for the outbound tour: organized, planned and controlled. "Organized" means that Chinese citizens must go abroad as a group at their own expense; travel agencies do not deal with the individual's outbound tour; and the whole group is required to enter and leave a country together; "planned" means that our country determines the scale of the outbound tour each year according

旅游的人数和创汇额,考虑国内市场的需求,确定每年出国旅游的规模,以保证旅游业外汇收入的增长大于支出;有控制是指对出境旅游实行总量控制和配额管理,并对特许经营出国旅游业务的旅行社进行审批和数量控制。

to the number of inbound tourists and the amount of foreign exchange earned, taking into account the needs of the domestic market, so as to ensure that the growth of foreign exchange income of the tourism industry is greater than the expenditure; "controlled" refers to the implementation of total amount control and quota management of the outbound tour, and the approval and quantity control of travel agencies that are franchised to operate the outbound tour.

8.5 出境旅游知识链接

出境旅游:组团社组织的以团队旅游的方式,前往中国公布的旅游目的地国家/地区的旅行游览活动。

出境旅游产品:组团社为出境旅游者提供的旅游线路及其相应服务。

出境旅游合同:组团社与旅游者(团)双方共同签署并遵守、约定双方权利和义务的合同。

同业合作:组团社之间互为代理对方的出境旅游产品,或者组团社委托其零售商代理销售其出境旅游产品并代为招徕出境旅游者的业务合作活动。①

✂ **ETIAS(欧洲旅行信息和授权系统)**

欧洲于 2023 年推出了新的免签证系统。欧洲旅行信息和授权系统(ETIAS)允许游客在申根区内旅行90 天。符合条件的国家的公民可以出差、过境、旅游、接受医疗服务或进行商务活动。从 2023 年开始,游客必须申请欧洲旅行信息和授权系统豁免签证。该计划增强了申根区 27 个成员国的安全。欧洲旅行信息和授权系统已用于预先筛选希望前往欧洲的个人。然而,如果计划在欧洲学习或工

8.5 Knowledge link of outbound tour

Outbound tour: It is a group tour organized by the tour wholesaler to the countries/regions among the tourist destinations announced by China.

Outbound tour product: It refers to the tour routes and corresponding services provided by the tour wholesaler for outbound tourists.

Outbound tour contract: It refers to the contract signed and observed by the tour wholesaler and the tourist (group) and where both parties agree on their rights and obligations.

Travel agencies' community cooperation: It refers to business cooperation activities in which the tour wholesalers act as agents for each other's outbound tour products, or the tour wholesalers entrust their retailers to sell their outbound tour products and attract outbound tourists.

✂ **ETIAS (The European Travel Information and Authorization System)②**

Europe launched a new Visa Waiver System in 2023. ETIAS permits visitors to travel within the Schengen Zone for a period of 90 days. Citizens of the eligible countries can travel for business, transit, tourism, health, or commerce. Starting from 2023, they have had to apply for an ETIAS visa waiver. This program has increased security within the Schengen region's 27 members. The European Travel Information and Authorization System (also known as ETIAS) is used for pre-screening individuals who wish to travel to Europe. If you plan to study or work in Europe, however, you will need a student

---

① 国家旅游局 2002 年发布的《旅行社出境旅游服务质量》,界定了以上几个概念。
② What is ETIAS? https://www.eurovisa.info/, 2022/7/9,略有修改。

作,你需要一个学生或工作签证。为了确定是否准备好前往欧洲,无论是商务旅行还是休闲旅行,旅行者必须首先查看欧洲旅行信息和授权系统要求。欧洲旅行信息和授权系统适用于所有符合条件的国家的公民。你必须持有有效的护照。

or work visa. To determine if you are ready to travel to Europe, whether for business or leisure, the traveler must first check the ETIAS requirements. ETIAS is available to citizens of all eligible countries. You must have a valid passport. It is important to plan for this change as soon as possible.

8.6 出境旅游需要的证件

8.6 Documents required for outbound tour

出境旅游需要的证件包括:护照、签证、国际预防接种证明书和国际旅行健康证等。

法律依据:《中华人民共和国出境入境管理法》第九条 中国公民出境入境,应当依法申请办理护照或者其他旅行证件。

中国公民前往其他国家或者地区,还需要取得前往国签证或者其他入境许可证明。但是,中国政府与其他国家政府签订互免签证协议或者公安部、外交部另有规定的除外。

Documents required for the outbound tour include passports, visas, international vaccination certificates and health certificates for international travel.

Legal basis: Article 9 of *The Exit and Entry Administration Law* stipulates that Chinese citizens shall apply for passports or other travel documents according to law. Chinese citizens who travel to other countries or regions also need to obtain visas or other entry permits for the country of destination. However, if the Chinese government has signed visa exemption agreements with other governments or the Ministry of Public Security and the Ministry of Foreign Affairs have otherwise stipulated, you do not have to apply for a visa.

8.6.1 护照和护照申办程序

8.6.1 Passport and passport application procedure

护照是一个国家的公民出入本国国境和到国外旅行或居留时,由本国发放的一种证明该公民国籍和身份的合法证件。2018年9月1日起,中国全国异地可换补护照。自2019年4月1日起,中华人民共和国普通护照实行"全国通办",即内地居民可在全国任一出入境管理窗口申请办理出入境证件,申办手续与户籍地一致。

申请人需要提交居民身份证、户口簿及复印件;在居民身份证领取、换领、补领期间,可以提交临时居民身份证。未满16周岁的居民携带本人户口簿(集体户口提交《常住人口登记表》)、其监护人居民身份证原件以及能证明监护关系材料的原件(如户口

A passport is a legal document issued by a country to prove the nationality and identity of a citizen when he/she enters or leaves the country and travels or stays abroad. From September 1, 2018, passports can be replaced and reissued in a place other than one's own hometown across China. From April 1, 2019, the ordinary passports of the People's Republic of China (PRC) will be subject to "nationwide unified application", that is, the residents of Chinese mainland can apply for exit and entry certificates at any exit and entry management window in the country, and the application procedures are the same as those of the registered residence.

The applicant's resident identity card, household register and its photocopy need to be submitted, and temporary resident identity cards may be submitted during the period of receiving, renewing and reapplying for resident ID cards. Residents under the age of 16 should bring their own household register (persons with the collective household

簿、出生证等），并由其监护人陪同前往办理。①

中华人民共和国往来港澳通行证旧版（2015年之前）封面蓝色，为五年有效，需要签注。新版为卡式，有效期10年。

持中国公民有效护照经香港前往其他国家或地区的过境旅客，若符合一般的入境规定，包括持有前往目的地的有效入境证件及在海外旅行所需的续程机票和船票，可在每次入境时在港逗留七天。

8.6.2 签证的申请

签证是一国政府机关依照本国法律规定为申请入出或通过本国的外国人颁发的一种许可证明。签证一般都签注在护照上，也有的签注在代替护照的其他旅行证件上，有的还颁发另纸签证（单独签注在一张专用纸上，但必须和护照同时使用）。随着科技的进步，有些国家已经开始签发电子签证和生物签证，大大增强了签证的防伪功能。个人签证指在每个申请人的护照或其他国际旅行证件上的签证。团体签证是指在一个团体名单上的签证。持用同一团体签证的人员必须随团一同入出境。②

签证除了有效期、停留期之外，还规定有效次数。一般分为一次有效签证、两次和多次有效签证等。一次有效签证是指该签证在有效期内，使用一次就失效。两次有效签证，即在签

register should submit the Permanent Resident Registration Form), the original of their guardian's resident ID card and the original materials that can prove the guardianship (such as the household register, birth certificate, etc.), and be accompanied by their guardian to go through the formalities.

PRC's Exit/Entry Permit for Traveling to and from Hong Kong and Macao: the old version (before 2015) with a blue cover is valid for five years and requires endorsement; the new version is a card with a validity of 10 years.

The transit passengers who pass through Hong Kong with valid passports of Chinese citizens to other countries or regions may stay in Hong Kong for seven days at the time of each entry if they satisfy the general entry requirements, including holding valid entry documents to the destination, onward air tickets and ship tickets required for overseas travel.

8.6.2 Visa application

The visa is a permit issued by a government agency of a country for foreigners who apply for entry to or exit from or pass through the country in accordance with the provisions of the country's laws. Visas are generally endorsed on passports, some on other travel documents instead of passports, and some are issued with separate paper visas (a kind of visa signed on a special piece of paper separately, but it must be used together with the passport). With the progress of science and technology, some countries have begun to issue electronic visas and biological visas, greatly enhancing the anti-counterfeiting function of visas. The individual visa refers to the visa on each applicant's passport or other international travel documents. The group visa refers to the visa on a group list. Persons holding the same group visa must enter and leave a country with the group.

In addition to the period of validity and the duration of the stay, the visa also stipulates the number of entry times. It is generally divided into visas for one entry, visas for two entries and visas for multiple entries. Visas for one entry can be used once within the validity period. Visas for two entries can be used twice within the validity period of the visa. The visa for

① 《普通护照签发服务指南》，国家移民管理局政务服务平台，https://s.nia.gov.cn/mps/bszy/gmcrg/slpthz/201903/t20190313_1011.html，2023/5/16。
② 出国签证，中国领事服务网，http://cs.mfa.gov.cn/zggmcg/cgqz/cgqzjj_660464/，2023/5/16。

证有效期内可以使用两次。多次有效签证,即在签证有效期内持照人可以多次出、入其国境。

multiple entries means that within the validity period of the visa, the holder can enter and leave a country many times.

8.6.3 港澳的签注

签注是进入港澳地区的入境许可。如果是港澳游,在前往港澳之前必须取得内地公安部门签发的前往港澳的签注。签注分为探亲签注(T)、商务签注(S)、团队旅游签注(L)、个人旅游签注(G)、其他签注(Q)和逗留签注(D)。

持证人必须持有港澳通行证并在签注有效期内,按照规定的次数和停留时限往来香港和澳门。个人旅游签注(G):目前有49个城市的居民可以"个人游"的身份前往香港旅游。旅游签注可以分为三个月或一年,一次、两次或多次(仅限深圳户籍,有效期为一年)有效,每次可以逗留七天。团队旅游签注(L):团队旅游签注可以分为三个月一次或两次、一年一次或两次,每次可以逗留七天,需随团出入境。①

8.6.3 Endorsement of Hong Kong and Macao

The endorsement is the entry permit for entering Hong Kong and Macao. If you are traveling to Hong Kong and Macao, you must obtain the endorsement issued by the public security department of Chinese mainland before going to Hong Kong and Macao. Endorsements include the family visit endorsement (T), business endorsement (S), group travel endorsement (L), personal travel endorsement (G), other endorsements (Q) and endorsement for staying (D).

The bearer must hold an Exit/Entry Permit for Traveling to and from Hong Kong and Macao and, within the period of validity of the endorsement, travel between Hong Kong and Macao according to the prescribed number of times and duration of the stay. Individual travel endorsement (G): At present, residents of 49 cities can travel to Hong Kong as "individual tourists". Tourism endorsement can be divided into three months or one year in terms of the period of validity, once, twice or more (only for registered residence in Shenzhen, valid for one year) in terms of the entry times, and visitors can stay for seven days each time. Group travel endorsement (L): The group travel endorsement can be divided into one time or two times within three months and one time or two times within one year. Each time visitors can stay for seven days, and it is necessary to enter and exit with the group.

8.6.4 申根签证

申根签证是一种短期停留签证,允许个人前往申根区的任何成员国,每次停留最多90天,用于旅游或商务目的。申根签证是欧洲最常见的签证。它使其持有人能够从任何申根成员国进入申根区、在申根区内自由旅

8.6.4 Schengen visa

A Schengen visa is a short-stay visa that allows a person to travel to any member of the Schengen Area, per stay up to 90 days for tourism or business purposes. The Schengen visa is the most common visa for Europe. It enables its holder to enter, freely travel within, and leave the Schengen Zone from any of the Schengen member countries. There are no border controls within the Schengen Zone.

---

① 《往来港澳通行证和签注签发服务指南》,国家移民管理局政务服务平台,https://s. nia. gov. cn/mps/bszy/wlgaot/sqgowl/201903/t20190313_1002. html,2023/5/16。

行和离开申根区。申根区内没有边境管制。①

1985 年 6 月 14 日签署的《申根协定》是一项导致大多数欧洲国家废除国家边界的条约,旨在建立一个被称为"申根区"的无边界欧洲。该协议最初只有五个欧盟国家在卢森堡签署,该协议所涵盖的地区现在仍然是世界上最大的终止成员国之间边境管制的地区之一。该协议由五个欧洲国家——法国、德国、比利时、卢森堡和荷兰,在位于卢森堡南部的一个小村庄——申根签署。申根区的真正实施终于在 1995 年 3 月 26 日开始,7 个申根成员国——法国、德国、比利时、卢森堡、荷兰、葡萄牙和西班牙决定取消其内部边境检查。

截至 2023 年 1 月,申根的成员国增加到 27 个:奥地利、比利时、丹麦、芬兰、法国、德国、冰岛、意大利、希腊、卢森堡、荷兰、挪威、葡萄牙、西班牙、瑞典、匈牙利、捷克、斯洛伐克、斯洛文尼亚、波兰、爱沙尼亚、拉脱维亚、立陶宛、瑞士、列支敦士登、马耳他、克罗地亚。②

▶❂ 8.6.4.1 申根签证办理所需材料

1.护照和先前的签证记录:必须提供有效护照和护照上所有签证记录的复印件。

2.签证申请表:可以从相关大使馆或领事馆网站上下载。需要白底彩照 2 张,尺寸为 3.5 厘米×4.5 厘米。

3.旅游行程表:包括日期、旅游景点、住宿、交通等信息。

4.往返机票订票单:国际机票售

The Schengen Agreement signed on June 14, 1985 is a treaty that led most of the European countries towards the abolishment of their national borders and to build a Europe without borders, known as the "Schengen Area". The agreement was signed in Luxembourg, initially by only five EU countries and the area covered remains one of the world's biggest areas that have ended border control between member countries. The Agreement was signed by the five European countries—France, Germany, Belgium, Luxembourg, and the Netherlands—in Schengen, a small village in Southern Luxembourg. The real implementation of the Schengen Area finally started on March 26 1995, where 7 Schengen member countries—France, Germany, Belgium, Luxembourg, the Netherlands, Portugal, and Spain decided to abolish their internal border checks.

As of January 2023, the member states of the Schengen visa have increased to 27 countries: Austria, Belgium, Denmark, Finland, France, Germany, Iceland, Italy, Greece, Luxembourg, the Netherlands, Norway, Portugal, Spain, Sweden, Hungary, the Czech Republic, Slovakia, Slovenia, Poland, Estonia, Latvia, Lithuania, Switzerland, Liechtenstein, Malta and Croatia.

▶❂ 8.6.4.1 Materials required for Schengen visa application

1. Passport and previous visa records: A valid passport and all visa records of the passport must be provided.

2. Visa application form: It can be downloaded from the website of the relevant embassy or consulate. Two color photos on a white background, measuring 3.5 cm × 4.5 cm are needed.

3. Tour itinerary: including dates, scenic spots, accommodation, transportation, and other information.

4. Round-trip air ticket booking form: It can be offered by the booking office or ticket agent for international flight tickets.

---

① Schengen Visa Information,https://www.schengenvisainfo.com/,2023/5/16.
② Schengen Agreement,https://www.schengenvisainfo.com/schengen-agreement/,2023/5/16.

票处或者机票代理均可出具。

5.签证保险一份:保险金额为三万欧元或三十万人民币以上,需覆盖旅行全程。旅行社可以代旅游者购买该保险,费用另计。

6.在职证明原件和英语版本:需出具单位在职证明原件(列明申请人的职务、入职时间、月薪及准假等信息,用所在单位抬头信纸打印,加盖公章)和英语版本。退休人士需提供退休证原件以及复印件。

7.户口簿:需提供原件和复印件。

8.个人经济担保:有效的存款证明,或房产证等。

9.身份证:需要原件及复印件。

8.6.4.2　申根签证的申请办法

1.申根签证的短期入境 C 类签证,允许有效期内一次、两次或多次入境。

2.只前往某一申根成员国,应申办该国的申根签证。

3.前往几个申根成员国,应申办主要访问成员国或停留时间最长的成员国的申根签证;无法确定主访国时,申请即将访问的第一个国家的申根签证。

4.在入境申根国前所有申请人必须事先购买并出示医疗保险,保额至少 3 万欧元。

5.若被拒签,不退签证费,然而可以申诉。

8.6.5　赴美国旅游签证申请所需材料

1.填写非移民签证电子申请表(DS-160)。

2.因私护照原件,护照有效期需

5. Visa insurance：The insurance amount is more than 30 000 euros or 300 000 RMB, which needs to cover the whole trip. Travel agencies can purchase the insurance for tourists at an additional cost.

6. The original on-the-job certificate and English version：The original on-the-job certificate of the organization in which one works and its English translation shall be provided (stating the applicant's position, time of entry, monthly salary and leave approval, etc., printed on the paper with the letterhead of the organization in which one works and stamped with the official seal). The retiree shall provide the original and photocopy of the retirement certificate.

7. Household register：Both the original and its photocopy are required.

8. Personal financial guarantee：the valid bank statement or property certificate, etc.

9. ID card：Both the original and its photocopy are required.

8.6.4.2　Application approaches to Schengen visa

1. Type C of the Schengen visa is for short-term entry that allows for one, two, or more entries during its validity period.

2. If you only travel to a certain Schengen member country, you should apply for a Schengen visa for that country.

3. To travel to several Schengen member states, one should apply for a Schengen visa for the main visiting member state or the member state with the longest stay; when the host country cannot be determined, apply for a Schengen visa for the first country to be visited.

4. All applicants must purchase and present medical insurance for a minimum amount of 30 000 euros before entering a Schengen member state.

5. If the visa is refused, the visa fee will not be refunded, but an appeal can be made.

8.6.5　Materials required for applying for a tourist visa to the United States

1. Fill in the electronic application form for the non-immigrant visa (DS-160).

2. The original passport for private use must be valid for more than 6 months, and the passport must be signed. The

要在 6 个月以上,护照后需有本人签名;持换发护照者,需提供所有旧护照原件,护照后也需有本人签名。

3. 提交一张 2 寸的近半年拍摄的不戴眼镜的白底彩照。

4. 身份证原件和身份证正反面复印件、申请人户口本原件和整本复印件。已婚人员和离异人员需分别提供结婚证原件和离婚证原件。

5. 提交资产证明,包括当前收入证明、房产证、购车证、企业产权证等。提供至少 10 万元的存折或存单或有价证券原件及复印件(活期存折需显示半年以上的交易记录,定期存单的存期应在半年以上,银行卡需打印至少半年以上的对账单明细并加盖银行业务用章)。

6. 旅游行程表和/或其他有关旅行计划的说明。

7. 需出具单位在职证明原件(列明申请人的职务、入职时间、月薪及准假等信息,用所在单位抬头信纸打印,加盖公章)。

8. 单位营业执照复印件加盖公章(若所在单位为政府部门、事业单位、大型企业可不提供)。

9. 非在职人士需提供街道出具的居住证明、经济依附人的存款证明及收入证明、与经济依附人的关系证明。

10. 退休人士需提供退休证原件以及复印件、退休福利证明文件原件以及复印件(如退休金、医疗补助等)。

11. 不满 18 岁人士、在校学生需提供学校出具的准假证明原件及学生证复印件。

12. 缴纳签证申请费用。

holder of a new passport shall provide the original of all the old passports, and the passports shall also be signed.

3. Submit a 2-inch white-background color photo without glasses taken in the last half year.

4. The original ID card and the copy of the front and back of the ID card, the original and full copy of the applicant's household register shall be provided; married and divorced persons shall provide the original marriage certificate and divorce certificate respectively.

5. Submit the asset certificate, including the proof of current income, real estate certificate, car purchase certificate, enterprise property right certificate, etc. Provide the original and photocopy of a bankbook or deposit receipt or negotiable securities of at least 100 000 RMB (the checking account shall display the transaction record of more than half a year; the deposit period of the saving account shall be more than half a year; one shall print the statement details of the bank card for at least half a year and affix the bank business seal).

6. Tour itinerary and/or other relevant travel plans.

7. The original on-the-job certificate of the organization in which one works shall be provided (stating the applicant's position, time of entry, monthly salary and leave approval, etc. printed on the paper with the letterhead of the organization in which one works and stamped with the official seal).

8. A copy of the business license of the organization in which one works stamped with the official seal (not required if the organization is a government department, public institution or large enterprise) shall be provided.

9. The unemployed shall provide the proof of residence issued by the neighborhood committee, the bank statement and proof of income of the person to depend on financially and proof of relationship between them.

10. The retiree shall provide the original and photocopy of the retirement certificate as well as the original and photocopy of the certificate of retirement benefits (such as the pension, medical subsidy, etc.)

11. Persons under the age of 18 and students at school shall provide the original leave of absence issued by the school and the photocopy of the student ID card.

12. Pay the visa application fee.

8.6.6　知识拓展①

◐ 申根签证所需要的旅游保险

问：我买保险是用于办理签证的，购买的时候应该注意哪些事项？

答：（1）为了使您的签证更加顺利，建议您选择旅行日期时延长2天的出行天数。（一般情况下意大利要求前后各延长2天，比利时使馆要求结尾延长2天。具体天数请以领事馆要求或者信件通知为准。）

（2）我们将为每位被保险人单独出具保单。

（3）按照使领馆要求"申根签证保险的医疗保险金额保障不得低于3万欧元"，欧洲签证旅游保险医疗费用补偿全部在3万欧元以上，您可以任意选择套餐。

（4）本产品提供的电子保单格式规范并附有公司签章，经彩色打印后可用于办理签证（具体以使馆要求为准）。请您使用彩色激光打印机在普通A4纸上打印此保单，请勿使用喷墨打印机进行打印。建议您提前准备一份保单复印件给使馆备份。

问：在境外出险，如何获取紧急援助？

答：24小时全球援助热线：＋86 7559 5511。

出险后请您拨打全球援助热线报案，以便保险公司和救援公司尽快为您提供医疗救援服务。若未拨打救援热线报案而自行处理，可能将无法理赔。

问：如果签证拒签，我该如何退保？

答：（1）保险生效前，未索要纸质保单及发票，可登录"会员中心"办理退保。

8.6.6　Knowledge expansion

◐ Tourism insurance required by Schengen visa

Q：I am going to buy insurance for visa application. What should I pay attention to when purchasing it?

A：(1) In order to make your visa application smoother, it is recommended to extend the travel time by 2 days when choosing a travel date. In general, Italy requires an extension of 2 days before and after the trip, while the Belgian embassy requests an extension of 2 days after the trip. The specific number of days should be determined by the consulate's request or letter of notification.

(2) We will issue a separate policy for each insured person.

(3) According to the requirements of the embassy and consulate, the medical insurance amount for Schengen visa insurance shall not be less than 30 000 euros. Our medical expense compensation for tourism insurance in application for the European visa shall be over 30 000 euros, so you can choose any package.

(4) The electronic insurance policy provided by this product has a standardized format with the company's signature and seal. After color printing, it can be used to apply for a visa (subject to the requirements of the embassy). Please use a color laser printer to print this policy on regular A4 paper. Do not use an inkjet printer for printing. We suggest that you prepare a copy of the insurance policy in advance for the embassy to backup.

Q: How can I obtain emergency assistance in case of an overseas accident?

A：24-hour global assistance hotline：＋86 7559 5511.

When an accident arises, please call the global assistance hotline to report the case, so that the insurance company and rescue company can provide you with medical services as soon as possible. If you handle the case without calling the rescue hotline, you may not be able to settle the claim.

Q: If my visa is refused, how should I withdraw it?

A：(1) Before the insurance takes effect, if you do not request a paper policy and invoice, you can log in to the "Member Center" to process the cancellation.

---

① 下载自平安保险网站，英语版本为编写者翻译，https://baoxian. pingan. com/pa18shopnst/quote/pc/index. html＃/ZP020414？ bd_vid=6644752543975424857&.WT. mc_id=T00-LYBD1-PPC-000652，2023/5/16。

（2）保险生效前，已索要纸质保单及发票，请携带拒签证明、纸质保单、发票、投保人身份证、投保人借记卡至当地平安门店办理全额批退，详情可致电：4008895512＊2客服咨询。

问：保险起期如何选择？

答：由于使馆要求或时差原因，为保证您的签证可以更加顺利地办理，建议选择的保险起止期在您的出行日期的基础上前后各增加两天，例如：出行日期为5月3日至5月10日，建议选择保险起止期为5月1日至5月12日，具体以领事馆要求为准。

问：如去多个国家，该如何选择目的地？

答：投保境外旅游保险后，在全世界各国家和地区（除不承保地区外）均可享受保障。填写目的地国家时只需填写主目的地国家或主签国＋申根国家即可，无需选择全部目的地国家。（最新不承保地区信息以登录 http://baoxian. pingan. com/dangerous_zone/war. shtml 的查询结果为准。）

问：多人出行必须分多次为每人投保吗？

答：不需要。您一次最多可为50人投保，我们将为每位被保险人单独出具保单。如需为多于50人投保，可在确认50人保险信息并生成投保申请号后关闭页面，重新填写其他人的投保信息后进入网站会员专区，将待支付保单合并支付，多张保单，只支付一次，为您的投保节省时间。

备注：平安欧洲签证旅游保险E款二代（单次）（互联网版）：经济型58元。

（2）Before the insurance takes effect，if you have requested a paper policy and invoice，please bring the refusal certificate，paper policy，invoice，policyholder's ID card，and policyholder's debit card to the local Ping'an store to process a full refund. For more information，please call customer service 4008895512 * 2 for consultation.

Q：How should I choose the insurance starting period?

A：Due to embassy requirements or time differences，in order to ensure that your visa can be processed more smoothly，it is recommended to choose the insurance's starting and ending dates two days earlier and later than your travel dates. For example，if the travel dates are from May 3rd to May 10th，it is recommended to choose the insurance's starting and ending period from May 1st to May 12th，which is subject to the requirements of the consulate.

Q：How should I choose a destination if going to multiple countries?

A：After applying for overseas tourism insurance，you can enjoy protection in various countries and regions around the world（except for non insured areas）. When filling in the destination country，you only need to fill in the main destination country or the main signatory country＋Schengen country，without selecting all destination countries. The latest information for non insured regions can be accessed at http://baoxian. pingan. com/dangerous_zone/war. shtml. The search results shall prevail.

Q：Do I have to insure one person at a time in multiple trips?

A：No. You can insure up to 50 people at a time，and we will issue a separate policy for each insured person. If you need to purchase insurance for more than 50 people，you can close the page after confirming the insurance information of 50 people and the system generating the insurance application number. After filling in the insurance information of the other people，you can enter the website's membership section and combine the payment of the policies to be settled. Multiple policies can be paid only once.

Note：Second generation of Type E of Ping'an tourism insurance（single time）required by application of the European visa（internet version）：economy type 58 RMB.

❋ Exercises

Ⅰ. Fill in the blanks with proper forms of words.

1. If a travel agency _____ (obtain) a business license for more than two years and has not been fined or _____ (punish) by the administrative organ for _____ (infringe) upon the legitimate rights and interests of tourists, it may apply for _____ (operate) of the outbound tour.

2. The travel agencies _____ (operate) the outbound tour shall not organize tourists to travel to countries and regions other than the outbound tour destinations of Chinese citizens _____ (announce) by the tourism administration department of the State Council.

3. A passport is a legal document _____ (issue) by a country to prove the nationality and identity of a citizen when he/she _____ (enter) or _____ (leave) the country and travels or stays abroad.

4. The Schengen Agreement _____ (sign) on June 14, 1985 is a treaty that led most of the European countries towards the _____ (abolish) of their national borders and to build a Europe without borders, _____ (know) as the "Schengen Area".

Ⅱ. Translate the following Chinese sentences into English.

1. 签证一般都签注在护照上,也有的签注在代替护照的其他旅行证件上,有的还颁发另纸签证(单独签注在一张专用纸上,但必须和护照同时使用)。

2. 多次有效签证,即在签证有效期内持照人可以多次出、入其国境。

3. 香港团队旅游签注可以分为三个月一次或两次、一年一次或两次,每次可以逗留七天,需随团出入境。

4. 随着科技的进步,有些国家已经开始签发电子签证和生物签证,大大增强了签证的防伪功能。

Ⅲ. Translate the following English sentences into Chinese.

1. A Schengen visa is a short-stay visa that allows a person to travel to any member of the Schengen Area, per stay up to 90 days for tourism or business purposes. The Schengen visa is the most common visa for Europe. It enables its holder to enter, freely travel within, and leave the Schengen Zone from any of the Schengen member countries. There are no border controls within the Schengen Zone.

2. The Schengen Agreement signed on June 14, 1985 is a treaty that led most of the European countries towards the abolishment of their national borders and to build a Europe without borders, known as the "Schengen Area".

3. Europe will launch a new Visa Waiver System in 2023. ETIAS will permit visitors to travel within the Schengen Zone for a period of 90 days. Citizens of the eligible countries can travel for business, transit, tourism, health, or commerce. From 2023, they will have to apply for an ETIAS visa waiver.

4. Due to embassy requirements or time differences, in order to ensure that your visa can be processed more smoothly, it is recommended to choose the insurance's starting and ending dates two days earlier and later than your travel dates.

Ⅳ. Questions and answers.

1. If a travel agency located in a certain city or county does not have the qualification to operate the outbound tour, can customers register for the outbound tour there?

2. If transit passengers who pass through Hong Kong with valid passports of Chinese citizens to other countries or regions join a 15-day tour to Singapore，Malaysia，Thailand and Hong Kong，do they have to show other materials besides a passport?

第❾单元　出境旅游业务(2)
Unit ❾　Outbound Tour Business(2)

📖 **教学目标**

⇨ 掌握出境旅游报价的基本程序
⇨ 掌握出境计调业务操作程序
⇨ 掌握出境游成团业务操作程序
⇨ 掌握境外接团社的选择与管理方法
⇨ 掌握出境旅游组团社与境外接团社
　合同范本
⇨ 掌握预订机票的注意事项

📖 **Teaching objectives**

⇨ To master the basic procedures for the quotation of the outbound tour
⇨ To master the operating procedures for planning the outbound tour
⇨ To master the operation procedures of the outbound tour group
⇨ To master the selection and management method of overseas travel agencies
⇨ To master the contract sample between the outbound tour wholesaler and overseas travel agencies
⇨ To master the precautions for booking air tickets

9.1　情景对话

🔲 **出境游报价**

> A. 中国环球旅行社的王先生
> B. 法国某旅行社的玛丽

A：早上好，我是王先生。玛丽在吗？我来自中国环球旅行社。

B：早上好，王先生，是我。今天有什么能帮你的吗？

A：我想请你报价2023年6月8日至2023年6月22日期间前往法国、意大利、瑞士、德国和卢森堡等5个西欧国家的12天旅行。团队共有36人。

B：好的，我会在30分钟后回复你。

A：(30分钟后)玛丽，你现在可以把报价单发给我吗？

B：当然可以。请稍等。

A：我收到了你的报价。然而，与另一家旅行社的报价相比，你报的价格不够有竞争力。你能为你的报价每

9.1　Situational dialogue

🔲 **Quotation of an outbound tour**

> A. Mr. Wang from Global Travel Agency in China
> B. Mary from a French travel agency

A：Good morning, this is Mr. Wang speaking. May I speak to Mary? I am from Global Travel Agency in China.

B：Good morning, Mr. Wang, it is me. How can I help you today?

A：I would like you to quote a 12-day tour to five Western European countries, including France, Italy, Switzerland, Germany and Luxembourg from June 8, 2023 to June 22, 2023. There are 36 persons in the group.

B：Okay, I will respond to you 30 minutes later.

A：(30 minutes later) Mary, could you send me the quotation now?

B：Sure. Just a second, please.

A：I got your quotation. However, compared with the quotation of another travel agency, the price you quoted is not competitive enough. Could you reduce 30 euros each person for your quotation?

人减少 30 欧元吗?

B:竞争激烈,利润很低。考虑到我们之间长期的业务关系,我将每人减少 20 欧元。

A:好的,请给我一份详细的行程表。我稍后会传真确认。

B:再见。稍后再聊。

A:再见。

9.2 角色扮演训练

任务 1:请设计新马泰港澳 15 日全包价游。该团队总共 30 人,全程要求四星级酒店,要求旅行社在泰国不安排自费旅游项目。香港为第一站,最后一站为澳门。旅游行程顺序为香港、曼谷、芭提雅、新加坡、吉隆坡、马六甲、澳门,其中福州—香港、香港—曼谷、曼谷—新加坡、吉隆坡—香港需要安排相应的航班。

各地一些景点包括:

香港:海洋公园、浅水湾、尖沙咀、维多利亚港、太平山、黄大仙庙、香港会展中心

泰国曼谷:大皇宫、玉佛寺、湄南河;**芭提雅:**格兰岛

新加坡:花芭山、鱼尾狮公园、旧高等法院、旧国会大厦、莱佛士铜像、滨海艺术中心、圣淘沙岛

马来西亚吉隆坡:黑风洞、国家英雄纪念碑、国家清真寺、苏丹皇宫(外观)、双峰塔;**云顶高原**(马来西亚最受欢迎的高原度假胜地,拥有马来西亚最大的娱乐城、体育设施);**马六甲:**荷兰红屋、圣保罗教堂、三宝庙

澳门:大三巴牌坊、妈阁庙、西望洋山、金莲花广场

任务 2:要求你设计欧洲德国、法

B: Competition is fierce and the margin is low. Considering the long-term business relationship between us, I will give you a reduction of 20 euros each person.

A: Okay, please send me a detailed itinerary as well. I will fax my confirmation a little time later.

B: Bye. Talk to you later.

A: Bye.

9.2 Role playing training

Task 1: Please design a 15-day package tour of Singapore, Malaysia, Thailand, Hong Kong and Macao. The group consists of a total of 30 people and requires a four-star hotel throughout the entire journey. The travel agency is required not to arrange self-funded tourism projects in Thailand. Hong Kong is the first stop, and the last stop is Macao. The tour itinerary sequence is Hong Kong, Bangkok, Pattaya, Singapore, Kuala Lumpur, Malacca, and Macao, with corresponding flights arranged from Fuzhou to Hong Kong, Hong Kong to Bangkok, Bangkok to Singapore, and Kuala Lumpur to Hong Kong.

Some scenic spots in the regions include:

Hong Kong: Ocean Park, Repulse Bay, Tsim Sha Tsui, Victoria Harbor, Tai Ping Shan, Wong Tai Sin Temple, Hong Kong Convention and Exhibition Center

Bangkok, Thailand: Bangkok Grand Palace, Wat Phra Kaew, Chao Phraya River; **Pattaya:** Koh Lan

Singapore: Mt. Faber, Merlion Park, Old Supreme Court, Old Parliament House, Raffles Bronze Statue, Esplanade—Theaters on the Bay, Sentosa Island

Kuala Lumpur, Malaysia: Batu Caves, National Monument, National Mosque, Sultan Palace (exterior), Petronas Twin Towers; **Genting Highlands** (the most popular plateau resort in Malaysia, boasts the largest entertainment city and sports facilities in Malaysia); **Malacca:** Dutch Square, St. Paul's Church, Sanbao Temple (a memorial temple to Zheng He, an outstanding navigator of the Ming Dynasty in China)

Macao: Ruins of St. Paul's, A-Ma Temple, Penha Hill, Golden Lotus Square

Task 2: You are requested to design a 10-day package tour

国、荷兰、比利时、卢森堡、瑞士 10 日全包价游。该团队总共 30 人。该团队起点站为福州,福州与巴黎之间往返。旅游行程顺序为福州、巴黎、卢森堡、布鲁塞尔、阿姆斯特丹、科隆、法兰克福、因特拉肯、第戎。由第戎返回巴黎后飞福州。

各国主要景点:

卢森堡:大公馆、卢森堡大峡谷、英雄纪念碑

比利时布鲁塞尔:原子塔(为 1958 年世界博览会设计)、布鲁塞尔广场、小于连雕像

荷兰阿姆斯特丹:库肯霍夫公园、水坝广场、国家纪念碑、阿姆斯特丹皇宫(外部)、新教堂(外部)

德国科隆:科隆大教堂(德国最宏伟、最完美的哥特式大教堂)

德国法兰克福:罗马贝格广场(市政厅大楼、圣保罗教堂和正义女神)

瑞士因特拉肯:瑞士中部的一个可以眺望欧洲屋脊——少女峰的小镇,也是欧洲著名的度假胜地。它以其优美的雪山、清澈的湖水、宁静的小镇和引人注目的风景而闻名。

法国巴黎:蒙帕纳斯大厦、埃菲尔铁塔、协和广场、凯旋门、卢浮宫博物馆

to Europe, including Germany, France, the Netherlands, Belgium, Luxembourg, and Switzerland. The tour group consists of a total of 30 people. The starting city of the group is Fuzhou, with a round-trip travel between Fuzhou and Paris. The tour itinerary covers Paris, Luxembourg, Brussels, Amsterdam, Cologne, Frankfurt, Interlaken and Dijon. After returning to Paris from Dijon, the group will fly to Fuzhou.

Main tourist attractions in various countries are as follows.

Luxembourg: Grand Ducal Palace, Alzette Valley, Monument of Remembrance

Brussels, Belgium: The Atomium (designed for the 1958 World Expo), Brussels Square, Manneken Pis

Amsterdam, the Netherlands: Keukenhof, Dam Square, the National Monument, Royal Palace Amsterdam (exterior), the New Church(exterior)

Cologne, Germany: Cologne Cathedral (the most magnificent and perfect Gothic cathedral in Germany)

Frankfurt, Germany: Römerberg (City Hall Building, St. Paul's Church and Statue of Justice)

Interlaken, Switzerland: a small town which commands a fine distant view of the Roof of Europe—Jungfrau in central Switzerland and a famous holiday destination in Europe. It is well-known for its graceful snowy mountains, clear lake water, quiet town, and eye-catching scenery.

Paris, France: Montparnasse Tower, the Eiffel Tower, Concorde Square, Arc de Triomphe, the Louvre Museum

9.3 出境计调业务操作程序

9.3.1 设计出境旅游产品

出境旅游产品的设计,是指根据旅游者对出境旅游产品的需求,结合旅游目的国家的旅游资源分布情况以及接待旅行社的产品设计,制作出符合旅游市场需求的产品。需要考虑旅游目的国家的签证情况是否稳定、航线是否具备条件,尽可能避开高峰期和会展高峰。可以采用旅行社现有的经典出境线路、采用境外接待社提供

9.3 Operating procedures for the planning and dispatching of outbound tour

9.3.1 Design outbound tour products

The design of outbound tourism products is to produce products that meet the needs of the tourism market by mainly considering the needs of tourists for outbound tour products and combining them with the distribution of tourism resources in the destination countries and the product design of the local tour operator. It is necessary to consider whether the visa result of the destination country is stable and whether the air route meets the conditions. Avoid the peak period and

的出境旅游线路、根据客人的具体需求设计出境旅游线路。

9.3.2 向境外旅行社询价

选择合适的境外旅行社报价至关重要。询价时需要提供所有相应信息：人数、出发日期、详细行程、酒店等级、用车要求、用餐情况、景点门票、特殊服务项目等。选择两家以上境外旅行社报价以便对比。

9.3.3 向旅游者报价

力求制作出的行程与报价能够满足旅游者对旅游天数、旅游内容与价格的要求，实现旅游者对旅游的期望。设计出多层次、多种类的旅游线路，满足不同旅游者的不同需求。出境旅游线路价格构成包括：出发城市与境外目的地城市间往返交通费、旅行社境外接待费（包括交通费、住宿费、餐费、景点门票费、导游服务费等）、签证费、领队费用、国内市内接送费用、保险费（出境旅游意外保险费通常 30 元/人，保额 30 万人民币；欧洲旅游意外保险费略高）、操作费用（利润）。①②

9.3.4 收取并审核旅游者的相关材料

1.旅游者提供本人签名的 6 个月以上的有效因私护照原件；若是换发护照需提供旧护照；有拒签史的旅游者，需要提供拒签说明。

exhibition peak as much as possible. You can use the existing classic outbound tour itinerary provided by travel agencies, the outbound tour itinerary provided by overseas tour operators, and design the outbound tour itinerary on the basis of the specific needs of customers.

9.3.2 Make inquiries to overseas travel agencies

It is very important to select the appropriate quotation of the overseas travel agency. All relevant information shall be provided in inquiry: the number of people, departure date, detailed itinerary, hotel grade, vehicle requirements, dining conditions, scenic spot tickets, special service items, etc. Select more than two overseas travel agencies for comparison.

9.3.3 Offer quotation to tourists

Strive to make the itinerary and quotation that can meet the requirements of tourists in terms of the number of days, content and price of the trip, and can meet the expectations of tourists for tourism, and design multi-level and multi-class itineraries to meet the different needs of different tourists. The price composition of the outbound tour itinerary includes: round-trip transportation fees between the departure city and the overseas destination city, the travel agency's overseas reception fees (including transportation fees, accommodation fees, meal fees, scenic spot admission fees, tour guide service fees, etc.), visa fees, fees for the outbound tour escort, domestic city transfer fees, insurance fees (the outbound tour accident insurance usually costs 30 RMB/person, with a coverage amount of 300 000 RMB; the outbound tour accident insurance for the European tour is slightly higher), and operating expenses (profits).

9.3.4 Collect and review relevant materials of tourists

1. Tourists need to provide a valid original passport for the private purpose and signed by the holder. The passport should have the validity of more than 6 months. If the passport

---

① 张春莲，盖艳秋 主编，《旅行社计调操作实务》，北京：中国旅游出版社，2017：152.

② 叶娅丽，陈学春 主编，《旅行社经营与管理》，北京：北京理工大学出版社，2018：153-156.

2.加盖单位公章的机构或企业营业执照复印件。有单位抬头的单位在职证明原件,内容包括申请人的姓名、性别、出生年月、年龄、护照号码,从何时起在本单位任职,现任职务,需负责人签名并加盖单位公章。事业单位任职人员需提供组织机构代码证复印件,加盖单位公章。

3.申请人户口簿原件与复印件(原件经确认后返还)。

4.申请人身份证原件与复印件(原件经确认后返还)。

5.申请人银行存款证明原件与复印件。如有房产证、行驶证等可提供复印件作为辅助材料;如提供配偶资产,需提供结婚证复印件。

6.学生需提供学生证或者在校证明。

7.夫妻参团需提供结婚证复印件。

8.出团前需提供保证金,具体数额根据旅游者情况而定。

9.退休人员申请时需提供退休证。

🎴 9.3.5 签订出境旅游合同

出境计调人员收齐旅游者材料并审核无误以后,与旅游者签订中国公民出境旅游合同。合同签订之后,计调员将旅游者所交团款交至财务部,出具发票给旅游者。

9.4 出境游成团业务操作

🎴 9.4.1 签证办理程序

及时将签证申请材料转交负责签证办理人员,时刻关注签证办理进展。

is changed, the old passport shall be provided; tourists with a history of visa refusal need to provide a visa refusal description.

2. A copy of the business license of an organization or enterprise with the official seal; the original of the on-the-job certificate with the letterhead of the organization or enterprise, including the name, gender, date of birth, age, passport number of the applicant, the date of employment in the organization or enterprise, and the current position, which should be signed by the person in charge and affixed with the official seal. The staff of the public institution shall provide a copy of the organization code certificate and affix the official seal of the institution.

3. The original and copy of the applicant's household register (the original will be returned after confirmation).

4. The original and copy of the applicant's ID card (the original will be returned after confirmation).

5. The original and copy of the applicant's bank statement. If there are real estate certificates, driving licenses, etc., the copies can be provided as supporting materials; if the spouse's assets are provided, a copy of the marriage certificate shall be provided.

6. Students must provide the student ID card or in-school proof.

7. A copy of the marriage certificate is required for couples to join the tourist group.

8. A deposit shall be provided before the tour, and the specific amount depends on the situation of tourists.

9. Retirees need to provide retirement certificates when applying.

🎴 9.3.5 Sign outbound tour contract

The planning and dispatching personnel for the outbound tour shall sign the outbound tour contract with the tourists after receiving the tourists' materials and verifying them. After the contract is signed, the planning and dispatching staff deliver the traveling expenses of the tourists to the finance department and issue an invoice to them.

9.4 Business operation of outbound tour group

🎴 9.4.1 Visa application procedures

Timely transfer visa application materials to the visa processing personnel and keep an eye on the progress of visa processing. If the embassy or consulate requests supplementary

若使领馆要求补充材料、面试等,需要及时通知客人。办理美国和英国等国家签证,需要先向使领馆或签证中心预约。办理签证之前需要向客人收取相关费用。①

🎴 9.4.2 核对护照页与签证页的内容是否相符

旅游团出境前,出境旅行社若发现差错需要告知相关使领馆。使领馆通知本国入境管理处,旅游者可能顺利入境。若在入境时才发现差错,使领馆不会采取措施纠错。

🎴 9.4.3 制作出境旅游团队名单表

出境旅游计调人员登录所在省旅游政务网,输入出境旅游团队名单、线路、出入境旅游时间等信息,等待旅游行政部门审核。旅游行政部门审核之后出境旅行社领取出境旅游专用团队名单表,请旅行社总经理签字,盖旅行社出境旅游专用章,然后请旅游行政部门加盖出境旅游审验章。

🎴 9.4.4 预订国内外全程机票并确认

在旅游者的旅游意向基本确定时,出境组团社计调人员应向有关航空公司落实机位情况、航班时间、机票价格、机型等是否可以满足旅游行程的需求;在与出境旅游者签订合同之后,出境组团社计调人员向航空公司传真名单(包括旅游者基本信息,如姓名、性别、出生年月、护照号码与有效期等)以及订票要求(出发和返程日期与航班号等)。② 查收航空公司的书面回复,涉及航班、人数、价格确认以及出票时间要求,与对方确认机位。

materials, interviews, etc., it is necessary to promptly notify the guests. To apply for visas to countries such as the United States and the United Kingdom, you need to make an appointment with the embassy or visa center first. Before applying for a visa, you need to charge the guest relevant fees.

🎴 9.4.2 Check whether contents of passport and visa are consistent

Before the outbound tour group leaves China, the outbound tour wholesaler should inform the relevant embassy and consulate if it finds any errors. The embassy and consulate will inform the immigration administration of its country, and tourists may enter the country smoothly. If an error is found only at the time of entry, the embassy and consulate will not take measures to correct the error.

🎴 9.4.3 Make a name list of the outbound tour group

The planning and dispatching personnel of the outbound tour wholesaler log in to the provincial tourism administration website, enter the name list of the outbound tour group, itinerary, traveling time and other information, and wait for the approval of provincial tourism administration. After the review of the provincial tourism administration, the outbound tour wholesaler shall obtain the name list of the outbound tour group, the general manager of the outbound tour wholesaler shall sign and affix the special outbound tour seal of the travel agency, and then the provincial tourism administration shall affix the outbound tour verification seal.

🎴 9.4.4 Booking and confirmation of domestic and international air tickets

When the tourist's travel intention is basically determined, the planning and dispatching personnel of the outbound tour wholesaler should confirm with the relevant airlines whether the flight seat, flight time, ticket price, aircraft type, etc. can meet the needs of the tour itinerary. After signing the contract with the tourists of the outbound tour, the planning and dispatching personnel of the outbound tour wholesaler shall fax the list (including the basic information of the tourists, such as the name, gender, date of birth, passport number and expiry date) and the booking requirements (departure and return dates, and flight numbers, etc.) to the airline. Check the written reply of the airline, involving the flight number, number of people, price confirmation and ticket time requirements, and confirm the seat with the airline.

---

① 吕海龙、刘雪梅 主编,《旅行社计调业务》,北京:北京理工大学出版社,2017:230-231.
② 叶娅丽、陈学春 主编,《旅行社经营与管理》,北京:北京理工大学出版社,2018:165.

待团队办妥签证后,出境组团社计调人员需确认旅游者是否已缴纳全额旅游费用,通知航空公司出票。团队机票价格与散客机票价格差别较大,因此团队机票一旦出票,人数不可增减,不能退票、签转、变更航班、更改名字。验票也是避免发生差错的一个重要环节。

After the visa of the tourist group is ready, the planning and dispatching personnel of the outbound tour wholesaler should confirm whether the tourists have paid the full amount of traveling expenses and notify the airline to issue the air ticket. The price of the group ticket is quite different from that of the individual ticket. Therefore, once the group ticket is issued, the number of people cannot be increased or decreased, the ticket cannot be refunded and transferred, and the flight number and the name of ticket holder cannot be changed. Ticket checking is also an important step to avoid mistakes.

9.4.5 与境外旅行社确认

给境外旅行社传真旅游团日程确认书,包括酒店分房表、行程表、旅游者名单、旅游者特殊要求等,等待境外接待旅行社确认回复(包括酒店、餐厅名称、导游姓名与电话等)。确认之后向境外旅行社索取团队账单,需要立刻付款的需要与财务人员提前预约费用。

9.4.5 Confirm with overseas travel agencies

Fax the confirmation letter for the itinerary of the tourist group to overseas travel agencies, including the hotel room list, itinerary, name list of tourists, special requirements of tourists, etc., and wait for their confirmation reply (including the name of the hotel and the restaurant, name and telephone number of the tour guide, etc.). After confirmation, ask the overseas travel agencies for the group's bill. If you need to pay certain expenses immediately, you need to make an appointment with the financial staff and tell them to prepare money in advance.

9.4.6 核实材料

确认旅游费用、保证金以及担保函是否收齐,核对成本预算;核对团队名单与行程表(电子版),核实行程表出发日期、航班时间、景点安排等;核实接待旅行社信息、接团确认书、接待旅行社计调人员的联系方式、接待信息、订房数量;核对机位订单和行程。

9.4.6 Verification of materials

Confirm whether the traveling expenses, deposit and guarantee letter are collected, and check cost budgeting; check the group's name list and itinerary (electronic version), and verify the departure date, flight time, scenic spot arrangement, etc. of the itinerary; double-check the information of local tour operators, the confirmation letter of reception, the contact information of the planning and dispatching personnel of local tour operators, the reception information and the number of rooms booked; check air tickets' order and their schedule.

9.4.7 制作出团通知书

出团通知书包括旅行团编号、出发的确切时间与地点、领队的姓名与手机号码、旅游者未能按时抵达集合地点的解决方案、航班号和起飞时间、返程时间与地点、所需携带物品。

9.4.7 Make a notice of departure

The notice of departure includes the serial number of the tourist group, the exact time and place of departure, the name and mobile phone number of the outbound tour escort, the solution to the tourists' failure to arrive at the meeting spots on time, the flight number and departure time, the return time and place, and the required personal belongings.

9.5 境外接团社的选择与管理①

组团社应对境外旅行社进行评审,在满足下列条件的旅行社中优先选用,并与其签订书面接团协议,以确保组团社所销售的旅游产品质量的稳定性:

(1)依法设立;

(2)在目的地国家/地区旅游部门指定或推荐的名单内;

(3)具有优良的信誉和业绩;

(4)有能够满足团队接待需要的业务操作能力;

(5)有能够满足团队接待需要的设施和设备;

(6)有能够满足团队接待需要且符合当地政府资质要求的导游人员队伍,并不断对其进行培养和继续教育,以使其不断提高其履行出境旅游合同约定的意识和服务技能,持续改进服务质量;

(7)订立了符合出境旅游合同要求的导游人员行为规范,并能在导游人员队伍中得到有效实施。

组团社应定期对境外旅行社进行再评审,并建立境外旅行社信誉档案。评审间隔不应超过1年。相关的记录应予保存。境外旅行社落实团队接待计划的确认信息的书面记录应予保存。

团队计划落实妥当后,计调人员应做好如下工作并保存相应的移送交接记录:

(1)将如下信息如实告知领队人员,并提供相应的书面资料:团队计划落实情况,如团队行程、团队名单、旅

9.5 Selection and management of overseas travel agencies

The tour wholesaler shall review the overseas travel agencies, give priority to those that meet the following conditions, and sign a written tour agreement with them to ensure the stability of the quality of the tourist products sold by it:

(1) Established according to law;

(2) Listed in the name list of the travel agencies designated or recommended by the tourism department of the destination country/region;

(3) Enjoying good reputation and performance;

(4) Having the business operation ability to meet the reception needs of the tourist group;

(5) Possessing the facilities and equipment that can meet the reception needs of the tourist group;

(6) Boasting a team of tour guides who can meet the reception needs of the tourist group and the qualification requirements of the local government, and continue to receive training and further education, so that they can continuously improve their awareness and service skills in performing the outbound tour contract, and continuously improve service quality;

(7) Setting up the code of conduct of tour guides that meets the requirements of the outbound tour contract and can be effectively implemented in the tour guide team.

The tour wholesaler shall regularly re-evaluate the overseas travel agencies and establish their reputation file. The review interval shall not exceed 1 year. Relevant records shall be kept. The written record of the confirmation information of the overseas travel agencies' implementation of the tourist group's reception plan shall be kept.

After the tourist group's plan is properly implemented, the planning and dispatching personnel shall do the following work and keep the corresponding transfer and handover records:

(1) Inform the outbound tour escort of the following information truthfully and provide corresponding written materials: the implementation situation of the group plan,

---

① 《旅行社出境旅游服务规范》,全国标准信息公共服务平台,http://c. gb688. cn/bzgk/gb/showGb? type＝online&hcno＝574AE910CA53FFE9D9375664D1B9DAE3,2023/5/13。

游者的特殊要求；

（2）向领队移交：团队的旅游证件、团队机票、团队出入国境时需使用的有关表格、公安边检查验用的团队名单表、另纸签证（需要时）、团队的其他相关资料。

such as the itinerary of the tourist group, the name list of the group, special requirements of tourists;

（2）Hand over to the outbound tour escort: the group's travel documents, the group's air tickets, relevant forms to be used by the group when entering or leaving relevant countries, the group's name list to be used by the public security for inspection, the separate visa (if necessary), other relevant information of the group.

9.6　出境旅游组团社与境外接团社的合同范本示例

出境旅游组团社与境外旅行社合同[①]

合同编号：

甲方：_____（以下简称甲方）具备中国公民办理去_____旅游业务旅行社之资格。依法享有中国公民赴_____旅游的经营权。总部设在_____。

乙方：_____（以下简称乙方）具备中国公民来_____从事观光活动业务旅行社之资格。依法享有中国公民赴_____旅游的经营权。总部设在_____。

甲乙双方为发展共同的事业，本着平等互利的原则，经友好协商，为组织、接待中国公民赴_____旅游事宜，明确双方的权利义务，订立本合同。

本合同和合同附件为不可分割的整体，合同正文与合同附件的条款具有同等的效力。

第一条　甲方同意将组织成行的旅游团交由乙方接待，乙方同意按甲方提出的接待标准，安排旅行团的旅行游览活动。

第二条　甲方应在旅行团进入_____之日起20天前向乙方确认，乙方应在接到确认函之日起5个工作日内予以确认。

甲方应在旅行团进入_____之日前7个工作日内，以书面形式向乙方提供下列数据：

1. 接待标准；
2. 旅游安排；
3. 旅游者名单（含姓名、性别、出生年月、职业、国籍、证件名称和号码）；
4. 所需房间数；
5. 入境航班或车次。

第三条　甲方应在旅游团离开_____之日后30天内，用电汇方式把旅游团的全部旅行费用汇入乙方账户，旅行费用以_____支付。

[①]　赵爱华 主编，《旅行社计调业务》，北京：中国旅游出版社，2021：175-176. 合同标题、内容有调整。

汇款账户

银行名称：

银行地址：

银行代号(SWIFT code)：

户名：

分支机构代号： 账号：

第四条 如甲方失误造成旅游团行程延误、更改、取消,所产生的经济损失由甲方承担。

第五条 乙方应该按照本合同和合同附件约定的接待标准和日程安排为旅游团提供服务。除人力不可抗拒的因素外,如乙方未按照本合同和合同附件约定的接待标准和日程安排为旅游团提供服务,应当为旅游团提供补偿服务或将低于服务标准的费用差额退还甲方并赔偿由此造成的经济损失。

除人力不可抗拒的因素外,如因乙方造成旅游行程、交通工具、食宿标准等的变更所增加的费用由乙方承担。

第六条 乙方应当为旅游团委派持有导游证的导游人员提供服务。乙方导游不得强迫或诱导旅游者购物;旅游者在乙方指定的商店购物,经鉴定,如属假冒伪劣商品或质价不符的,乙方有责任随时退换。乙方导游不得诱导旅游者涉足色情场所和赌博场所,不得强迫旅游者参与自费项目。

第七条 甲方旅游团成员搭乘飞机、轮船、汽车或在饭店、餐厅等各项旅游设施中受到损害,如不属乙方责任,乙方也应尽人道主义义务协助甲方处理;如属乙方责任,乙方应承担损害赔偿责任。

第八条 甲方旅游团在进入_____ 被阻时,除旅游者自身的原因外,乙方应当积极协助处理;如属乙方原因,乙方应承担赔偿责任。

第九条 若乙方未按接待标准为旅游团提供服务,造成旅游者经济损失,乙方应承担赔偿责任。甲方有向乙方旅游管理机构投诉并要求赔偿的权利。

第十条 乙方如因特殊原因需调整双方已经确认的旅游团报价,应当在旅游团进入_____ 之日起10天前通知甲方。

第十一条 乙方有责任使甲方知晓_____ 的法律和有关规定。甲方应当要求旅游者遵守_____ 的法律和有关规定。

第十二条 乙方对旅游团的报价,经甲方书面认可后,可作为本合同的附件。

第十三条 本合同的订立、变更、解除、解释、履行和争议的解决受中华人民共和国法律的管辖。

第十四条 本合同自双方签订之日起生效,有效期至_____。有效期前30天,若双方都无意终止合同或更改合同内容,可以无限期延长合同期限。如果在合同期间,双方的法人名称、地址、电话、联系人发生变化,请提前1个月告知对方。

第十五条 本合同有中文和_____ 文两种文本,两种文本具有同等效力。在两种文本解释不一致时,以中文文本为准。

第十六条　乙方每月将发团计划按直客价、同行价、总部价报给甲方，甲方集本社的客源交予乙方操作。

附：乙方营业执照复印件、经营许可证复印件并且加盖公章。

甲方：　　　　　　　　　　　　　　乙方：

甲方代表签字：　　　　　　　　　　乙方代表签字：

签订地点：　　　　　　　　　　　　签订地点：

签订时间：　　年　月　日　　　　　签订时间：　　年　月　日

9.6　Example of contract between outbound tour wholesaler and overseas travel agency

Contract between Outbound Tour Wholesaler and Overseas Travel Agency[①]

Contract No. :

Party A：_____ （hereinafter referred to as Party A） is a qualified outbound tour wholesaler to handle Chinese citizens' tour to _____. With its headquarters based in _____, the outbound tour wholesaler is entitled to the operation of Chinese citizens' tour to _____ according to Chinese law.

Party B：_____ （hereinafter referred to as Party B） is a qualified travel agency to engage in Chinese citizens' inbound tour to _____. With its headquarters based in _____, the travel agency is entitled to the operation of Chinese citizens' tour to _____ according to law.

In order to develop the common cause，based on the principle of equality and mutual benefit，Party A and Party B have entered into this contract through friendly negotiation to organize and receive Chinese citizens to travel to _____, and have clarified the rights and obligations of both parties.

The contract and its appendices are inseparable as a whole，and the text of the contract and the articles of its appendices have the same effect.

Article 1　Party A agrees to hand over the organized tour group to Party B for reception，and Party B agrees to arrange the tour activities of the tour group according to the reception standards proposed by Party A.

Article 2　Party A shall confirm with Party B 20 days prior to the date of the group's entry into _____；Party B shall confirm within 5 working days upon the receipt of the confirmation letter.

Party A shall provide the following data to Party B in writing within 7 working days prior to the date of the group's entry into _____：

---

① 　原合同为中文版，英语版合同为编写者翻译。

1. Reception standards;

2. Tour arrangements;

3. List of tourists (including name, gender, date of birth, occupation, nationality, name of ID and number);

4. Number of rooms required;

5. Inbound flight or train number.

Article 3 Party A shall remit all travel expenses of the tour group to Party B's account by telegraphic transfer within 30 days after the group's departure of _____. The payment of travel expenses shall be made in _____.

Account for remittance

Bank name：

Bank address：

Bank's SWIFT code：

Account name：

Branch code：　　　　　　　Account No.：

Article 4 Party A shall bear the economic losses arising from the delay, change and cancellation of the tourist group caused by Party A's fault.

Article 5 Party B shall provide services for the tourist group in accordance with the reception standards and itinerary agreed in this contract and the appendix to the contract. In addition to force majeure, if Party B fails to provide services for the tourist group according to the reception standards and itinerary agreed in this contract and the appendix to the contract, it shall provide compensatory service for the tourist group or return the difference of the service charge to Party A and compensate for the economic losses caused thereby.

In addition to the force majeure, Party B shall be liable for the increased expenses if Party B's fault results in the change of the tour itinerary, transportation, accommodation standards, etc.

Article 6 Party B shall provide the tourist group with tour guides with tour guide certificates. Party B's tour guide shall not force or induce tourists to shop; Party B shall be liable for returning and exchanging commodities the tourists bought at the stores designated by Party B any time if they are found to be fake and inferior commodities or their prices do not match their quality. Party B's tour guide shall not induce tourists to set foot in pornographic places and gambling houses, and shall not force tourists to participate in self-funded items.

Article 7 If the members of Party A's tourist group are hurt in various tourist facilities such as hotels, restaurants, etc. or the plane, ship and car they travel by, even if it is not Party B's responsibility, Party B shall also perform its humanitarian obligation to assist Party A in their handling of such situations; if it is the responsibility of Party B, Party B shall be liable for compensation.

Article 8   Party B shall actively provide assistance in case of Party A's tour group being blocked from entry into _____ except for tourists' own faults; if it is Party B's faults, Party B shall be held accountable for compensation.

Article 9   If Party B fails to provide services for the tourist group according to the reception standards and causes economic losses to tourists, Party B shall be liable for compensation. Party A has the right to complain to Party B's tourism administration and claim for compensation.

Article 10   If Party B needs to adjust the quotation of the tourist group confirmed by both parties due to special reasons, it shall notify Party A 10 days prior to the tour group's entry into _____.

Article 11   Party B has the responsibility to make Party A understand _____ laws and relevant regulations. Party A shall require tourists to comply with _____ laws and relevant regulations.

Article 12   The quotation of Party B for the tourist group shall be attached to this contract after being approved in writing by Party A.

Article 13   The conclusion, modification, cancellation, interpretation, performance and dispute settlement of this contract shall be governed by the laws of the People's Republic of China.

Article 14   This contract shall come into force from the date of signing by both parties and shall be valid until _____. If both parties have no intention to terminate the contract or change the contract content 30 days before its validity expires, the duration of the contract can be extended indefinitely. If the name of legal persons, address, telephone number and contact person of one party change while the contract is being implemented, it shall inform the other party one month in advance.

Article 15   This contract is written both in Chinese and _____, both of which have the same effect. In case of any discrepancy between the two versions, the Chinese version shall prevail.

Article 16   Party B shall submit the tourist groups' plan to Party A monthly according to the direct customer price, peer price and headquarters price, and Party A shall hand over its customer source to Party B for operation.

Appendix: the copy of Party B's business license, copy of its operating license with the official seal.

Party A: Party B:

Signature of Party A's representative: Signature of Party B's representative:

Signed at: Signed at:

Date: Date:

9.7 知识链接

▨▨《中国公民出国旅游团队名单表》①

第七条 国务院旅游行政部门统一印制《中国公民出国旅游团队名单表》(以下简称《名单表》),在下达本年度出国旅游人数安排时编号发放给省、自治区、直辖市旅游行政部门,由省、自治区、直辖市旅游行政部门核发给组团社。

组团社应当按照核定的出国旅游人数安排组织出国旅游团队,填写《名单表》。旅游者及领队首次出境或者再次出境,均应当填写在《名单表》中,经审核后的《名单表》不得增添人员。

第八条 《名单表》一式四联,分为:出境边防检查专用联、入境边防检查专用联、旅游行政部门审验专用联、旅行社自留专用联。

组团社应当按照有关规定,在旅游团队出境、入境时,将《名单表》分别交有关部门查验、留存。

9.7 Knowledge link

▨▨ "The Name List of Chinese Citizens' Outbound Tour Group"

Article 7 The tourism administrative department of the State Council uniformly prints "The Name List of Chinese Citizens' Outbound Tour Group" (hereinafter referred to as the list), which is numbered and distributed to the tourism administrative departments of provinces, autonomous regions and municipalities directly under the Central Government when the national department assigns the number of tourists of the outbound tour for the current year, and then issued to outbound tour wholesalers by the tourism administrative departments of provinces, autonomous regions and municipalities directly under the Central Government.

The outbound tour wholesaler should organize outbound tour group according to the approved number of outbound tourists and fill out "name list". Tourists and outbound tour escort who leave China for the first time or leave again are expected to fill out the "name list" and no extra person can be added to the approved "name list".

Article 8 The list is made in four sheets of the same form, which are divided into the special sheets for the border inspection of the tourist group's departure and return, the veirfication by the tourism administration department and the filing of the travel agency respectively.

The outbound tour wholesaler shall, in accordance with the relevant regulations, submit the list to the relevant departments for inspection and preservation at the time of the group's departure and return.

9.8 知识拓展

预订机票的注意事项

根据拟定的团队线路,至少应该提前一个半月左右将航班及飞行的方式(直航或转机、经停)报给票务,并掌握机票价格信息。团队和散客订票具有差异性。散客需提供名单预订机位,10人以上的团队可以事先预订机位,确认好之后再提供名单;然而在旅游旺季,部分航空公司要求提供旅客名单方可出票,因此需要根据具体情况落实。国际机票尽量购买大型航空公司的直航航班。

需要了解出机票时间与签证完成时间是否吻合,是否存在时间冲突。妥善安排出境被拒

---

① 《旅行社出境旅游服务规范》,全国标准信息公共服务平台,http://c.gb688.cn/bzgk/gb/showGb? type=online&hcno =574AE910CA53FFE9D9375664D1B9DAE3,2023/5/16。

签客人的机票处理(免收费还是按比例收取订金)、机票改签的处理(向航空公司了解是免费改签或是收费改签)。了解团队机票申请的订金每位多少,旅客是否有特殊预订要求(如有婴儿、小孩,要求乘坐经济舱、商务舱等)。在售票处通知必须确认出票,否则机票价格会提高的情况下,需要根据签证能否通过以确定是否可以出机票。出票前核对旅客名单、账单、付款方式(转账或支票),出票之后向票务索取电子行程单、订票号、发票。需要记录航空公司、票务的紧急联络方式,以便遇到紧急情况可以及时协调处理。

9.8.1 国际航班知识

9.8.1.1 航空公司代码

航空公司代码分为两位和三位,如美国联合航空公司 UA,德国汉莎航空公司 LH。航班号通常使用航空公司的两个英语字母和三个阿拉伯数字来表示,如 CA981,CA 为中国国际航空公司,9 表示国际航班,8 表示中美航线,1 表示飞往美国。

9.8.1.2 航班起止点

按照国际惯例,在国际航空中通常采用世界各大城市或机场的英语缩写的前三个字母为该城市的代号,例如从北京到纽约,即 PEK—NEW。

表 9-1　主要国际航空公司与代码
(Table 9-1　Major international airlines and codes)

中文名称 (Chinese name)	英文名称 (English name)	2 位代码 (2-letter code)	3 位代码 (3-letter code)
大韩航空公司	Korean Air	KE	KAL
日本航空公司	Japan Airlines	JL	JAL
全日空航空公司	All Nippon Airways	NH	ANA
新加坡航空公司	Singapore Airlines	SQ	SIA
泰国国际航空公司	Thai Airways International	TG	THA
美国联合航空公司	United Airlines	UA	UAL
英国航空公司	British Airways	BA	BAW
荷兰皇家航空公司	Klm Royal Dutch Airlines	KL	KLM
德国汉莎航空公司	Lufthansa German Airlines	LH	DLH
法国航空公司	Air France	AF	AFR
瑞士航空公司	Swissair	SR	SWR
奥地利航空公司	Austrian Airlines	OS	AUA
俄罗斯国际航空公司	Aeroflot Russian International	SU	AFL
澳洲航空公司	Qantas Airways	QF	QFA
芬兰航空公司	Finnair Airlines	AY	FIN
意大利航空公司	Italia Airlines	AZ	AZA
斯堪的纳维亚(北欧)航空公司	Scandinavian Airlines	SK	SAS
印度尼西亚鹰航空公司	Garuda Indonesia Airlines	GA	GIA
新加坡胜安航空公司	Singapore Silk Air	MI	MMP

中文名称 (Chinese name)	英文名称 (English name)	2位代码 (2-letter code)	3位代码 (3-letter code)
马来西亚航空公司	Malaysian Airlines	MH	MAS
以色列航空公司	Ei Ai Israel Airlines	LY	ELY
澳门航空公司	Air Macau	NX	AMU
国泰航空公司	Cathay Pacific Airways	CX	CPA
阿拉伯联合酋长国航空公司 (阿联酋航空)	Emirates Airline	EK	UA

9.8.1.3　航班基本信息

了解并掌握国际航班的起飞城市、经停城市、目的地城市、航空公司、成人票价、儿童票价、婴儿票价、退票条件、税金及燃油附加费等基本信息。

9.8.1.4　订票的相关规定

出境旅游的国际机票一般为联程机票。机票的有效期通常为一年,然而旅游团的机票为团体票,因此并没有一年的有效期,况且,团队机票不可退票、改期和更换。

9.8.1.5　国际机票的税费

在各大网站查询到的只是机票款,不包括税费以及燃油附加费,这两笔费用在出票时才支付。国际机票的税费可以分为三类:离境费、入境费和过境费。个别国家还征收其他名目的税费,如美国除了征收上述税费,还征收海关使用费、机场费、动植物卫生检验费等。有些国家不征收类似税费,如中国和菲律宾。日本不征收入境费,但征收离境费。

9.8　Knowledge expansion

9.8.1　Points for attention in air tickets' booking

According to the proposed tour itinerary, the flight number and flight mode (direct flight, transfer or stopover) should be reported to the booking office at least one and a half months in advance, and information of the ticket price should be mastered. There arises the difference of ticket booking between group and individual passengers. Individual passengers need to provide a name list to reserve seats, and the tour group with more than 10 people can reserve seats in advance and then provide the list after confirmation. However, in the peak season of tourism, some airlines require you to provide a passenger list before issuing tickets, so you need to deal with the booking according to the specific situation. For international air tickets, try to buy direct flights from large airlines.

It is necessary to know whether the time of ticket issuance matches the time of visa completion and whether there is time conflict. Properly deal with the ticket of the guests whose visa is refused (free of charge or proportional deposit) and the ticket rescheduling (ask the airline whether rescheduling is free or charged). How much is the deposit for the air ticket application of each member of the tour group? Do passengers have special reservation requirements (such as taking the baby, child with them or requiring the economy class, business class，etc.）? When the booking office notifies that the ticket issuing must be confirmed，or the ticket price will increase，it is necessary to determine whether the ticket can be issued according to whether the visa can be approved. Check the passenger list，bill and terms of payment（transfer or check）before the ticket issuing. After the ticket issuing，ask the booking office for the electronic itinerary，booking number and invoice. It is necessary to record the emergency contact information of the airline and the booking office，so as to coordinate and handle emergency in time.

9.8.2　International flight knowledge

9.8.2.1　Airline code

The airline code is divided into two-letter code and three-letter code，such as United Airlines—UA and Lufthansa—LH. The flight number is usually expressed by two English letters standing for the airline and three Arabic numbers，such as CA981. CA is Air China，9 represents international flights，8 represents Sino-US routes，and 1 represents flights to the United States.

9.8.2.2　Flight starting and ending points

According to international practice，the first three letters of English abbreviations of major cities or airports in the world are usually used as the code of the city in international aviation. For example，from Beijing to New York is expressed as PEK—NEW.

9.8.2.3　Basic flight information

Learn about and master the basic information of the departure city，stopover city，destination city，airlines，adult fares，child fares，infant fares，refund conditions，taxes and fuel surcharges of international flights.

9.8.2.4　Relevant regulations on ticket booking

International air tickets for the outbound tour are generally connecting air tickets. The validity period of the air tickets is usually one year. However，the air tickets of tour groups are group tickets，so there is no validity period of one year. In addition，group tickets cannot be refunded，rescheduled or replaced.

9.8.2.5　Taxes on international air tickets

What is found on all major websites is only the air ticket price，excluding taxes and fuel surcharges，which will only be paid when the ticket is issued. The taxes and fees of international air tickets can be divided into three categories：the departure fee，entry fee and transit fee. Some countries also levy other taxes. For example，in addition to the above taxes，the United States also charges customs use fees，airport fees，animal and plant health inspection fees. Some countries do not levy similar taxes，such as China and the Philippines. Japan does not levy an entry fee，but charges a departure fee.

Exercises

Ⅰ. Fill in the blanks with proper forms of words.

1. The design of outbound tourism products is _____ （produce） products that meet the needs of the tourism market by mainly _____ （consider） the needs of tourists

for outbound tour products and _____ (combine) them with the distribution of tourism resources in the destination countries and the product design of the local tour _____ (operate). You can use the _____ (exist) classic outbound tour itinerary _____ (provide) by travel agencies, the outbound tour itinerary provided by overseas tour operators, and design the outbound tour itinerary on the _____ (base) of the specific needs of customers.

2. Check the _____ (write) reply of the airline, _____ (involve) the flight number, number of people, price _____ (confirm) and ticket time _____ (require), and confirm the seat with the airline.

3. In addition to force majeure, if Party B _____ (fail) provide services for the tourist group according to the reception standards and itinerary _____ (agree) in this contract and the appendix to the contract, it shall provide _____ (compensate) service for the tourist group or return the difference of the service charge to Party A and compensate for the economic losses _____ (cause) thereby.

4. The tourism administrative department of the State Council uniformly prints "The Name List of Chinese Citizens' Outbound Tour Group" (hereinafter referred to as the list), which _____ (number) and _____ (distribute) to the tourism administrative departments of provinces, autonomous regions and municipalities directly under the Central Government when the national department _____ (assign) the number of the tourists of the outbound tour for the current year, and then _____ (issue) to outbound tour wholesalers by the tourism administrative departments of provinces, autonomous regions and municipalities directly under the Central Government.

Ⅱ. Translate the following Chinese sentences into English.

1. 选择合适的境外旅行社报价至关重要。询价时需要提供所有相应信息：人数、出发日期、详细行程、酒店等级、用车要求、用餐情况、景点门票、特殊服务项目等。选择两家以上境外旅行社报价以便对比。

2. 旅游者提供本人签名的 6 个月以上的有效因私护照原件；若是换发护照需提供旧护照；有拒签史的旅游者，需要提供拒签说明。

3. 出境旅游计调人员登录所在省旅游政务网,输入出境旅游团队名单、线路、出入境旅游时间等信息,等待旅游行政部门审核。

4. 可以采用旅行社现有的经典出境线路、采用境外接待社提供的出境旅游线路、根据客人的具体需求设计出境旅游线路。

Ⅲ. **Translate the following English sentences into Chinese.**

1. In order to develop the common cause, based on the principle of equality and mutual benefit, Party A and Party B have entered into this contract through friendly negotiation to organize and receive Chinese citizens to travel to France, and have clarified the rights and obligations of both parties.

2. If Party B fails to provide services for the tourist group according to the reception standards and causes economic losses to tourists, Party B shall be liable for compensation. Party A has the right to complain to Party B's tourism administration and claim for compensation.

3. According to reports from the European Travel Commission on June 1, 2023, as the summer season approaches, over 50% of respondents in China, Brazil, Australia, Canada, and the US expressed optimism about traveling overseas. Among them, Europe remains a top choice for long-haul trips in May—August 2023. Nearly half of those planning to visit the region are repeat visitors, indicating Europe's ability to cultivate a positive reputation, satisfy travellers, and entice them to return.

4. Established in 1948, the European Travel Commission is a unique association in the travel sector, representing the National Tourism Organizations of the countries of Europe. Its mission is to strengthen the sustainable development of Europe as a tourist destination.

Ⅳ. Questions and answers.

1. What fees are included in the quotation of an outbound tour wholesaler?

2. What important points do you need to pay attention to in the selection and management of overseas travel agencies?

第❿单元 出境旅游接待
Unit ❿ Outbound Tour Reception

📖 **教学目标**

⇨掌握欧洲购物退税的基本程序

⇨了解出境旅游领队相关规定

⇨掌握出境旅游领队职责

⇨掌握出境游领队工作程序

⇨学会出境旅游突发事件的处理方法

📖 **Teaching objectives**

⇨To master the basic procedures for shopping tax refunds in Europe

⇨To learn about the relevant regulations for the outbound tour escort

⇨To master the responsibilities of the outbound tour escort

⇨To master the work procedures of the outbound tour escort

⇨To learn the handling ways of emergencies in the outbound tour

10. 1 情景对话

10.1.1 入境手续

> A. 欧洲之旅中国领队
> B. 机场工作人员

B：请出示护照。

A：这是我的护照。

B：你此行的目的是什么？

A：我是来旅游的。我是 36 人欧洲之旅的中国领队。

B：你打算待多久？

A：整个旅行总共 12 天。

B：你的欧洲之旅包括几个国家？

A：它包括五个国家：法国、意大利、瑞士、德国和卢森堡。

B：祝你旅途愉快。

A：谢谢你的祝福。

10.1.2 办理退税

> A. 欧洲游中国领队
> B. 一家法国商店的店员

A：早上好，我是张先生，欧洲游中国领队。你们的商店提供退税服务吗？法国对退税的基本要求是什么？

B：同一个人在同一天在同一家商

10. 1 Situational dialogue

10.1.1 Entry formalities

> A. Chinese outbound tour escort for a Europe tour
> B. airport staff

B：Could/May I have your passport, please? / Passport, please.

A：Here it is.

B：What's the purpose of your visit?

A：I am here for sightseeing. I am a Chinese outbound tour escort for a Europe tour of 36 people.

B：How long are you going to stay?

A：It is 12 days for the whole tour.

B：How many countries are included in your Europe tour?

A：It includes five countries：France, Italy, Switzerland, Germany and Luxembourg.

B：Have a pleasant trip.

A：Thank you for your good wishes.

10.1.2 Handling tax refund

> A. Chinese outbound tour escort for a Europe tour
> B. clerk in a French store

A：Good morning, I am Mr. Zhang, a Chinese outbound tour escort for a Europe tour. Does your store provide tax refund service? What are the basic requirements for the tax refund in France?

B：The total amount of shopping by the same person at the

店购物的总额必须达到 175 欧元（包括增值税），才能在法国获得退税。

A：客户如何在法国申请退税？

B：当顾客购买的东西超过175 欧元时，他们需要向商店申请一式三份的退税表和相应退税公司的信封。填写完表格后，一份由商家保存，另外两份将在消费者出境时随货物一起提交给海关人员。海关人员将在退税单上盖章，其中一份将用信封寄回退税公司，第三份由客户自己保存。一般来说，退税适用于有"免税购物"、"退税"或"免欧元税"标志的商店。

A：可以提供多少种退税方式？

B：退税方式包括现金退款、信用卡退款和支票退款。

A：以上三种方法的优点和缺点是什么？

B：现金退税的优点是可以在办理退税的机场直接领取，缺点是需要排队。信用卡退款的退税率可能高于现金退款，但退款要到回国后两个月左右才能收到。

A：如何在机场获得海关印章/货物清关验证？

B：请您持购买的物品、收据和护照到海关服务台，并让他们在您的免税表上盖章。请不要将购买的货物装进您的托运行李中，这是由于您需要向海关工作人员出示。请在飞机起飞前留出足够的时间办理退税手续。

A：欧洲主要的退税公司是什么？如果现金或信用卡退款在海关退款柜台盖章后没有在当地机场及时处理，那么回国后还能退款吗？

B：Global Blue、Premier Tax Free 和 Tax Refund SPA 是欧洲三家主要的退税公司。Global Blue 已经在北京、上海、广州和香港设立了现金退税点。只要保留在欧洲消费的单据和 Global Blue 的退税表，就可以在国内退税点处理现金退税。

A：非常感谢你的解答。

B：不客气。

same store on the same day must reach 175 euros (including TVA) so that one can receive a tax refund in France.

A：How can customers apply for the tax refund in France?

B：When what customers buy exceeds the amount, they need to request a tax refund form in triplicate from the store and the envelope of the corresponding company for the tax refund. After filling out the form, one copy will be kept by the merchant, and the other two copies will be presented to customs personnel along with the goods when the consumer leaves the country. The customs personnel will stamp the tax refund form, one of which will be sent back to the tax refund company in an envelope, and the third copy will be kept by the customers themselves. Generally speaking, the tax refund is applicable to stores with the signs of "Tax Free Shopping", "Tax Refund" or "Euro Free Tax".

A：How many tax refund approaches can be provided?

B：Tax refund approaches include the cash refund, credit card refund, and check refund.

A：What are the advantages and disadvantages of the above three approaches?

B：The advantage of the cash tax refund is that it can be directly received at the airport where the tax refund is processed, while the disadvantage is that you need to line up. The tax refund rate for the credit card refund may be higher than that for the cash refund, but the refund will not be received until about two months after returning to China.

A：How can I obtain the customs stamp/cargo clearance verification in the airport?

B：Please bring your purchased items, receipts, and passport to the customs desk and have them stamp your tax refund form. Please do not pack the goods you purchased into your checked luggage as you need to show them to customs staff. Please spare sufficient time before the plane takes off to process the tax refund.

A：What are main tax refund companies in Europe? If the cash or credit card refund is not processed in a timely manner at the local airport after the tax refund form is stamped at the customs refund counter, can I still get the refund after returning to China?

B：Global Blue, Premier Tax Free and Tax Refund SPA are three main tax refund companies in Europe. Global Blue has set up some places for the cash tax refund in Beijing, Shanghai, Guangzhou, and Hong Kong. As long as the documents for consumption in Europe and the tax refund form of Global Blue are retained, cash tax refunds can be processed at some places for the domestic tax refund.

A：Thank you so much for your explanation.

B：It is my pleasure.

10.2 角色扮演训练

任务：假如你是一位出境游领队，需要熟悉机场服务和机上服务的一些基本表述，如机场办理登机手续、飞机延误、航空公司广播等。

一些有用的可供参考的表述如下。

1. 我想为我的团队办理登机手续。

2. 让我数一下。我们团队总共有25件行李要托运。

3. 能给我一个靠过道的座位吗？那样我就可以更方便地走动。

4. 这是你们的机票、护照和登机牌。你们的行李提取存根粘贴在相应的机票上。

5. 对不起，恐怕我的行李超重了。我该怎么办？

6. 你可以从托运行李中取出一些东西作为随身行李。手提行李将不予称重。这将减轻托运行李的重量。手提行李的限额是8公斤。

7. 这是您的行李领取标签和护照。

8. 我们在曼谷转机。行李会直接运送到目的地吗？

9. 是的。会直达巴黎。

10. 离港乘客应立即前往25号登机口。

11. 各位乘客请注意。飞往曼谷的泰航TG635航班，已经开始登机。第15排到20排的旅客请前往第9号登机门。

12. 可以帮我把行李放进头顶置物箱吗？

13. 女士们，先生们，机长已经关闭了系好安全带的标志，你们现在可以在机舱里走动了。然而，我们始终建议您在就座时系好安全带。过一会儿，我们将为您提供茶、咖啡和其他软饮料。欢迎您做出选择。请把您面前

10.2 Role play training

Task：If you are an outbound tour escort, you need to be familiar with some basic expressions of airport services and onboard services, such as airport check-in, flight delay, airline broadcasting, etc.

Some useful expressions for reference are as follows.

1. I'd like to check in for my group, please.

2. Let me count. Altogether our group has got 30 pieces of luggage to check.

3. Could you give me an aisle seat so that I can move around more easily if it is available?

4. Here are your air tickets, passports and boarding passes. Your luggage claim stubs are attached to respective tickets.

5. Excuse me, I am afraid my luggage is overweight. What should I do?

6. You can take something out of your checked luggage as carry-on baggage. Carry-on baggage will not be weighed. Thus it will reduce the weight of the checked luggage. The allowance for the carry-on baggage is 8 kg.

7. Here are claim tags for your luggage and your passport.

8. We're changing aircraft in Bangkok. Will the luggage be transferred automatically?

9. Yes, it's checked through to Paris.

10. Departing passengers should proceed to Gate 25 immediately.

11. May I have your attention, please? Thai Airlines flight TG 635 to Bangkok is now boarding. Passengers from Row 15 to 20, please proceed to Gate 9.

12. Could you help me put my luggage into the overhead compartment?

13. Ladies and gentlemen, the Captain has turned off the Fasten Seat Belt sign, and you may now move around the cabin. However, we always recommend you to keep your seat belt fastened while you're seated. In a few moments, we will be serving you the meal with tea, coffee and other soft drinks. Welcome to make your choice. Please put down the table in front of you. For the convenience of the passenger behind you, please return your seat back to the upright position during the meal service. Thank you!

的桌子放下。为了方便后面的乘客，请在送餐时将座椅靠背调直。谢谢！

14. 各位旅客请注意，本班机即将行经乱流区。请您回到您的座位，并系好安全带。

15. 我能喝一杯咖啡/橙汁/椰奶/红茶吗？

16. 我们的晚餐有什么选择？

17. 你能给我一条毯子和一个耳机吗？有点冷，并且这个耳机坏了。

18. 能给我的团队入境卡、报关单和离境卡吗？

14. Ladies and gentlemen, we are approaching an area of turbulence. For your own safety, please go back to your seat and fasten the seat belt. Thank you.

15. Can I have a cup of coffee/ orange juice/ coconut milk/ black tea?

16. Do we have any options for our dinner?

17. Can I get a blanket and a pair of earphones? It is a little cold and this pair of earphones doesn't work.

18. Can I have the arrival card/ landing card, customs declaration form and departure card for my group?

10.3 出境旅游领队相关规定

《旅游法》第三十六条规定，旅行社组织团队出境旅游或者组织、接待团队入境旅游，应当按照规定安排领队或者导游全程陪同。①

《旅行社条例实施细则》有关出境旅游领队的规定如下所示：②

第三十一条 旅行社为组织旅游者出境旅游委派的领队，应当具备下列条件：

（一）取得导游证；

（二）具有大专以上学历；

（三）取得相关语言水平测试等级证书或通过外语语种导游资格考试，但为赴港澳台地区旅游委派的领队除外；

（四）具有两年以上旅行社业务经营、管理或者导游等相关从业经历；

（五）与取得出境旅游业务经营许可的旅行社订立劳动合同。

赴台旅游领队还应当符合《大陆

10.3 Relevant regulations on outbound tour escorts

Article 36 of Tourism Law stipulates that when organizing outbound tours or organizing and receiving inbound tours, travel agencies shall arrange an outbound tour escort for the outbound tour or a tour guide for the inbound tour throughout the journey.

The relevant provisions of *The Detailed Rules for the Implementation of the Regulations on Travel Agencies* on outbound tour escorts are as follows:

Article 31 An outbound tour escort appointed by a travel agency in its organizing the tourists of the outbound tour shall meet the following conditions:

（1）Obtaining a tour guide certificate;

（2）Graduate of college with two-to-three-year study program or above;

（3）Obtaining relevant certificates of the language proficiency test or passing the foreign language tour guide qualification test, except for the outbound tour escort appointed to travel to Hong Kong, Macao and Taiwan;

（4）Having more than two years of experience in the business operation, management or tour guiding of travel agencies;

（5）Having signed employment contract with the travel agency that has obtained the business license for outbound tour.

① 《旅游法》，国家文化和旅游部网站，https://zwgk.mct.gov.cn/zfxxgkml/zcfg/fl/202105/t20210526_924763.html，2023/5/17。

② 《旅行社条例实施细则》，国家文化和旅游局网站，https://zwgk.mct.gov.cn/zfxxgkml/zcfg/bmgz/202012/t20201204_905330.html，2023/5/17。

居民赴台湾地区旅游管理办法》规定的要求。

第三十二条 旅行社应当将本单位领队信息及变更情况,报所在地设区的市级旅游行政管理部门备案。领队备案信息包括:身份信息、导游证号、学历、语种、语言等级(外语导游)、从业经历、所在旅行社、旅行社社会保险登记证号等。

第三十三条 领队从事领队业务,应当接受与其订立劳动合同的取得出境旅游业务许可的旅行社委派,并携带导游证、佩戴导游身份标识。

第三十四条 领队应当协助旅游者办理出入境手续,协调、监督境外地接社及从业人员履行合同,维护旅游者的合法权益。

第三十五条 不具备领队条件的,不得从事领队业务。

领队不得委托他人代为提供领队服务。

第三十六条 旅行社委派的领队,应当掌握相关旅游目的地国家(地区)语言或者英语。

Outbound tour escorts for the Taiwan tour should also meet the requirements of *Measures for the Administration of Trips by the Residents of Chinese Mainland to Taiwan*.

Article 32 A travel agency shall report the information and changes of its own outbound tour escort to the tourism administrative department of the city with districts for the record. The recorded information of the outbound tour escort includes: identity information, the tour guide certificate number, educational background, language type, language level (the foreign language tour guide), employment experience, travel agency he/she works at, social insurance registration number of the travel agency, etc.

Article 33 When working, outbound tour escorts shall accept the appointment of the travel agency that obtained the business license for the outbound tour and signed an employment contract with them, carry the tour guide certificate and wear the tour guide identification.

Article 34 The outbound tour escorts shall assist the tourists in handling the formalities for border inspection, coordinate and supervise the performance of the contract by the overseas travel agencies and employees, and safeguard the legitimate rights and interests of the tourists.

Article 35 Those who do not meet the requirement for outbound tour escorts are prohibited from providing relevant service. Outbound tour escorts shall not entrust others to provide relevant service, either.

Article 36 The outbound tour escorts appointed by a travel agency shall master the language of the relevant destination country (region) or English.

10.4 出境游领队职责

《出境旅游领队服务规范》对出境游领队职责作了如下规定:①

1.恪守职业道德,遵守外事纪律;

2.为旅游者提供全程陪同服务;

3.在旅游行程的各个环节向旅游者宣讲文明旅游注意事项;

4.代表组团社监督地接社和地陪导游履行旅游合同,按照组团社的行

10.4 Responsibilities of outbound tour escort

The Service Standards for Outbound Tour Escort stipulates the responsibilities of outbound tour escorts as follows:

1. Adhering to professional ethics and foreign affairs discipline.

2. Providing full accompanying services for tourists.

3. Providing sensible tourism precautions to tourists at all stages of the tour.

4. Working as the representative of the tour wholesaler to supervise the local tour operator and the local guide to fulfill

① 《出境旅游领队服务规范》,国家文化和旅游部网站,https://zwgk. mct. gov. cn/zfxxgkml/hybz/202302/t20230210_939033. html,2023/5/17。

程计划兑现接待服务承诺,监督其执行接待标准和保证服务质量,维护组团社和旅游者合法权益;

5.与地接社和地陪导游共同实施旅游接待计划,协助处理旅游行程中的突发事件、纠纷及其他问题;

6.在旅游过程中随时向旅游者发出安全提示;

7.维护国家利益和民族尊严,并提醒旅游者抵制任何有损国家利益和民族尊严的言行;

8.向旅游者说明旅游目的地法律法规、风土人情及风俗习惯等;

9.关心旅游团中的老年人、儿童、残障人士等特殊旅游者,需要时提供必要的照顾;

10.协调处理旅游者之间的纠纷及行程中旅游者提出的投诉;

11.做好各段行程之间衔接工作。

10.5 出境游领队工作程序

领队应认真履行领队职责,按旅游合同的约定完成旅游行程计划。

10.5.1 出团准备

领队接收计调人员移交的出境旅游团队资料时应认真核对查验。出境旅游团队资料通常包括团队名单表、旅游证件、旅游签证/签注、交通票据、接待计划书、联络通讯录等。领队应提前到达团队集合地点,召集、率领团队按时出发,并在适当的时候代表组团社致欢迎词。①

the tour contract and realize reception service commitment according to the tour itinerary of the tour wholesaler. Supervising the implementation of reception standards and ensuring service quality, and safeguarding the legitimate rights and interests of the tour wholesaler and tourists.

5. Collaborating with the local tour operator and local tour guides to implement tour reception plans and assisting in handling unexpected events, disputes, and other issues in the tour.

6. Providing safety reminders to tourists at any time in the tour.

7. Safeguarding national interests and national dignity, and reminding tourists to resist any words or actions that harm national interests and national dignity.

8. Explaining the laws and regulations, local customs and habits of the tourist destination to tourists.

9. Caring for special tourists such as the elderly, children, and disabled in the tour group, and providing necessary care when needed.

10. Coordinating and handling disputes between tourists and complaints raised by tourists during their tour.

11. Doing a good job in connecting different segments of the itinerary.

10.5 Work procedures for outbound tour escort

The outbound tour escort should conscientiously fulfill their duties and complete the tour itinerary according to the provisions of the tour contract.

10.5.1 Preparation for group tour

The outbound tour escort should carefully check and verify the outbound tour group's information handed over by the planning and dispatching personnel. The outbound tour group's information usually includes the group's name list, travel documents, tourist visas/endorsements, transportation documents, reception plan, address book, etc. The escort should arrive at the group's meeting spot in advance, convene and lead the group to depart on time, and give a welcome speech on behalf of the tour wholesaler at an appropriate time.

① 《旅行社出境旅游服务规范》,全国标准信息公共服务平台,http://c.gb688.cn/bzgk/gb/showGb?type=online&hcno=574AE910CA53FFE9D9375664D1B9DAE3,2023/5/17。

▩ 10.5.2　出入境服务

领队应告知并向旅游者发放通关时应向口岸的边检/移民机关出示/提交的旅游证件和通关资料(如:出入境登记卡、海关申报单等),引导团队依次通关。向口岸的边检/移民机关提交必要的团队资料(如:团队名单、团体签证、出入境登记卡等),并办理必要的手续。

领队应积极为旅游团队办妥乘机和行李托运的有关手续,并依时引导团队登机。飞行途中,领队应协助机组/空乘人员向旅游者提供必要的帮助和服务。①

▩ 10.5.3　旅行游览服务

领队应按组团社与旅游者所签的旅游合同约定的内容和标准为旅游者提供符合要求的旅游行程接待服务,并督促接待社及其导游员按约定履行旅游合同。入住饭店时,领队应向当地导游员提供团队住宿分房方案,并协助当地导游员办好入店手续。②

在旅游途中,领队应:

1.积极协助当地导游为旅游者提供必要的帮助和服务;

2.劝谕引导旅游者遵守当地的法律法规,尊重当地风俗习惯;

3.随时注意团队安全。

旅游行程结束时,应通过向旅游者发放并回收《游客旅游服务评价表》征询旅游者对旅游行程服务的意见,并代表组团社致欢送词。

▩ 10.5.2　Entry and exit service

The outbound tour escort should inform the tourists and distribute to them the travel documents and customs clearance documents (such as entry and exit registration cards, customs declaration forms, etc.) that should be presented/submitted to the border inspection/immigration authorities at the locality of entry during customs clearance, guiding the group to clear customs in sequence. The outbound tour escort should also hand over the group's information such as the name list, group visa, entry and exit registration card, etc. to the border inspection/immigration authorities at the locality of entry, and handle necessary procedures.

The outbound tour escort should actively handle the relevant procedures for boarding and luggage check-in for the tour group, and guide the group to board the plane on time. During the flight, the outbound tour escort should assist the crew/flight attendants in providing necessary assistance and services to tourists.

▩ 10.5.3　Sightseeing service

The outbound tour escort should provide tourists with qualified reception service according to the content and standards stipulated in the tour contract signed between the outbound tour wholesaler and tourists, and supervise the overseas tour operator and its tour guides to fulfill the tour contract as agreed. When checking into a hotel, the outbound tour escort should provide the local tour guide with the group's rooming list and assist the local tour guide in the group's check-in.

In the trip, the outbound tour escort should:

1. Actively assist local tour guides in providing necessary assistance and services to tourists;

2. Encourage and guide tourists to comply with local laws and regulations, and respect local customs and habits;

3. Always pay attention to the group's safety.

At the end of the trip, tourists should be consulted for their opinions on the trip by the distributing and collecting the "Tourist Service Evaluation Form", and a farewell speech should be delivered on behalf of the outbound tour wholesaler.

---

① 《旅行社出境旅游服务规范》,全国标准信息公共服务平台,http://c.gb688.cn/bzgk/gb/showGb? type＝online&hcno
＝574AE910CA53FFE9D9375664D1B9DAE3,2023/5/17。

② 《旅行社出境旅游服务规范》,全国标准信息公共服务平台,http://c.gb688.cn/bzgk/gb/showGb? type＝online&hcno
＝574AE910CA53FFE9D9375664D1B9DAE3,2023/5/17。

10.6 出境游行前说明会

说明会的主要内容包括:代表旅行社致欢迎词,表示欢迎,自我介绍;旅行团具体出发时间及集合地点;向旅游者讲解旅游行程单内容,包括境外的食宿标准、交通安排、景点概况等;前往国历史、天气、货币、特产、风俗习惯等基本情况;旅途中的安全问题,包括护照、贵重物品的保管,确认旅游者在国内的紧急联系人、联系方式等;应携带的个人物品及海关的一些规定、换汇事宜;落实有关分房、特殊要求等事项;旅行团境外纪律规定;发放旅行纪念品如旅行包等;解答参团者的各种疑问。因特殊原因未能安排行前说明会的,或参团旅游者未能参加说明会的,领队应在团队出发集合地点组织行前说明会。

10.6 Pre-departure briefing for outbound tour

The main content of the briefing includes: expressing welcome on behalf of the tour wholesaler, and introducing oneself; the specific departure time and meeting spot of the tour group; explaining the tour itinerary to tourists, including the overseas accommodation standards, transportation arrangements, and overview of tourist attractions; basic information on the history, weather, currency, specialties, customs and habits of the destination country; security issues during travel, including the safekeeping of passports and valuable items, confirmation of the tourists' emergency contacts in China and their contact information, etc; personal belongings that should be carried, as well as some customs regulations and issues on currency exchange; implementing matters related to room allocation and special requirements; disciplinary regulations for outbound tour groups; distributing souvenirs such as traveling bags; answering various questions from participants. If a pre-departure briefing cannot be arranged due to special reasons, or if the group tourists are unable to attend the briefing, the outbound tour escort should organize a pre-departure briefing at the departure and meeting spots of the group.

10.7 出境游境外住宿服务

境外住宿服务包括:[①]

1. 告知旅游者领队所住房间号,提醒旅游者保存并随身携带领队及地陪导游联系方式;

2. 告知旅游者饭店基本设施、免费提供的服务内容和需要另付费的项目及收费标准;

3. 与地陪导游一起检查房间设备、设施,需要时指导旅游者使用;

4. 宣布早餐的时间、地点;

10.7 Overseas accommodation service for outbound tour

Overseas accommodation service includes:

1. Informing tourists of the number of the room where the outbound tour escort is staying, and reminding them to keep and carry with them the contact information of the outbound tour escort and local tour guide;

2. Notifying tourists of the hotel's basic facilities, free services, items that require additional payment, and amount of fees;

3. Checking the room equipment and facilities with the local tour guide, and guiding tourists to use them when necessary;

4. Announcing the time and location for breakfast;

---

① 《出境旅游领队服务规范》,国家文化和旅游部网站,https://zwgk. mct. gov. cn/zfxxgkml/hybz/202302/t20230210_939033. html,2023/5/17。

5.离店前告知旅游者次日办理退房手续的相关程序与注意事项；

6.告知旅游者离店集合时间与地点；

7.离店时领队应提示旅游者带齐所有行李物品,检查有无遗留物品；

8.提示旅游者结清自费项目或商品费用；

9.敦促并协助地陪导游为旅游者办理离店的相关手续。

10.8　出境游境外用餐服务

境外用餐服务包括：①

1.团队用餐时,领队应监督地接社与地陪导游按照旅游合同的约定兑现用餐安排和用餐标准；

2.告知或要求地陪告知旅游者用餐后集合的时间、地点；

3.与地陪导游一道引导旅游者按照餐位就座用餐；

4.在用餐过程中进行巡视,了解旅游者的用餐情况及对餐食的意见；

5.检查旅游者的特殊预订要求(如清真餐、素食)是否得到落实；

6.在行程中如餐食需旅游者自理的,领队应提前要求地陪导游向旅游者介绍可用餐的地点及相关信息；

7.与地陪导游协商处理好旅游者在用餐过程中反映的问题,做好相关协调工作。

5. Familiarizing tourists with the relevant procedures and precautions for checking out the next day before leaving the hotel；

6. Telling tourists the departure time, meeting time, and location；

7. When leaving the hotel, the outbound tour escort should remind tourists to bring all their luggage and items，and check whether there is anything left；

8. Reminding tourists to settle the cost of self-funded items or goods；

9. Urging and assisting the local tour guide in handling the relevant procedures for tourists to check out.

10.8　Overseas dining service for outbound tour

Overseas dining service involves the following：

1. When a tour group dines, the outbound tour escort should supervise the local tour operator and the local tour guide to fulfill the meal arrangements and standards as agreed in the tour contract；

2. Informing or requesting the local tour guide to inform the tourists of the time and place to gather after meals；

3. Together with the local tour guide, guiding the tourists to take their seats and have meals；

4. Conducting inspections during the dining process to learn about the dining situation of the tourists and their opinions on the food；

5. Checking if the special booking requirements of the tourists (such as halal meals and vegetarian meals) have been implemented；

6. If the tourists need to pay for their own meals during the tour, the outbound tour escort should request the local tour guide in advance to introduce the available dining locations and relevant information to the tourists；

7. Discussing with the local tour guide to handle the issues reported by tourists during the dining process and coordinating relevant work.

---

① 《出境旅游领队服务规范》,国家文化和旅游部网站,https://zwgk. mct. gov. cn/zfxxgkml/hybz/202302/t20230210_939033. html,2023/5/17。

10.9 出境游境外游览服务

出境游境外游览服务包括：①

1. 领队应监督地陪导游执行行程游览计划，保证合同约定的游览时间；

2. 全程提示文明旅游注意事项，提示旅游者遵守游览须知；

3. 留意观察周边环境，评估安全隐患，全程提示安全注意事项，劝阻旅游者不安全的行为；

4. 始终与旅游者在一起活动，随时清点人数，以防旅游者走失；

5. 领队应敦促地陪导游带领旅游者游览，做好景点讲解；

6. 景点景区对参观游览有特别要求或安全注意事项时，对旅游者宣讲，建议游客根据自身状况决定是否参加具有较高风险的游览项目，充分告知风险；

7. 旅游者参加较高风险的游览项目时，重点宣讲安全事项，要求旅游者严格遵守项目的操作指引和安全提示；

8. 团队自由活动前，领队应着重提示安全注意事项，并告知旅游者集合时间及地点；

9. 团队集合时，领队应先行到达集合地点，清点人数，主动联系并寻找迟到的旅游者。

10.10 出境游另行付费旅游项目

领队不应擅自安排另行付费旅游项目。如旅游者要求安排另行付费旅游项目，领队应在行程计划中"自由活

10.9 Overseas sightseeing service for outbound tour

Overseas sightseeing service for the outbound tour includes：

1. The outbound tour escort should supervise the local tour guide to carry out the tour itinerary, ensuring the agreed tour time in the contract；

2. Remind tourists of the precautions for sensible tourism throughout the entire process, and remind them to comply with the travel instructions；

3. Observe the surrounding environment, evaluate safety hazards, remind the tourists of safety precautions throughout the process, and discourage unsafe behaviors of tourists；

4. Always stay with tourists and count the number of people at any time to prevent them from getting lost；

5. The outbound tour escort should urge the local tour guide to accompany the tourists and provide a good explanation of the scenic spots；

6. When scenic spots have special requirements or safety precautions for sightseeing, the outbound tour escort should inform the tourists and advise them to decide whether to participate in high-risk tourism items on the basis of their own conditions, and fully inform them of the risks；

7. When tourists participate in high-risk tourism items, the outbound tour escort should focus on informing them of safety precautions and require them to strictly follow the items' operational guidelines and safety tips；

8. Before the tour group is involved in free activities, the outbound tour escort should emphasize safety precautions and inform the tourists of the meeting time and location；

9. When the group gathers, the outbound tour escort should arrive at the meeting spot first, count the number of people, actively contact and search for late tourists.

10.10 Additionally paid tourism items for outbound tour

The outbound tour escort should not arrange additionally paid tour items without authorization. If tourists request additionally paid tourism items, the outbound tour escort

---

① 《出境旅游领队服务规范》，国家文化和旅游部网站，https：//zwgk. mct. gov. cn/zfxxgkml/hybz/202302/t20230210_939033. html，2023/5/17。

动"时段内组织实施且不影响其他旅游者行程安排。在另行付费旅游项目实施前,领队应要求旅游者签署旅行社规定制式的书面协议。领队应及时制止地陪导游擅自安排另行付费旅游项目。①

should organize and implement them during the "free activities" period without affecting the itinerary of other tourists. Before implementing an additionally paid tourism item, the outbound tour escort should require the tourists to sign a written agreement in the prescribed format by the travel agency. The outbound tour escort should promptly prevent the local tour guide from arranging additionally paid tourism items without authorization.

10.11　出境游境外购物安排

领队应严格按照旅游合同约定的购物活动安排购物服务,不应擅自增、减购物安排或强迫旅游者购物。购物时,领队应监督地接社和地陪导游严格执行在旅游合同或其附件中对购物安排的约定,不擅自延长购物时间、不擅自增加购物场所,对地接社或地陪导游的违约行为及时制止。提示旅游者遵守购物须知,并保留购物凭据。需要时,向旅游者介绍退税相关规定,协助旅游者办理退税手续。旅游者坚持要求安排行程计划之外的购物活动且影响到原计划的执行时,要求旅游者签订旅行社规定制式的行程变更确认单。如有旅游者不同意变更则不安排。②

10.11　Overseas shopping arrangements for outbound tour

The outbound tour escort should strictly arrange shopping service in accordance with the shopping activities stipulated in the tour contract, and should not arbitrarily increase or decrease shopping arrangements or force tourists to shop. When shopping, the outbound tour escort should supervise the local tour operator and local tour guide to strictly comply with the shopping arrangements stipulated in the tour contract or its attachments, and not extend the shopping time or add shopping venues without authorization. Any breach of contract by the local tour operator or local tour guide should be promptly stopped. Remind tourists to follow the shopping instructions and keep their shopping receipt. When necessary, introduce relevant tax refund regulations to tourists and assist them in handling tax refund procedures. When tourists insist on arranging shopping activities outside of the itinerary, which affects the performance of the original itinerary, they are required to sign a travel agency's prescribed itinerary change confirmation form. If there are tourists who do not agree to the change, no arrangements will be made.

10.12　知识拓展

10.12.1　出境游突发事件处理

10.12.1.1　航班延误或取消

遇航班延误或取消,领队应向航

10.12　Knowledge expansion

10.12.1　Emergency handling for outbound tour

10.12.1.1　Flight delay or cancellation

In case of flight delay or cancellation, the outbound tour

①　《出境旅游领队服务规范》,国家文化和旅游部网站,https://zwgk.mct.gov.cn/zfxxgkml/hybz/202302/t20230210_939033.html,2023/5/17。
②　《出境旅游领队服务规范》,国家文化和旅游部网站,https://zwgk.mct.gov.cn/zfxxgkml/hybz/202302/t20230210_939033.html,2023/5/17。

空公司证实延误的原因,落实预计起飞的时间;报告旅行社团队操作人员;向航空公司索取延误或取消证明,提示旅游者保管好保险理赔所需证据;安抚旅游者,需要时协助安排旅游者的食宿;为旅游者向航空公司争取合法合理的赔偿。①

escort should confirm the reason for the delay with the airline and confirm the estimated departure time, report to the group operators of the tour wholesaler; request proof of delay or cancellation from the airline and remind tourists to keep the necessary evidence for making claims to the insurance company; comfort tourists and assist in arranging their accommodation and meals when needed; strive for legal and reasonable compensation from airlines for tourists.

▶ 10.12.1.2　托运行李延误与丢失

托运行李出现延误,领队应协助旅游者取得承运人出具的相关证明及联系方式;协助旅游者对延误的行李进行追踪。托运行李丢失,领队应详细询问行李的丢失细节;协助旅游者与航空公司交涉,并提供所需的联系方式;协助旅游者购买临时必需品;行李无法找回,协助旅游者向运输公司/保险公司(如需)索赔。②

▶ 10.12.1.2　Delay and loss of checked baggage

If there is a delay in checked luggage, the outbound tour escort should assist the tourist in obtaining relevant evidence and contact information issued by the carrier and assist tourists in tracking delayed luggage. If the checked baggage is lost, the outbound tour escort should inquire about the details of the lost baggage, assist tourists in negotiating with the airlines and provide necessary contact information, and assist tourists in purchasing temporary necessities. If the luggage cannot be retrieved, assist tourists in claiming compensation from the transportation company/insurance company (if necessary).

▶ 10.12.1.3　旅游者身份证件遗失

要尽快去当地的警察局报案挂失,开具护照遗失证明。持护照遗失证明补办护照或旅行证。在中国大使馆或领事馆补办护照,签发时间为自受理申请之日起15个工作日,等待时间较长,因此不推荐。可办理旅行证。正常情况下中国大使馆或领事馆办理旅行证只需4个工作日,加急只需2个工作日。旅行证有效期为2年。

旅行证不等同于护照。原则上,旅行证只能供回国使用,不允许跨国旅行。比如在中国驻意大利大使馆办好了旅行证,那么只被允许从意大利

▶ 10.12.1.3　Tourist's loss of identity document

Report the loss to the local police station as soon as possible and obtian a passport loss certificate. Present the passport loss certificate to apply for a replacement of passport or travel certificate. To apply for a new passport in a Chinese embassy or consulate takes 15 working days from the date of acceptance of the application, and the waiting time is relatively long, so it is not recommended. The tourist can apply for a travel certificate. To apply for a travel certificate in a Chinese embassy or consulate usually takes 4 working days, and only 2 working days for expedited service. The validity period of the travel certificate is two years.

The travel certificate is not equivalent to the passport. In principle, the travel certificate can only be used for returning to China and cross-border travel is not allowed. For example, if a travel certificate is obtained from the Chinese Embassy in

---

① 《出境旅游领队服务规范》,国家文化和旅游部网站,https://zwgk.mct.gov.cn/zfxxgkml/hybz/202302/t20230210_939033.html,2023/5/17。

② 《出境旅游领队服务规范》,国家文化和旅游部网站,https://zwgk.mct.gov.cn/zfxxgkml/hybz/202302/t20230210_939033.html,2023/5/17。

回国。如果时间允许,可以去意大利的市政厅重新申请签证。需要注意的是,旅行证必须和护照复印件及所在国警方出具的护照遗失证明共同使用。部分国家还要求旅游者在持有旅行证的基础上,前往移民局补办入境签证。出国前最好先将相关身份证明做好备份,并随身带上复印件。最好的办法是将身份证、护照首页和签证页、户口本、机票拍照,备一份在电邮中和手机上。

有一种情况允许旅游者持旅行证去别的国家,但旅游者必须有充分的理由。所谓充分的理由就是去这个国家只为了经停回国。在这种情况下,出入境人员将会放行,让旅游者前往这个国家,但旅游者除了出示旅行证、护照复印件、签证复印件和遗失证明之外,还应该出示从目的国家回国的机票。香港和内地之间也需要出入境手续,所以持临时证件的游客不能从香港入境,最好从报失国直飞回国。

Italy, the tourist will only be allowed to return from Italy to China. If time permits, the tourist can reapply for a visa at an Italian city hall. It should be noted that a travel certificate must be used together with a copy of the passport and a passport loss certificate issued by the local police. In some countries, besides a travel certificate, the tourist also needs to go to the immigration office to apply for a new visa. The tourist had better make a backup of the relevant identification documents before going abroad and bring a copy with him/her. The best way is to take a photo of the ID card, the first page of the passport, visa page, household register and flight ticket, and keep a copy in the email and mobile phone.

There is a situation where it is still possible to travel to another country with a travel certificate, but the tourist must have a sufficient reason. The so-called sufficient reason is that the tourist goes to this country for tranfer and return to his/her home country. In such case, the entry-exit personnel will allow the tourist to go to this country. However, in addition to presenting the travel certificate, copies of the passport and visa, and the loss certificate, the tourist should also present the flight ticket from the destination country to his/her home country. There are also entry formalities between Hong Kong and Chinese mainland, so tourists holding temporary documents cannot enter Hong Kong. It is best for the traveler to fly directly from the country where he/she reported loss to the home country.

❈ Exercises

Ⅰ. Fill in the blanks with proper forms of words.

1. Article 36 of Tourism Law stipulates that when _____ (organize) outbound tours or organizing and _____ (receive) inbound tours, travel agencies _____ (arrange) an outbound tour escort for the outbound tour or a tour guide for the inbound tour throughout the journey.

2. When working, outbound tour escorts shall accept the _____ (appoint) of the travel agency that _____ (obtain) the business license for the outbound tour and _____ (sign) an employment contract with them, carry the tour guide certificate and wear the tour guide _____ (identify).

3. Those who do not meet the requirement for outbound tour escorts _____ (prohibit) from providing relevant services. Outbound tour escorts shall not entrust

others _____ (provide) relevant service, either.

4. The outbound tour escort should inform the tourists and distribute to them the travel documents and customs _____ (clear) documents 〔such as entry and exit registration cards, customs _____ (declare) forms, etc.〕 that should be _____ (present) / _____ (submit) to the border inspection/immigration authorities at the locality of entry during customs clearance, guiding the group _____ (clear) customs in sequence.

5. The outbound tour escort should provide tourists with _____ (qualify) reception service according to the content and standards _____ (stipulate) in the tour contract _____ (sign) between the outbound tour wholesaler and tourists, and supervise the overseas tour operator and its tour guides _____ (fulfill) the tour contract as _____ (agree).

Ⅱ. **Translate the following Chinese sentences into English.**

1. 出境游领队代表组团社监督地接社和地陪导游履行旅游合同,按照组团社的行程计划兑现接待服务承诺,监督其执行接待标准和保证服务质量,维护组团社和旅游者合法权益。

2. 出境游领队与地接社和地陪导游共同实施旅游接待计划,协助处理旅游行程中的突发事件、纠纷及其他问题。

3. 领队不应擅自安排另行付费旅游项目。如旅游者要求安排另行付费旅游项目,领队应在行程计划中"自由活动"时段内组织实施且不影响其他旅游者行程安排。在另行付费旅游项目实施前,领队应要求旅游者签署旅行社规定制式的书面协议。领队应及时制止地陪导游擅自安排另行付费旅游项目。

4. 团队用餐时,领队应监督地接社与地陪导游按照旅游合同的约定兑现用餐安排和用餐标准。与地陪导游协商处理好旅游者在用餐过程中反映的问题,做好相关协调工作。

Ⅲ. Translate the following English sentences into Chinese.

1. The English newspaper *China Daily*'s reported on May 11, 2023, "China has so far resumed outbound group tours to 60 countries and regions, according to the Ministry of Culture and Tourism. Southeast Asian countries remain the most popular destinations for Chinese tourists, and countries such as Egypt and the United Arab Emirates are becoming increasingly sought after by Chinese consumers, Tuniu found."

2. According to the English newspaper *China Daily*'s report on May 11, 2023, the travel market witnessed a bonanza during the five-day May Day holiday, with the strongest customer demand in the past three years; pent-up demand to travel abroad is expected to be further released in the second half of the year, while the summer vacation period is likely to see greater travel demand from families who haven't taken trips for a long time, according to Tuniu Corp., an online travel agency.

3. According to the English newspaper *China Daily*'s report on May 11, 2023, more people have inquired about and booked cruise tours in Europe and the polar regions for the latter half of the year, with most of the trips lasting more than 15 days and carrying a high price tag, according to Tuniu.

"Chinese travelers now favor small and private group tours more, and young consumers in particular are looking for high-quality experiences. They prefer high-end catering, transport and accommodation options," said Li Peng, director of long-haul outbound tourism at Tuniu.

4. China and Brazil are the two markets with the highest intent to travel to Europe in the short term. In China, 73% of respondents hope to visit the region over the summer—this level of assurance harks back to the early months of 2020 before the COVID-19 crisis. Of these travelers, about 52% demonstrated a strong certainty in realizing their plans. In Brazil, 52% of respondents said they intend to visit Europe in the coming months, of which 32% expressed a strong likelihood.

In Australia, Canada and the United States, travel sentiment is relatively similar, with 38%, 37% and 36% of respondents, respectively, intending to visit Europe between May—August 2023. The positive sentiment is primarily driven by people below the age of 50.

Japan shows the weakest travel intent, with only 26% of surveyed respondents planning to travel outside of East Asia, and only 15% of them intending to travel to Europe. [1]

Ⅳ. Questions and answers.

1. What are the outbound tour escort's main duties for entry and exit service and overseas sightseeing service?

2. As an outbound tour escort, what are the key points in dealing with additionally paid tourism items for the outbound tour?

3. How will an outbound tour escort handle emergency for the outbound tour?

---

[1] https://etc-corporate.org/news/long-haul-travellers-to-europe-become-more-cost-conscious/, 2023/5/18。

习题答案

Unit ❶

Ⅰ. 1. joining, covered   2. paid, provided

3. credibility, timely, payment, receiving, to avoid

4. will be exempted, will be charged

Ⅱ. 1. The functional organizational structure of China's travel agencies can be divided into three types established according to the business process, according to the source market and according to the business category.

2. The liaison department in some travel agencies is also known as market department, sales department or marketing department. The main business is to design and sell the travel agency's products.

3. The full name of the planning department is planning and dispatching department with its main duty being planning and dispatching reception services.

4. The evaluation of customers needs to be based on the analysis of detailed information and data of previous customer files to ensure the objectivity of the evaluation.

Ⅲ. 1.散客旅游产品是指旅游人数低于10人的旅游产品。

2.客户关系的巩固对旅行社的可持续发展具有更重要的意义。可以采用多样化的策略。

3.客户档案是旅行社在经营过程中与供应商、分销商、旅游者、其他相关部门与企业开展业务合作的历史记录。

4.外联部门与旅游客户经过洽谈,就旅游产品的内容、价格、付款方式和优惠条件进行协商并达成一致意见,最后签订合作意向书、合同书或委托书等书面协议,建立业务合作关系。

Ⅳ. 1. see 1.5.1, 1.5.3   2. see 1.5.4.1

Unit ❷

Ⅰ.1. locality, entry, wholesaler 2. planning, scheduling, to purchase, catering
3. procurement, detailed 4. confirmed, compensation
5. holding, covered 6. operator, established

Ⅱ.1. The functions of this department are mainly reflected in the following aspects: functions to select, to sign contracts, to communicate and coordinate, and to collect statistics.

2. The procurement business of the planning and dispatching department refers to the action of the planning and dispatching personnel of the travel agency to purchase single tourism service products from relevant tourism product suppliers at a certain price in order to combine them into a certain tourism product.

3. If the contract cannot continue to be performed due to one party's breach of contract or the influence of force majeure, both parties shall terminate the cooperation. The transfer of this agreement is invalid.

4. The planning and dispatching department works out a detailed tourist group reception plan and implements various ordering tasks. It completes and sends all kinds of advance orders, changed orders and canceled orders, and explains various special requirements of the tourist group.

Ⅲ.1.地接社应配合组团社关于接待费用结算的要求及时填写结算单,并加盖地接社财务专用章,送达组团社财务部门。

2.未经组团社书面同意,地接社不得以任何方式将组团社组织的旅游者与其他旅游者合并接待,或者转交任何第三方接待。

3.一方因不可抗力等不可归责于合同任何一方的事由不能履行合同的,应当及时通知另一方,并在合理期限内提供证明。双方应采取合理适当措施防止损失扩大。

4.若不可抗力等不可归责于合同任何一方的事由导致行程延滞,组团社和地接社应及时与旅游者协商、调整行程,所增加的费用,同意旅游者不承担的部分由组团社和地接社协商承担。

Ⅳ.1. see 2.5 2. see 2.3.4

Unit ❸

Ⅰ.1. represented, to occupy　2. disseminating, talented

3. accessible, driver, sustainability

4. representative, preserved, mountainous, technically, defensive, reflection

Ⅱ. 1. Throughout the development of Fujian culture, the main sources of its formation are the heritage of Minyue culture, the introduction of central China's culture, the spread of religious culture and the impact of overseas culture.

2. Fujian in the Song Dynasty (960—1279) was one of the famous cultural provinces in the south, which made outstanding achievements in imperial examinations, academies, publishing and other fields. In the intangible cultural industry, there arose many famous poets, writers, historians and scientists in Fujian in the Song Dynasty, creating a magnificent cultural wave.

3. Wang Shenzhi (862—925) was a sensible statesman in the period of Five Dynasties (907—960) and Ten States (902—979). During his rule of more than 30 years, he took history as a lesson and put people first. He had made outstanding contributions to economy, agriculture, education, talent training, commerce and overseas trade, and had greatly promoted the development of Fujian in all aspects, so Fujian became a relatively stable and prosperous place in the country at that time. Consequently, he was also called "the ruler of the Min State, who developed Fujian" by later generations, and was deeply loved by the people.

4. Culturally-loaded words contain rich cultural connotations and we cannot find equivalent expressions in the target language, resulting in cultural default. Explanatory translation is undoubtedly the translation strategy of culturally-loaded words.

Ⅲ.1.简而言之,入境旅游是指外国人或非居民访问某个国家,而出境旅游指的是某个国家的居民离开本国,访问另一个国家。

2.当一个国家吸引大量入境旅客时,游客会在酒店、餐饮、景点、纪念品和其他设施上花钱。这创造了就业机会,并通过消费税为该国的国库增加了额外的资金。

3.如果一个国家的入境旅游多于出境旅游,那么它就有旅游贸易顺差。一个具有旅游贸易顺差的国家可能认为旅游业是一个非常有利可图的出口行业。对美国来说,国际旅行作为一个整体不断促进美国就业增长,并有助于平衡该国的贸易,这是其最大的服务出口。

4.该系列遗产作为一个整体,由其组成部分和要素组成,真实地描述了宋元时期泉州作为全球海上商贸中心的总体布局、宋元时期的贸易体系的功能、历史和社会结构、史实。

Ⅳ. 1. see 3.4.1　2. see 3.4.2

Unit ❹

Ⅰ. 1. fermentation，non-fermentation，semi-fermented

2. endangerment 3. Pestled，produced

4. Hidden，symmetrical，objectively，glorifying，humanistic

Ⅱ. 1. Mount Wuyi is the birthplace of black tea and oolong tea. The tea custom accompanied by Wuyi rock tea production technique enjoys strong local characteristics. The customs of shouting to mountain to bless a bumper harvest of tea production，tea contest and tea ceremony etc. are popular among the public in this area.

2. The tea growers in Anxi absorbed the principle of the full fermentation of black tea and the non-fermentation of green tea，and invented a semi-fermented tea-making process. Anxi Tieguanyin is one of the six major types of tea in China.

3. Pestled tea represents a special tea culture produced by Hakkas in order to survive and avoid the attack of southern plague.

4. The two constituent elements of cultural imagery are physical images and connotation. The physical image is a carrier of information，reflecting people's perception of a certain object；the connotation refers to the extended meaning or cultural meaning of objects in a specific cultural context，which is the reflection of cultural imagery.

Ⅲ. 1. 武夷山是世界上最杰出的亚热带森林之一。这是一个规模最大、最具代表性的保护得最好的森林，包括中国亚热带森林和华南雨林的多样性，植物多样性高。

2. 武夷山是理学的摇篮，理学在东亚和东南亚国家占据主导地位长达几个世纪，并影响了世界大部分地区的哲学和政府。

3. 鼓浪屿是厦门装饰风格的起源和最佳代表。厦门装饰风格（Amoy Deco Style）以厦门当地的方言"Amoy"命名，指的是一种建筑风格和类型，最早出现在鼓浪屿，体现了来自当地建筑传统、早期西方尤其是现代主义的影响以及闽南移民文化的灵感的融合。基于这些，厦门装饰风格展示了传统建筑类型向新形式的转变，后来在整个东南亚被作为参照物，并在更广泛的地区流行。

4. 具有历史意义的景观的完整性得以保持，主要是由于对具有历史意义的建筑结构的持续保护和对新建筑的高度、体积和形式的有效开发控制。

Ⅳ. 1. see 4.3 2. see 4.4.1

Unit ❺

I. 1. primarily, attractive, complimentary   2. attendees, conferencing, located
3. commonly, is established, wholly-owned, independently, to manage
4. are agreed, signed, to ensure, managed   5. known, equipped, to live, used

II. 1. Suite hotels are the latest trend and the fastest-growing segments of the hotel industry. Such hotels provide a living room and a separate bedroom for the hotel guest.

2. Residential hotels provide long-term or permanent accommodation for guests. Usually the guest makes a lease with the hotel for a minimum of one month up to a year. The room of residential hotels generally includes a living room，bedroom, kitchen, private balcony, washing machines, kitchen utensils, etc. Unlike normal hotels，residential hotels only provide weekly housekeeping service.

3. Another new type or segment of the hospitality industry is the timeshare hotels. Timeshare hotels are where the guests purchase the ownership of accommodations for a specific period. These owners may also have the unit rented out by the management company that operates the hotel.

4. The executive suite generally refers to the suite on the administrative floor. Some hotels have executive floors specifically designed for business guests and are equipped with dedicated business centers and coffee shops. There is an independent front desk for quick check-in and check-out.

III.1.每年"品牌金融"对5 000个最大的品牌进行评估,并发布大约100份报告,对所有行业和国家的品牌进行排名。该公司评选出的"2022年50强酒店"排行榜中包括了全球价值最高、实力最强的50大酒店品牌。

2."香格里拉"这个名字唤起了一个遥远而美丽的景观形象,在这里与自然的和谐接近完美。我们力图不辜负"香格里拉"这个名字,为此,我们将环境可持续性纳入新的发展项目和资产增强计划。我们还努力促进酒店日常运营中的环境管理。

3.华邑酒店与度假村是洲际酒店集团的一个酒店品牌。华邑酒店与度假村是一个以中国消费者的风俗习惯为核心打造的国际高端酒店品牌。华邑酒店与度假村为客人提供身临其境的中国文化体验,并将中国美学和文化遗产引入日常生活。它通过"饮食"和"聚会"展示了中国的好客之道。

4.如今,人们普遍认为,酒店业的下一步倾向于个性化。无论如何,为了实现高水平的个性化服务,必须保持与客人的持续而优质的沟通。值得庆幸的是,技术让酒店经营者更容易与客人沟通,这是由于现在有很多直接联系他们的方式,如社交媒体和定位通知。

IV. 1. see 5.3.3.3   2. see 5.3.3.4   3. see 5.3.4

Unit ❻

Ⅰ. 1. calculated, initially, hoped to, have inherited, commitment, accommodation
2. listed, founded, headquartered, has been selected
3. upgraded, providing, highly
4. was launched, extended
5. has been rooted, to enter, has... adhered 6. had opened, had entered, has been cultivated, has laid

Ⅱ.1. A total of 6 hotel brands under Marriott International Group, including Ritz-Carlton, JW Marriott, Marriott, Renaissance, Marriott and Marriott Executive Apartments, have entered the Chinese market. Marriott International Group is also expected to welcome the opening of the 500th hotel in China in early 2023, further demonstrating Marriott International's commitment to continue to develop the Chinese market.

2. InterContinental Hotels Group is a famous global hotel group. It operates and franchises more than 6 000 hotels in more than 100 countries and regions around the world with 18 brands. It has more than 60 years of international hotel management experience.

3. Hilton is one of the largest and fastest growing hotel companies in the world, with 19 brands and 7 215 hotels in 122 countries and regions. Hilton International Hotel Group (HI), a branch of Hilton Group, headquartered in the United Kingdom, has the right to use the "Hilton" trademark worldwide except in the United States.

4. Accor Hotel Group enjoys 40 hotel brands and 5 400 hotels in 110 countries worldwide, which can meet the needs of different customers. Accor offers the largest brand portfolio in the hotel industry comprised of internationally acclaimed luxury and premium brands as well as popular midscale and economy brands.

Ⅲ. 1.即使客人离开了一处酒店,他们仍然是顾客。这意味着酒店经营者不应该停止所有沟通。后续沟通有助于建立品牌信任和忠诚度。

2.客人离开酒店后发一封感谢邮件。客人离开酒店后直接跟进是至关重要的。给他们提供一种直接反馈的方式。如果客人体验不佳,这就有可能避免他们的线上差评,酒店经营者就可以开始改善服务从而建立忠诚度。如果客人对酒店有反馈意见,那么根据反馈意见采取行动同样重要。当客人知道酒店经营者正在倾听并适应他们的需求时,他们会建立对品牌的忠诚度。

3.凯悦酒店的文化建立在同理心的实践之上,以倾听为基础,以关怀为动力。它努力创造归属感和社区意识:重视彼此之间、和客人以及和社区之间的关系,每天都在践行尊重、诚信、创造力、谦逊、同理心和快乐的价值观。

4.欧洲旅游协会(ETOA)是欧洲旅行社和供应商的贸易协会,从全球品牌到当地独立企业。会员包括旅游社和在线运营商、中介和批发商、欧洲各国旅游局、酒店、景点、科技公司以及其他旅游和商业服务提供商。

Ⅳ. 1. see 6.3.1.1   2. see 6.3.1.2   3. see 6.3.2

Unit ❼

Ⅰ. 1. drafting，is drafted，is… submitted，approval，taken
2. required，are implemented，processed，verification
3. accepting，understand，canceling，to consolidate
4. offered，organized，aiming，ensuring，determination，utilization
5. pricing，competitiveness，indicators，corresponding，basis

Ⅱ. 1. The confirmed reservation usually refers to the reservation that is confirmed in writing，but the guest has not yet made the advance payment or paid deposit. For guests who have made confirmed reservations and come to register for accommodation，the risk of collecting debt from them is relatively low.

2. In order to prevent guests from temporarily cancelling their reservations and causing losses due to the failure to rent out their rooms，hotels may require guests to prepay a deposit or use other means to ensure their booking requirements. That is called guaranteed reservations.

3. In order to improve the accuracy of reservations and the occupancy rate of the hotel，it is necessary to conduct multiple checks with the guests before they arrive at the hotel. The staff should ask if the guest can arrive on schedule，whether there are any changes in the number of people staying，time and requirements，etc. The check is usually conducted three times.

4. For hotels with a certain scale，the sales department of the hotel is responsible for booking rooms. At the same time，the front desk also accepts room reservations. The reservation is a very important task of the front desk.

Ⅲ. 1.美国酒店行业协会是代表酒店业各个领域的独特声音,包括主要连锁酒店、独立酒店、管理公司、房地产投资信托基金、廉价酒店、行业合作伙伴等。它致力于成为美国酒店业的代表,提供必需的资源,为必需的资源提供支持并保护必需的资源,以建立一个充满活力和团结的酒店业,为美国经济提供动力。

2.根据美国酒店行业协会和牛津经济研究院 2023 年 6 月 4 日发布的一项经济分析,美国酒店为 830 万个美国工作岗位提供了支持,相当于美国每 25 个工作岗位中就有近 1 个酒店的岗位。这项研究包括对酒店业在每个州和国会选区的经济影响的细分,全面审视了酒店如何为全国各地的社区做出贡献。

3.酒店业直接影响的组成部分是:

酒店运营:代表酒店的收入(如客房、食品和饮料等)加上某些税收(住宿税和其他销售税);酒店客人辅助支出:代表酒店客人在目的地其他业务上的支出;资本投资:代表新建酒店、装修和现有酒店维护的持续资本支出。

Ⅳ. 1. see 7.9　　2. see 7.12　　3. see 7.11.3—7.11.4

Unit ❽

Ⅰ. 1. has obtained, punished, infringing, operation 2. operating, announced
3. issued, enters, leaves 4. signed, abolishment, known

Ⅱ. 1. Visas are generally endorsed on passports, some on other travel documents instead of passports, and some are issued with separate paper visas (a kind of visa signed on a special piece of paper separately, but it must be used together with the passport).

2. The visa for multiple entries means that within the validity period of the visa, the holder can enter and leave a country many times.

3. Hong Kong's group travel endorsement can be divided into one time or two times within three months and one time or two times within one year. Each time visitors can stay for seven days, and it is necessary to enter and exit with the group.

4. With the progress of science and technology, some countries have begun to issue electronic visas and biological visas, greatly enhancing the anti-counterfeiting function of visas.

Ⅲ. 1.申根签证是一种短期停留签证,允许个人前往申根区的任何成员国,每次停留最多90天,用于旅游或商务目的。申根签证是欧洲最常见的签证。它使其持有人能够从任何申根成员国进入申根区、在申根区内自由旅行和离开申根区。申根区内没有边境管制。

2.1985年6月14日签署的《申根协定》是一项导致大多数欧洲国家废除国家边界的条约,旨在建立一个被称为"申根区"的无边界欧洲。

3.欧洲将于2023年推出新的免签证系统。欧洲旅行信息和授权系统(ETIAS)将允许游客在申根区内旅行90天。符合条件的国家的公民可以进行商务、过境、旅游、健康或商业旅行。从2023年开始,他们必须申请欧洲旅行信息和授权系统豁免签证。

4.由于使馆要求或时差原因,为保证您的签证可以更加顺利地办理,建议选择的保险起止期在您的出行日期的基础上前后各增加两天。

Ⅳ. 1. see <u>8.2</u> 2. see <u>8.2</u>

Unit ❾

Ⅰ. 1. to produce, considering, combining, operator, existing, provided, basis

2. written, involving, confirmation, requirements

3. fails to, agreed, compensatory, caused

4. is numbered, distributed, assigns, issued

Ⅱ. 1. It is very important to select the appropriate quotation of the overseas travel agency. All relevant information shall be provided in inquiry: the number of people, departure date, detailed itinerary, hotel grade, vehicle requirements, dining conditions, scenic spot tickets, special service items, etc. Select more than two overseas travel agencies for comparison.

2. Tourists need to provide a valid original passport for the private purpose and signed by the holder. The passport should have the validity of more than 6 months. If the passport is changed, the old passport shall be provided; tourists with a history of visa refusal need to provide a visa refusal description.

3. The planning and dispatching personnel of the outbound tour wholesaler log in to the provincial tourism administration website, enter the name list of the outbound tour group, itinerary, traveling time and other information, and wait for the approval of the provincial tourism administration.

4. You can use the existing classic outbound tour itinerary provided by travel agencies, the outbound tour itinerary provided by overseas tour operators, and design the outbound tour itinerary on the basis of the specific needs of customers.

Ⅲ. 1.甲乙双方为发展共同的事业,本着平等互利的原则,经友好协商,为组织、接待中国公民赴法国旅游事宜,明确双方的权利义务,订立本合同。

2.若乙方未按接待标准为旅游团提供服务,造成旅游者经济损失,乙方应承担赔偿责任。甲方有向乙方旅游管理机构投诉并要求赔偿的权利。

3.根据欧洲旅游委员会 2023 年 6 月 1 日的报道,随着夏季的临近,中国、巴西、澳大利亚、加拿大和美国超过 50% 的受访者对出国旅行表示乐观。其中,欧洲仍然是 2023 年 5 月至 8 月长途旅行的首选。计划访问该地区的游客中,近一半是回头客,这表明欧洲有能力树立良好的声誉,满足游客,并吸引他们重游故地。

4.欧洲旅游委员会成立于 1948 年,是旅游业的一个独特协会,代表欧洲各国的国家旅游组织。其使命是加强欧洲作为旅游目的地的可持续发展。

Ⅳ. 1. see 9.3.3 2. see 9.5

Unit ❿

Ⅰ.1. organizing, receiving, shall arrange

2. appointment, obtained, signed, identification   3. are prohibited, to provide

4. clearance, declaration, presented, submitted, to clear

5. qualified, stipulated, signed, to fulfill, agreed

Ⅱ. 1. The outbound tour escort works as the reprensentative of the tour wholesaler to supervise the local tour operator and the local guide to fulfill the tour contract and realize reception service commitment according to the tour itinerary of the tour wholesaler. The escort supervises the implementation of reception standards and ensures service quality, and safeguards the legitimate rights and interests of the tour wholesaler and tourists.

2. The outbound tour escort collaborates with local tour operators and local tour guides to implement tour reception plans and assists in handling unexpected events, disputes, and other issues in the tour.

3. The outbound tour escort should not arrange additionally paid tourism items without authorization. If tourists request additionally paid tourism items, the outbound tour escort should organize and implement them during the "free activities" period without affecting the itinerary of other tourists. Before implementing an additionally paid tourism item, the outbound tour escort should require the tourists to sign a written agreement in the prescribed format by the travel agency. The outbound tour escort should promptly prevent the local tour guide from arranging additionally paid tourism items without authorization.

4. When a tour group dines, the outbound tour escort should supervise the local tour operator and the local tour guide to fulfill the meal arrangements and standards as agreed in the tour contract. The escort should discuss with the local tour guide to handle the issues reported by tourists during the dining process, and coordinate relevant work.

Ⅲ. 1.英文报纸《中国日报》2023 年 5 月 11 日报道:"根据文化和旅游部的数据,到目前为止,中国已经恢复了 60 个国家和地区的出境团队游。途牛发现,东南亚国家仍然是最受中国游客欢迎的目的地,埃及和阿拉伯联合酋长国等国家越来越受到中国消费者的追捧。"

2.据英文报纸《中国日报》2023 年 5 月 11 日报道,在为期五天的五一假期期间,旅游市场火爆,客户需求是过去三年来最强劲的;据在线旅行社途牛公司称,被压抑的出国旅行需求预计将在今年下半年进一步释放,而暑假期间,长期没有旅行的家庭可能会有更大的旅行需求。

3.据英文报纸《中国日报》2023年5月11日报道,途牛表示,今年下半年,越来越多的人询问并预订了欧洲和极地的游轮旅行,其中大多数旅行持续时间超过15天,价格高昂。

途牛远程出境旅游经理李鹏表示:"中国游客现在更喜欢小型和私人团体游,尤其是年轻消费者正在寻找高质量的体验。他们更喜欢高端餐饮、交通和住宿选择。"

4.中国和巴西是短期内前往欧洲意愿最强的两个市场。在中国,73%的受访者希望在夏季访问该地区,这一水平与2020年初新冠肺炎危机之前的几个月持平。在这些旅行者中,约52%的人在实现他们的计划时表现出了强烈的确定性。在巴西,52%的受访者表示他们打算在未来几个月访问欧洲,其中32%的人表示很有可能。

在澳大利亚、加拿大和美国,旅游心理相对相似,分别有38%、37%和36%的受访者打算在2023年5月至8月期间访问欧洲。主要是由50岁以下的人做出这种积极反应。

日本市场的旅行意愿最弱,只有26%的受访者计划前往东亚以外的地方旅行,只有15%的受访者打算前往欧洲。

Ⅳ. 1. see <u>10.4</u>, <u>10.5.2</u>, <u>10.5.3</u>, <u>10.9</u>　　2. see <u>10.10</u>　　3. see <u>10.12</u>

参考文献

文件法规：

1. 国务院关于修改《旅行社管理条例》的决定，中央人民政府网站，http://www.gov.cn/gongbao/content/2002/content_61771.htm

2. 境内旅游组团社与地接社合同（示范合同），中国政府网，http://www.gov.cn/govweb/foot/2014－04/17/content_2661652.htm

3. 《中国公民出国旅游管理办法》，国家文化和旅游部网站，https://zwgk.mct.gov.cn/zfxxgkml/zcfg/xzfg/202012/t20201204_905494.html

4. 《旅行社条例》，国家文化和旅游部网站，https://zwgk.mct.gov.cn/zfxxgkml/zcfg/xzfg/202012/t2020120

5. 《旅游法》，国家文化和旅游部网站，https://zwgk.mct.gov.cn/zfxxgkml/zcfg/fl/202105/t20210526_924763.html

6. 《旅行社条例实施细则》，国家文化和旅游部网站，https://zwgk.mct.gov.cn/zfxxgkml/zcfg/bmgz/202012/t20201204_905330.html

7. 《出境旅游领队服务规范》，国家文化和旅游部网站，https://zwgk.mct.gov.cn/zfxxgkml/hybz/202302/t20230210_939033.html

8. 《中华人民共和国出境入境管理法》，国家移民管理局网站，https://www.nia.gov.cn/n741440/n741547/c1013311/content.html

9. 《普通护照签发服务指南》，国家移民管理局政务服务平台，https://s.nia.gov.cn/mps/bszy/gmcrg/slpthz/201903/t20190313_1011.html

10. 《往来港澳通行证和签注签发服务指南》，国家移民管理局政务服务平台，https://s.nia.gov.cn/mps/bszy/wlgaot/sqgowl/201903/t20190313_1002.html

11. 《旅行社出境旅游服务规范》，全国标准信息公共服务平台，http://c.gb688.cn/bzgk/gb/showGb? type＝online&hcno＝574AE910CA53FFE9D9375664D1B9DAE3

著作：

1. 福建省地方志编纂委员会 编，《福建省志》，北京：方志出版社，2002

2. 高燕 主编，《旅行社经营管理与实务》，杭州：浙江大学出版社，2014

3. 李伟清 主编，《酒店经营管理实务》，北京：中国旅游出版社，2021

4. 刘伟，《酒店管理》，北京：中国人民大学出版社，2022

5. 吕海龙，刘雪梅 主编，《旅行社计调业务》，北京：北京理工大学出版社，2017

6. 叶娅丽，陈学春 主编，《旅行社经营与管理》，北京：北京理工大学出版社，2018

7. 张春莲,盖艳秋 主编,《旅行社计调操作实务》,北京:中国旅游出版社,2017

8. 赵爱华 主编,《旅行社计调业务》,北京:中国旅游出版社,2021

9. 朱晔,问建军 主编,《旅行社经营与管理业务》,西安:西安交通大学出版社,2014

论文:

1. 蔡雄彬,从明清时期装饰艺术看当时闽南民居文化,广东园林,2012,(6)

2. 陈东,船政文化在近代中国文化重组中的作用,闽江学院学报,2005,(4)

3. 陈榕三,王审知与闽台根亲文化的研究,现代台湾研究,2009,(2)

4. 戴志坚,闽文化及其对福建传统民居的影响,南方建筑,2011,(6)

5. 邓文金,马照海,福建土楼文化三论,闽台文化研究,2009,(1)

6. 林更生,客家擂茶探源,茶叶科学技术,2009,(1)

7. 王冬凌,福州船政学堂及其科学教育,大连海事大学学报(社会科学版),2004,(1)

8. 徐晓望,论宋代福建经济文化的历史地位,东南学术,2002,(2)

9. 卓娜,福建民居三坊七巷的装饰木雕艺术,南京工程学院学报(社会科学版),2010,(3)

网络文章:

1. Brand Finance：HOTELS 50 2022，https：//brandirectory. com/rankings/hotels/

2. Explore Our Brands，https：//www. marriott. com/marriott-brands. mi

3. Fujian tulou，https：//whc. unesco. org/en/list/1113

4. Jordan Hollander，What Is a Boutique Hotel? A Clear Definition with Examples，January 26，2022，https：//hoteltechreport. com/news/boutique-hotel

5. Kulangsu，a Historic International Settlement，https：//whc. unesco. org/en/list/1541/

6. Mount Wuyi，https：//whc. unesco. org/en/list/911/

7. Our Story of Innovation，https：//www. marriott. com/about/culture-and-values/history. mi

8. Quanzhou：Emporium of the World in Song-Yuan China，https：//whc. unesco. org/en/list/1561

9. The American Hotel & Lodging Association，A New Era for U. S. Hotels—2023 State of the Hotel Industry Report，https：//www. ahla. com/sites/default/files/AHLA. SOTI_. Report. 2023. final_. 002. pdf? inf_contact_key＝b0761d7a09db3213fa8aa6ca34c764ff

10. The Criteria for Selection，https：//whc. unesco. org/en/criteria/

11. The World Tourism Organization，https：//www. unwto. org/about-us

12. What Do Hotel Stars Mean in Europe? https：//www. hotrec. eu/industry-projects/hotel-stars/

13. What Is the Difference Between Inbound and Outbound Tourism? https：//www. reference. com/world-view/difference-between-inbound-outbound-tourism-6760686bcb6e64b0

14. What Is Intangible Cultural Heritage? https：//ich. unesco. org/en/what-is-intangible-heritage-00003

15. 深耕中国市场,凯悦酒店集团大中华区开业 109 家酒店,网易,2022 年 2 月 26 日,https://www. 163. com/dy/article/H13FAL6E05389YET. html

16. 温德姆酒店集团亚太区以强劲势头开启 2022 年,搜狐网,2022 年 4 月 10 日,http://news. sohu. com/a/536750092_393368

17. 乌龙茶制作技艺(铁观音制作技艺),福建省非物质文化遗产保护中心网站,http://www. fjfyw. net/daibiaozuo/2015-01-16/1270. html

18. 乌龙茶制作技艺(铁观音制作技艺),中国非物质文化遗产网,http://www. ihchina. cn/project_details/14620/

19. 武夷岩茶(大红袍)制作技艺,中国非物质文化遗产网,http://www. ihchina. cn/project_details/14373/